THE M1903 SPRINGFIELD RIFLE AND ITS VARIATIONS

2ND EDITION, REVISED AND EXPANDED

BY

JOE POYER

EDITED BY

ED FURLER, JR.

North Cape Publications®, Inc.

The author wishes to thank all those who helped, directly or indirectly, in the research for this book. He would especially like to mention John Beard; Ken Catero; Ed Cote; Nick Ferris; Chris Gayman Leinicke, Director, Rock Island Arsenal Museum; James Gronning, Grüning Precision Gunsmith; Gary James, Editor, Military Classics Illustrated; an old friend who is sorely missed, the late Stephen Johns; Roy Marcot, Old Fort Lowell Press; Mike Metzgar and Ken Fladrich, Armory of Orange; Remington Arms Company; Larry Reynolds; Craig Riesch; Phil Siess, S&S Guns; and Woody Travis for their direct help and support.

He would also like to thank Ed Furler, Jr., for his hours of patient copy-editing, extensive advice and searching red pencil. Any mistakes or typos remaining are solely the fault of the author.

This publication is designed to provide authoritative and accurate information of the subject matter covered. However, it should be recognized that serial numbers and dates, as well as other information given within, are necessarily limited by the accuracy of source materials, the experimental nature of certain developments and procedures and the military nature of the basic rifle/ammunition system.

ISBN #1-882391-30-6

North Cape Publications®, Inc. P.O. Box 1027, Tustin, California 92781
714 832-3621, Fax 714 832-5302
E-mail: ncape@ix.netcom.com
Internet Website http://www.northcapepubs.com

Printed by Delta Printing Solutions, Valencia, California 91355-1111

Table of Contents

Appendices

Tables

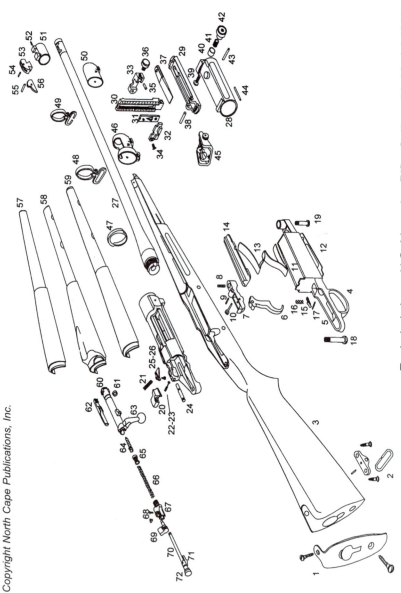

Exploded view---U.S. Magazine Rifle, Caliber .30, Model 1903

Copyright North Cape Publications, Inc.

XII

U.S. Rifle, Caliber .30, Model 1903 Exploded View

1. Butt plate and screws
2. Rear sling swivel assembly
3. Stock
4. Trigger guard
5. Trigger guard plate
6. Trigger
7. Sear
8. Sear spring
9. Sear pin
10. Trigger pin
11. Magazine well
12. Magazine floor plate
13. Magazine spring
14. Magazine follower
15. Floor plate catch
16. Floor plate catch spring
17. Floor plate catch pin
18. Rear guard screw
19. Front guard screw
20. Cutoff
21. Cutoff screw
22. Cutoff plunger spring
23. Cutoff plunger
24. Cutoff spindle
25. Ejector
26. Ejector pin
27. Barrel
28. Rear sight fixed base
29. Rear sight moveable base
30. Rear sight leaf
31. Rear sight drift slide
32. Rear sight slide
33. Rear sight slide cap
34. Rear sight slide cap screw
35. Rear sight slide binding pin
36. Rear slide screw
37. Rear sight base spring
38. Rear sight joint pin
39. Rear sight windage screw
40. Rear sight windage screw collar
41. Rear sight windage spring
42. Rear sight windage knob
43. Rear sight fixed base pin
44. Rear sight fixed base spline
45. Rear sight, Model 1903A3
46. Upper barrel band
47. Barrel guard ring (M1903A3)
48. Lower band/sling swivel
49. Upper barrel band (M1903A3)
50. Bayonet lug mount (M1903A3)
51. Front sight stud or band
52. Front sight stud screw
53. Front sight moveable stud
54. Front sight pin
55. Front sight stud pin
56. Front sight
57. Handguard (rod bayonet rifle)
58. Handguard (M1903, M1903A1)
59. Barrel cover or guard
    (M1903A3)
60. Bolt sleeve
61. Extractor collar
62. Extractor
63. Bolt handle
64. Striker
65. Firing pin sleeve
66. Mainspring
67. Bolt sleeve
68. Bolt sleeve lock assembly
69. Safety lock
70. Firing pin rod
71. Cocking piece
72. Cocking knob

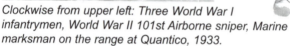

Clockwise from upper left: Three World War I
infantrymen, World War II 101st Airborne sniper, Marine
marksman on the range at Quantico, 1933.

Model 1903 Springfield Rifle and Its Variations

Introduction

The United States Magazine Rifle, Caliber .30, Model of 1903 replaced the U.S. Magazine Rifle, Caliber .30, Model of 1898 (Krag-Jorgensen) as the issue rifle of the U.S. Army in 1903 and the U.S. Navy and Marine Corps in 1911. Its design was based on the Mauser Model of 1898. It had a five-round box magazine, a double-lugged bolt with an additional safety lug and an open rear sight. It was originally designed to fire a bullet with a diameter of 0.308 inch weighing 220 grains. It used a rod bayonet that was carried under the barrel in the stock. The first of the new rifles were issued to the Corps of Cadets at the U.S. Military Academy at West Point, New York, in 1904.

Almost immediately two major problems were encountered. Although, as president of the United States, Theodore Roosevelt had pushed hard for the development of the new rifle, he objected strenuously to the rod bayonet, calling it useless. He based his opinion on dispatches from the Russo-Japanese War in which the bayonet had assumed unexpected importance in the trench warfare that had developed. Production was stopped at Springfield and Rock Island Arsenals and design changes were made to permit the use of a knife bayonet similar to that used on the M1898 Krag rifle, only longer.

The second problem was the speed with which barrels in the new rifle eroded. Subsequent studies showed that the combination of the powder being used and the heavy bullet was to blame. By the time this was determined, the rifle design had been altered for the knife bayonet and production had just been resumed. Production was halted a second time. A new cartridge had been developed using a 150-grain bullet and a less erosive powder. The new cartridge case was 0.7 inch shorter than the original .30-M1903 case. A new barrel had to be designed and manufactured, existing barrels shortened and rechambered, and stocks shortened to match.

Model 1903 Springfield Rifle and Its Variations

A new cartridge also meant different ballistics which required that the sights be recalibrated. The Army had never been entirely satisfied with the M1903 front and rear sights selected for the new rifle. The peep on the rear sight was too difficult to use and obscured the area on either side of the immediate target. The front sight was set on a fixed stud extending from a barrel band and only a minimum of lateral adjustments for windage could be made which produced a high barrel rejection rate. The Ordnance Department took advantage of the second halt in production to redesign the sight system. The result was the Model 1905 front and rear sights with the former mounted on a moveable stud dovetailed to the sight post on the barrel band to permit a wider range of lateral adjustment. The new rear sight provided an open battle sight of 530 yards (increased in 1911 to 547 yards), an aperture sight and it was calibrated to a range of 2,850 yards.

Assembly of new production rifles resumed in mid-1906 and within a year the new rifle was being distributed throughout the Army. Alteration of existing rifles was carried out simultaneously as new rifles were being produced at Springfield Armory and Rock Island Arsenal. In 1911, the U.S. Navy and Marine Corps also adopted the M1903 rifle.

Between 1906, when the design of the rifle in .30-M1906 caliber was finalized and it was equipped with the Model 1905 bayonet and M1905 sights, and 1927 when the last M1903 service rifle left the assembly line at the Springfield Armory, only minor changes were made to the rifle. Somewhere around 1.5 million Model 1903 service rifles were manufactured at the Springfield Armory in Springfield, MA, and as many as 451,133 at the Rock Island Arsenal at Rock Island, IL. The rifle served as the front-line personal weapon of millions of American soldiers, sailors, marines and airmen during a series of wars and hostile actions that included the Mexican Punitive Expedition, Honduras, World War I, Nicaragua and China Service.

When the U.S. entered World War II, the '03 was still in service, in spite of having been superceded by the M1 Garand in 1936. An additional 1.3-1.4 million Model 1903, 1903 (Modified) and 1903A3/A4 rifles were produced by the Remington Arms Company

Model 1903 Springfield Rifle and Its Variations

and by the L.C. Smith Corona Typewriter Company between 1941 and 1944. The M1903A3 was a simplified version of the original M1903 and included some 29,000 M1903A4 sniper rifles. Production of the '03 Springfield, as it had come to be known by soldiers and civilians alike, ended in June 1944. The last spare parts were produced the following year. See Appendix A for a full discussion of totals.

The M1903 rifle was held in such high regard by soldiers, sailors and marines that resistance to the change to the M1 Garand was greater than for any other combat rifle, before or since. The Marines did not adopt the M1 Garand until after the U.S. Army demonstrated its superior firepower over the M1903 in late 1942 on Guadalcanal.

Along the way, the M1903 also served as one of the finest match target rifles of the first five decades of the 20th century. Another variant served as an excellent .22-caliber training rifle. The .30-M1906 cartridge, minus its bullet, also served as the primer for the Navy's 14- and 16-inch battleship guns.

More than sixty years after its official demise, the M1903 Springfield still evokes images of courageous Army and Marine rifleman throwing enemy troops back in disarray with rapid, accurate rifle fire from Belleau Wood to Edson's Ridge. A large piece of American history and valor is wrapped up in the '03 Springfield.

CONVENTIONS

1. Following the editorial practice of North Cape Publications, Inc., major changes to parts are classified as "Types." For instance, "two kinds of lower barrel bands were developed and used. The first is designated as Type 1 and the second as Type 2," etc. This system is used for the convenience of collectors only and was never used by the U.S. Ordnance Department.

2. Much of the specific documentation pinpointing changes in manufacture, shape, markings, etc. for the M1903 Rifle no longer exists. Facility closures, downsizing and destruction of outdated documents have obscured many of the changes to the M1903 rifle in the century and more since the rifle was conceived. Much of the data concerning

production and changes that was saved was due to the diligence of Clark S. Campbell and Lt. Col. William S. Brophy. Collectors and historians owe them a great debt of gratitude.

At the National Armories, changes were implemented by work orders approved by the Ordnance Department. Following a practice established at the Springfield National Armory at the end of the eighteenth century, manufactured parts were used up first when safety was not a concern, before a new part was introduced. Parts were drawn from bins or racks and assembled into finished rifles. These were replenished at intervals, not when they were empty. Thus an "old" part could lie in the bottom of the bin or at the back of a rack for several weeks or even months before being drawn out and used.

With very few exceptions, changes to the M1903 cannot be pinpointed to a specific serial number. Thus most parts' changes are described as taking place at "circa serial number XXX." Circa means "about." All "circa serial number XXX" ranges have been established according to observations made by the author and by many other researchers in the past. Those are credited when known.

3. All markings on a rifle part are shown in quotation marks, i.e., "escutcheon/SA/05-18." The quotation marks were not part of the marking unless so noted.

4. When measurements are given from a point to a hole or other opening, that measurement is understood to be to the center of the hole or opening, unless otherwise noted.

5. All reference directions are given from the shooter's standpoint while looking toward the muzzle with the rifle shouldered. Thus right side refers to the side with the bolt handle, etc.

6. Line drawings of parts are often used in preference to photographs for clarity or to emphasize certain aspects. Occasionally, a drawing or part of a drawing is exaggerated to emphasize a point. Where exaggeration is used it is noted in the text and/or caption.

Model 1903 Springfield Rifle and Its Variations

7. The M1903 rifle and its variations were manufactured to the English measurement system. All dimensions are given in decimal inches. Non-North American readers can easily convert measurements from decimal inches to millimeters by multiplying by 25.4. Example: 2.3 inches x 25.4 = 58.4 millimeters or 5.84 centimeters.

8. Information may be repeated several times in the text at different points so the reader does not have to page back and forth.

A Word about Models and Nomenclature

During the forty-two-year production life of the M1903 rifle, some twenty-six distinct types of the rifle were manufactured, many of which had minor variations. They break down into seven categories: 1) service rifles, 2) target rifles, 3) sporting rifles, 4) sniper rifles, 5) one spotting rifle, 6) special use rifles and 7) gallery rifles. All are described at some length in Chapter 1. The heading for each model provides the official Ordnance Department designation.

While the M1903 service rifle is called by a number of names, the correct Ordnance Department nomenclature is as shown in Table 1. Note how the official designation changed over the years. The correct nomenclature for all rifle types other than service rifles is listed in the individual descriptions in Chapter 1.

Table 1 U.S. Ordnance Department Nomenclature M1903 Service Rifle	
1903 to 1917:	U.S. Magazine Rifle, Caliber .30, Model of 1903
1917 to 1939:	United States Rifle, Caliber .30, Model of 1903
After 1927:	United States Rifle, Caliber 30, Model 1903A1 (if equipped with a "C" stock)

Model 1903 Springfield Rifle and Its Variations

Table 1, cont. U.S. Ordnance Department Nomenclature M1903 Service Rifle	
1940 to 1943:	U.S. Rifle, Caliber .30, M1903 U.S. Rifle, Caliber .30, M1903A1 U.S. Rifle, Caliber .30, M1903 (Modified) U.S. Rifle, Caliber .30, M1903A3 U.S. Rifle, Caliber .30, M1903A4
1944:	Rifle, Caliber .30, M1903 Rifle, Caliber .30, M1903A1 Rifle, Caliber .30, M1903 (Modified) Rifle, Caliber .30, M1903A3 Rifle, Caliber .30, M1903A4

Chapter 1
The Model 1903 Springfield Rifle

"Model 1903 Springfield" is the generic term applied by collectors and others to the **United States Magazine Rifle, Caliber .30, Model of 1903** or the **U.S. Rifle, Cal. .30, Model 1903A3.** The Model 1903 is not one but a sequence of models produced at the National Armory at Springfield, MA, Rock Island Arsenal, IL, the Remington Arms Company and at the L.C. Smith Corona Typewriter Co. during World War II. Nowhere in official U.S. military nomenclature is the rifle referred to by the name of the Arsenal or company manufacturing it but as it is a collector's convenience, we shall do so in this book.

The M1903 Rifle entered production in 1903 at Springfield Armory and in late 1904 at Rock Island Arsenal. Production of service rifles ended in 1913 at Rock Island, was resumed in 1917, and ended finally in 1919, although a few rifles were assembled from parts in 1920. Production of the M1903 service rifle ended in Fiscal Year 1927 at Springfield Armory but rifles for target shooting and sport continued to be assembled until 1942. Receiver production ended at Springfield Armory in 1939 but production of other spare parts continued into 1942 and was resumed again in 1944 and 1945.

During World War II, four variations of the M1903 service rifle were manufactured by Remington Arms and one by Smith Corona. Remington Arms manufactured the M1903 and M1903 (Modified), the M1903A3 and the M1903A4 Sniper Rifle. They also manufactured a final run of spare parts under two contracts in 1944 and 1945. Smith Corona manufactured only the M1903A3.

Table 2 provides a complete listing of all "variations" of the United States Magazine Rifle, Caliber .30, Model of 1903, their production dates and numbers produced. The reader should note that totals cannot be added to arrive at a final figure as certain models and variations were rebuilt from existing rifles.

Although a detailed history of the design and production of the Model 1903 rifle is beyond the scope of this book, a synopsis of

Model 1903 Springfield Rifle and Its Variations

Table 2 U.S. Magazine Rifle, Cal. .30, Model 1903 and U.S. Rifle, Cal. .30, Model 1903A3 All Models and Major Variations by Production Dates		
Model	**Production Dates**	**Total Produced**
United States Magazine Rifle, Caliber .30, Model of 1903 (Designation Used 1903-1917)		
1903 "Rod Bayonet" .30-M1903, Springfield	1903-1905	76,689
1903 "Rod Bayonet" .30-M1903, Rock Island (Parts)	1904-1905	1,600
1903 "Rod Bayonet" .30-M1903 altered to "Knife Bayonet" (1st Alteration), Springfield	1906-1907	209,183
1903 "Rod Bayonet" .30-M1903 altered to "M1905 Bayonet" (1st Alteration), Rock Island	1908-1910	49,000 - 62,000 (1)
1903 .30-M1903 "Knife Bayonet" altered to ".30-M1906 with M1905 Sights" (2nd Alteration), Springfield	1907-1910	207, 446
1903 .30-M1903 "Knife Bayonet" altered to ".30-M1906 with M1905 Sights" (2nd Alteration), Rock Island	1907-1910	62,540
1903 Magazine Rifle, .30-M1906, Springfield	1908-1927	947,404
1903 Magazine Rifle, .30-M1906, Rock Island	1908-1913 and 1917-1919	172,918-185,918 (1)(2) 113,600
1903 Magazine Rifle, .22, Hoffer-Thompson	1907	3,000
United States Rifle, Caliber .30, Model of 1903 (Designation Used 1917-1939)		
1903 Rifle, Air Service	1918	910
1903 Magazine Rifle, Mark I, Springfield	1918-1920	101,775 to 145,000 (3)
M1922 Cal. .30 "Heavy Barrel" Rifle, Springfield	1922-23	133

Model 1903 Springfield Rifle and Its Variations

	Table 2, cont. U.S. Magazine Rifle, Cal. .30, Model 1903 and U.S. Rifle, Cal. .30, Model 1903A3 All Models and Major Variations by Production Dates	
Model	**Production Dates**	**Total Produced**
M1922 "Gallery Rifle, Cal. .22," Springfield	1922-1924	2,020
M1922 Cal. .30 International Match Rifle	1922	13
M1903 "Target Rifle, Star-Gauged Barrel"	1922-1924	1,256
M1903 "NRA Sporter Rifle," Springfield	1924-1932 1937-1938	6,518 29
M1924 International Match Rifle, Cal. .22	1924	12
M1922M1 "Gallery Rifle, Cal. .22"	1925-1934	20,020
M1903 "Special Target" Rifle	1926-1929	2,595
M1903 "NRA-NBA Sporter Rifle," Springfield	1926	589
M1922M2 "Gallery Rifle, Cal. .22," Springfield	1934-1944	21,118 (3)
M1903 "National Match Rifle," Springfield	1921-1928	19,995 (4)
M1903 "International" Rifle	1929-1930	40
M1903 "Style T"	1930	100
M1903 "National Match, Style B"	1925-1928	150
United States Rifle, Caliber .30, Model 1903A1 (Designation used after 1927 if equipped with "C" Stock)		
M1903A1 Magazine Rifle, Springfield	1928-1945	Unknown
M1903A1 "National Match Rifle," Springfield	1929-1940	8,912 (4)

9

Model 1903 Springfield Rifle and Its Variations

Table 2, cont. U.S. Magazine Rifle, Cal. .30, Model 1903 and U.S. Rifle, Cal. .30, Model 1903A3 All Models and Major Variations by Production Dates		
Model	**Production Dates**	**Total Produced**
U.S. Rifle, Caliber .30, Model of 1903; U.S. Rifle, Caliber .30, Model 1903 (Modified); U.S. Rifle, Caliber .30, Model 1903A3; U.S. Rifle, Caliber .30, Model 1903A4 (5)		
M1903, Remington Arms	1941	133,444
M1903 (Modified), Remington Arms (6)	December 1941 to May 1942	214,641/ 231,509
M1903, .30-M1906, "Bushmaster Carbine"	1942	4,725
M1903A3, Remington Arms (6)	November 1942 to 1944	707,629/ 783,844
M1903A3, Smith Corona (6)	1942-1944	233,998/ 236,831
M1903A4, Remington Arms (6)	1943-1944	28,365/ 29,964

1. Data from official and unofficial sources is contradictory. These figures are cited in various Ordnance Department reports and total 234,918 for all RIA production.
2. Brophy provides a total RIA production figure of 376,973 based on a study of serial numbers.
3. Exact number is unknown. Figures are based on published sources and observed serial numbers.
4. Includes National Match rifles rebuilt at least once.
5. In 1944, the official nomenclature was changed a final time to: "Rifle, Cal. .30, M1903," "Rifle, Cal. .30, M1903A1," "Rifle, Cal. .30, M1903 (Modified)," "Rifle, Cal. .30, M1903A3," and "Rifle, Cal. .30, M1903A4."
6. Campbell and Brophy disagree on the totals produced by Remington and Smith Corona. Figures from both authors are included here.
NOTE: "Totals Produced" will not add to total production as certain models were built from existing rifles and an unknown number of "spare" receivers were also built.

major models is provided below. A brief developmental history is also provided and particular methods of identification are listed. References to parts by type will be explained in Chapter 2, Parts. Collectors interested in pursuing the history of the rifle in detail are advised to consult two excellent reference works, *The '03 Springfield* or the later edition, *The '03 Era,* both by Campbell, and *The Springfield 1903 Rifles,* by Brophy. See Appendix I, Bibliography.

UNITED STATES MAGAZINE RIFLE, CALIBER .30, MODEL OF 1903 (.30-M1903)

Many readers may question the need for detailed information on the M1903 rod bayonet rifles as they are almost nonexistent. Few rod bayonet equipped rifles were ever issued to troops and those were recalled and altered between 1906 and 1910.

The information is included for three reasons: 1) You should know how their development affected the U.S. Magazine Rifle, Caliber .30, Model of 1903 as it was redesigned for the M1905 Knife Bayonet and .30-M1906 cartridge; 2) it will help you detect the many M1903 Rod Bayonet Rifle fakes and assembled-from-parts rifles on the current collector's market and 3) it will help you determine whether or not a rifle with a serial number and barrel date before 1911 is correct as issued, reassembled from parts or an out-and-out fake.

For those interested in pursuing the M1903 rod bayonet rifle and its alterations further, the author recommends two excellent books, *Springfield Model 1903 Service Rifle, Production and Alteration, 1905-1910* (Ferris and Beard) and *The Rock Island '03* (Ferris). See Appendix I, Bibliography.

The first rifle in the 1903 series was designed to fire the .30-M1903 caliber cartridge containing a 220-grain round-nose bullet. This rifle originally had a sliding rod bayonet under the barrel similar to that used by the M1888 .45-70 Springfield Rifle, an M1903 front sight and a rear sight modeled after the Model 1902 rear sight developed for the Krag rifle. It had an overall length of 43.41 inches, a nominal weight of 8.937 pounds including the rod bayonet and a 24-inch-long

Model 1903 Springfield Rifle and Its Variations

barrel with a 1:10 inch rifling twist. See Figure 1-1 A-D.

The Model 1903 in .30-M1903 caliber was approved by Secretary of War William Taft on June 19, 1903; production began at Springfield Armory in November 1903, and continued to July 1, 1904. During this production period, minor changes were made to the rifle: 1) a new modified safety lock; cocking piece and bolt sleeve that provided a larger camming surface and a locking plunger to provide better wear were incorporated; 2) the addition of a peep sight to the rear sight and 3) the lengthening of the magazine follower to prevent jamming during single loading.

This rifle was also produced at the Rock Island Arsenal beginning in May 1904. But the first complete rifle was not ready until December and was not accepted until January 1905. The delay was due to the fact tools, equipment and fixtures had to be obtained from Springfield and workers hired and trained.

The initial distribution of the new rifle (all manufactured at Springfield) was limited to the Corps of Cadets at the U.S. Military Academy at West Point and to units of the Alaskan and Philippine commands. The .30-caliber (.30-40) Krag round was still in wide distribution and limiting the new rifle to these commands avoided logistic problems.

The identifying characteristics of the M1903 rod bayonet rifle are as follows:

1. Barrels were not stamped with the armory name, escutcheon or month and year
2. The bolt body was bright but not highly polished while the bolt handle retained the dark heat treatment color
3. The extractor had a purplish hue from overheating during the hardening and tempering process
4. Rear Sight (M1903) very similar to the M1902 Krag Rear Sight
5. Smooth, non-grooved trigger
6. Smooth, non-checkered butt plate
7. Stacking swivel had a flat ground on one side of the mounting screw lug

Model 1903 Springfield Rifle and Its Variations

Fig. 1-1C. Address, model and serial number.

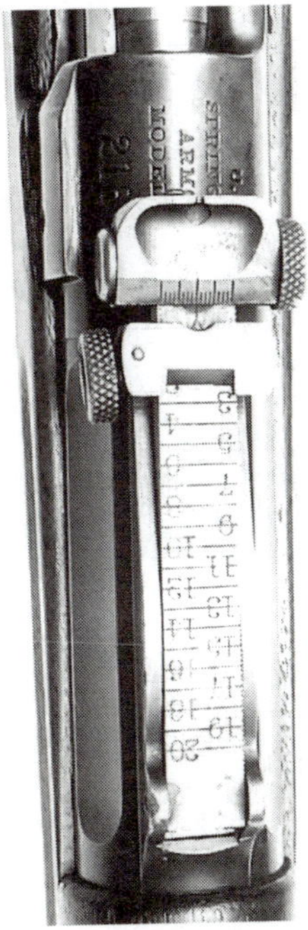

Fig.1-1B. Cartouche "ILA/1904."

Fig. 1-1A. U.S. Magazine Rifle, Caliber .30, Model of 1903 (a.k.a.) rod bayonet rifle. Courtesy, Gary James.

Fig. 1-1D. Model 1903 rear sight.

Model 1903 Springfield Rifle and Its Variations

8. Lower band was solid

9. Upper band was narrow, similar to the lower band and lacking a bayonet mount

10. Magazine follower had a square-cut end

11. The rod bayonet was contained in a channel cut in the underside of the forearm. The latch mechanism was fixed in the stock and not brazed to the barrel as it was in the M1888 .45-70 Springfield Rifle.

Almost as soon as distribution of the new rifle began, the first two major sets of changes were implemented. The first change involved the adoption of the Model 1905 knife bayonet and a new front and rear sight, and the second the adoption of a new, shorter cartridge with a 150-grain spire point bullet.

UNITED STATES MAGAZINE RIFLE, CALIBER .30, MODEL OF 1903 — 1ST ALTERATION (.30-M1903)

On January 4, 1905, Secretary of War William Taft received a letter from President Theodore Roosevelt objecting to the "ramrod" bayonet in the new service rifle. Since the end of the Civil War, the bayonet had fallen from favor in the U.S. Army and was seen largely as a means for controlling prisoners and mobs. But during the Russo-Japanese War then in progress in the Far East, the new machine gun and quick-firing artillery pieces had driven opposing troops into trenches. The bayonet played a significant role in the trench warfare tactics that were evolving, particularly in night fighting.

President Roosevelt, then engaged in helping to negotiate a peace treaty between Russia and Japan, was fully cognizant of the tactical situation. It took very little to persuade the Ordnance Department that he was right and consequently, on January 11, production of the rod bayonet rifle was halted at Springfield and Rock Island while a committee of five general staff officers began evaluating new bayonet designs. They completed their work on March 28, 1905 and recommended that a 16-inch knife bayonet with scabbard be adopted for the new rifle. Five days later, on April 3, 1905, Secretary Taft approved the new bayonet and ordered it adopted. See Figure 1-2.

Model 1903 Springfield Rifle and Its Variations

To adapt the knife bayonet to the rifle, the ramrod bayonet and its locking device in the stock were removed, the forearm was shortened and the area formerly occupied by the locking device was plugged. A shorter handguard was manufactured as well as a new front barrel band which was considerably longer than the original band. It resembled that used on the Krag rifle with a Krag-style bayonet stud mounted beneath. See Figure 1-3.

On April 17, 1905, Brigadier General Crozier, head of the Ordnance Department, also recommended that a new rear sight be developed during the retooling period for the new bayonet. A board was appointed to reevaluate two designs, the Model 1901 and the Model 1902. Many officers and enlisted men objected to the "peep" sight then in use on the Model 1903 rear sight as it restricted their field of view. Consequently, a style based on the Model 1901 Krag rear sight, but with a windage modification, was adopted. The new sight design had a leaf hinged at the rear and a sliding sight bar, and incorporated a "V-Notch" on the aperture bar and two apertures on a slide that moved up and down in

Fig. 1-2. The 16-inch Model 1905 knife bayonet with leather scabbard as approved on April 3, 1905. Mike Metzgar collection.

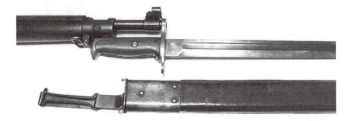

Fig. 1-3. Forearm of the M1903 Magazine Rifle with the M1905 bayonet mounted.

15

the leaf to adjust for range. Both the M1905 front and rear sights were placed into production but assembly to rifles was held up while the sight gradations were worked out.

The M1903 front sight was made in two pieces. The lower part was a band which clamped around the barrel and was secured with a pin. A platform integral with the band had a slot cut into its top. The front sight blade was pinned into the slot. The construction of the front sight band allowed only a very small amount of adjustment for windage during targeting, and consequently, barrel rejection rates were high.

A new three-piece front sight (Figure 1-4) consisting of a barrel band (1), stud (2) and front sight blade (3) was developed. The stud was mounted on the barrel band in a dovetail and the blade was pinned in the stud. This permitted lateral adjustments of up to 0.025 inch right or left, thus reducing the high number of rejected barrels.

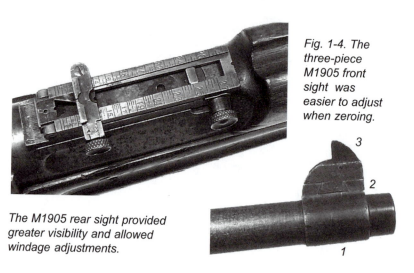

Fig. 1-4. The three-piece M1905 front sight was easier to adjust when zeroing.

The M1905 rear sight provided greater visibility and allowed windage adjustments.

Note: M1903 rifles chambered for the .30-M1903 cartridge but altered to accept the M1905 knife bayonet are referred to as the "M1903

Model 1903 Springfield Rifle and Its Variations

1st Alteration" throughout this book. The reader need only remember that it referred to the change to M1905 Bayonet.

UNITED STATES MAGAZINE RIFLE, CALIBER .30, MODEL OF 1903 — 2ND ALTERATION (.30-M1906)

The French army had adopted a lighter, pointed bullet, the *Balle D*, for their 8 mm Lebel rifle in 1898, creating a flurry of concern among the world's armies. The new cartridge's 198-grain pointed, solid bronze bullet provided a flatter trajectory and thus greater accuracy as well as longer range. Germany, not to be outdone by their arch-rival, adopted the "*spitzeschoss*" (spire point) bullet in 1904. Most other major European powers quickly followed suit.

This, plus that fact that the .30-M1903 cartridge produced an unacceptable amount of erosion in the barrel chamber, prompted the United States Army's Ordnance Department to develop a 150-grain spire point bullet that performed better than the round-nose 220-grain bullet originally used in the .30-M1903 cartridge (see Figure 1-5). A new powder reduced barrel erosion to a more acceptable amount. But as the new 150-grain bullet was shorter than the 220-grain round-nose bullet, it had to be set back further in the case mouth. To eliminate the long jump from case mouth to barrel lands this created, the barrel was shortened by 0.2 inch.

By the time the new cartridge was adopted as the Cartridge, Ball, Cali-

Fig. 1-5. New spire point bullets, l-r: Russian M1909, French Balle D M1898; German spitzeschoss M1904 and U.S. 30-Model 1906 cartridges.

Model 1903 Springfield Rifle and Its Variations

ber .30, Model of 1906 (a.k.a. .30-M1906), some 271,000 barrels chambered for the longer .30-M1903 cartridge had been manufactured at Springfield and Rock Island. The government could ill afford to discard over $1.5 million dollars of finished barrels ($810 million in today's dollars). The decision was made to rechamber all rifles. Any new barrels manufactured after that point were to be chambered for the new cartridge.

All existing barrels (24.206 inches long) chambered for the .30-M1903 cartridge were rechambered for the new cartridge by the simple expedient of cutting 0.20 inch off at the breech end to make the barrels 24.006 inches long. This shortened the throat of the existing chamber. The shoulder was also moved ahead 0.20 inch by re-reaming and two more barrel threads were added. The feeding cone and the extractor slot were recut as well.

Because the shoulder was moved ahead 0.20 inch, the notch for the M1905 rear sight pin had to be recut 0.20 inch ahead of the existing notch. Two rear sight pin notches in the underside of the barrel are the best way to identify .30-M1903 barrels rechambered for the .30-M1906 cartridge.

The trajectory of the .30-M1906 spire point bullet was flatter than that of the round-nose .30-M1903 bullet so new firing tables were prepared by marksmen shooting at specified ranges to 1,200 yards. The ranges beyond 1,200 yards were calculated rather than being fired. With the completion of ballistic tests on the new cartridge, rear sight leaf graduations were calculated and the height of the front blade was established. The new rear sight leaf was graduated to 2,825 yards with a notch at the very top for 2,850 yards as compared to 2,400 yards for the .30-M1903 cartridge. The battle sight on the new Model 1906 rear sight was established as 547 yards from 1911 on.

Not until actual experience was obtained in 1917-1918 in France was it discovered that an error had been made in the calculations and the range was actually a third shorter than the tables specified. The problem did not affect riflemen who rarely fired beyond 1,000 yards but did have a great effect on machine gunners. The Model 1906 cartridge, using the calculated sights, actually had only a little more than half the range of the British Mark VII .303 174-grain bullet or the German 7.92 196-grain boattail bullet adopted for the machine gun cartridge.

As above, these rifles (whether the rod bayonet or 1st Alteration) converted to the .30-M1906 cartridge and equipped with the Model 1905 front and rear sights and the M1905 bayonet are referred to throughout this book as the Model 1903 Rifle, 2nd Alteration.

ALTERING THE M1903 ROD BAYONET AND M1903-1905 (.30-M1903) RIFLES

As confusing as the work done to alter both the M1903 rod bayonet rifle to use the M1905 knife bayonet and then to the new M1906 cartridge and M1905 sights is, specifying the time period(s) and manner in which the work was done is even more complicated.

First, it should be recognized that very few of the M1903 rod bayonet rifles were ever issued because of the problems of supplying two different types of ammunition. The M1898 Krag rifle was still in the hands of the troops, both regulars and national guard, and it fired a rimmed cartridge known as the U.S. Cartridge, .30 caliber, Model of 1892. Issuing a different cartridge was certain to cause great confusion. By 1905, only the Corps of Cadets at West Point and troop units stationed in Alaska and the Philippines, where the issuance of ammunition could be closely controlled, had received the new rifle. The M1903 rifle was not issued to the U.S. Navy, Marines or Coast Guard until after 1911 when the M1906 Rifle was adopted by those services.

Orders to alter the rifles first for the M1905 knife bayonet, then to rechamber them for the new M1906 .30-M1906 cartridge and add the M1905 rear and front sights, delayed further issues of the M1903 rifle to the Army. Springfield continued to manufacture finished rifles but because of the problems involved in first designing and then calibrating the new rear sight, the completed rear sights could not be installed until mid-1907. Rock Island, during this period, continued to manufacture M1903 rifle parts but did not assemble them. The parts were placed in storage with the barrels only being stored by month of production.

The M1903 rifle was reissued after alteration in the following manner:

1) With the changes of 1905: i.e., modified to accept the M1905 knife bayonet but chambered for the .30-M1903 caliber (1st Alteration), rifles were issued to the Regular army through the end of Fiscal 1907 (July 1, 1906 to June 30, 1907). These were recalled beginning the following calendar year for further alteration.

2) Issues of the *new production* M1903 rifles *manufactured* in .30-M1906 caliber and equipped with the M1905 knife bayonet and M1905 sights began in Fiscal 1908 (July 1, 1907 to June 30, 1908) to the Corps of Cadets at West Point and were completed throughout the Regular Army in early 1909.

3) The M1903 rifles *altered* to accept the M1905 knife bayonet, the .30-M1906 cartridge and with the M1905 sights (2nd Alteration) were issued from 1910 on; the majority may have gone to the U.S. Navy and Marine Corps when they adopted the U.S. Magazine Rifle, .30 Caliber, Model 1903 in 1911.

It bears repeating that production of new rifles chambered for the .30-M1906 cartridge and equipped with the knife bayonet and the new sights was begun in calendar year 1907 and continued at the same time as previous rifles were altered, being only temporarily delayed until the new rear sight leaves became available.

The timeline in Table 3 below detailing the alteration and production program should provide a less confusing picture to the reader. Figures 1-6, A-G illustrate some of these changes.

NOTE: Alterations were not made on one rifle at a time nor in serial number sequence. Rather, all rifles undergoing alteration were completely disassembled, inspected and useable parts stored in bins. Rifles were then reassembled substituting altered and new parts as required.

Model 1903 Springfield Rifle and Its Variations

Table 3 Production and Alteration of the M1903 Rod Bayonet and M1903-1905 (.30-M1903) Rifles	
November 1903	Production begins at Springfield and reaches 400 rod bayonet rifles per day.
December 1904	RIA completes first finished rod bayonet rifle (accepted and inspected in 1905)
January 11, 1905	Parts production associated with rod bayonet rifles stopped at Springfield and RIA. Production of other parts continued. Springfield turned into stores 17,000 finished rifles by this date. RIA turned into stores 1,600 rod bayonet rifle parts sets by this date.
January 30, 1905	RIA reached their target production rate of 125 rod bayonet rifle parts sets per day.
April 3, 1905	M1905 knife bayonet approved.
April 17, 1905	Production of M1903 rear and front sights halted.
June 30, 1905	All 1,800 rod bayonet rifles (1,600+200) manufactured since the start of production at RIA turned into stores as unassembled parts.
July-August 1905	M1905 rear and front sights approved. Decision made to apply Armory/Date stamp to all barrels.
July-October 1905	Springfield and RIA retool for production of the M1905 knife bayonet (1st Alteration).
November 1905 to September 1906	Rifle production of new M1903 .30-M1903 caliber rifles with 1905 bayonet and M1903 sights resumed at Springfield. Rifles assembled from new and accumulated rifle parts sets. Springfield barrels show only Armory/Escutcheon/Year on all pre-1906 barrels, (Fig. 1-6F); Armory/Escutcheon/Month-Year on all 1906 and later barrels
May 1906	Rifle (.30-M1903 caliber) production resumed at RIA (49,628 rifles assembled) with provision for the M1905 bayonet. RIA barrels show RIA/Escutcheon/Month/Year, (Fig. 6-1G).

Model 1903 Springfield Rifle and Its Variations

Table 3, cont. Production and Alteration of the M1903 Rod Bayonet and M1903-1905 (.30-M1903) Rifles		
	M1906 cartridge with 150-grain spire point bullet adopted.
October 15, 1906	Production of M1903 .30-M1903 rifles with M1905 bayonet halted at Springfield and RIA. RIA turned into storage 13,165 rifles assembled from new parts. None issued.
January-February 1907 to June 10, 1910	Springfield begins altering rod bayonet rifles for the M1906 cartridge, M1905 bayonet and M1905 sights. Barrel is shortened, rethreaded and rechambered. Front of stock is shortened, plugged and stamped "S." M1903 rear sight and base replaced by M1905 rear sight and base. Handguards with swell to protect M1905 rear sight manufactured and stamped with small "S" on rear of swell. Installation of rear sight leaves calibrated for the .30-M1906 cartridge begins. Barrels are stamped as follows: Armory/Escutcheon/Year, pre-1906 barrels (Figure 1-6F); Armory/Escutcheon/Month-Year on all 1906 and later barrels.
February 1907 to June 30, 1909	RIA begins altering rod bayonet rifles for the M1906 cartridge following the exact procedure used at Springfield. The date this process began is unknown but is thought to be February 1907. Barrels stamped with Armory/Escutcheon/Month-Year (Figure 6-1G).

UNITED STATES MAGAZINE RIFLE, CALIBER .30 (M1906)-MODEL OF 1903

With the start of production in late 1907 of new Model 1903 rifles chambered for the .30-M1906 cartridge and equipped with the new Model 1905 front and rear sights and the Model 1905 bayonet, the service rifle assumed the shape it would retain until 1942 when the Remington Arms Company (and the following year, Smith Corona) began to produce the Model 1903A3. Minor changes were made to the

Model 1903 Springfield Rifle and Its Variations

Fig. 1-6A. Springfield Caliber .30-M1903 rod bayonet rifle altered to Caliber .30-M1906 with the M1905 knife bayonet and M1905 front and rear sights. Craig Riesch collection.

Figs. 1-6B and C. The altered rod bayonet stocks were shortened, plugged and stamped "S." Handguards were newly manufactured and stamped "S" below the sight protector swell. Note the early M1905 rear sight graduated to only 2,400 yards. Craig Riesch collection.

23

Model 1903 Springfield Rifle and Its Variations

Fig. 1-6D. An "M" was struck beside the cartouche on the wrist of altered Springfield stocks. Craig Riesch collection.

Fig. 1-6E. The underside of the stock wrist showing the "A" stamped above the proof mark. Craig Riesch collection.

Fig. 1-6F. Altered Springfield barrel marked only with the year of manufacture. Craig Riesch collection.

Fig. 1-6G. Altered Rock Island barrel marked with the month and year of manufacture. Ed Furler collection.

Model 1903 Springfield Rifle and Its Variations

Model 1903 rifle in the years after 1906 but they did little to alter the familiar contours, see Figure 1-7.

Springfield receivers and bolts were originally made of the same Class C steel as the older Model 1892 Krags. The old single heat treatment method gave way to a double heat treatment method in 1917 (circa serial #800,000 at Springfield and #285,507 at Rock Island). The transition to a nickel steel alloy began during World War I at Rock Island but not until 1927 at Springfield. After 1936, the gas vent in the right side of the receiver was transferred to the left side of the receiver and enlarged. Many earlier rifles still in service and returned to the Springfield Armory for repair or refurbishing had the gas vent added to the left side, see Figure 1-8.

The standard stock was termed the "S" stock, possibly because of the "S" stamped on .30-M1903 stocks shortened at Springfield and Rock Island to accept the Model 1905

Fig.1-7. The M1903 Springfield assumed its familiar basic shape after the completion of the 1st and 2nd sets of alterations starting in 1906. North Cape Publications collection.

Model 1903 Springfield Rifle and Its Variations

Fig.1-8. After 1936, the gas vent was drilled in the left side of the receiver through the locking lug shoulder. Earlier production rifles often had the new gas vent added during repair.

bayonet. It had a straight, smooth grip behind the trigger guard, see Figure 1-9. Not until 1929 with the advent of the Model 1903A1 and its "C" stock did it gain a pistol grip (Figure 1-10), although the "S" stock continued to be used for almost all production of service-style rifles until 1941 when

assembly of service rifles was resumed at Springfield Armory. Stocks (and handguards) were dipped in a logwood dye before being saturated with linseed oil until 1928. This provided the characteristic reddish stock color of the early Springfield '03. From

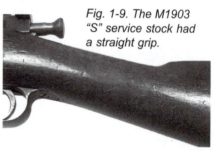

Fig. 1-9. The M1903 "S" service stock had a straight grip.

Fig. 1-10. In 1928, the Ordnance Department ordered the use of the "C" stock with a pistol grip.

1928 to the end of production, the M1903 received only the linseed oil finish which produced a deep brown to maroon color.

In 1910, a sight clearance channel was cut in the top side of the handguard to make it easier for the rifleman to see the front sight, see Figure 1-

Model 1903 Springfield Rifle and Its Variations

11. Reinforcing clips were added to the underside of the handguard at the same time, see Figure 1-12. A total of 12 different handguards were used on the M1903 service rifle alone. All are described in Chapter 2, Parts — Handguards.

Fig. 1-11. Sight clearance channel added to the handguard in 1910.

Stock reinforcing bolts were added, the first behind the magazine in 1908 and the second behind the receiver front lug in late 1919, see Figure 1-13.

In 1918, the bolt handle was swept back at a shallow angle to make it easier for the rifleman to manipulate, see Figure 1-14. Starting in 1917, the bolt received the same double heat treatment as the receiver. The bolt handle was no longer blackened after 1905 but polished until the start of World War II.

Fig. 1-12. Because the thin handguards had a tendency to split, metal reinforcing clips were added to the underside.

Receivers, bolt sleeves, cocking pieces, followers, triggers, butt plates, rear sight leaves and bases were case-hardened in oil which provided a blackish, somewhat mottled color. Bolt assemblies and the forward face of rear sight leaf were blackened until World War II and production began at Remington Arms. The process was referred to as "carburization" and involved soaking the part in oil and burning it off. The magazine cutoff and the safety thumbpiece were color case-hardened in water. The trigger guard, floor plate, front sight stud, butt swivel, lower band and spring and magazine spring were all niter blued (dipped in molten potassium

Model 1903 Springfield Rifle and Its Variations

nitrate). Parkerizing was approved in 1917 but was apparently not applied to new rifle manufacture until 1919. Rifles or rifle parts earlier than 1919 that are Parkerized have been refinished. Any of the rifle parts named in this chapter as having been case-hardened or niter blued prior to 1919 and which are now Parkerized have been refinished.

Fig. 1-13. The rear stock reinforcing bolt was added in 1908 and the front in 1919. Earlier rifles were often retrofitted.

UNITED STATES MAGAZINE RIFLE, CALIBER .30, MODEL OF 1903 FOR NATIONAL BOARD FOR THE PROMOTION OF RIFLE PRACTICE

In 1905, Congress formed the National Board for the Promotion of Rifle Practice to encourage civilian target shooting in the hope that it would reduce the time and money needed to train future soldiers. The program was carried out through the Director of Civilian Marksmanship in cooperation with the National Rifle Association. In 1910, the distribution of M1903 service rifles began. In 1915, the Chief of Ordnance, General Crozier, directed that rifles distributed or sold for this purpose through the NRA be marked on the trigger guard plate with the Ordnance Department flaming bomb symbol above the letters "N.R.A." The marking was done with a steel die. The letters were 0.08 inch high and the ordnance escutcheon was 0.8 inch high, see Figure 1-15. The standard service rifle was advertised and sold as the "Style S." The service rifle with a star-gauged barrel signifying that the variation in bore diameter and the width and height of the lands and grooves did not exceed 0.0001 inch of established specifications was designated the "Style SS." These bar-

Fig. 1-14. Learning from the British SMLE rifle, the M1903 bolt handle was bent slightly to the rear to make it easier for the rifleman to manipulate. Woody Travis collection.

rels were not marked with the "star" symbol but the star-gauge record was sent with the rifle.

Sales — and marking — of these rifles ended with the entry of the United States into World War I.

NOTE: The marking of star-gauged barrels on the muzzle with an eight-pointed "star" began in 1921.

Fig. 1-15. National Rifle Association marking on pre-World War I rifle.

UNITED STATES MAGAZINE RIFLE, CALIBER .30, MODEL OF 1903 — MK. I

The failure of the 1917 Allied offensives with their consequent huge loss of life prompted the U.S. Allied Expeditionary Force com-

Model 1903 Springfield Rifle and Its Variations

mander-in-chief, General John Pershing, to demand from the War Department an effective weapon that would multiply the firepower of the individual rifleman.

A total of 65,000 conversion units officially designated the "U.S. Pistol, Cal. .30, Model of 1918," but better known to collectors as the "Pedersen Device," were manufactured for the M1903 Springfield, see Figure 1-16. A few test units were made also for the Model 1917 Enfield and the Mosin-Nagant rifles. Production began in strict secrecy in 1918 for use in the Spring offensive scheduled for 1919.

Fig. 1-16. The M1903 MARK I rifle modified to use the "U.S. Pistol, Cal. .30, Model of 1918" also known to collectors as the "Pedersen Device." Photo courtesy of Remington Arms and Roy Marcot.

Model 1903 Springfield Rifle and Its Variations

M1903 rifles set up for the "Pedersen Device" have an oval ejection port milled into the left side of the receiver. The stock line on the left side of the receiver was lowered to make room for the ejection port. Such rifles were designated the Model of 1903 Mark I and "MARK I" was stamped on the right side of the receiver ring, between "MODEL 1903." and the serial number. Other differences were a modification to the magazine cutoff which held the device in place when turned down, or to the "OFF" position. The spindle on the second variation was adjustable by a screwdriver slot at the opposite end. An additional sear was added to the trigger lever that released the device's firing pin.

M1903 Mk. I rifles were manufactured and assembled from early 1918 to 1920. The earliest observed was March 1918 and the latest was May 1920. The serial number ranges observed to date are: 1,034,502 (Remington), 1,197,834 (Brophy). Serial number and barrel dates as late as 1921 have been reported but not observed by the author. See Appendix F, The Pedersen Device for further details on this extremely interesting answer to trench warfare.

U.S. Rifle, Caliber .30, Model 1903A1

The Model 1903A1 service rifle was approved on March 15, 1928. The only difference between it and its predecessors was the addition of a pistol grip to the stock which was designated as "Stock, Cal. .30 Model 1903A1" (a.k.a. the "C" stock). Since assembly of service rifles had ended in Fiscal Year 1927 and regulations called for the sizeable inventory of "S" stocks to be used up first, "C" stocks were primarily installed on National Match rifles and some service rifles submitted for rebuild and repair, see Figure 1-17. In addition, "C" stocks were sold through the DCM from 1932-1940 for $3.75 each.

Many "C" stocks are marked with the drawing number on the bottom, either D1836 or D35379, between the lower swivel and grip; some National Match Rifles with the "C" stock also have the rifle serial number added.

Model 1903 Springfield Rifle and Its Variations

Fig. 1-17. The M1903A1 rifle is distinguished by its "C" pistol-gripped stock. North Cape Publications collection.

When the United States entered World War II after the Japanese attack at Pearl Harbor, Springfield Armory was ordered to assemble as many M1903A1 rifles as possible, drawing from their large stock of receivers and spare parts. Campbell estimates that there may have been as many as 60,000 receivers in inventory in late 1941 as receiver serial numbers into the 1,590,000s have been reported, nearly 60,000 higher than the last reported serial number of the last complete rifle assembled at Springfield Armory in 1939 (see also Appendix A concerning the highest serial number reported). How many of these rifles saw actual combat is impossible to say. It is known that Nationalist Chinese units on Taiwan were armed with the M1903A1 in the 1950s, and many more were sold through the DCM after the war. Large quantities of M1917 Enfield and M1903 Springfield rifles are known to have been shipped to the Nationalist Chinese during World War II.

U.S. Rifle, Cal. .30, Non-Standard Adaptions

The M1903 rifle formed the basis of several interesting but not official weapons during its years of service. It was employed as an anti-tank training gun and was rebuilt as a carbine.

Training crews of armored vehicles to hit their targets is an expensive proposition, even with today's computer and laser assisted devices. One way to reduce the cost of target training is to use a device that simulates the trajectory of the rifled gun round. The M1903

Model 1903 Springfield Rifle and Its Variations

was first adapted for this purpose in 1918 and again in the early 1940s. The M1903 rifle in both .30- and .22-caliber configurations with their stocks and sights removed were installed in special gun mounts. Tank crews used the "subcaliber" guns to fire at fixed and moving targets, thus sparing the expense and logistical effort of supplying full caliber tank gun rounds. M1903 .30-caliber rifles were redesignated as U.S. Rifle, Cal. .30, M1903A2. M1903 Hoffer-Thompson .22-caliber rifles and M1922, M1922M1 or M2 rifles were redesignated Rifle, Subcaliber, Cal. .22, M2A1. The .30-caliber rifles were stamped "A2" by hand on the receiver after the "M1903" marking. After the war, they were reconverted to their former configurations and the additional markings were either lined out or ignored.

A second non-standard use of the M1903 was designated officially, "Carbine, Improvised, Cal. .30." Today, collectors know it as the "Bushmaster Carbine." U.S. Army troops stationed in Panama during World War II had the task of guarding the Panama Canal. Because so much of Panama is rain forest, they conducted continuous patrols in the heavily jungled country to prevent the infiltration of Axis sabotage teams. To make it easier to maneuver in the dense forests, the Panama Canal Department was instructed on June 10, 1942 to convert 4,725 M1903 rifles into carbines by shortening barrels. They were then designated "Carbine, Improvised, Cal. .30." "Bushmaster" was an unofficial nickname.

All work was done in the U.S. Army armory shops in the Canal Zone in 1942. Barrels were shortened to 18 inches and the forend cut back about nine inches (1.75 inches ahead of the rear barrel band). The M1905 front sight was reinstalled on the barrel. The front barrel band and bayonet mount were discarded. The handguard was reduced in length to match the stock. No bayonet was used. The Carbines were used by the 158th Regiment (Oklahoma National Guard) and by elements of the Sixth Army Air Force as part of the "Caribbean Defense Command" until September 1944 when they were ordered turned in and were replaced by the M1 Carbine.

The collector should beware when offered an "original" Bushmaster carbine. Instructions had been issued on May 9, 1945 to destroy them "by dumping in the ocean." Some Bushmaster carbines were apparently issued to the Sixth Army Air Force until the M1 Carbine became available. Another order required that 4,500 Bushmaster Carbines be turned into the Raritan Ordnance Depot, but so far no evidence has come to light to suggest that they were. In short, it is not known exactly what happened to them but the scarcity of specimens suggests that most were destroyed or at the very least, broken down for parts.

Any markings indicating that a rifle was converted to "Bushmaster Carbines" are unknown and the recorded serial numbers taken from U.S. Army reports and correspondence show that the Bushmasters were made from rifles ranging from the rod bayonet series to the very end of M1903 production.

NATIONAL MATCH RIFLES

The National Matches were first organized and fired in 1873 at the National Rifle Association range at Creedmore, Long Island. Both civilian and military shooters participated in one of the oldest continuing sporting events in the United States, see Figure 1-18. The National Matches were fired annually from 1873 to 1916, 1918 to 1941 and 1950 to the present, but were not fired during World War I and World War II and for four years thereafter.

The National Matches were established in their present home at Camp Perry, Ohio, in 1907. The Krag rifle and carbine were used in the National Matches until 1908 when the Springfield M1903 became the official rifle. In 1910, the use of "star-gauged" barreled, selected rifles was authorized and in 1913, the sale of the M1903 rifle was authorized through the Director of Civilian Marksmanship via the National Rifle Association, see Figure 1-19.

The requirements for a special "National Match" rifle were first established in 1921 (see Appendix E, The National Match Rifle) and updated periodically thereafter. Specifications were established for every major part of the rifle and from 1910 on all barrels were

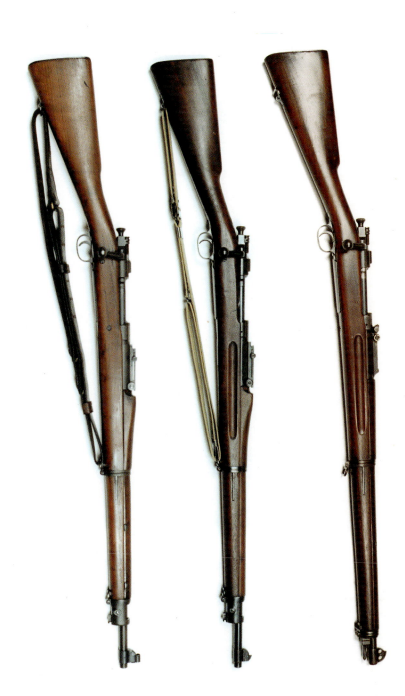

Top to Bottom: M1903 rod bayonet rifle, Gary James collection; M1903 manufactured in 1909 and M1903 manufactured in 1911, both from the North Cape Publications collection.

Top to bottom: Remington Model 1903A3 and M1903A4 sniper rifle, North Cape Publications collection and M2 .22 caliber gallery rifle, James Gronning collection.

Model 1903 Springfield Rifle and Its Variations

Fig. 1-18. Distinguished Marksmen, U.S. Army Rifle Team, 1889. (L-r) Front: J.P. Kelly, L. Roper, John Wolford, E. Stevens, and J. Gromley. Second Row: G.N. King, W. Williams, W.A. Mercer, W.D. Umphray, and R.C. Van Vliet. North Cape Publications collection.

star-gauged and so marked on the muzzle starting in 1921. The rules for the National Match Rifle required that the "current" service rifle be used. In practice this meant that while the external shape and the actual function of the rifle could not be modified, armorers could and did pay very careful attention to selecting and assembling parts, seating the action in the stock bed and adjusting trigger function and pull to produce the most accurate rifle possible. The bolt body was also given a high polish.

Other changes put into effect in 1921 included a new, longer front sight hood that completely enveloped the sight assembly. The bigger sight cover not only protected the front sight, muzzle and bore but because many riflemen of that era used carbide lamps to blacken the front sight against sun glare, it also prevented the carbon coating from smearing when the rifle was not being used. Because the longest distance fired in the National Matches was 1,000 yards, the 2,850-yard notch at the top of the leaf was eliminated on all National Match rifles.

Fig. 1-19. U.S. Army shooting team at National Matches, Camp Perry, Ohio, in 1927. Every man is holding an M1903 National Match rifle. Note the "S" stocks. North Cape Publications collection.

In 1922, new proof standards were developed for the National Match rifles. A proof cartridge producing 75,000 psi was used; five service cartridges were fired followed by twenty-five to thirty more service cartridges fired at the rate of ten rounds per minute.

Other changes followed including a reversed safety and a headless cocking piece to speed up lock time. Starting in 1924, the practice of engraving the serial number of the rifle on the bolt by electric pencil became standard practice. In 1929, the stock was changed from the straight-grip "S" stock to the pistol grip "C" stock and the nomenclature for those rifles so equipped became the "Rifle, U.S. Cal. .30, Model 1903A1 National Match," see Figure 1-20.

In 1930, the headless cocking piece was eliminated and use of the knurled knob cocking piece was resumed for safety considerations—the knob deflected gas away from the shooter's face in case of a ruptured cartridge. A new nickel steel ejector and a sear and extractor of chrome-vanadium steel were used to increase the life of those parts.

Model 1903 Springfield Rifle and Its Variations

Fig. 1-20. In 1929, the "C" stock with the pistol grip became the standard issue for the National Match rifle. North Cape Publications collection.

The ejector was marked "N.S." and the sear and extractor were marked "C.V." Nickel steel bolts were also introduced that year and were marked "N.S." on top of the bolt handle root.

In 1936, regulations called for an extra gas escape hole to be drilled in the left side of the receiver ring but in practice few National Match rifles show this change. Production of the National Match rifle was discontinued after 1940.

National Match rifles are characterized by a heavily oiled stock (the specifications called for them to be dipped in linseed oil four times) with two stock bolts, and smooth, dark-grey or almost black Parkerizing. Stocks show both the Armory inspector's cartouche and the "P" in a circle proof mark in accordance with the practice of the time (see Appendices C and D for proof marks). Bolt assemblies were polished bright and, after 1921, all barrels were "star" marked on the muzzle signifying that they had been gauged.

Of the 28,907 National Match rifles produced at Springfield in the twenty-year period between 1921 through 1940, an estimated 23,200 or more were used by the U.S. military for intra-, inter-, and extra-service matches. A National Match rifle was considered to have a service life of one season including practice and matches and so Springfield records show that a total of 25,377 National Match rifles were rebuilt at least once.

Rebuilt National Match rifles should not be considered in any way inferior to newly built rifles. At the end of the match season (the National Matches at Camp Perry) all National Match rifles issued that year were turned in for rebuilding. All barrels on all rifles were replaced (which explains why so many National Match rifles have barrel dates that do not agree with receiver dates), stocks were scraped and sanded to bare wood, then reoiled (which explains why so many National Match rifles have stocks that look as if they have been refinished – they have) and other metal parts replaced as needed.

It might seem as if 28,907 National Match rifles is an unbelievable number but Brophy quotes a Springfield Armory report for 1930: "At the National matches this year, there will be used 3,129 caliber .30 rifles, M1903 (NM1930) . . ." The report stated that 1,000 of the National Match rifles ". . . are of entirely new manufacture and 2,129 are reconstructed from rifles used in the 1929 matches . . . all have new barrels, ejectors, firing pin assemblies, main springs, sears and front sights, 300 new bolts, 278 new receivers, and 250 new stocks . . . they are to all intents and purposes new guns and are classed as manufactures."

The reader should keep in mind that shooters reaching Camp Perry formed only a small number of those civilians and military personnel participating annually during the match season. Matches were held across the country on both civilian and military ranges and on U.S. military bases in Puerto Rico, Guam, the Philippines and American Samoa with rifles issued to local and state clubs, Reserve Officer Training Corps, National Guard and Reserve military units. At the end of the National Matches at Camp Perry, competitors could purchase a "new" National Match rifle or the one they had been issued for use during the matches. While they were referred to as "new" manufacture, they were in the strictest sense, rebuilt rifles.

Between 5,800-6,000 National Match rifles were also sold through the Director of Civilian Marksmanship Program before the entry of the United States into World War II. Many DCM rifles had the Lyman 48B or C receiver rear sight installed. Springfield Armory did not install these sights on National Match rifles used in National Match competition as the rules required that the rifle's original service sights be used but they could be used in NRA and other competition. Nor did they install them on receivers already hardened. But

Model 1903 Springfield Rifle and Its Variations

they would on request install them on National Match rifles intended for civilian sale through the DCM program or on those intended for use on the "National Match Special" rifles.

The NM rifles retained by the Services were, sad to say, recycled into military service during World War II. Most National Match parts were removed and replaced by standard service parts. Stocks were retained or replaced as necessary and the resulting rifles were reissued as standard Model 1903A1 service rifles.

After World War II, those remaining National Match rifles converted to service rifles followed the standard path of inspection, overhaul with parts replacement as necessary, storage as war reserve rifles and finally surplus sales through the Director of Civilian Marksmanship Program from the early 1950s through the early 1960s.

NATIONAL MATCH "STYLE B" RIFLES

In addition to the standard National Match rifles, Springfield Armory also produced a National Match "Style B" rifle which used the M1922 Type 5 stock with the flattened pistol grip and full-length forend without finger grooves, see Figure 1-21. The Type 6 handguard was used

Fig.1- 21. The National Match "Style B" rifle can be identified by its full-length forend combined with a flattened pistol grip.

as well—observed examples have a pronounced convex curve from the sight protector hump to the lower barrel band cut. The "Style B" was manufactured for sale through the DCM. It had a National Match receiver, star-gauged barrel mounted in the "B" stock. The firing pin assembly was the service type. The receiver was tapped and drilled for the Lyman 48C receiver sight. The stock did not show an Armory inspector's cartouche as it was not intended for military use but did have the "P" in a circle in the usual place on the pistol grip to signify that it had been proof-tested. The Type 5 butt plate for the M1922 stock was used.

SPECIAL TARGET RIFLES

Four distinct types of target rifles totaling 3,851 were produced, see Table 4. They were manufactured from 1922 through 1935 for use by the regular military and National Guard for non-National Match competition and were also sold through the Director of Civilian Marksmanship Program to civilian shooters. From 1922 through 1927, they were made up from standard service rifles, many equipped with star-gauged barrels. From 1928 through 1935, they were National Match rifles that were not reconditioned for use the following season. The

Table 4		
Special Target Rifles Nomenclature and Special Features		
1922-1924	U.S. Rifle, Caliber .30, Model 1903, Star-Gauged	Service rifle with star-gauged barrel
1926-1927	U.S. Rifle, Caliber .30, Model 1903, Style S, Special Target	Service rifle with star-gauged barrel
1928-1930	U.S. Rifle, Caliber .30, Model 1903, Special Target	Reconditioned National Match rifles, reversed safety and headless cocking piece replaced with service parts
1931-1935	U.S. Rifle, Caliber .30, Model 1903A1, Special Target	Reconditioned National Match rifles, reversed safety and headless cocking piece replaced with service parts

reversed safeties and headless cocking pieces of the National Match rifles were replaced with service-configured parts and they were re-designated the "U.S. Rifle, Cal. .30, M1903, Special Target" or, after 1931, "U.S. Rifle, Cal. .30, M1903A1, Special Target." They retained all other National Match parts. When military and National Guard rifles could no longer be used in competition or training, they were returned to the Springfield Armory where they were recondi-tioned as standard service rifles.

NATIONAL MATCH "SPECIAL"

The National Match "Special" rifle was available through the Direc-tor of Civilian Marksmanship Program. Its official description was "U.S. Rifle, Caliber .30, Style NM Special." They were built from National Match rifles that were not sold after the conclusion of the National Matches. They were restocked in the M1922 stock (Type 4H) with the full-length forend. The National Match Type 5 butt plate was installed. The receiver was drilled and tapped, and the stock cut for the Lyman 48C receiver sight. The firing pin assembly was the standard service type. The National Match "Special" rifles were avail-able from 1924 through 1928 and a total of 277 were sold. These rifles did not have the Arsenal inspector's cartouche but did show the "P" in a circle proof mark to show that they had been proof-fired.

The collector should be aware that the "Stock, Cal. .30, NRA Special" was available for separate purchase to National Rifle Asso-ciation members from 1922 through 1932. A great many standard service rifles ultimately wound up in these stocks. They are not and should not be considered "National Match Special" rifles. The droop and contour of the buttstock plus the non-star-gauged barrel should serve to identify them.

U.S. RIFLE, CAL. .30, "STYLE T"

The term, "Special T" (Target) or "Style T" (Target) is somewhat of a misnomer. When this series of rifles was first made available for

Model 1903 Springfield Rifle and Its Variations

sale through the Director of Civilian Marksmanship, it was referred to as a "Match Springfield." Manufactured from 1922 until 1924, they had a 24-inch, .30-caliber heavy match barrel. Some of the early "Match Springfields" may have been mounted in the Type 4F "NRA" stock with finger grooves. They were also inletted for the Lyman Model 48B receiver sight.

In 1925 very similar rifles, produced under the same authority, were referred to by the Commanding Officer of the Springfield Armory as "Special Target" rifles. From 1925 through 1927, they were called "Special Target" rifles by the Springfield Armory but the Ordnance Department referred to them as the "Match Springfield." Those sold through the DCMP were referred to as "Special Target" rifles from 1922 to 1926. In 1927, the DCM listed them as "Style T." They were officially designated the "U.S. Rifle, Cal. .30, Style T" in 1930.

From 1922 through 1927, 1,238 were sold with barrel lengths of 26, 28 and 30 inches. An additional 1,357 were built in 1928 and 1929 and it is assumed that various barrel lengths were still available. They were mounted in the Type 4G stocks without finger grooves. Final production occurred in 1930 when 100 were manufactured and 70 sold through the DCM.

Fig. 1-22. Winchester globe sights were often dovetailed into the BAR front sight and mounted on the "Style T" rifles.

Special target rifles made through 1925 and those rebuilt from National Match rifles that retained their original barrels should show the star-gauge mark on the muzzle.

Telescope blocks for the Winchester A5 or Lyman Model 5A telescopic sight were mounted on many of these rifles; the rear block is mounted on the receiver ring and the forward block on the barrel on 7.2-inch centers. Many of the "Style T" rifles had Winchester globe front sights mounted on the Browning Automatic Rifle barrel fixed stud, see Figure 1-22. Headless cocking pieces were installed on all rifles sold before 1931 and flared head cocking pieces on those sold after 1931 or retrofitted or repaired after that date.

INTERNATIONAL M1903 MATCH RIFLES

The U.S. military competed in various international matches during the 1920s and early 1930s, including the Olympics, which at that time still included long-range, high-power rifle competition. International Match rules applied and the Ordnance Department was persuaded to supply four types of rifles for these competitions which were designated as "Rifle, U.S., Caliber .30, Model 1921 International Match"; "Rifle, U.S., Caliber .30, Model 1922 International Match"; " Rifle, U.S., Caliber .30, Model 1924 International Match" and "Rifle, U.S., Caliber .30, Model 1927 International Match." Each series contained enhancements suggested by the preceding model. The collector should keep in mind that international teams were comprised of between five and ten officers and enlisted men and so the number of rifles produced was very low. And many of these rifles were rebuilt for use in succeeding years — the U.S. participated in International Competition from 1919 to 1925 and 1927 to 1930. Matches were not held in 1926.

All International Match rifle barrels had to meet National Match specifications and were marked with the eight-pointed star on the muzzle indicating that they had been individually tested with the star-gauge apparatus.

U.S. military riflemen first took part in international competition in 1919 firing customized service rifles fitted with stocks customized for each shooter, including one with a pistol grip and another with a butt plate hook. They also were equipped with the Lyman 48B receiver rear sight, a cocking piece from which the flared head had been ground and a 24-inch heavy barrel. The American team won that year by using the sling in the prone position. European military shooters did not use the sling as a shooting aid. Following is a description of each year's model.

Model 1903 Springfield Rifle and Its Variations

Rifle, U.S., Caliber .30, Model 1921 International Match was the first attempt to build a special-purpose rifle for the international matches, see Figure 1-23. The basic design used a straight taper heavy barrel 1.5 inches in diameter at the receiver and 1 inch in diameter at the muzzle in an "S" stock with the forend cut off and rounded up ahead of a modified M1917 Enfield barrel band. The Lyman 48B receiver sight (long slide) was used in conjunction with the standard undercut M1905 front sight. Rifles are said to have averaged 12.75 lbs. in weight. Three variations in the stock were made to fit the individual shooters. The first had a Schuetzen-style butt plate, the second had a pistol grip and the third was the "S" stock with the forend reduced. All rifles had a standard service trigger which had been smoothed and lightened at the Springfield Armory. Brophy noted that only two examples of this rifle appear to have survived.

Fig. 1-23. M1921 International Match Rifle. Springfield Armory collection.

Rifle, U.S., Caliber .30, Model 1922 International Match incorporated the lessons learned during the 1921 season. The M1922 NRA .30-caliber stock was modified to include an adjustable forward sling swivel, sporting-type butt plate with a hook attached to the stock, cork-ball palm rest under the magazine, headless cocking piece, lightened firing pin, double-lever set trigger manufactured in Germany, and the Lyman 48B receiver rear sight. Originally, barrel length was set at 24 inches but team members were allowed to pick the barrel length with which they were most familiar. These rifles were used in both 1922 and 1923.

Model 1903 Springfield Rifle and Its Variations

Rifle, U.S., Caliber .30, Model 1924 International Match was similar to the M1922 but used commercial barrels from Remington, Pope and Winchester, see Figure 1-24. Also changed was the front sight. The Browning Automatic Rifle barrel fixed stud was used to mount the Winchester globe front sight (refer to Figure 1-22) and the firing pin assembly was replaced by the Garand Super Speed Firing Mechanism. Two trigger assemblies were used, one of which was a new two-lever system designed at the U.S. Marines Small Arms Arsenal and Armory and the other of which was designed and built by Frank Rimkunas, also at the USMSAAA. Both were based on the German two-lever design used in the M1922 International rifles. A new aluminum butt plate with hook was used. The butt plate could be adjusted vertically.

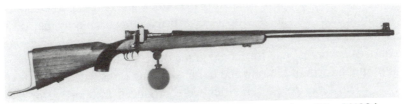

Fig. 1-24. Believed to be one of the few existing examples of the M1924 International Match Rifle. Original Pope barrel replaced by a 28-inch Springfield barrel. From the collection of the late Stephen Johns.

The Garand Super Speed Firing Mechanism had a travel of 0.4 inch to impact the primer and did so in 0.0022 second. The service rifle firing pin traveled 0.6 inch in 0.0057 second. Complete details of the Garand Super Speed Firing Pin can be found in *Hatcher's Notebook*.

Rifle, U.S., Caliber .30, Model 1927 International Match was very similar to the M1924 International Match Rifle. Barrel length was set at 28 inches and a new, four-lever set trigger was added that had been designed by Captain George A. Woody. Other than an article in *The American Rifleman* by Julian S. Hatcher in April 1927, little more has been published about these rifles.

Model 1903 Springfield Rifle and Its Variations

This was the last M1903-based International Match rifle. Those used in 1928 and 1929 were based on the Hammerli Martini action. The M1927 International Match rifles were intended to be used in the prone stages of the 1930 matches, but the condition of the firing line did not allow that and so the M1928 Hammerli Martini action rifles were used instead. The U.S. did not participate in the International Matches after that year.

M1903 AND M1903A1 .30-CALIBER SPORTER RIFLES (A.K.A. NRA SPORTER)

The practice of providing service rifles for sale to military officers for hunting and target practice began in the post-Civil War era. During the 1870s and 1880s, the Springfield Armory designed an M1873 .45-70 Springfield Rifle with a sporting rifle stock and tang-mounted aperture sight and sold it to officers at a price comparable to that of a commercial rifle of like quality. While expensive—often the equivalent of 1-2 months' pay for a field grade officer—they provided recreation in the form of hunting and target shooting on isolated posts.

No Krag-Jorgensen rifles were produced as sporting or target rifles, although many Krags were used by military and civilian shooting teams and individuals from 1894 through 1907.

After World War I, there were few commercial sporting rifles in .30-M1906 caliber available. So, in 1924, the Director of Civilian Marksmanship authorized the sale of .30-caliber barrels shaped to the contour of the .22-caliber barrel for use in the M1922 stock (Type 4I). The demand was high enough and the supply of the sporting barrels limited so that the sale of M1922 stocks with or without inletting for the M1905 sight base was later authorized to allow the use of standard service barrels. In November 1924, complete rifles became available from the Director of Civilian Marksmanship Program. National Match actions, barrels and trigger assemblies were used.

Barrels were star gauged and ground to the same contour as the .22-caliber barrels to fit the M1922 stock. The front sight assembly was the standard M1905 front sight; the rear sight was the Lyman

Model 1903 Springfield Rifle and Its Variations

48B before 1926 and the Lyman 48C after. The owner of the rifle was expected to shorten the stock to fit, see Figure 1-25.

The bolt was polished bright as was the follower but the bolt runways were not as the rifle was blued (browned). The butt plate, trigger guard and floor plate were blackened using the carburizing process.

The .30-caliber sporter rifles were available through the DCM from late 1924 through 1932. After that, only parts were sold. In 1934, parts sales were further limited to those who had actually purchased a

Fig. 1-25. Model 1903A1 Sporting Rifle sold through the DCMP in 1924. From the collection of the late Stephen Johns.

complete rifle. A final production run of twenty-nine rifles was made in 1937-1938 for the Department of Justice. Total production was 6,547.

The collector should note that these "sporter rifles" were intended to be sold to experienced shooters, both military and civilian, with the idea that they would custom fit the stocks and sights to their particular needs. These rifles were never used in military service.

U.S. Rifle, Caliber .30 Sporting Type (NBA Sporter)

A total of 529 sporter rifles were manufactured in 1926 and equipped with the Model 1922 M1 stock. The stock, which was refitted with the two reinforcing screws, had the characteristic flat pistol grip of the Model 1922 M1 stock. These rifles were characteristically equipped with the Lyman 48B or C receiver sight and without the Model 1905 rear sight on the barrel. The designation, "NBA," had nothing to do with the National Basketball Association since that organization was not founded until 1946.

Model 1903 Springfield Rifle and Its Variations

Gallery Practice Rifles, .22 Caliber

As early as the 1870s, the New York National Guard had used .22-caliber rimfire versions of their issue rifles (the Remington Rolling Block) for indoor shooting and target practice or where space was too limited for a larger range. The U.S. Navy followed much the same practice in the 1880s using their M1870 rolling block rifles.

Other National Guard units used .22-caliber Krag rifles as modified by the J. Stevens Arms and Tool Company with barrels made by Harry M. Pope at the turn of the 20th century. The Pope barrels centered the muzzle in the barrel but the bore was slanted so it emerged close to the top of the receiver ring, see Figure 1-26. This allowed the Krag extractor to grip the cartridge properly and the firing pin to strike the rim of the cartridge.

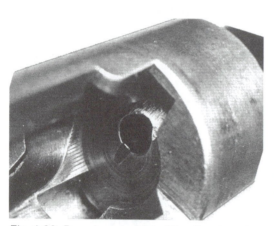

Fig. 1-26. Breech end of the .22-caliber barrels manufactured by Harry M. Pope for the Krag rifle. Hal Bolefahr collection.

The Ordnance Department developed a .22-caliber rimfire version of the M1903 rifle that used the same offset bore principle developed by Pope, but in which the bore ran from the center of the muzzle to the bottom of the receiver. An auxiliary extractor was used to remove the cartridge cases from the chamber and the side of the receiver was relieved to make it easier to insert the .22 cartridge. When this design did not prove satisfactory, further work led to the design of the "Hoffer-Thompson Cartridge Holder" by Major J.E. Hoffer.

Model 1903 Springfield Rifle and Its Variations

U.S. GALLERY PRACTICE RIFLE, CALIBER .22, MODEL OF 1903 (HOFFER-THOMPSON)

The Hoffer-Thompson Cartridge Holder was shaped like the .30-M1906 cartridge but with a long neck in place of the bullet, see Figure 1-27. The .22-caliber short cartridge was inserted into the holder which was then placed in the M1903 Springfield. The bolt's firing pin struck the back of the cartridge holder which in turn drove a spring-loaded double firing pin to strike on the rim of the cartridge. The new system was adopted in 1907 and designated the "U.S. Gallery Practice Rifle, Caliber .22, Model of 1903." The rifle was a standard M1903 except for the barrel which had a .22-caliber bore and the receiver's chamber which was slightly shorter and wider in diameter to prevent the accidental chambering of .30-M1906 cartridges. The cartridge holders, in turn, were slightly larger in diameter than the .30-M1906 cartridge. The advantage of the Hoffer-Thompson system lay in the fact that the cartridge holders could be loaded into a magazine one at a time or inserted into the cartridge clip. Also, with the exception of the barrel and receiver, all parts were standard M1903 parts which kept costs down. Some 3,000 rifles were manufactured in late 1907 at Springfield Armory. Special clips with bronze springs and no tabs were used with the Hoffer-Thompson cartridge holder. Twenty-five holders were issued with each rifle, also an ejection tool

Fig. 1-27. Hoffer-Thompson .22-caliber rimfire cartridge holder. Phil Siess collection.

which was essentially a straight rod with a screwdriver-style handle to remove the spent cases from the holder. The rifles were marked "22" on the receiver bridge and other parts such as the bayonet lug, bolt safety lug and the front of the stock—but not consistently.

Model 1903 Springfield Rifle and Its Variations

The Hoffer-Thompson cartridge holder system did not work as well in practice as in theory. It was a pain in the neck to load the holders and even worse to unload the empties. The salts in the rimfire cartridge primers caused excessive corrosion and rusting, no matter how carefully they were cleaned and oiled. After several rifles had inadvertently been shipped overseas and other mistakes in issue had been made, many of them were restocked with birch stocks finished with a light oil in the hope that the difference in color and wood grain would prevent further mixups.

The Hoffer-Thompson system continued in use through World War I, supplemented by a purchase of 4,428 falling block .22-caliber rifles from Winchester, known as the Winder Musket. A further 2,000 Hoffer-Thompson rifles were ordered in 1919 and issued to DCM-affiliated clubs. Many of these muskets continued in use through 1928. The majority of Hoffer-Thompson rifles and military-issue Winder Muskets were recalled in the 1920s and destroyed. Gallery practice was already being conducted with a special .30-M1906 low-power cartridge designated Cartridge, Gallery Practice, Cal. .30, M1919 which was fired through the standard service rifle.

U.S. RIFLE, CALIBER .22, M1922

Starting in 1922, Springfield Armory was directed to work with the National Rifle Association to develop a .22-caliber rifle that could be used by DCM-affiliated rifle clubs and by high-school, college and Reserve Officer Training Corps (ROTC) shooting teams.

NOTE: The M1922, M1922 M1 and M2 rifles were each serial numbered in their own sequence, starting with "1." The highest serial numbers that have been observed are: M1922—2,018, M1922 M1—20,020, and M2 —21,082 (receiver only).

The first design used a standard M1903 rifle with a .22-caliber barrel. A five-round magazine fed cartridges through a cut in the floor plate, the bolt was extensively modified with a rotating head and extractor and a standard service stock was used. In all, three variations were tried, culminating in a prototype with a sporter stock, the Lyman 48 rear sight and a flared head cocking piece.

Fig. 1-28. M1922 .22-Caliber gallery rifle. North Cape Publications collection.

The new gallery rifle was standardized in 1922 as "Rifle, Caliber .22, M1922," see Figure 1-28. It had a 24-inch barrel that had a slightly concave taper ahead of the breech to the muzzle. Rifling was four lands and grooves of equal width with a twist of 16:1. Minimum and maximum land and groove height and depth was specified as 0.2175-0.2180 and 0.2225-0.2230 inch, respectively. The Lyman 48B rear sight replaced the M1905 rear sight although the M1905 front sight was retained. If requested, telescopic sight blocks were installed on 7.2-inch centers on the barrel. The two-piece bolt made use of the rotating head with extractor developed in the prototypes. The "throw of the bolt" (the length of pull required to open and draw the bolt back to its full extent) was made to simulate the throw of the M1903 .30-caliber bolt. The sporting stock was the "Stock, Model of 1922," also known as the NRA stock. During the first month or so of production only, the stock was made with finger grooves. The barrel and receiver were blued (browned) and the other parts niter blued or "carbonia blackened" a.k.a. carburized. The bolt and extractor were polished bright. The receivers were marked U. S./ SPRINGFIELD/ ARMORY/MODEL OF 1922/CAL. .22/XXXX.

A total of 2,032 receivers were manufactured between 1922 and 1924 — 2,000 for DCM sales; 20 for U.S. Army evaluation and

12 receivers were used to build twelve .22-caliber International Match Rifles.

INTERNATIONAL MATCH RIFLE, CALIBER .22, MODEL 1924

The U.S. Free Rifle Team decided at a late date to enter the 1924 international small bore matches and Springfield Armory personnel scrambled to come up with a rifle for them. The basic M1922 rifle was used with some changes made to the bolt, barrel and stock. The double striker was dropped in favor of a single striker attached to the firing pin rod which reduced lock time. A 30-inch heavy barrel tapering from 1.25 inches at the breech to 0.9 inch at the muzzle was installed. The Browning Automatic Rifle fixed sight stud was used and the magazine was dispensed with. The palm rest was attached to the magazine well. Rifling was six groove, 16:1. Twelve of these rifles were manufactured using the M1922 receiver.

U.S. RIFLE, CALIBER .22, M1922M1

The Army conducted extensive testing of the M1922 gallery rifle before a decision was reached in May 1923 to adopt the .22-caliber gallery rifle in place of the Hoffer-Thompson system. Due to shortcomings in the M1922, developmental work continued on the gallery rifle concept. A new rifle, designated the Rifle, Caliber .22, M1922M1, was adopted in 1925, see Figure 1-29. In 1936, the designation was changed to "M1."

A new bolt retained the separate bolt head but used the single-point striker (as developed for the M1924 International .22 Rifle) attached to the firing pin rod. The bolt throw again simulated that of the M1903 .30-caliber rifle. The chamber was reduced in both diameter and length and the rifling diameter was slightly enlarged by 0.0005 inch. Minimum and maximum land and groove height and depth was specified as 0.2180 - 0.2185 and 0.2230-0.2235 inch, respectively. The new gallery rifle also received a slightly altered stock. The Lyman 48C rear sight replaced the Lyman 48B. The chamber, lock time and

Model 1903 Springfield Rifle and Its Variations

Fig. 1-29. Military M1922M1s used a modified M1922 stock with a flattened pistol grip and slightly longer pull. DCM rifles used the M1922 stock as shown here. John Turner collection.

rifling changes provided exceptional accuracy. Specifications called for group sizes of one inch at 50 yards.

A new stock—"Stock, M1922M1, Caliber .22," also known as the "B" stock"— replaced the earlier M1922 stock. It was basically the service rifle "S" stock with the short forend and without the handguard. The pull was 0.375 inch longer, had slightly less drop at the comb, finger grooves and a squared-off or abbreviated, flat-bottomed pistol grip.

The "Stock, M1922M1, Caliber .22" was used for military gallery rifles and had the standard service rifle butt plate. The DCM-NRA sales rifle used the M1922 stock without finger grooves, although the military-style finger groove stock could be ordered instead. DCM-NRA sales rifles in the M1922 stock were equipped with the National Match butt plate.

The bolt was polished bright and serial numbered to the receiver with an electric pen. The rest of the metal was Parkerized until 1926 when the receiver finish was changed to carbonia blackening. A new five-shot magazine that fit almost flush with the bottom of the receiver was used.

M1922 rifles returned for repairs or refurbishment received the upgraded bolt and firing pin/striker assembly, new magazine and Lyman 48C rear sight. The receiver was then stamped "MI" (the capital letter "I" was used to denote a modification) after the "M1922" and an "A" was added to the serial number to prevent duplication.

Model 1903 Springfield Rifle and Its Variations

After receiver serial number 17,267, the receiver and bolt steel were changed to nickel steel. The bolt root was stamped "N.S." A total of 114 DCM-NRA M1922M1 rifles were later rebuilt as M1922MII rifles. A "B" was added to their serial numbers. Production of the M1922 M1 ended in 1934 but DCM-NRA sales continued through 1937. A total of 20,020 M1922 M1 rifles were built, 14,680 for military use and 5,330 for sales through the DCM-NRA.

U.S. RIFLE, CALIBER .22 M2

The M2 rifle (Figure 1-30) differs in many regards from its two predecessors. The barrel was set further back into the receiver and a new bolt, stock and magazine were used. The bolt was redesigned to eliminate the locking latch and the cuts needed in the safety lug to support it. The M2 bolt head locked into the bolt via a cut ground on the forward edge of the safety lug and a raised rim at the rear of the bolt head. Two types of M2 bolt bodies were used during M2 production. The first, in use until 1934, was not adjustable for head space, while the second, used after 1934, was. A set screw adjusted the spacing between the bolt and bolt head.

Fig. 1-30. M2 .22-caliber Gallery Rifle. James Gronning collection.

A nut secured the firing pin in the bolt. The nut had a flared head to deflect gas from the shooter's eye in case of a ruptured cartridge. The stock was modified slightly with less drop to the comb and a shorter, thinner pistol grip. As with the M1922M1 stock, those intended for service use had a service-style butt plate while those for civilian sale had a squared butt and used the National Match butt plate.

Model 1903 Springfield Rifle and Its Variations

Markings are more complicated in this series. Those M1922 rifles not having been previously upgraded now received the M2 bolt, firing pin/striker assembly and magazine and were stamped "M2" after the "M1922" marking. M1922 rifles upgraded to "MI" and now upgraded again to M2 status had "MII" or "MI1" stamped after the "M1922" marking and an "A" was added to their serial number. M1922 M1 rifles had an extra "I" or "1" added to their marking and a "B" added to their serial number.

An estimated 3,800 M2 rifles were built using the first style of M2 nonadjustable bolt and the balance with the second type of M2 adjustable bolt. DCM-NRA sales were 7,660 M2 rifles which started in 1938 and ended in 1940. Production of M2 parts continued into 1942 with all of the post-1940 production going to the military services. Barrels manufactured in 1942 were 23.5 inches long, 0.5 inch shorter than the pre-1942 M2 barrels. The muzzle crown was changed in early June 1942 to a countersink, as it was on the service rifle .30-caliber barrels. Barrels dated 1942 were used in large quantities to re-barrel rifles returned for repairs or refurbishing during and after World War II. No production figures are available for M2 rifles manufactured after 1942 but receivers as high as serial number 21,181 have been observed. M2 receivers and other parts were sold through the DCM after World War II.

The production of the M2 rifle was discontinued as it proved cheaper to purchase the Winchester M75, Stevens 416 and Remington M513T rifles for gallery practice. It also freed up production and assembly space at Springfield Armory for higher-priority war work.

U.S. Model 1903 Service Rifle, Final Production

Assembly of U.S. Model 1903 Service Rifles ended, for all intents and purposes, in Fiscal Year 1927 with the assembly of 2,000 rifles. M1903 .30-caliber rifles continued to be assembled until 1941 but only for sale through the Director of Civilian Marksmanship (DCM) Program or for use in the National Matches. During the fiscal years 1934-1935 the process of tooling up for the M1 Garand occupied the facili-

Model 1903 Springfield Rifle and Its Variations

ties and work force at Springfield Armory and no M1903 .30-caliber rifles were assembled or parts manufactured.

The manufacture of M1903 parts, including receivers, was resumed in 1936 and continued at Springfield Armory until late in 1941 or early 1942 when Remington Arms Company began producing M1903 parts. The last receiver appears to have been manufactured in 1939 but is the subject of some controversy as noted below. When Remington shifted to the manufacture of M1903A3 Rifles, Springfield Armory produced additional M1903 spare parts in 1944 and 1945. It is unlikely that any receivers were included in this last manufacturing run.

Late wartime Springfield M1903 barrels can be identified not only by their dates but also by the substitution of a countersunk muzzle in place of the crowned muzzle and the heavy undercuts on either side of the front sight stud.

After the Korean War, parts for the M1903 Springfield were made available for civilian sale through the Director of Civilian Marksmanship Program. Over the years, the DCM Program included complete rifles as well as spare parts. Rifles and parts sold through the DCM were required to meet current standards for the M1903 or M1903A3/A4 and consequently, the vast majority of the rifles were updated or refurbished at various Ordnance facilities before being transferred to the DCM.

As late as this writing, some M1903 parts are still available through the successor to the DCM, the Civilian Marksmanship Program.

The question of the last serial-numbered receiver for the M1903 has confounded scholars and writers for years. Major General Julian S. Hatcher, in his *Hatcher's Notebook* published in 1947, stated that the last receiver was manufactured in October 1939 with the serial number 1,532,878. Certainly if anyone should have known what the highest number receiver produced at Springfield was, it would have been Major General Hatcher. However, serial-numbered receivers higher than that have turned up with disconcerting regularity.

Model 1903 Springfield Rifle and Its Variations

Clark Campbell reported serial number 1,592,563 in *The '03 Era* (1994), 59,685 numbers higher. John Beard, in a well-reasoned and researched article appearing in the *U.S. Martial Arms Collector*, No. 91, suggests that the last M1903 serial-numbered receiver manufactured at Springfield was probably 1,536,XXX, recorded sometime in 1940. This agrees nicely with a rifle reported in the collection of Mr. Joseph Lyon which carries the serial number 1,536,281 and a Springfield barrel date of "10/42."

Rather than nearly 60,000 receivers over that reported by Major General Hatcher as suggested by some, the total number is probably closer to 3,500 or less. For a more thorough discussion of the problem of the high-numbered receivers, see Appendix A.

U.S. RIFLE, CALIBER. 30, M1903 (REMINGTON ARMS COMPANY)

As early as September 1939, British military authorities became concerned about their lack of small-arms production capability. In the years following World War I, successive British governments had reduced the British military and arms production to dangerous levels. Warnings against resurgent German militarism went unheeded until too late. When Germany attacked Poland in 1939, both Great Britain and France declared war on Germany but were unable to do more than offer moral support and conduct an ineffective bombing campaign against German military targets along the North Sea.

In April 1940, Germany attacked and occupied Denmark and Norway in a blitzkrieg-style operation. British and French troops were sent to Norway and British destroyers won a major naval battle off Trondheim, sinking eight German destroyers. Allied troops which had landed along the western coast and pushed inland were unable to hold against superior German forces and withdrew in June 1940.

In early May of that same year, Germany invaded the Low Countries and France. In little more than three weeks, the British Expeditionary Force, which had been on the Continent since the previous autumn, found itself trapped against the English Channel at

Model 1903 Springfield Rifle and Its Variations

Dunkirk and Calais. Only an extraordinary effort by military and civilian mariners allowed more than 350,000 British, French and Belgian troops to be rescued by sea. But they were forced to leave their heavy armament and most of their small arms behind. Then just as France was falling to the German blitzkrieg, Mussolini ordered Italian troops into southern France and invaded British possessions in North Africa and Ethiopia.

Great Britain now faced Germany and Italy alone with only a small, poorly armed army, a tough but small Air Force and a Navy weakened by two decades of budget reductions and downsizing while waiting for what they hoped was the inevitable entry of the United States into the war, see Figure 1-31. In July, German submarines intensified their undersea offensive against British shipping and in Au-

Fig. 1-31. The attack on Pearl Harbor on December 7, 1941 thrust the United States into World War II. U.S. Navy photo.

gust the Luftwaffe began a major air offensive. Operation Sea Lion, the invasion of the British Isles, was set to jump off as soon as the Luftwaffe gained control of the skies over the English Channel and the invasion beaches.

Great Britain, lacking the production capacity to produce sufficient small arms for its military forces, turned to the United States and Canada. A contract was granted to the Savage Arms Company's Stevens Division to produce the No. 4 Mk. 1* Rifle. Next, the Remington Arms Company was approached to produce 500,000 rifles for British forces at the rate of 1,000 per day. The rifle was to be the "U. S. Rifle, Caliber .30, Model 1903" but modified to .303 British caliber with rear aperture sight, Enfield-style front sight with protectors and the barrel muzzle modified to accept the Enfield No. 4 bayonet.

Remington leased the tooling and fixtures for the Model 1903 rifle that had been in storage at Rock Island for 19 years. They also procured from Rock Island 600,000 blanks for stocks and handguards as a trade against cartridges to be manufactured later. Remington engineers worked with the British to redesign the components necessary to meet the British requirements.

President Franklin Roosevelt then signed the Lend-Lease Act in March 1941, easing the weapons situation in Great Britain. The contract for the converted rifles was canceled on September 17, 1941, and all small-arms procurement became the province of the Ordnance Department. The Ordnance Department reissued the contract to Remington for 134,000 M1903 rifles in .30-M1906 caliber for use by the U.S. military forces. As the rifles were built on Rock Island tooling and fixtures, they were almost identical to the rifles (except for markings) produced at that armory between 1917 and 1921. They were equipped with the M1905 knife bayonet and the M1923 web sling, see Figure 1-32. This contract was subsequently increased to 174,000.

Model 1903 Springfield Rifle and Its Variations

NOTE: While the "C" stock was approved for the Remington M1903 as it was for the Springfield M1903A1, only a few thousand Remington-made rifles were so equipped and the "S" stock was the principal stock supplied with the Remington M1903. Some 600,000 stock blanks that had been in storage at Rock Island Armory had been procured but they were not large enough to make the pistol-gripped "C" stock. The "S" stocks produced by Remington were very similar to those made at Springfield and Rock Island but they lacked finger grooves and were slightly thicker by 0.1 to 0.15 inch in the wrist and forearm.

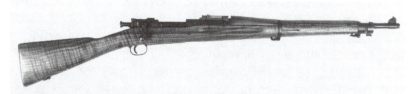

Fig. 1-32. Remington-manufactured M1903 rifle. Photo courtesy of Remington Arms Company and Roy Marcot.

Production of the Remington Model 1903 began in September 1941 with the delivery of ten trial rifles. During this period, engineers and designers in the Ordnance Department and at Remington Arms were working on ways to simplify production of the rifle. Approvals were given by the Ordnance Department and the change to the modified version of the M1903 took place in May-June 1942 circa serial #3,133,444. Table 5 provides a list of all Post-Springfield Armory rifle models and their production figures.

U.S. RIFLE, CALIBER. 30, M1903 (MODIFIED)
REMINGTON ARMS COMPANY

In early March 1942, a third supplement to the original contract with Remington Arms designated the new model as U.S. Rifle, Cal. .30, M1903 (Modified) and doubled the quantity of rifles to be produced. Late March to early April 1942 saw the start of production of the Remington M1903 (Modified) which continued through August 1942.

Model 1903 Springfield Rifle and Its Variations

Manufacturer	Model	Serial Number Range[1]	Campbell[2]	Brophy[3]
		Table 5 **Post-Springfield Armory M1903, M1903A3 and M1903A4 Production Estimates** Clark S. Campbell and Lt. Col. W. S. Brophy, USAR, Ret.		
Remington	1903	3,000,000 - 3,133,444	133,444	133,444
	1903 (Modified)	3,133,445 - 3,364,954	214,641	231,509
	1903A3	3,364,955 - 3,407,087	707,629	783,844
		3,427,088 - 4,168,800[4]		
	1903A4	3,407,088 - 3,427,087	28,365	29,964
		4,000,001 - 4,015,000[5]		
		4,992,001 - 4,999,045		
Remington Production			**1,084,079**	**1,178,761**
Smith Corona	1903A3	3,608,000 - 3,707,000	234,580	236,831
Smith Corona	1903A3	4,708,000 - 4,485,831		
Smith Corona Production				
Total Post-Springfield Model 1903 Production			**1,318,659**	**1,415,592**

1. Serial number ranges issued by the Ordnance Department.
2. Campbell's figures are from the Remington Arms Company.
3. Brophy's totals were compiled from production records and reports.
4. Although this block supposedly ended at serial #4,168,800, the author has Remington M1903A3 serial #4,206,757, dated 9/43, a serial # overrun that required the use of the "Z" prefix in the next block assigned to prevent duplicate serial numbers. Apparently, Remington did not include the 2,920 overrun rifles in their totals.
5. Only 2,920 M1903A4s from this block built, all with "Z" serial number prefixes.

This variation continued to resemble the M1903 as produced at Rock Island during WWI with its M1905 barrel-mounted rear sight. But the first of the changes, or "modifications" was made in December 1941 when the lightening cuts in the forward tang of the trigger guard and

Model 1903 Springfield Rifle and Its Variations

the sides of the rear sight base were eliminated, see Figure 1-33. The M1903 (Modified) is rightly regarded as the transition model between the M1903 and the M1903A3. Over the next several months additional changes were introduced as shown in Table 6.

Stocks for the Remington M1903 (Modified) between December 1941 and August 1942 show a gradual transition from the finely made and fitted Remington M1903 stocks to the more crudely cut and finished stocks of the M1903A3. In January 1942, the receiver bedding had been opened up by 0.2 inch to ease seating problems. The scraping and sanding procedures were also eased, leaving the stocks with a rough, grainy appearance. The last 1,909 M1903 (Modified)

Table 6
Remington M1903 to Remington M1903 (Modified) Changes
Phased in between December 1941 and August 1942

No lightening cuts under receiver tang. (December 1941)*
Profile cuts on the receiver shoulder front eliminated. (December 1941)
Bolt stop eliminated. (March 1942)
Rear guard screw drilled through tang. (March 1942)
Gas hole on right side of receiver eliminated. (Feb/March 1942)
Butt plates---cyanide case-hardening eliminated. (March 1942)
Front guard screw drilled into receiver ring. (March 1942)
Cutoff seat profile changed to milled cut. (March 1942)
Stamped components replaced milled components (April 1942) including:
    Lower band
    Lower band retaining spring
    Upper sling swivel
    Extractor collar
    Magazine follower
    Butt swivel assembly
Fixed stud key replaced the integral spine. (April 1942)
Bolt turned below body diameter in the following areas: (April 1942)
    Around bolt handle (0.7 inch from rear of bolt body)
    Around safety lug (1.6 to 2.7 inches from front of body)
    Around front lugs (0.7 inch from front of body)
Cocking piece neck was left straight instead of sloping downward. (April 1942)
The height of the bolt sleeve was raised to 1.072 inches from 1.025 inches above
    its centerline. (April 1942)
Integral trigger guard and magazine housing. (Approved April 1942)
Upper and lower band, guard and cutoff screw threads changed from "V" to
    rounded. (April 1942)
M1903A3 stock. (August 1942)

*Dates in parentheses are authorization dates and not necessarily introduction dates.

Model 1903 Springfield Rifle and Its Variations

Rifles were delivered in March 1943.

U.S. RIFLE, CALIBER .30, M1903A3

Changes to manufacturing procedures, tools, fixtures, jigs and parts that had been in the works since December 1941 had gone far enough forward that on May 21, 1942, the Ordnance Department authorized the new Model

Fig. 1-33. Remington M1903 (Modified) rifles incorporated changes to simplify production, i.e., eliminating the lightening cut in the trigger guard plate, among others.

1903A3 rifle, see Figure 1-34. The M1903A3 stock was authorized on June 8 and the first stock deliveries were made to the assembly line on August 3, 1942. The most significant alteration was the change from a barrel-mounted open rear sight to a receiver bridge-mounted aperture sight with a 0.07-inch-diameter "peep." The fixed-base rear sight mount with its M1905 rear sight was eliminated. The first 1,909 M1903A3 rifles were delivered in December 1942.

Fig. 1-34. The M1903A3 was a simplified production model of the M1903 rifle. Extensive use was made of parts stamped from sheet steel rather than milled from bar stock to increase production. North Cape Publications collection.

The receiver bridge rear sight consisted of a "U"-shaped mount, the "windage yoke," which held a slide aperture that moved

Model 1903 Springfield Rifle and Its Variations

left or right by means of a screw to adjust for windage. The slide aperture itself was "L" shaped and bolted to the base and moved up and down inside the side of the windage yoke to adjust the range from 100 to 800 yards in 50-yard increments. The aperture was 0.07 inch in diameter. The windage could be adjusted in 1 minute of angle increments by turning the windage knob on the right side of the windage yoke, see Figure 1-35.

The front sight was also changed. The combination of barrel band base and moveable sight stud was discarded. The front sight band was extruded instead of milled and the blade was pinned in place. The base was indexed to the barrel with a pin. As the receiver bridge rear sight was higher than the barrel-mounted sight, the front sight blade heights were changed. Five blades were used ranging in height from 0.477 to 0.537 inch.

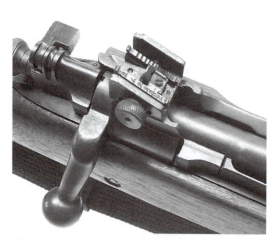

Fig. 1-35 The M1903A3 receiver mounted rear sight with a 0.07-inch aperture replaced the M1905 barrel-mounted rear sight.

Since the Model 1905 rear sight and its base had been eliminated, the barrel contour ahead of the receiver was also changed. Where the diameter of the M1903 service barrel was 1.140 inches for 1.03 inches ahead of the receiver, the M1903A3 barrel was now 1.200 inches in diameter for only 0.749 inch ahead of the receiver. The M1905 rear sight base cannot be mounted on the M1903A3 barrel.

The original specifications for the Remington M1903 had called for a "C"-type stock with a pistol grip. Remington's acquisition of

64

Model 1903 Springfield Rifle and Its Variations

600,000 stock blanks forced a compromise as the blanks were not large enough to produce a pistol-grip stock. On May 12, 1944, authorization was given to use either the straight-grip ("S" stock) or the "scant-grip" stock, see Figure 1-36. This last was a "C"-configuration stock with the line of the stock bottom extended through the pistol-grip area to produce a blunt or partial

Fig. 1-36. M1903A3 stocks, top to bottom: "Scant-Grip," "C" and "S" types.

pistol grip. Apparently the Remington Arms and Smith Corona companies produced only the "S" stock while the "C" stocks and "scant-grip" stocks were produced by subcontractors like American Bowling and Keystone Manufacturing. The drawing number for the World War II "S" stock was D35539. The "C" stock drawing (D28366) was modified to the "Scant-Grip" stock.

The straight-grip stock appears to have been used in far greater numbers than the scant-grip stock on original production M1903A3 rifles as might be expected given that the scant-grip stock was not approved until May 1944, only a few months from the end of M1903A3 production. The scant-grip stocks appear in large numbers as replacement stocks but were also used as original stocks on the M1903A4 Sniper Rifle in the serial number range 4,000,001 to 4,003,000 along with the "S"-style stock. M1903A3 stocks can be identified by the transverse groove cut ahead of the magazine well. To hold the new "barrel cover" securely at the receiver end of the M1903A3 rifle, a barrel guard ring had been added, see Figure 1-37. It was stamped from sheet steel and had a rear facing lip or tenon that fitted under the

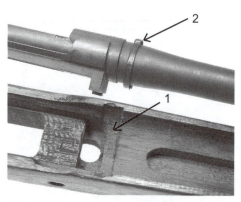

receiver ring and a forward lip that held the barrel cover tenon. The ring encircled the barrel. To allow the stock to be seated with the barrel guard ring present, the M1903A3 stock had a cut milled around the inside of the stock. Even though the Model 1905 rear sight had been eliminated, both versions of the M1903A3 stock retained the clearance cuts for the fixed-base rear sight

Fig. 1-37. A transverse groove was cut in the stock for the barrel guard ring, arrows 1 & 2.

mount so that it could also serve as a replacement of the M1903 service rifle.

The M1903A3 stock had two stock bolts. Early production used a smaller-diameter transverse screw with a nut that looked very much like a pin but later production used the early type stock bolt and nut. A new "barrel cover" replaced the handguard used on the M1903. It was longer and its rear tenon was held in place by barrel guard ring, see Figure 1-38.

Fig. 1-38. With the M1903A3 rear sight moved to the receiver bridge, a longer barrel cover was required; top, M1903A3 barrel guard, below, M1903 handguard.

Model 1903 Springfield Rifle and Its Variations

The M1903A3 cocking piece was similar to that used on the M1903 with the exception of the head or cocking knob. The M1903 cocking knob had one row of knurling and 5 grooves cut around its circumference to make it easier to grasp. The M1903A3 cocking knob was knurled only, see Figure 1-39.

The M1903A3 trigger guard screws were increased 0.1 inch in length (M1903 — 0.9, M1903A3 — 1.0 inch). M1903A3 trigger guard screws should not be used on the M1903 as they will bottom against the receiver, prevent proper bedding and may destroy accuracy.

Fig. 1-39. Cocking knobs: top, M1903, bottom, M1903A3.

The final change occurred at the end of December 1942 when the Ordnance Department ordered that the trigger guard be increased in diameter for cold-weather use with gloves, see Figure 1-40. The change was not introduced into production until mid-June 1943. All remaining changes were phased into production between August 1942 and December 1943 (see Table 7).

Fig. 1-40. M1903A3 trigger guards: top, Type 3 "Arctic" or "Winter" trigger guard; bottom, Type 2 early trigger guard.

Model 1903 Springfield Rifle and Its Variations

Table 7
Remington M1903 (Modified) to M1903A3 Changes
Phased in between August 1942 and December 1943
Receiver-bridge mounted aperture sight.
Front sight and mount combined in one extruded part.
Higher front sight blade.
Barrel contour changed to 1.200 x 0.749 inches.
Barrel cover replaced by handguard.
"C" and scant-grip stocks used as replacements.
Barrel guard ring added.
Stock pins to replace stock bolts introduced at end of Modified production (10-11/42).
Stock bolts replace stock pins by 7/43.
Three-part cocking piece (pentagonal shaft).
Long front guard screws (0.9 to 1.0 inch).
Increased-diameter trigger guard for gloved hands.

NOTE: The Model 1903A3 was manufactured by both Remington Arms Company and L.C. Smith Corona Typewriter Company. There is little difference between the two rifles except in markings which are detailed in the appropriate parts sections. Some overlap in serial numbers did occur at the beginning and end of serial number blocks. This was handled by marking a "C" before duplicated serial numbers on the Smith Corona-manufactured rifles.

MODEL 1903 SNIPER RIFLES

Both Germany and Great Britain deployed snipers to great effect in World War I. When the United States entered the war in 1917, the U.S. Army reactivated the sniper rifle sight first built in small quantities in 1908 as the "Telescopic Musket Sight, Model of 1913." The telescopic sight was mounted on left side of the M1903 service rifle.

TELESCOPIC MUSKET SIGHT, MODEL OF 1908

The development of a standard sniper rifle had begun as early as June 1900 when Springfield Armory began testing telescopic sights for the M1898 Krag rifle. The results were favorable and in 1906 the Small Arms Firing Regulations called for expert riflemen to be furnished with telescopic sights. To provide a more compact sight than the long, straight tubes tested to date, Frankford Arsenal worked with the Warner & Swasey Company of Philadelphia to design and manufacture a prismatic telescopic sight. This type of sight used prisms to bend the light path between the lenses and thus reduce the overall length of the telescopic sight. A total of 1,000 of the Warner & Swasey sights were delivered to Springfield Armory in 1909 and mounted on rifles with star-gauged barrels (but not marked on the barrel—such marking did not start until 1921) and some were sent out for trial, see Figure 1-41. The trial reports were favorable with minor changes requested. In 1910, the telescopic sighted rifle was issued at the rate of two per infantry company or cavalry troop. The Maxim silencer was fitted to most of them.

Fig. 1-41. M1903 rifle equipped with the Warner & Swasey Telescopic Musket Sight. North Cape Publications collection.

The M1908 Warner & Swasey telescopic sight was 6X but with only a 20 mm objective, which meant it did not allow all of the light the eye could use to pass through except in broad daylight. And the erecting prisms used in the body absorbed enough light to dim the image even more. The mount consisted of a bracket attached to the left side of the rifle with two 0.8-inch locking notches spaced one inch apart. A removable base on the scope itself slid over the bracket (both were machined into a dovetail) and a plunger engaged the chosen notch but did not lock into place. A disk at the front of the removable base provided elevation adjustment which acted against a spring at the rear of the bracket to tilt the scope. A windage screw on the bracket pressed against the mount. Elevation adjustments could be made in theory to 3,000 yards. But much past 400 yards, play in the mounting system introduced accuracy errors. The detachable mount was made of steel and the scope housing of brass and bronze. The entire assembly was painted with a glossy black enamel.

The theory was good in certain respects, but the technology was just not available to make it work properly. The field of view was quite good at 7 yards wide per 100 yards of distance. But the prisms, besides absorbing too much light, were easily knocked out of alignment. The eye relief was only 1.5 inches and required the use of a soft rubber eyecup which was easily lost. It also stuck to the shooter's face. The reticle was etched on glass and as the rifle was fired, carried and banged around, flakes of enamel detached from the interior surface and accumulated on its surface.

TELESCOPIC MUSKET SIGHT, MODEL OF 1913

In 1913, the Warner & Swasey scope (Figure 1-42) was slightly redesigned. The magnification was lowered to 5.2X which increased the

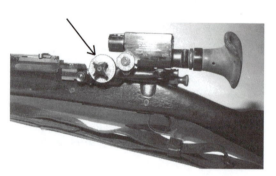

image brightness. A clamping screw was added to secure the eyepiece adjustment and a cruciform elevation screw replaced the older knurled version. But the sight still weighed 2 lbs. and no one thought to provide a raised cheek rest for the stock to make it more comfortable to

Fig. 1-42. M1913 Warner & Swasey Telescopic Musket Sight. Note the large clamping screw (arrow).

shoot. On the range, the Telescopic Sight, Model of 1913 performed acceptably, but under field conditions, it proved to be finicky, delicate, heavy and too difficult to use. The Warner & Swasey sight saw limited use in Europe during World War I with American forces. Brophy has estimated that at least 1,550 *M1908* Warner & Swasey sights were installed on M1903 rifles (and marked with the receiver serial number). Of the 5,041 *M1913* Warner & Swasey sights purchased by the Ordnance Department, at least 4,000 were installed on M1903 rifles and not marked with the receiver serial number.

In the interwar years, both the Army and Marine Corps experimented with a variety of telescopic sights and mounts, the most popular of which was the Winchester A5, a 5X straight tube telescope. This scope was mounted so that it could slide in its mount to reduce the effects of recoil on the delicate crosshairs. The Army subsequently adopted the same system but by time the U.S. entered World War II, they had long been obsolete. The Winchester A5 was also installed on several of the .30-caliber sporting rifles and the .22-caliber gallery rifles on request through the DCM. The manufacturing rights were later purchased by the Lyman Gun Sight Corporation (now Lyman Products Corporation).

U.S. RIFLE, CAL. 30, M1903A4 (SNIPER'S)

When the United States entered World War II on December 8, 1941, no branch of the U.S. military had an issue sniper rifle. Production Order S-1066 on 18 January 1943 instructed Remington Arms to set aside 20,000 M1903 rifle receivers to be converted to sniper rifles. The Weaver 330C 2.5X power telescopic sight was selected to be mounted on the Redfield Jr. commercial mount and rings. During the bolt forging process, the bolt handle was forged into a concave bend and ground to clear the scope when opened. The stock had a semicircular cut milled under the bolt handle to allow it to close fully. The rifle, scope and Model 1907 sling, but without ammunition, weighed 9.125 lbs. (according to specification), see Figure 1-43.

Receivers were to continue to be marked "Model 03-A3" so that any rejected for accuracy could be used as service rifles. The markings were, however, to be split with "U.S./Remington/Model 03-A3" on the left side of the receiver and the serial number on the

Model 1903 Springfield Rifle and Its Variations

Fig. 1-43. The M1903A4 Sniper Rifle was a standard '03A3 rifle equipped with a 2.5X telescopic sight. Some 28,500 were manufactured in 1943 and 1944 by Remington Arms Company. North Cape Publications collection.

right. This left the center blank as it would be covered by the telescopic mount. It is interesting to note that the majority of these first 20,000 receivers were actually from M1903 (Modified) rather than M1903A3 production.

Three blocks of serial numbers were allocated to Remington Arms for the M1903A4 (Smith Corona did not build M1903A4s). The first block ran from serial numbers 3,407,088 to 3,427,087. They were stocked with the Springfield-made "C" stocks marked "S" in the magazine cutoff recess. The barrel guard ring and bolt clearance cuts were made at Remington Arms, according to Campbell. The first block of M1903-A4 rifles were equipped with both Weaver 330C commercial 2.5X telescopic sights and the "Telescope, M73B1," see Figure 1-44. This was the military version of the 330C adjustable for 1/4 minute angle changes in elevation and windage. The scope was officially designated "Sight, Telescopic, M73B1." The commercial scopes had either a crosshair or tapered post reticle while the M73B1s had a crosshair only.

Fig. 1-44. The scant-grip stock was used on certain M1903A4 sniper rifles. The telescopic sight was a Weaver 330 designated "M73B1." North Cape Publications collection.

Model 1903 Springfield Rifle and Its Variations

A second block of serial numbers was assigned in June 1943; 4,000,001 to 4,015,000. M1903A3 production, running ahead of schedule by two days, ran into this block and duplicate serial numbers were inadvertently produced. Only the 2,920 M1903A4s from the block were built and they had a "Z" stamped before the serial number. These Z-prefixed M1903A4 rifles have either 2- or 4-groove barrels, are equipped with the M73B1 telescopic sight and are stocked with either "S" or "Scant-Grip" stocks marked "S" for Springfield or "K" for Keystone.

The third and final block of serial numbers issued for the M1903A4 ran from 4,992,001 to 4,999,045. They were equipped very much like the Block 2 M1903A4s. But only an estimated total of 6,300 M1903A4s were made in this block before production of the M1903 ended. The last M1903A4 rifles left the Remington Arms production line in June 1944, making it the last M1903 rifle of any variation to be produced. Stocks were marked "S" or "K."

The actual number of M1903A4s produced is in dispute. Campbell, using Remington's figures, suggests a total of 28,365 while Brophy sets the number at 29,964.

Sometime late in 1942, a fifteen-round magazine is believed to have been produced for the M1903A4, see Figure 1-45. It was made either by reducing Air Service twenty-five-round magazines by cutting off the bottom portion or was newly made in the exact same manner but was shorter in length. The fifteen-round magazine

Fig. 1-45. An experimental 15-round magazine for the M1903A4 rifle, based on the "Air Service" detachable magazine. North Cape Publications collection.

zine locked into the M1903 trigger guard plate in place of the normal floor plate. The author has one of these magazines in his collection; it

Model 1903 Springfield Rifle and Its Variations

Fig. 1-46. During the Korean War, some M73B1 telescopic sights were replaced with Lyman M73E1 Alaskan scopes equipped with sun shades. North Cape Publications collection.

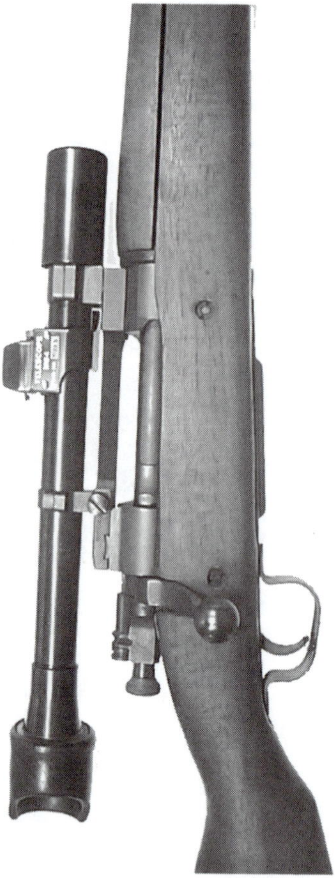

Fig. 1-47. A small but un-known quantity of M1903A4 rifles were refurbished in the late 1950s and early 1960s. The M84 telescopic sight mounted with 1-inch rings was substituted. A number of these sniper rifles saw service in Vietnam. North Cape Publications collection.

was identified for him by a World War II army veteran who served as a rifle instructor at Fort Benning, Georgia, in 1942-43 and later as a sniper in Europe. He recalled that they received ten such magazines for testing but never saw them again after the tests were completed.

The M1903A4 continued in service into and after the Korean War. Some were reissued with the Lyman Alaskan telescopic sight, see Figure 1-46. After the Korean War ended, those M1903A4s still in service were reequipped with the M84 2.2X telescopic sight with larger rings, see Figure 1-47. A number of these saw employment in the early stages of the Vietnam War, see Chapter 4.

MODEL 1903A1 (SNIPER) US MARINE CORPS

As noted above, neither the Army nor the Marine Corps had a sniper rifle in service as the U.S. entered World War II. After some experimentation during 1941 with both M1922 .22-caliber rifles equipped with Lyman M48C rear and Lyman 17A aperture front sights, approval was given on January 6, 1943 to build 1,000 Model 1903A1 .30-caliber Springfield Rifles equipped with the new Unertl 8X telescope and mounts. The intention was to allocate nine of the sniper rifles to each rifle company and four per headquarters company in the 1st and 2nd Marine Raider Battalions. The rifles were assembled at the Marine Corps' Philadelphia Armory, see Figure 1-48.

Barrels dating from 1922 and that met National Match specifications were selected and assembled to receivers that ranged from reheat-treated "below 800,000" serial numbers to nickel steel receivers manufactured in the 1930s. Bolt runways were polished as were bolts and followers. Bolts were polished and blued to eliminate glare and had the rifle's serial number etched on top with an electric pencil. This, plus the fact that many barrels were star-gauged, has given rise to the misconception among collectors that all USMC M1903A1 sniper rifles were built on National Match rifles. Many were, but not all, as the Marine Corps did not possess that many National Match rifles.

The stocks were Springfield-manufactured "C" stocks equipped with National Match butt plates, although some "S" stocks

Model 1903 Springfield Rifle and Its Variations

have been observed. Specifications call for the stocks to be varnished but not all were. The stocks showed the "P" in a circle proof. Most of the rifles had the Springfield Armory cartouche for David A. Lyle (D.A.L.) if they were made from National Match rifles with stocks dating from before 1936. Most later rifles had the SA/S.P.G cartouches. Other stocks will have no cartouches or proof mark if the stocks were acquired by the Marine Corps as replacement stocks.

The telescopic sight had been developed and manufactured by John C. Unertl of Philadelphia, PA. It was the "Target Scope" model, was 7.8X, had a 1.25-inch objective lens and a tube 24 inches long. Adjustment was in 1/4 minute of angle clicks although a few with 1/2 minute of angle clicks have been observed by the author and others. The reticle was a crosshair with a center dot. Its eye relief was short, only 2.25 to 2.75 inches, and its field of view was eleven feet at one hundred yards. It was marked "USMC-SNIPER," stamped into the tube body which was 0.75 inch in diameter. The scopes were serial numbered but not to the rifle. Serial numbers seem to run between 1,000 and 2,800. The mounts were made of duraluminum with case-hardened steel bases and mounting screws. The rear base mounted on the receiver ring immediately behind the standard 1905 rear sight and base (which was left intact) and the front base was mounted on the barrel 7.2 inches ahead of the rear base. The handguard was reshaped to remove the front part of the convex swell leading to the barrel band groove, see Figures 1-49 and 1-50.

Their first combat use came with the Raider Battalions in the jungles of New Georgia. But after-action reports disparaged the delicate scopes and mounts and pointed out that scoped rifles were of little use in that kind of terrain. The Marine Corps Commandant, who had previously supported the sniper rifle concept, concurred and in February 1944, the acquisition of further Unertl Scopes was ended. At least one hundred of the sniper rifles were transferred to the Navy for use in mine-sweeping.

In the spring of 1945, a review was undertaken of the Unertl-equipped sniper rifles. The outcome was more favorable and they

Model 1903 Springfield Rifle and Its Variations

Fig. 1-49. USMC M1903A1 sniper rifle rear mount detail.

Fig. 1-50. Front mount detail.

Fig. 1-48. The U.S. Marine Corps issued the M1903A1 rifle with a Unertl 8X telescopic sight to the 1st and 2nd Marine Raider Battalions in 1943. They also saw use during the Korean War. Larry Reynolds collection.

were authorized for issue once again in August of that year. It was noted that when the supplies of M1903A1 Sniper Rifles were exhausted, they would be replaced with the M1C Garand sniper rifles. The M1903A1 USMC sniper rifles were to see action once again during the Korean War before being declared obsolete and eliminated from inventory.

Those few USMC M1903A1 sniper rifles that survived World War II and the Korean Conflict, along with surplus and now obsolete USMC-owned M1903s, M1903A1s and M1903A3s, appear to have all been sold in late 1954 to members of the Marine Corps.

M1903 Spare Parts–Final Production

After production of the M1903 service rifle ended in Fiscal Year 1927, the Springfield Armory continued to produce receivers and other parts which were used primarily for the National Match rifle and its variants, the .30-caliber sporting rifles and the .22-caliber gallery rifles. The Armory also produced spare parts for the M1903 service rifles until 1934 when production was suspended for two years while tooling up for M1 Garand production was carried out. Starting again in 1936, receivers, barrels and stocks for the M1903 service rifle plus .30- and .22-caliber rifles for DCM sales and .22-gallery rifles for military training were again produced until 1939 when receiver production ended. The production of spare parts continued until 1942 when Remington Arms production of the M1903 and M1903 (Modified) was sufficient to supply spares as needed. When Remington Arms Company made the production switch from the M1903 (Modified) to the Model 1903A3, Springfield resumed production of all M1903 parts except receivers in both 1944 and 1945.

Two contracts were granted to the Remington Arms Company late in World War II to manufacture additional spare parts for stockpiling. The first contract was termed an "All Time Buy" and included 95,000 barrels and 1,859 bolts as well as other parts except, again, receivers. The final contract was termed the "End Buy" and was the last contract awarded for any M1903 or M1903A3 part. It should be noted that all barrels produced under this contract were four-groove barrels with the countersunk rather than the crowned muzzle.

Additional contracts had been awarded as well to private manufacturers—Johnson Automatics (JA), Sedgley (S) and High Standard (HS) to produce replacement barrels. With the exception of the High Standard barrels which appear on Smith Corona M1903A3s, the Sedgley and Johnson Automatics barrels were primarily used as replacement barrels during the post-World War II period.

Chapter 2
Parts

Butt Plates

The M1903 butt plate was derived from the Krag Rifle butt plate. Nine types in all were used: six manufactured by Springfield and Rock Island, two by Remington and one by Smith Corona. Only Remington butt plates were marked with an "R" on the interior surface, but occasionally, a Springfield-manufactured butt plate will show an inspector's mark. All but two types had trapdoors for the cleaning kit or spare firing pin. The first two types were installed on the standard infantry rifle, the last three on special target or other variations. The following paragraphs explain each type, and Table 8 provides a summary. See Figure 2-1.

Common parts of the butt plate are: 1) toe, 2) tang, 3) cap hole, 4) cap ears, 5) cap pin holes, 6) spring lug, 7) large butt plate screw hole, 8) small butt plate screw hole, 9) cap spring, 10) butt plate cap screw, 11) small butt plate screw, 12) butt plate cap, 13) butt plate cap pin and 14) large butt plate screw.

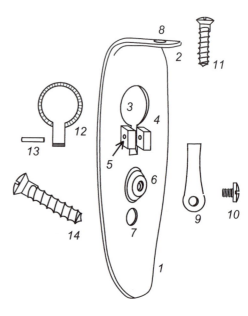

Fig. 2-1. Butt plate assembly.

Type 1. The original butt plate was used on both the M1903 .30-M1903 and the M1903 .30-M1906 until 1909 and again in 1918-1919. It was milled from plate steel and not checkered, see Figure 2-2. The lack of checkering sped

Model 1903 Springfield Rifle and Its Variations

production during World War I. Manufactured by Springfield and Rock Island.

Two variations were made. **Type 1A** butt plate was blued and manufactured from 1903 to 1909. **Type 1B** was Parkerized and manufactured in 1918-1919.

Type 2. The Type 2 butt plate was really the Krag rifle butt plate which was installed on some early M1903 .30-M1903 rifles and on some 1903 .30-M1903 rifles altered to .30-M1906 caliber between 1907 and 1910. It can be identified by its smaller butt trap, Krag assembly numbers on the inside and grinding marks on the toe where it was altered to fit the M1903 .30-M1906 stock, see Figure 2-3. The butt plate cap will be a lighter gray blue color than the butt plate

Fig. 2-2. Type 1 butt plate in use from 1903 to 1909 and again in 1918-1919. This early butt plate was not checkered.

as it was case-hardened in water whereas the butt plate itself was case-hardened in oil and assumed a darker color.

Type 3. Similar to Type 1 but checkered 20 lines/inch. Brophy suggests its use between 1910 to 1917 and again, from 1920 to the end of production in 1939, but rarely if ever seen in this later period. Manufactured by Springfield and Rock Island, see Figure 2-4.

Fig. 2-3. Type 2 altered Krag butt plate (right) compared to a Type 1 M1903 butt plate (left).

Some sub-variations were made. **Type 3A** was blued and manufactured from

Model 1903 Springfield Rifle and Its Variations

1910 to 1917. **Type 3B** was Parkerized and manufactured from 1920 to the end of production in 1939 *but may not exist*. **Type 3C** was identical to the Type 3A but was smooth and uncheckered with a large butt trap. It was in use from 1917 to 1942 and manufactured at Springfield.

Type 4. Made from plate steel and milled to final shape, checkered 12 lines/inch, manufactured with a trapdoor and Parkerized. It was installed on the National Match and the 1st 6,000 M1922 M1 rifles not sold through the Director

Fig. 2-4. Type 3A butt plate used from 1910 to 1917.

of Civilian Marksmanship. The Type 4 butt plate was also installed on all USMC M1903A1 sniper rifles assembled by Marine Corps armorers at the Philadelphia Navy Yard. The Type 4 was in use from 1925 to the end of production in 1939 and again in 1942 by the USMC for the sniper rifle. Manufactured only by Springfield, see Figure 2-5.

Type 5. The first of the "special" M1903 butt plates. It was "forged" from steel and then machined to shape. It lacked the trapdoor and was checkered 12 lines/inch, see Figure 2-6. It was installed on all M1922 .22-caliber rifles, .30-caliber Sporter rifles using

Fig. 2-5. The Type 4 butt plate is often called the "National Match Butt Plate." It was checkered 12 lines per inch.

Model 1903 Springfield Rifle and Its Variations

the M1922 stock, the National Match "Style B" and M1922M1 .22-Caliber Rifles (except the first 6,000 which received the Type 4 butt plate) and M2 rifles manufactured for sale through the Director of Civilian Marksmanship via the National Rifle Association. The butt plate was in production and use from 1922 through the end of production in 1939. All were Parkerized. Manufactured by Springfield.

Fig. 2-6. M1903 Type 5 Butt Plate without butt trap for M1922 and M1922M1 .22-caliber gallery rifles, .30-caliber Sporters and National Match "B" Rifles.

Type 6. Milled from plate steel or cast and then milled to final shape, checkered 10 lines/inch, made without a trapdoor and Parkerized. They were installed on all military issue M1922 M1 and M2 rifles, not intended for sale through the Director of Civilian Marksmanship. Manufactured by Springfield. In use from 1925 through 1942 when production of the M2 .22-caliber gallery rifle ended. These butt plates will sometimes show an inspector's initial or number on the inside surface, see Figure 2-7.

Fig. 2-7. Type 6 butt plate intended to be installed on military issue M1922, M1922M1 and M1922M2 gallery rifles. John Turner collection.

Type 7. Manufactured by Remington Arms and installed on the M1903 and M1903 (Modified) rifles. Milled from plate steel, not checkered, with trapdoor and Parkerized. Marked "R" on the interior surface. Used on Remington rifles built in November 1941 to May-June 1942, see Figure 2-8.

83

Model 1903 Springfield Rifle and Its Variations

Fig. 2-8. Type 7 butt plate used on the Remington M1903 and M1903 (Modified). Usually marked "R" on the interior.

Type 8. Manufactured by Remington Arms and installed only on the M1903A3 and A4 rifles. Stamped from sheet steel, checkered 16 lines/inch, with trapdoor and blued. Marked "R" on the interior surface. Manufactured from May-June 1942 to 1944, see Figure 2-9. The butt trapdoor is distinguished by a vertical indentation on the tail to reinforce the hinge area and by the round rivet head above the lower screw hole. The rivet attached the trapdoor spring to the butt plate. The Type 8 butt plate can further be identified by the *twelve* stamped squares on the right side of the butt trap cover neck (arrows).

Type 9. Manufactured by Smith Corona and installed only on their M1903A3 rifles. Stamped from sheet steel, checkered 10 lines/inch, with trapdoor and blued. Other than the fact that they were unmarked, they were identical to the Type 8 Remington-made M1903A3 butt plates. Manufactured from December 1942 to February 1944. They can also be identified by examining the area on either side of the butt trap cover neck for *seven* stamped squares on either side.

Fig. 2-9. Type 8 was used on M1903A3 and M1903A4 rifles. Notice the vertical indentation on the trapdoor and the rivet head above the lower screw hole.

84

Model 1903 Springfield Rifle and Its Variations

	Table 8 M1903, M1903A1 and M1903A3/A4 Butt Plates	
Type	**Years in Use**	**Identification**
1	1903-1909	1A not checkered
	1918-1919	1B Parkerized, not checkered
2	1907-1910	Not checkered, small butt trap, assembly numbers
3	1910-1917	3A Checkered 20 lines/inch, blued
	1920-1939	3B* Checkered 20 lines/inch, Parkerized
	1917-1942	3C Not checkered, large butt trap assembly
4	1925-1939 1942	Checkered 12 lines per inch, Parkerized (a.k.a. National Match butt plate)
5	1922-1939	Checkered 12 lines/inch, Parkerized
6	1925-1942	Checkered 10 lines/inch, no trap, Parkerized, on military gallery rifles
7	11/41 to 5-6/1942	Not checkered, marked "R," manufactured by Remington Arms for M1903 and M1903 (Modified), Parkerized
8	5-6/42 to 1944	Checkered 16 lines per inch, manufactured by Remington Arms for M1903A3/A4, blued, marked "R"
9	12/42-2/44	Checkered 10 lines per inch, manufactured for Smith Corona M1903A3/A4, blued, unmarked

* Brophy cites the use of this butt plate. But observation suggests that the Type 3C was actually used.

Model 1903 Springfield Rifle and Its Variations

Stocks

Stocks for the Model 1903 series of rifles were made at Springfield Armory, Rock Island Arsenal and at various subcontractors during World War II for Remington and Smith Corona. One of the principal contract stock makers was Keystone, known primarily for their stocks for the M1903A3 and M1903A4 Sniper Rifle. Springfield stocks may be, but not always, marked "S," "B" or "R" before 1920 on the forend tip or in the magazine cutoff groove and "S" intermittently thereafter. Keystone stocks can be identified by the letter "K," Remington stocks by the letter "R" and Smith Corona stocks by the letter "E," on the forearm tip and inside the barrel channel.

Basically, there are four classes of the M1903 service stock that were used during the production of the rifle and one non-service variation, see Figures 2-10 and 2-11. They were the 1) rod bayonet stock, 2) the "S" stock, 3) the "C" stock, 4) the M1903A3 stock and 5) the M1922 stock which was used with the .22-caliber gallery rifles from 1922 on as well as on special target or match rifles. Within these five classes are numerous variations and all are described below.

Nine types of stocks were installed on the M1903 and M1903A3 series rifles and are described in Table 9 below and in the following paragraphs.

COMMON FEATURES OF ALL M1903 STOCKS

The Model 1903 series stocks were made from American black walnut. Although a bidder's form dated July 1, 1916 allowed birch or gumwood, no M1903 series stocks ever appear to have been of anything but American black walnut. Early M1903 stocks were treated with a dye made from logwood which gave the wood a reddish hue and then dipped in heated linseed oil and air-dried. The use of the dye was discontinued in 1928 according to the fiscal year annual report from Springfield Armory. The principal parts of the stock (Figure 2-12) were 1) butt, 2) wrist (called the "small"), 3) receiver and maga-

Model 1903 Springfield Rifle and Its Variations

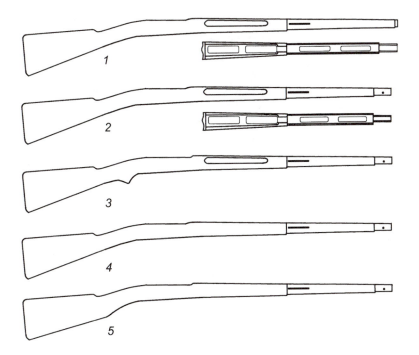

Fig. 2-10. Composite image of all five classes of the M1903 stock.

zine well, 4) barrel bed, 5) air chamber, 6) butt plate tang inletting, 7) trigger and sear inletting, 8) inletting for receiver recoil lug, 9) rear sight base inletting, 10) grasping or finger grooves, 11) rear barrel

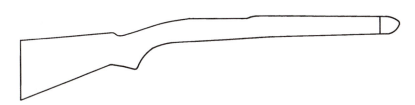

Fig. 2-11. The M1922 stock.

band shoulder, 12) barrel band spring inletting, 13) forward barrel band screw hole, 14) lightening channels, 15) front barrel band shoulder, 16) lightening hole, 17A) lightening hole, 17B) cleaning case hole, 18) pistol grip, 19) relief cut for the receiver ring (M1903A3 and M1903A4) stocks and Springfield replacement stocks made in 1944-45 only, 20) rear recoil bolt, 21) front recoil bolt (also called stock screws). The rod bayonet stock had two additional features: 22) inletting for the rod bayonet stud and an inletted slot for the lug on the rod bayonet stud, not shown.

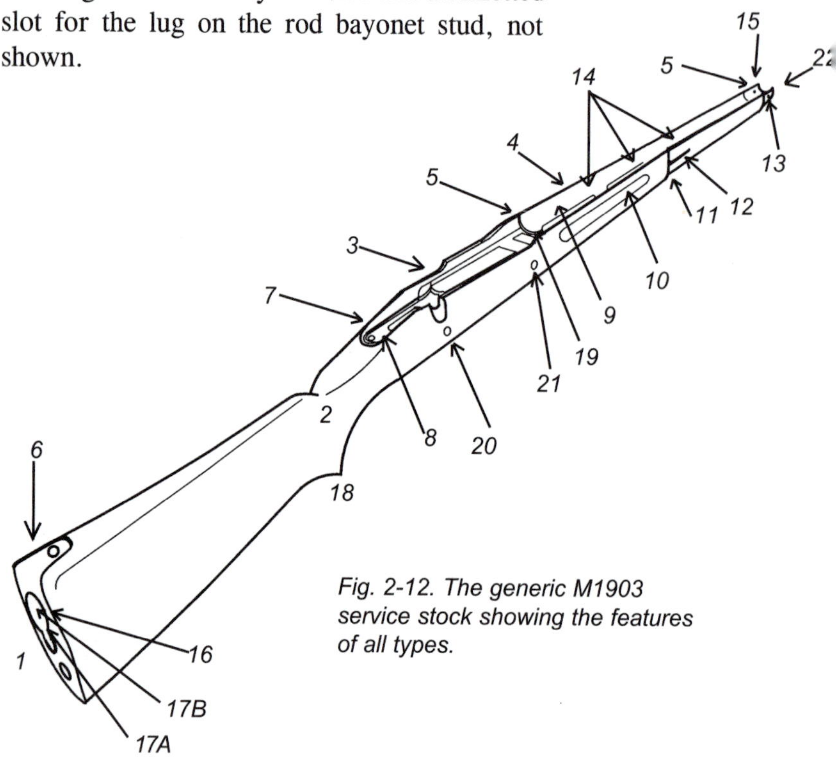

Fig. 2-12. The generic M1903 service stock showing the features of all types.

All M1903 stocks were inletted for the barrel, magazine assembly and trigger assembly and all stocks manufactured, or altered for the .30-M1906 caliber rifles are interchangeable through the end of final spare parts production in 1945 regardless of manufacturer but with these two exceptions:

Model 1903 Springfield Rifle and Its Variations

1) Stocks manufactured before the U.S. entry into World War I in 1917 may require some handfitting around the tang, barrel bed and receiver recoil bolt, or screw, as these stocks were bedded to the rifle. This also applies to National Match and other target or sporting rifles produced at Springfield between 1919-1939.

2) Model 1903 A3/A4 stocks will accept Model 1903 barreled actions, magazine assemblies and trigger assemblies but M1903 stocks will not accept Model 1903A3/A4 barreled actions, magazine assemblies and trigger assemblies without fitting as the pre-M1903A3 stocks lack the milled cut for the receiver ring.

The initials of the ordnance inspector were stamped into the left side of the stock in a cartouche above and slightly behind the trigger. Rifles made in the first decade of the 20th century will often show the cartouche struck in script letters inside a rectangular box with clipped corners above the calendar year of manufacture. After 1910, in an effort to save money and tool maker labor, the inspector's initials with periods were struck in sans serif type, see Figure 2-13, most often inside a rectangular box. To the left of the inspector's cartouche, the Ordnance Department's cartouche, crossed cannons superimposed on a belted wheel, was struck after 1939. See Appendices C and D for a discussion of inspection procedures and markings.

Fig. 2-13. The inspector's cartouche was stamped on the left side of the stock, above the trigger.

Model 1903 Springfield Rifle and Its Variations

Once the rifle was assembled and fired with a proof cartridge, a "P" in a circle was struck on the inside of the stock wrist, see Figure 2-14.

Behind the trigger guard, various armory inspectors stamped a single initial or number.

Fig. 2-14. After the proof cartridge was fired, a "P" inside a circle was stamped on the stock wrist.

The right side of the stock, 0.43 inch below the top of the stock, or the rail, and 8.8 inches behind the nose, was inletted for the barrel band retaining spring. The inletting was in the form of a slot 2.5 inches long and 0.13 inch wide. The forward end of the slot was drilled through to accept the anchoring arm of the spring, refer to Figure 2-12, 12.

The stock had a 0.14-inch-diameter hole drilled through 0.95 inch behind the nose for the forward barrel band screw on all but the rod bayonet stocks, refer to Figure 2-12, 13.

The stock was carefully inletted for the barreled receiver, magazine assembly and trigger assembly. The magazine well was 3.6 inches long. It was 0.97 inch wide at the front and 1.07 inches wide at the rear. The four corners were rounded slightly to match the corners of the magazine box.

A stock bolt bushing was used to prevent the stock wood from being crushed when the rear stock bolt was tightened, refer to Figure 2-12, 3, 4 and 7. It was a steel tube 1.10 inches long by 0.270 inch in diameter driven through the stock at the end of the inletting for the tang.

Model 1903 Springfield Rifle and Its Variations

Four lightening cuts were made in the forearm to remove unnecessary wood, see Figure 2-12, 14. The first lightening cut was 2.3 inches long x 0.46 inch wide, the second was 2.3 inches long x 0.465 inch wide, the third was 3.1 inches long x 0.53 inch wide and the fourth was 3.5 inches long x 0.6 inch wide.

Finger grooves are present on all "service" rifle "S" stocks including the very earliest (first month of production) Remington Model 1903 rifles. The finger grooves were 6.5 inches long, 0.5 inch high and 0.1 inch deep, refer to Figure 2-12, 10.

Rear recoil bolts, or stock screws, were installed on all M1903 series rifles from circa serial #390,000 (1910) except the .22-caliber M1922, M1922M1 and M2 Series Rifles. Refer to Figure 2-12, 20.

Front recoil bolts were installed on all M1903 series rifles manufactured at Springfield Armory from circa serial #650,000 (1917) and at circa serial #238,000 on all M1903 rifles manufactured at Rock Island Arsenal, refer to Figure 2-12, 21. Only the Springfield-manufactured .22-caliber M1922, M1922M1 and M2 series Gallery Rifles did not have the reinforcing stock bolts.

See Table 9, overleaf, for a summary of stock types.

TYPE 1—MODEL 1903 STOCK

Two alterations were made to the Model 1903 rod bayonet rifle in .30-M1903 caliber that affected the stock: first they were altered to the Model 1905 knife bayonet and then altered again for the .30-M1906 cartridge with the 150-grain spire point bullet.

C.S. Ferris and John Beard have conducted extensive research on rod bayonet and altered Model 1903 .30-M1903 rifles which they have

Model 1903 Springfield Rifle and Its Variations

		Table 9 M1903 Stock Types and Variations (All dimensions in inches)
Type	**Length**	**Identification Points**
1A	41.2	Rod bayonet stock Front barrel band recess 0.5 inch long Forend inletted rod bayonet catch No stock bolts Finger grooves 6.5 long, 0.5 high
1B	41.2	New manufacture for 1st Alteration for M1905 knife bayonet Front barrel band recess 1.9 inches long for barrel band with bayonet stud Rod bayonet stud groove filled with wood plug Stamped "S" on nose Finger grooves 6.5 long, 0.5 high
1C	41.0	1st Alteration of existing rod bayonet stocks for M1905 knife bayonet Front barrel band recess 1.9 inches long for barrel band with bayonet stud Rod bayonet stud groove filled with wood plug Stamped "S" on nose Finger grooves 6.5 long, 0.5 high
1D	41.0	2nd Alteration of rod bayonet stocks for .30-M1906 cartridge. Screw hole for rod bayonet band filled and redrilled 0.2 inch behind original position Stock nose stamped "S" Forend tip to barrel band shoulder is 11.87 inches vs 11.375 inches for "S" stock Finger grooves 6.5 long, 0.5 high
1E	41.0	Type 1B/C further altered for .30-M1906 cartridge Rear reinforcing stock bolt added at circa serial #338,000 (Feb. 20, 1908) Finger grooves 6.5 long, 0.5 high

Model 1903 Springfield Rifle and Its Variations

	Table 9, cont. M1903 Stock Types and Variations (All dimensions in inches)	
Type	**Length**	**Identification Points**
2A	40.16	"S" Stock approved April 1905 Rear stock bolt approved Feb. 20, 1908 (actually installed at Springfield circa serial #338,000-1908. Rock Island Arsenal circa #165,000-1910) Finger groove 6.5 long, 0.5 high (Note: All "S" stocks have the same finger groove dimensions) Receiver tang routing lengthened by 0.1 to 0.4 inch
2B	41.0	"S" Stock Rectangular mortise milled on each side of rear lightening cut for M1905 rear sight base at circa serial #338,000 (April 1908) Finger grooves 6.5 long 0.5 high
2C	41.0	"S" Stock Curve on right side below serial number altered to slope after circa serial #398,276 (1910)
2D	41.0	"S" Stock Groove in cleaning kit hole bottom 0.130 inch wide x 0.1 inch deep circa serial #456,376 (1911)
2E	41.0	"S" Stock Front reinforcing stock bolt added after circa serial #650,000 (1917) at Springfield
2F	41.0	"S" Stock Installed on M1903 Mk. 1. Cut in lower left side of receiver 1.5 long, 0.1 deep behind receiver ring area. Intermittent from late 1917 through 1919

Model 1903 Springfield Rifle and Its Variations

Type	Length	Identification Points
Table 9, cont. M1903 Stock Types and Variations (All dimensions in inches)		
3A	41.0	"S" Stock (Rock Island Arsenal) Identical to 2B through 2D stocks, but manufactured at Rock Island Arsenal. Will show script "P" in circle proof and large "S" 0.18 inch high on stock nose. Circa serial #s 1 to 165,000
3B	41.0	"S" Stock (Rock Island Arsenal) Same as 3A except for the addition of the rear stock bolt at circa serial #165,000
3C	41.0	"S" Stock (Rock Island Arsenal) Identical to 3B except that proof changed to sans serif "P" in circle, "S" on nose eliminated and replaced by "RI." Second stock bolt ahead of magazine well added. Circa serial #s 234,435 (Feb. 25, 1917) through 430,742 (1920)
4A	31.5	M1922 Stock .22 caliber, short forend, finger grooves 6.5 inches long and 0.5 inch high, comb-heel drop 0.375 inch
4B	31.45	M1922 Stock .22 caliber, short forend, flat butt, no finger grooves, bullet-shaped pistol grip, comb-heel drop 0.4 inch
4C	31.1	M1922 Stock, installed on M1922M1 .22 caliber, short forend, service-style buttstock with forward angled toe, oval-shaped pistol grip, steeper comb-heel drop, finger grooves 6.5 inches long and 0.5 inch high
4D	31.1	M1922 Stock, installed on M1922M1 Stock (DCM use). .22 caliber, same as Type 4B, comb-heel drop 0.9 inch

Model 1903 Springfield Rifle and Its Variations

Table 9, cont. M1903 Stock Types and Variations (All dimensions in inches)		
Type	**Length**	**Identification Points**
4E	31.5	M1922 installed on M1922M2, .22 caliber, short forend, no finger grooves, circular cross-section pistol grip 1.53 inches in diameter, shallower comb-heel drop (0.743 inch)
4F	31.5	M1922 installed on Cal. .30 Match Springfield, short forend, finger grooves 6.5 long, 0.5 high. Inletted for Lyman 48 receiver sight, front and rear stock reinforcing bolts
4G	Not known	M1922 stock for "Style T" rifles, .30 caliber, short forend, no finger grooves. Inletted for Lyman 48 receiver sight, front and rear stock reinforcing bolts. See Table 10 for Type 4G Stock Variations
4H	Not known	M1922 stock for Cal. .30, NRA Special, .30 caliber, full-length military forend, no finger grooves, flat buttstock, inletted for M1905 rear sight, front and rear stock bolts
4I	31.5	M1922 stock for M1922, Cal. .30 Style NRA, Short forend, no finger grooves, front and rear stock bolts, flat butt, magazine cutoff recess
4J	31.5	M1922 stock for Cal. .30, "Style T," Identical to Type 4A but for .30 caliber
4K	Not known	M1922 stock, .30-Caliber, International Match, Short forend rounded and indented, no finger grooves, checkered pistol grip, flat butt with notch or groove for shoulder hook, forearm inletted for adjustable upper sling swivel rail, inletted for set trigger
4L	Not known	M1922-.30 Caliber, International Match, 1924, Short forend with rounded tip, no indentation, no finger grooves, checkered pistol grip, oval area on comb indented, flat butt for one-piece hooked butt plate, no notch or groove for hook

Model 1903 Springfield Rifle and Its Variations

		Table 9, cont. M1903 Stock Types and Variations (All dimensions in inches)
Type	**Length**	**Identification Points**
5	41.0	"B" Stock–.30 Caliber Flattened pistol grip, comb-heel drop 1.035 inches, full-length forearm, front/rear stock screws, National Match butt plate, not inletted for Lyman 48 receiver sight
6	41.0	"C" Stock–.30 Caliber Full pistol grip, may show drawing #s D1836 or D35379. May also show receiver serial #, comb 0.967 inch longer than "S" stock
7	41.0	7A Remington Model 1903 Stock Identical to Type 3 "S" stock, but with Remington markings and Ord. Department cartouche. Used on earliest production Remington M1903 rifles
	41.0	7B Remington Model 1903 Stock Identical to Type 7A but without finger grooves, installed on remainder of Remington M1903 and M1903 (Modified) rifles, receiver tang channel widened by 0.01 inch and lengthened to 0.5 inch
	41.0	7C Similar to Type 6 "C" Stock but without markings. Made by Remington; some modified with barrel guard ring when used as replacement stocks
8	41.0	8A Model 1903A3 Stock "S" Style No pistol grip, no finger grooves, barrel guard ring cut, inletting for Model 1905 rear sight band, used on M1903A3 rifles manufactured by Remington or Smith Corona
	41.0	8B Model 1903A3 Scant-Grip Style Abbreviated pistol grip, no finger grooves, no barrel guard ring cut, inletting for Model 1905 rear sight band. Stock bolts to November 1942

Model 1903 Springfield Rifle and Its Variations

Table 9, cont. M1903 Stock Types and Variations (All dimensions in inches)		
Type	**Length**	**Identification Points**
8	41.0	8C Model 1903A3 Stock Scant-Grip -- abbreviated pistol grip, stock pins, no finger grooves, barrel guard ring cut, inletting for Model 1905 rear sight band, manufactured by subcontractors, 5-42 to 7-43
	41.0	8D Model 1903A3 Stock Scant-Grip -- abbreviated pistol grip, no finger grooves, barrel guard ring cut, inletting for Model 1905 rear sight band, manufactured by subcontractors, 8/42 to 10/42 and 7/43 to end-of-production
9	41.0	9A Model 1903A4 Stock "C" Identical to Type 7C "C" stock with the addition of a recess milled on the right side for the M1903A4 convex bolt handle, Remington Arms or subcontractor
	41.0	9B Model 1903A4 Stock Scant-Grip Identical to the Type 8D Scant-Grip stock with the addition of a recess milled on the right side for the convex bolt handle of the M1903A4. Manufactured by subcontractors
10	41.0	10A Model 1903A3 Stock, "S" configuration. Manufactured by Smith Corona. Stock pins. Marked "E." Manufactured 10/11-42 to 7-43
	41.0	10B Model 1903A3 Stock, "S" configuration. Manufactured by Smith Corona. Stock bolts. Marked "E." Manufactured 7-43 to end of production

Sources: Actual measurements
Batha, *U.S. Martial .22 RF Rifles*; Brophy, *The Springfield 1903 Rifles;* Campbell, *The '03 Era*; Ezell, *Small Arms of the World,* 12th ed.; Smith, *The Book of Rifles.*

published in their book, *Springfield Model 1903 Service Rifle, Production and Alteration, 1905-1910* (see Appendix I, Bibliography). They have identified three variations which we have listed as "types" according to the North Cape Publications, Inc., format.

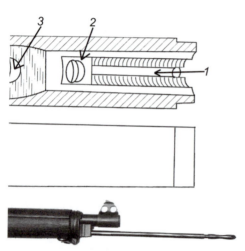

Fig. 2-15. Inletting for the rod bayonet catch. Top, overhead view of stock forend; middle, side view and bottom, actual view. 1) Relief for lug, 2) hole for bayonet catch, 3) hole for bayonet.

TYPE 1A

The original stock for the Model 1903 rod bayonet rifle in .30-M1903 caliber was 41.2 inches long and quite similar to the later 1903 (.30-M1906) stock from the forend back, although it did lack the reinforcing stock bolts which were not added until 1910 and 1917, refer to Figure 2-10. It can be recognized instantly by the fact that the recess at the front for the barrel band is only 0.5 inch long. There was also a groove cut into the stock nose for the rod bayonet stud and a slot for the lug on the rod bayonet stud, see Figure 2-15.

TYPE 1B

When the M1905 knife bayonet was approved on April 3, 1905, original .30-M1903 stocks manufactured for the rod bayonet were altered as follows: 1) The rod bayonet stud groove in the forend was squared and a filler block of wood glued and pinned in place. 2) The stock nose was cut back and machined for the Type 2 upper band. 3) Springfield-manufactured and altered stocks were stamped on the nose with a small capital "S" (0.12 inch high) and Rock Island-manufactured and altered stocks with a large capital "S" (0.24 inch high).

Model 1903 Springfield Rifle and Its Variations

TYPE 1C

When the M1903-06 cartridge was adopted on October 15, 1906, in order to salvage the 271,723 .30-M1903 barrels which had been manufactured to that time, the barrels were set back 0.2 inch and the threads back two turns. The chamber and extractor slot were recut. In order for the stock (and handguard) to match and allow the M1905 knife bayonet to be attached, the stock and handguard were also shortened by 0.20 inch to 41.0 inches overall. This stock is sometimes called the Model 1905 stock by collectors.

TYPE 1D

Those Types 1B and C stocks already altered for the M1905 bayonet were further altered for the .30-M1906 cartridge as follows. 1) The screw hole for the M1905 front band was plugged and a new front band screw hole drilled 0.20 inch behind the original one. 2) The stock nose was stamped with a capital "S" (0.12 inch high on Springfield stocks and 0.24 inch high on Rock Island stocks). 3) Cartouches: A new cartouche was apparently not stamped on rifles altered at Springfield Armory and they will therefore not show an additional cartouche. Rock Island altered stocks show the script "C.N." cartouche dated 1906 or 1908 (see Appendix D for M1903 inspector markings).

NOTE: If a Model 1903-03 stock has been altered, the distance from the forend tip to the barrel band shoulder will be 11.87 inches. If the stock was made for the M1903 originally chambered for the .30-M1906 cartridge, the distance will be 11.375 inches.

TYPE 1E

A reinforcing transverse stock crew, or bolt, was added behind the magazine at circa serial #338,000 to those Type 1 stocks undergoing alteration at the Springfield Armory, and at circa serial #165,000 at Rock Island Arsenal. Some previously altered stocks may have had a stock bolt added later, refer to Figure 2-12, 20.

Model 1903 Springfield Rifle and Its Variations

TYPE 2 —"S" STOCK

The "S" stock, approved on April 3, 1905, replaced the rod bayonet stock and was 40.16 inches long. From the axis point of the trigger to the heel of the buttstock, it was 12.740 inches long and the comb length was 7.7 inches. The drop from the top edge of the stock to the top of the heel was 2.089 inches and the drop from the front of the comb to the rear was 1.45 inches, refer to Figure 2-10 and see Table 11 later in this chapter.

The stock had a finger groove on either side under the barrel 6.5 inches long by 0.5 inch high measured at a point 1.0 inch from the front and 0.8 inch high measured at a point 1.0 inch from the rear.

Many "S" stocks produced at Springfield Armory have an "S" stamped in the magazine cutoff. Other initials observed are "B" and "R." Very few inspectors' initials are observed in the magazine cutoff after 1920.

Six variations of the Type 2 "S" stock were produced at Springfield Armory and two variations at Rock Island, as described below.

TYPE 2A — "S" STOCK

The original "S" stock to circa serial #335,000 (1908) lacked a rear reinforcing stock bolt and the line of the stock on the left ran straight from the handguard to the magazine cutoff. On February 20, 1908 at circa serial #338,000, a single reinforcing bolt was installed to reinforce the stock area just behind the receiver (below the magazine cutoff inletting), see Figure 2-12, 20. At the same time, the routing for the receiver tang was lengthened slightly to prevent this area from splitting during recoil.

NOTE: Type 1 rod bayonet and Model 1905 stocks undergoing alteration at both Arsenals received the rear stock bolt as well. And some Springfield and Rock Island stocks that had completed alteration also received the stock bolt during later inspection and repair.

Model 1903 Springfield Rifle and Its Variations

TYPE 2B— "S" STOCK

From circa serial #338,000 to the end of production, a rectangular mortise was milled on each side of the rear lightening cut to accommodate the Model 1905 rear sight base, see Figure 2-16.

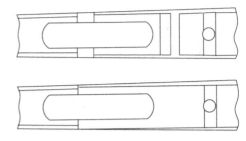

Fig. 2-16. Inletting for the solid M1905 rear sight barrel band. Top, with inletting; bottom, without.

TYPE 2C — "S" STOCK

The top edge of the stock on the right side, immediately below the serial number and gas vent on the receiver, was virtually straight until it descended in a shallow curve at the rear of the breech to circa serial #398,276 (1910). After, the shallow curve was changed to a slope, see Figure 2-17.

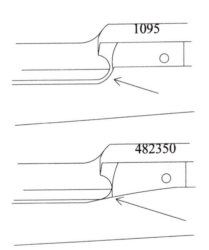

Fig. 2-17. Change to stock slope at rear of the breech to eliminate splitting.

TYPE 2D — "S" STOCK

At circa serial #456,376 (1911), a groove was cut in the bottom of the cleaning kit hole in the buttstock 0.130 inch wide and 0.1 inch deep for the spare parts container (Figure 2-12, 17B). The cleaning kit hole was 0.810 inch in diameter and 6.25 inches deep and located above the lightening hole. One half the soldiers in each company carried the oil bottle and cleaning kit and the rest, a walnut container with an extra striker, assembled firing pin rod with cocking piece and extractor. A part of the cocking piece was wider than the container and the storage hole drilled in the buttstock and so it was necessary to machine the groove.

101

Model 1903 Springfield Rifle and Its Variations

Stocks produced earlier than circa serial #456,376 often had the hole and groove cut during repairs or refurbishment.

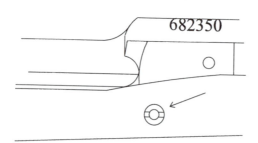

682350

TYPE 2E — "S" STOCK
After circa serial #650,000 (1917), a second reinforcing stock bolt was added above the front portion of the trigger guard bow and behind the front guard screw, see Figure 2-18.

Fig. 2-18. Forward stock reinforcing bolt.

Type 2F — "S" Stock
The "S" stock was installed on the Model 1903 Mk. 1 used with the Pedersen Device. The ejection port in the left side in of the receiver was lower than the line of the stock and therefore, a cut was made in the stock wood on the left side about 1.5 inches long and 0.1 inch deep starting where the stock line dips behind the receiver ring, see Figure 2-19. These stocks will also be found on non M1903 Mk. 1s refurbished and overhauled after the Pedersen Device was withdrawn.

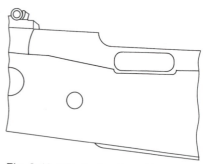

Fig. 2-19. "S" stock relieved for the ejection port on Mark I rifles.

TYPE 3 — "S" STOCK
The categorization of this stock type is for convenience and is purely arbitrary; they were never identified as such in Government service.

TYPE 3A — "S" STOCK, ROCK ISLAND
The Rock Island "S" stock, manufactured between 1907 and 1910,

is essentially the same as the Types 2B through 2D stocks with the following exceptions: 1) The proof mark on the wrist behind the trigger guard is a script "P" in a circle. 2) The stock forend tip is marked with a large "S" 0.18 inch high.

Type 3B— "S" Stock, Rock Island

This stock is very similar to the Type 3A Rock Island Arsenal stock but at circa serial #165,000 the rear reinforcing stock bolt was added below the line formed by the bolt handle and the magazine cutoff inletting.

Type 3C— "S" Stock, Rock Island

When the Rock Island Arsenal resumed Model 1903 production in 1917 at circa serial #234,435, the proof mark on the wrist, behind the trigger guard, was changed to a sans serif "P" in a circle. The stock forend tip was now marked "RI" in block letters 0.25 inch high. The second stock bolt was added in front of the magazine inletting. No further changes were made to the Rock Island stocks through the end of production of complete rifles in 1920 at circa serial #430,742

Type 4—Model 1922 Stock

The Model 1922 stock was developed originally for use with the .22-caliber gallery rifle and almost immediately was adopted for use on a range of .30-caliber rifles intended for marksmanship training, non-National Match competition and for sale through the Director of Civilian Marksmanship. It was often referred to at the time as the "NRA" stock as many of the rifles on which it was used were sold through the DCMP.

The M1922 is characterized by a pistol grip, flat butt for the Types 3 and 4 shotgun-style butt plate, a short forend extending only 1.5 inches beyond the barrel band cut (one exception) and a "pull" of 13.5 inches (distance from trigger face to butt plate). The flat butt allowed the stock to be cut to exact length for the individual shooter, refer to

Model 1903 Springfield Rifle and Its Variations

Figure 2-11 for a generic drawing and the figures below for specifics. Seven types of this stock with six variations were developed for the .22-caliber rifles and four for the .30-caliber rifles, as seen in the description below.

Six variations of the Type 4 .22-caliber stock were manufactured.

Type 4A—Model 1922 Stock

The Model 1922 **Type 4A** stock had finger grooves similar to those on the "S" stock and is generally thought to have been installed on those rifles used by the military for training or competition, see Figure 2-20. In actual fact, the finger grooves were eliminated from all M1922 stocks after a small, unknown quantity was produced. The flat sides on the new stock permitted purchasers to checker the forearm.

Fig. 2-20. Model 1922 stock, Type A.

Type 4B—Model 1922 Stock

The Model 1922 **Type 4B** stock lacked the finger grooves and was installed on all M1922 rifles used by the military after the Type 4A stocks (with finger grooves) were used up, refer again to Figure 2-11. Also on those rifles sold through the National Rifle Association or the Director of Civilian Marksmanship Program. It can easily be identified by the flat butt which could be shortened to the user's preference. The bottom of the pistol grip is shaped somewhat like a bullet and is nominally 3.56 inches long and 1.54 inches wide at its widest point. Two variations of the Type 4B stock were manufactured as noted:

Model 1903 Springfield Rifle and Its Variations

Variation 1 has hand-cut inletting for the Lyman 48 receiver sight (see Figure 2-21) but **Variation 2** lacks the inletting for the Lyman 48 receiver sight.

NOTE: All Model 1922 stocks used for .22-caliber gallery rifles were cut for the Lyman 48 receiver-mounted rear sight except for the M1922 Types 4B and 4H

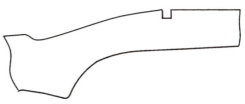

Fig. 2-21. Model 1922 Type 4 B, Variation 1 stock inletted for the Lyman 48 receiver sight.

stocks. Stocks sold individually through the Director of Civilian Marksmanship could be obtained in two variations: **Variation 1** with inletting for the Lyman 48 receiver sight and **Variation 2** without inletting for the Lyman 48 receiver sight.

TYPE 4C—MODEL 1922 STOCK

Two types of stocks were installed on the Rifle, Cal. .22, M1922M1. The **Type 4C** stock (Stock, M1922M1, Cal. .22) had a longer pull than the "S" stock and 0.36 inch less drop at the comb. It had a different pistol grip pattern (the bottom was an oval with flattened sides, 1.48 inches wide). The butt was cut for the service Type 3 butt plate with the toe angled forward 3.5 degrees from a vertical line running down from the heel. The stock had the characteristic short forend and also finger grooves. This stock was installed on the M1922M1 rifle intended for military service use.

TYPE 4D—MODEL 1922 STOCK

The **Type 4D** stock was also installed on the M1922M1 and those M1922M1 rifles converted to the M1922M2. It was very similar to the Type 4B stock installed on the original M1922 .22-caliber rifle with the flat butt to allow it to be shortened to fit the individual shooter. It had the full pistol grip and no finger grooves. M1922M1 rifles with

Model 1903 Springfield Rifle and Its Variations

this stock were used to replace the "Winder Muskets" lent to DCM-affiliated clubs two decades earlier, and were also sold through the NRA. These rifles were known as the M1922M1, NRA rifles. The stocks were also sold separately. Most of these sales occurred after 1928.

Type 4E—Model 1922 Stock
The **Type 4E** stock was installed on those gallery rifles manufactured originally as the M1922M2 .22-Caliber Rifle and not converted from the M1. This was essentially the same stock installed on the M1922 but with a modified pistol grip (bottom is circular, 1.53 inches in diameter) and a deeper thumbhole 0.75 inch below line of comb. The drop to comb and heel also differed. The butt plate used was the Type 6 without the trap.

Type 4F—Model 1922 Stock
The Model 1922 **Type 4F** stock with the short forend was installed on .30-caliber rifles equipped with the heavy barrel. It was identical to the Model 1922 Type 4A stock with finger grooves but it had two stock bolts in the same locations as the "S" stock. The stock was inletted for the Lyman 48 receiver sight. These are very rare stocks as they were only manufactured for a short time. They were installed on the .30-caliber rifle known as the "Match Springfield, M1922."

Type 4G—Model 1922 Stock
The following year, the **Type 4G** stock replaced the Type 4F for almost all applications. The Type 4G was identical to the Type 4F except that it did not have finger grooves. Installed on "Style T" rifles. Four variations of the Type 4G .30-caliber stock were manufactured at Springfield and sold to the public during the late 1920s and into the 1930s in the variations shown in Table 10.

Type 4H—Model 1922 Stock
On December 1, 1922, a variation of the M1922 stock for the .30-caliber rifle became available through the Director of Civilian Marks-

Model 1903 Springfield Rifle and Its Variations

Variation	Identification Points
Table 10 Type 4G Stock Variations	
Variation	Identification Points
1st	.30 Caliber, no inletting for the M1905 rear sight base
2nd	.30 Caliber, inletted for the M1905 rear sight base
3rd	Minimum barrel channel for handfitting, no 1905 rear sight base inletting, inletted for the Lyman 48 receiver sight
4th	Minimum barrel channel for handfitting, no inletting for Lyman 48 receiver sight
5th	.30 Caliber, no 1905 rear sight base inletting, flat pistol grip bottom like the Type 4 K stock, used on 529 NBA Sporter models in 1926. Standard stock nose and no checkering.

manship Program to National Rifle Association members. The Model 1922 **Type 4H** stock was identical to the Model 1922 Type 4A stock from the butt forward to receiver area (flat butt for sizing to the individual shooter) and had the Type 5 butt plate installed. But it had the full-length military forend without finger grooves. The stock was inletted for the M1905 rear sight and had both stock reinforcing bolts. It was referred to as the Stock, Caliber .30, NRA Special and was sold from 1922 through 1932, see Figure 2-22.

Fig. 2-22. M1922, Type 4H stock, a.k.a. "NRA Special" stock.

TYPE 4I—MODEL 1922 STOCK

The **Type 4I** was designated the Stock, Model of 1922, Cal. .30, Style NRA. It had the short forend, the magazine cutoff recess in the left side, no finger grooves and both stock bolts. The butt was flat so that

107

the shooter could shorten it to his or her length. It was used to stock the U.S. Rifle, Cal. .30, Style NRA, (a.k.a.NRA Sporter.) The stock was available to NRA members through the DCM from 1924 through 1932. In 1938-39, 29 more rifles were made for the Department of Justice. Type 4I stocks were sold from 1934 to 1939 as spare parts only to previous purchasers of the complete rifle, see Figure 2-23.

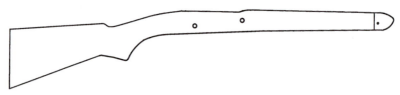

Fig. 2-23. Model 1922, Type 4J stock, a.k.a. "NRA Sporter" stock.

TYPE 4J—MODEL 1922 STOCK
The Model 1922 **Type 4J** stock was identical to the Model 1922 Type 4A stock including the shortened forend. The barrel channel was enlarged for the heavier .30-caliber barrel and it was installed on the .30-caliber "Style T" rifle.

TYPE 4K—MODEL 1922 STOCK
The Model 1922 **Type 4K** stock was installed on the .30-caliber International Match Rifles. It had a checkered pistol grip, red rubber butt plate with a cutout in the buttstock for a butt hook, see Figure 2-24.

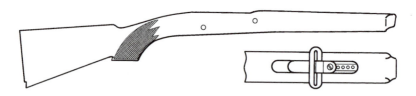

Fig. 2-24. M1922, Type 4K, International Match stock. Notice the cutout in the butt for the butt hook and the indented forearm.

Model 1903 Springfield Rifle and Its Variations

The bottom of the stock in the magazine area was inletted for a palm rest's threaded shaft. The forward part of the forearm was inletted for an adjustable upper sling swivel rail. The tip of the forend was indented at the front and sides. These rifles, equipped with set triggers made in Germany and barrels varying from 24 to 30 inches long, were used in 1922 only.

TYPE 4L—MODEL 1922 STOCK
The Model 1922 **Type 4L** stock was installed on the .30-caliber International Match rifles used in 1924. These stocks had the short rounded forend and adjustable forward sling swivel rail. The checkering on the pistol grip was in a slightly different form and the forend was not indented on either side of the nose. An oval-shaped area beneath the forward end of the comb was indented. A one-piece butt plate and hook replaced the separate butt plate and hook used on the M1922 international match rifle stock (Type 4K) and the butt was cut square vertically without the cutout previously needed for the separate butt hook, see Figure 2-25.

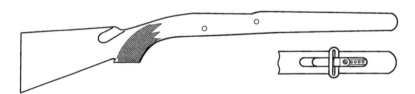

Fig. 2-25. M1922, Type 4L, International Match stock. Notice the vertical cut at the butt, lack of cutout for the separate butt plate hook and rounded nose.

TYPE 5— "B" STOCK
The "B" stock is instantly recognizable by its "flattened" pistol grip and greater droop to the buttstock, see Figure 2-26. The "B" stock had a full-length forearm and both front and rear stock screws. It was shaped for the same Type 5 butt plate, sling swivels and bands as used on the National Match Rifle.

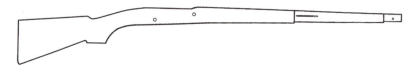

Fig. 2-26. The Type 5 "B" stock was used on a small number of National Match rifles made between 1925--1928 and sold through the DCM in 1931-

The "B" Stock was installed only on National Match "Style B" rifles manufactured between 1925-1928, and sold through the DCM-NRA in 1931-32.

TYPE 6—"C" STOCK

The Model 1903A1 stock was approved on March 15, 1928. The major difference between it and the "S" stock was the addition of a pistol grip which was 3.36 inches deep when measured from the top front of the comb to the bottom front edge of the pistol grip, see Figure 2-27. Minor dimensional changes were made as shown in Table 11 and Figure 2-28. True M1903A1 service rifles with the "C" stock are fairly scarce as Springfield Armory was instructed that all "S" stocks were to be used up first. From 1928 through 1939 most "C" stocks appear to have been installed only on some service rifles submitted for a complete rebuild. Most "C" stocks during this period (1929 on) were installed on National Match rifles.

Fig. 2-27. The M1903A1 "C" stock was installed primarily on National Match rifles before WWII. During the war, it was installed on refurbished M1903s.

Many "C" stocks are marked with the drawing number, either D1836 or D35379, between the lower swivel and pistol grip. In addition,

Model 1903 Springfield Rifle and Its Variations

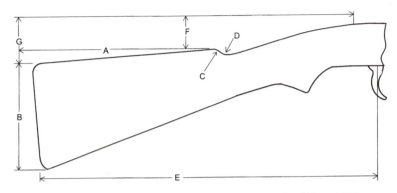

Fig. 2-28. Dimensional differences are shown between the "S" and "C" stocks. Consult Table 11 for the dimensions.

some National Match rifles with the "C" stock also had the rifle serial number added, see Figure 2-29.

Table 11 Dimensional Comparison "S" and "C" Stocks in Inches (See Figure 2-28)		
Feature	**"S" Stock**	**"C" Stock**
A. Comb Length	7.563	8.530
B. Vertical Height at Butt	4.704	4.702
C. Radius, Top of Comb	0.375	0.375
D. Radius, Bottom of Comb	0.750	0.658
E. Length of Pull, Trigger to Midpoint of Comb	12.740	12.900
F. Drop from Bore Centerline to Top of Comb	1.450	1.110
G. Drop from Bore Centerline to Top of Butt	2.089	1.407

Model 1903 Springfield Rifle and Its Variations

Fig. 2-29. *The receiver serial number was often stamped on the bottom of National Match "C" stocks.*

"C" stocks used on service rifles received the Type 3C butt plate (some suggest the Type 3B); those installed on National Match rifles received the heavily checkered Type 5 butt plate. "C" stocks were also sold through the DCM from 1932-1940 for $3.75.

NOTE: During World War II, "C"-type stocks were manufactured at Springfield and Remington and subcontractors such as Keystone for use on the Model 1903A3 and A4 rifles. These can be identified by the transverse groove cut into the stock just ahead of the receiver seat for the barrel guard ring that held the rear of the M1903A3 handguard in place. This allowed these stocks to be used on both the M1903 and M1903A3 rifles. The stocks used on the M1903A4 sniper rifle can be identified by the relief cut for the turned-down bolt handle. Keystone stocks can further be identified by the "K" stamped in the magazine cutoff groove.

TYPE 7—REMINGTON MODEL 1903 STOCK

The stocks used on the Remington series of rifles from M1903 through the M1903 (Modified) to the Model 1903A3 were developed over a period of seven months from November 1941 through May 1942 and included two types in the three variations as described below.

Three additional variations were used (Type 9) for the Model 1903A4 Sniper Rifle. These had a cutout on the right side for the turned-down bolt handle and are also described in the following paragraphs.

Model 1903 Springfield Rifle and Its Variations

TYPE 7A—REMINGTON MODEL 1903

Stocks made originally for Remington M1903 production rifles were identical to the Type 3B—"S" Stocks manufactured at the Rock Island Arsenal, including the finger grooves. Remington stocks were manufactured on machinery and fixtures that had been in storage at Rock Island Arsenal since the end of that factory's production. This stock was used only on the Remington Model 1903 rifles probably just during the first month or so of production, see Figure 2-30.

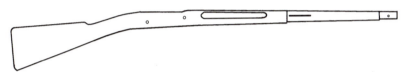

Fig. 2-30. Remington M1903, Type 7A, Stock for the Remington M1903 and M1903 (Modified).

TYPE 7B—REMINGTON MODEL 1903

Identical to the Type 7A stock but without finger grooves. This stock was installed on the majority of Remington M1903 and all Remington 1903 (Modified) rifles, see Figure 2-31.

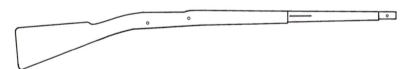

Fig. 2-31. Remington M1903, Type 7B, Stock for the Remington M1903 and M1903 (Modified).

NOTE: Types 7A and B stocks were not made with the barrel guard ring cut forward of the magazine well as were later Remington-made stocks for the M1903A3. It should be noted, however, that many of these stocks had the barrel guard ring milled in at a later time, refer to Figure 2-32.

113

Model 1903 Springfield Rifle and Its Variations

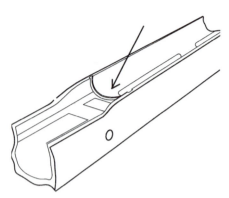

Fig. 2-32. The barrel guard ring (arrow) was cut in all M1903A3 stocks ahead of the receiver recoil lug mortise. It was also cut on all M1903 stocks manufactured during WWII, and was added to many pre-war M1903 stocks.

TYPE 7C—REMINGTON MODEL 1903

This was stock was similar to the Type 6 "C" stock manufactured by Springfield Armory for the M1903A1. Many of these stocks were installed on Remington M1903 and Remington M1903 (Modified) rifles as supplies warranted and also used as replacement stocks for earlier M1903 service rifles. These stocks were modified by having the barrel guard ring recess milled in as they were also used as replacement stocks for the M1903A3 service rifle, refer to Figure 2-32.

TYPE 8—REMINGTON MODEL 1903A3 STOCK

Specifications for the M1903A3 called for the stock to have the full pistol grip of the "C" stock. However, Remington had already purchased over 300,000 stock blanks in storage at Rock Island and contracted for 300,000 more. None proved large enough to allow the full pistol grip to be cut. As a consequence, on May 12, 1942, Remington was allowed to manufacture two variations of stock as described below. All Remington stocks will show inspectors' markings stamped in the area ahead of the trigger guard plate consisting of letters or numbers alone or in circles, triangles, boxes or ovals of varying sizes. Immediately behind the trigger guard plate will often be found the stock inspectors' numbers, "42," "43," or "44" or the letter "R." Many Remington 1903A3 stocks will not show the stock inspector's mark, however. The "P" in a circle proof is 0.375 inch in diameter and the letter "P" is 0.25 inch high. Most Remington-made M1903A3 stocks will show the ordnance escutcheon on the stock tip or the letter "K" stamped in the magazine cutoff groove for Keystone Company.

All M1903A3 stocks will have a slight flat cut under the bolt handle. All but the Type 8B stocks will have a milled recess for the handguard retaining band immediately ahead of the receiver face.

TYPE 8A—REMINGTON MODEL 1903A3 STOCK— "S" STYLE

This stock was similar to the M1903 "S" stock but without finger grooves as used on the Remington M1903 rifles and the M1903 (Modified) rifles, refer to Figure 2-31. It was slightly larger in all bedding dimensions to reduce handfitting both at the factory and at depots when replacement stocks were fitted. The finish was not as fine as pre-World War II stocks as the final sanding and filling was gradually eliminated.

TYPE 8B—REMINGTON MODEL 1903A3 STOCK—"SCANT-GRIP" STYLE

This stock was originally intended to be used as a replacement stock after it was discovered that the stock blanks were too narrow to permit a full "C-style" pistol grip to be cut. It was then manufactured with an abbreviated pistol grip referred to as the "Scant Grip" (Figure 2-33) by extending the line of the stock forward. The grip thus formed was 2.75 inches high when measured from the top front of the comb to the bottom front edge of the grip. The same measurement for the "C" stock was 3.36 inches. The **Type 8B** was used on some Remington M1903 and M1903 (Modified) rifles and did not have a recess cut for the barrel guard ring to hold the new barrel cover used on the M1903A3.

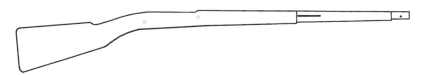

Fig. 2-33. Remington Type 8B Scant-Grip stock.

115

Model 1903 Springfield Rifle and Its Variations

The **Type 8C** scant-grip stock was similar to the Type 8B but had a recess cut for the barrel guard ring so that they could be used on Model 1903, M1903 (Modified) and M1903A3 rifles with any M1903 handguard. It used reinforcing stock pins and was manufactured by subcontractors from May 1942 to July 1943 when the stock bolt was reintroduced.

The **Type 8D** is the most common scant-grip stock. The reinforcing stock pins were found to weaken the stock and so the stock bolts were reintroduced. The Type 8D was manufactured from August 1942 to October 1942 and again from July 1943 to the end of production.

NOTE: Use of M1903A3 scant-grip stock was optional and used whenever the supply of "S" stocks ran low. Some Type 8B scant-grip stocks were installed on a few Remington Model 1903 and Model 1903 (Modified) rifles when Type 8A stocks were not available. Types 8B and 8D stocks were also used on some M1903A4 sniper rifles in the circa serial #3,708,000 to 4,707,999 and intermittently in the 4,992,001 to 5,784,000 ranges.

TYPE 9—REMINGTON MODEL 1903A4 STOCK

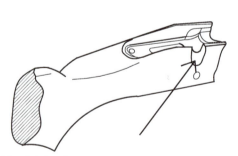

The stocks used for the Model 1903A4 sniper rifle were similar to the Type 7C "C" stock and Type 8B or 8D scant-grip stocks. They are distinguished only by the recess groove cut into the right side 2.3 inches ahead of the tang cut for the bolt handle, see Figure 2-34 (arrow) for a view of this cut. The recess is swept slightly to the rear

Fig. 2-34. M1903A4 sniper rifle with the cutout on the right side for the bent-down bolt handle. This is the only distinguishing feature of the M1903A4 stock.

Model 1903 Springfield Rifle and Its Variations

to match the sweep of the bolt handle. Beware of counterfeits which can almost always be detected through poor workmanship.

Type 9A—Remington Model 1903A4 Stock—"C" Configuration

This stock was the Type 7C but manufactured by Remington and Keystone and similar to the M1903 "C" stock made by Springfield Armory, but without finger grooves, and was the preferred stock for the M1903A4. It is thought that manufacture of this stock had ended by the time the first sniper rifles were assembled in late 1942 and early 1943 and that the recess for the bolt handle and the cut for the barrel guard ring were made prior to or during the later assembly of M1903A4 rifles. They were assembled to rifles in the first run of M1903A4 sniper rifles (serial # range 3,407,088 to 3,427,087) and intermittently as supply allowed during later M1903A4 production, particulary in the third run, serial number range 4,992,001 to 4,999,045.

Type 9B—Remington Model 1903A4 Stock—"Scant-Grip" Configuration

This stock was the Type 8D "Scant-Grip"-style stock but with the recess cuts for the bolt handle and barrel guard ring. These were originally intended for use as replacement stocks only on the M1903A4 but were used as original equipment stocks whenever the supply of Type 9A "C" stocks was not available. They were used on many M1903A4 rifles in the serial number range 4,000,000 to 4,003,000 and intermittently thereafter.

NOTE: M1903A3 and A4 original and replacement "C" and "Scant-Grip" stocks can be easily differentiated by examining both the left side of the wrist and the area ahead of the magazine well. If the stock was fitted to the rifle during manufacture it will show the Ordnance Department escutcheon (crossed cannons), the Ordnance Inspector's initials (FJA) and the Remington Arms factory mark, "RA" (Smith Corona did not produce the M1903A4). The area ahead of the magazine well will show the numerous small initials and numbers of the Remington factory inspectors. If the stock was installed as a replacement, it will not show the Ordnance Department escutcheon, the Remington "RA" factory mark, or the factory inspector marks. It may show an Ordnance Department inspector and will often show the initials of the armory or repair station—see Appendix D.

TYPE 10– SMITH CORONA MODEL 1903A3 STOCK–"S" CONFIGURATION

All stocks manufactured by Smith Corona for the M1903A3 were the "S" configuration without a pistol grip. They are quite similar to those M1903A3 stocks manufactured by Remington but can easily be identified as follows: 1) they will usually be stamped "E" on the tip of the forearm, 2) will usually have one or two "E"s stamped inside the barrel channel, 3) workmanship is rougher than the Remington M1903A3 stocks with machining and rasp marks visible on stocks that have not been refinished.

All **Type 10A** stocks will have a milled groove for the barrel guard retaining ring immediately ahead of the receiver face. Reinforcing stock pins were used in place of stock bolts from 10/11-42 to 7-43.

Type 10B stocks were identical to the Type 10A but stock bolts replaced the stock pins from 7-43 to the end of production.

Assembly markings will be stamped on the bottom of the stock. Those stamped ahead of the magazine well consist of numbers alone or are inside triangles, boxes, circles and

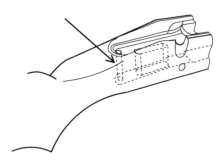

Fig. 2-35. Rear guard screw bushing shown in the stock (arrow).

118

Model 1903 Springfield Rifle and Its Variations

diamonds. No alphabetical letters have ever been noted by the author stamped ahead of the magazine well on Smith Corona stocks. Behind the trigger guard will be stamped the "P" in a circle proof, 1/2-inch diameter. The letter "P" will be 0.312 inch high. Between the proof and rear of the trigger guard plate will be found an inspector's initial, usually "F," "Q," "M" or "O."

Stock specifications for stocks used on the M1903 rifle only are shown in Table 12.

Table 12 M1903 Stock Specifications in Inches			
Stock Type	**Drop at Comb**	**Drop at Heel**	**Pull**
"S"—Types 2 and 3	1.450	2.089	12.74
"C"—Types 6 through 8	1.110	1.407	12.90
"B"—Type 5	1.090	2.215	13.21
M1922—Type 4A	1.875	2.250	13.50
M1922 (NRA) Type 4B	0.750	1.150	13.45
M1922 (with Forend and Pistol Grip) Type 4D	0.760	1.660	14.12
M1922M1 Type 4C	1.112	2.185	13.10
M2 Type 4E	0.997	1.750	13.10

Model 1903 Springfield Rifle and Its Variations

REAR GUARD SCREW BUSHING

The rear guard screw bushing is a steel tube 1.1 inches long by 0.270 inch in diameter (Figure 2-35) inserted into the stock at back of the trigger guard plate inletting. The rear guard screw passed through the bushing which allowed it to be tightened without danger of crushing the wood and loosening the wood-to-metal fit. This guard screw bushing was used in all variations of the M1903 rifle including the M1903A3/A4. The bushing was fitted during manufacture and rarely needed replacement.

STOCK SCREWS

Steel stock screws were added to reinforce the stock against the rearward movement of the receiver under recoil. The first stock screw was approved on February 20, 1908 and added at circa serial #342,000 just behind the magazine well. The second stock screw was added in early 1917 at circa serial #675,800. Refer to Figure 2-12, 20 and 21.

The stock screw had a flat, unslotted head and was inserted through the side of the stock with the head on the left. The rear screw was 1.6 inches long and the front screw was 1.45 inches long. A slotted nut was threaded onto the screw on the right side. The tip of the screw was upset to prevent it from backing out.

To save time and cost, the stock screw and nut were replaced with stock pins beginning circa October/November 1942 on the M1903 (Modified) rifle stocks. But it was found that the stock pins weakened the stock. Accordingly, the Ordnance Department returned to using the stock screw and nut about July 1943, and continued their use to the end of the production in 1944. The first six to seven months of M1903 (Modified) and M1903A3 production, as well as M1903A3 production by Smith Corona, will have stock pins instead of stock screws.

Handguards

When it comes to classifying M1903 parts, nothing is ever easy. Handguards are a prime example.

At least thirteen types of service handguards were made and used on all M1903 rifles from the rod bayonet rifle to the M1903A4. Handguards were manufactured at Springfield Armory, Rock Island Arsenal, Remington Arms and Smith Corona, and their various subcontractors. Except for the handguards used on the rod bayonet rifle, the M1903A3 and the M1903A4, changes are subtle and handguards should be examined carefully to determine exact type and period of use. See the paragraphs below for a general description of each type and Table 13 for identification details.

Handguards — General

All service rifles and service-style target rifles were equipped with handguards. Handguards *were not* used on rifles assembled with M1922 stocks in .22 and .30-M1906 caliber.

Like the stocks, all M1903 handguards were made of American black walnut. The walnut blanks were milled to shape, sanded and, until 1928, dipped in a logwood dye solution to impart a reddish hue. They were then dipped in a heated bath of linseed oil and dried. After 1928, the logwood dye was no longer included in the process.

Handguards, like stocks, were made at the two national arsenals and by subcontractors. During World War II, handguards and stocks were manufactured by Springfield as spare parts, and by Remington and Smith Corona. Remington also manufactured handguards as part of their spare-parts contracts to extend the life of the M1903 and M1903A3 rifles.

Model 1903 Springfield Rifle and Its Variations

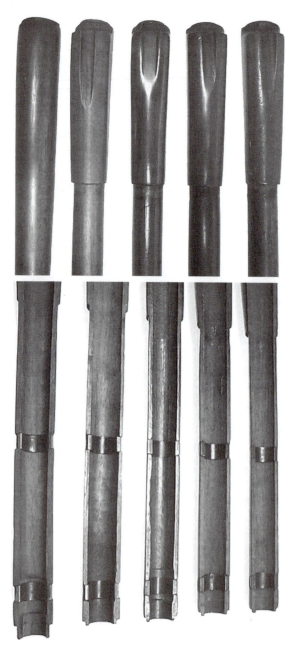

Handguard detail, right to left: Type 4 M1903 service rifle; Type 8 M1903A1 National Match rifle; Type 9, 1st Variation M1903 or M1903A1 replacement, note square end to sight clearance groove and oversized forward spring clip relief; Type 9, 3rd Variation M1903 or M1903A1 replacement, note extended sight clearance groove. Type 13 for the M1903A3 or M1903A4.

Model 1903 Springfield Rifle and Its Variations

Table 13 Models of 1903, 1903A1, 1903A3 and 1903A4 Handguards		
Model	**Characteristics**	**Manufacturer and Period**
Type 1. Model rod bayonet .30-M1903	18.6 inches long; no sight protector swell; a single handguard clip riveted (2) to the underside 6.2 inches behind front and rear tenons	Springfield and Rock Island, 1903-1905
Type 2. M1903 rod bayonet, 1st Alteration with M1905 knife bayonet only	15.4 inches long; no sight protector swell; a single handguard clip riveted (2) to the underside 6.2 inches behind front and rear tenons	Springfield, 1905 Rock Island ?
Type 3. M1903 rod bayonet, 1st Alteration with M1905 knife bayonet and M1905 front and rear sights	15.4 inches long; sight protector swell with concave slope to rear barrel band shoulder; no sight line clearance cut; no handguard clips; 1/3 arc windage knob cut 0.2-0.3-inch radius; three air chambers on underside; indexing cut at rear NOTE: These are new contemporary manufacture. No rod bayonet handguards are believed to have been altered at the Armories	Springfield, 1905-1906 Rock Island, 1906
Type 4. M1903 new production and M1903 rod bayonet, 2nd Alteration with M1905 knife bayonet, M1905 sights and .30-M1906 cartridge	15.2 inches long; sight protector swell with concave slope, no sight line clearance cut; two handguard clips; 1/3 arc windage knob cut, 0.3-0.4-inch radius; no air chambers; indexing cut at rear	Springfield, 1906-1910 Rock Island, 1907/08-1910

Model 1903 Springfield Rifle and Its Variations

Table 13, cont. Models of 1903, 1903A1, 1903A3 and 1903A4 Handguards		
Model	**Characteristics**	**Manufacturer and Period**
Type 5. Model 1903 Service Rifle	15.2 inches long; sight protector swell with concave slope, sight line clearance cut 0.53 inch wide, 2.4 inches long; handguard clips; semi-circular windage knob cut 0.3-0.4-inch radius; indexing cut at rear	Springfield and Rock Island, 1910-1919
Type 6. M1903 Service Rifle	15.2 inches long; sight protector swell assuming a convex shape that becomes more pronounced through the period. Sight line clearance cut 0.53 inch wide, 2.4 inches long; handguard clips; 1/3 arc windage knob cut, 0.3-0.4-inch radius. Index cut at rear in the first few months only, eliminated thereafter	Springfield, 1920-1929
Type 7. M1903A1 Service Rifle and National Match Rifle	15.2 inches long; sight protector swell with straight slope, sight line clearance cut 0.53 inch wide, 2.4 inches long; handguard clips; 1/3 arc windage knob cut, 0.3-0.4-inch radius; no indexing cut at rear	Springfield, 1929-1941
Type 8. M1903A1 National Match Rifle	15.2 inches long; sight protector swell with straight slope, sight line clearance cut 0.53 inch wide, 2.4 inches long;	Springfield, 1936-1941 (intermittent use)

Model 1903 Springfield Rifle and Its Variations

	Table 13, cont. Models of 1903, 1903A1, 1903A3 and 1903A4 Handguards	
Model	**Characteristics**	**Manufacturer and Period**
Type 8, cont.	handguard clips, 1/3 arc windage knob cut, 0.3-04-inch radius, no indexing cut at rear, excellent finish; drawing # D29179 stamped on top surface	
Type 9, 1st Variation replacement handguards	15.2 inches long; sight protector swell with concave slope with sight line clearance cut 0.59 inch wide by 3.25 inches long; handguard clips; elliptical knob windage knob cut, 0.2 inch wide	Springfield, 1942-1945
Type 9, 2nd Variation replacement handguards	15.2 inches long; high, thicker sight protector swell with convex slope, sight clearance groove 0.59 inch wide by 3.25 inches long, elliptical windage knob cut. Poor workmanship and rough, wartime finish	Springfield, 1944-1945 Keystone, 1944
Type 9, 3rd Variation replacement handguards	15.2 inches long; high, thicker sight protector swell with concave slope, sight clearance groove 0.47 inch wide by 2.76 inches long ending in parabola; elliptical windage knob cut	Probably Springfield 1944-45
Type 10. Model 1903 Service Rifle	15.2 inches long; sight protector swell with concave slope, sight clearance groove 0.59 inch wide by 2.5 inches long sight line and square end; semicircular windage knob cut, 0.3-.4-inch radius	Remington Arms, 1941

Model 1903 Springfield Rifle and Its Variations

Table 13, cont. Models of 1903, 1903A1, 1903A3 and 1903A4 Handguards		
Model	**Characteristics**	**Manufacturer and Period**
Type 11. M1903 (Modified) Service Rifle	15.2 inches long; sight protector swell with slight convex slope and sight line clearance cut 0.59 inch wide by 2.25 inches long; handguard clips; semicircular windage knob cut, 0.3-0.4-inch radius	Remington Arms, 1942-1943
Type 12. M1903A1 Sniper Rifle	15.2 inches long, sight protector swell 1.3 inches long with short, concave slope and flat apron to lower barrel band shoulder; no sight line clearance; 1 x 0.5 inch milled for Unertl telescopic sight mounting block	USMC, 1942-43
Type 13. Model 1903A3 Service Rifle Model 1903A4 Sniper Rifle	18.75 inches long; no sight protector swell; slight concave curve all the way to lower barrel band; no sight clearance cut; two handguard clips	Remington Arms, Smith Corona, 1943-1944 Remington Arms, 1943-1944

HANDGUARDS—ROD BAYONET RIFLE

The original handguard for the Model 1903 rod bayonet rifle in .30-M1903 caliber (**Type 1**) was made without a sight protector swell and was held in place by a tenon at the breach end and the upper and lower barrel bands, see Figure 2-36. The handguard had a single step for the middle band. It was 18.6 inches long and had a single handguard clip placed just forward of midway between the lower and upper bands in a milled depression on the underside (arrow). The handguard clip was made of spring steel and riveted with two iron countersunk rivets through the handguard. Only one type of this handguard was used on those rifles equipped with the rod bayonet from 1903-1905.

Model 1903 Springfield Rifle and Its Variations

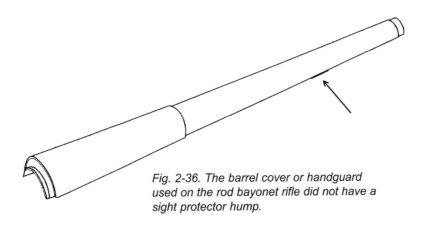

Fig. 2-36. The barrel cover or handguard used on the rod bayonet rifle did not have a sight protector hump.

HANDGUARDS—ALTERED M1903 RIFLES

The **Type 2** handguard was adopted and used briefly on those rod bayonet rifles that had been altered for the M1905 knife bayonet only and not the M1905 rear sight and which remained in .30-M1903 caliber. It was similar to the Type 1 handguard except that it was 3.2 inches shorter (15.4 inches long overall). It is not clear whether this handguard was manufactured new (or even existed) but it is not thought that they were altered from existing handguards.

The **Type 3** handguard was adopted and used briefly in late 1905-early 1906 on rifles altered for the M1905 knife bayonet and the M1905 sights (1st Alteration) but which remained chambered for the .30-M1903 cartridge. It was 15.4 inches long and was the first handguard to have the sight protector swell at the rear with a concave front slope (arrow 1) but did not have the later sight line clearance cut through the middle. A windage knob cut was made on the right, rearside of the swell in the form of 1/3 of an arc with a radius of 0.2 to 0.3 inch (arrow 2). It had front and rear tenons which fit under the front lip of the M1905 sight base and the rear section of the upper barrel band

Model 1903 Springfield Rifle and Its Variations

(arrows 3 and 4). Three shallow "air chambers" were inletted into the underside of the handguard: the first two inches forward of the breech end, the second in the center and the third 1.5 inches behind the front tenon (arrows 5, 6 and 7). An indexing cut (arrow 8) for exact placement on the milling machine in the shape of a rectangle with rounded ends was cut into the rear underside of the handguard, half in the barrel groove, half in the air chamber, see Figure 2-37.

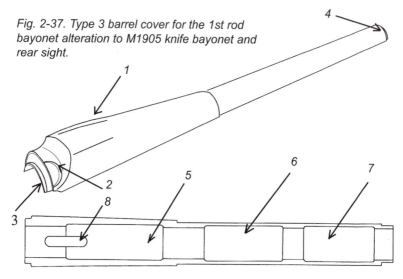

Fig. 2-37. Type 3 barrel cover for the 1st rod bayonet alteration to M1905 knife bayonet and rear sight.

The **Type 4** handguard type was installed on all new production M1903 rifles and on all rod bayonet rifles rechambered for the .30-M1906 cartridge and equipped with the Model 1905 knife bayonet and M1905 sight (2nd Alteration). It was used from 1906 to 1910, refer to Table 13. The Type 4 handguard was 15.2 inches, 0.2 inch shorter than the Type 3, reflecting the change in barrel length caused by the change to the .30-M1906 cartridge. It had front and rear tenons and the swell at the rear to protect the rear sight but no sight clearance cut. The forward slope to the barrel band cut was concave. This handguard lacked the air chambers but retained the indexing cut and added two steel spring clips at 1.0 and 5.2 inches behind the front end, see Figure 2-38

Model 1903 Springfield Rifle and Its Variations

(arrows 1 and 2). The spring clips were folded at the ends to slip over the hand-guard shoulders into semicircular milled cuts. The underside of the handguard was also relieved for the front clip but not the rear clip 0.02 inch deep by 0.5 inch wide. A windage knob cut

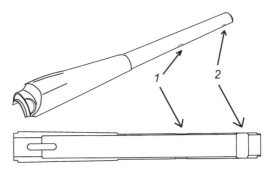

Fig. 2-38. The Type 4 handguard used on the 2nd Alteration and all originally produced M1903 rifles from 1906 to 1910 (refer to Table 13).

was made on the right, rear side of the swell in the form of 1/3 of an arc but with an enlarged radius of 0.3 to 0.4 inch.

HANDGUARDS—.30-M1906 SERVICE RIFLE

The **Type 5** handguard was adopted to provide a sight clearance cut to improve the sight picture, see Figure 2-39. The sight protector swell was slightly concave and cut through with a sight line 0.53 inch wide and 2.4 inches long. The end of the sight clearance cut forms a pa-rabola. The handguard was 15.2 inches long, had front and rear ten-ons, the indexing cut at the rear, and two steel clips 1.0 and 5.2 inches behind the front end. The spring clips were folded at the ends to slip over the handguard

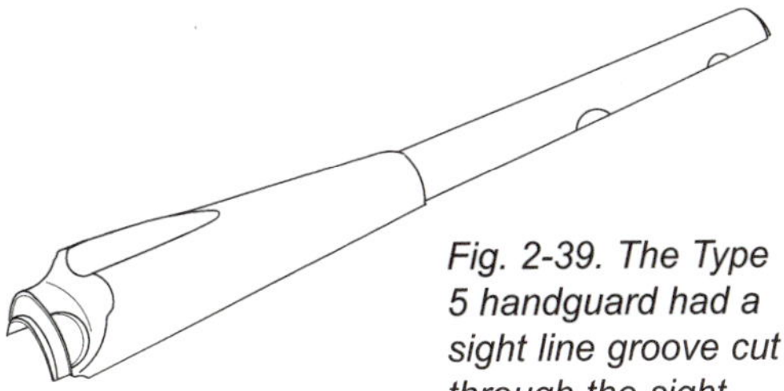

Fig. 2-39. The Type 5 handguard had a sight line groove cut through the sight protector hump.

shoulders into semicircular milled cuts. The underside of the hand-guard was also relieved 0.002 inch deep by 0.5 inch wide for the front clip but not the rear clip. This type was used from 1910 to 1919.

129

Model 1903 Springfield Rifle and Its Variations

Note: From Type 5 through Type 10, the chief difference between the various types of handguards appears to be the forward slope of the sight protector hump, see Figure 2-40. Types 3, 4, 5, 9-1 and 10 have concave front slopes; Types 6, 9-2 and 11 have convex front slopes and Types 7 and 8 have straight front slopes.

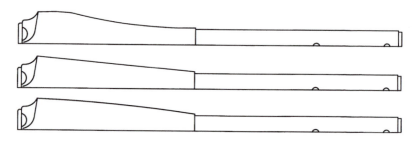

Fig. 2-40. Profiles of M1903 service rifle handguards, from the top—Concave: Types 3, 4, 5, 9-1 and -3 and 10; Straight: Types 7 and 8; Convex: Types 6, 9-2 and 11. Exaggerated for clarity.

Further, all pre-World War II sight clearance cuts end in a parabola (Types 4-8) while WW II-manufactured handguard sight clearance cuts are wider and end in a square cut with one exception, see Figure 2-41. All pre-World War II handguards (Types 3-8) have a windage knob adjustment cut that forms 1/3 of an arc and is 0.3 to 0.4 inch in radius with the exception of the Type 3 which is smaller at 0.2-0.3 inch in radius. Type 9 windage knob cuts are all elliptical and 0.2 inch wide. Types 10 and 11 windage knob cuts are semicircular and 0.3 to 0.4 inch in radius, see Figure 2-42.

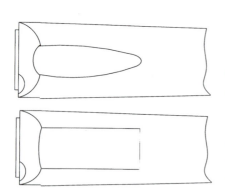

Fig. 2-41. Sight line clearance cut shape, top: Types 4-8; below, Types 9-11.

Model 1903 Springfield Rifle and Its Variations

The **Type 6** handguard was similar to the Type 5 but the curve ahead of the sight protector hump changed from concave to convex, refer to Figure 2-40. It was in use from 1920 to 1929.

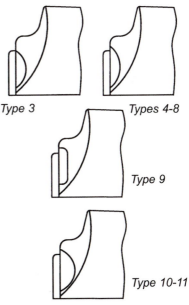

Type 3   *Types 4-8*

Type 9

Type 10-11

Fig. 2-42. Windage knob clearances: top to bottom: Type 3 (left) and Types 4-8 (right), then Type 9 followed by Types 10 and 11.

The **Type 7** handguard was used on the M1903A1 and on National Match Rifles. It was similar to the Type 6 but the slope ahead of the sight protector swell was a straight slope to the barrel band step, refer to Figure 2-40. The use of the interior indexing cut at the rear was discontinued. It was in use from 1929 through 1941 when production of the M1903A1 and National Match Rifles ended.

The **Type 8** handguard was identical to the Type 7 but had the drawing number, D29179, stamped on the top surface ahead of the barrel band step. It was used intermittently between 1936 and 1941 on National Match rifles until production ended.

Three variations of the **Type 9** handguard were used. They were similar to the Type 6 but with subtle differences. The **1st Variation** handguard was manufactured at Springfield in 1942 to 1945 as replacement handguards for M1903 rifles and had a slightly concave slope, refer to Figure 2-40. The major difference between it and the Type 5 is the shape of the windage knob cut which was elliptical in shape and 0.2 inch wide, refer to Figure 2-42. The sight clearance groove is 0.59 inch wide and 3.25 inches long, has a square end and often shows milling marks, refer to Figure 2-41.

Model 1903 Springfield Rifle and Its Variations

The **2nd Variation** handguard was manufactured as a replacement handguard in 1944-1945. It may have been manufactured by Springfield or Keystone, or both. The sight protector swell appears to be higher and thicker and the sight clearance groove is 0.59 inch wide and 3.25 inches long with a square end, refer to Figure 2-41. The slope from the sight protector swell to the barrel band step is convex, refer to Figure 2-40. The workmanship and finish is quite rough. They are often wider than the Type 5 handguard by 0.1-0.2 inch.

The **3rd Variation** of the Type 9 handguard was manufactured as a replacement handguard in 1944-1945. It is similar to the Type 9, 2nd variation but the slope is concave and the sight clearance groove is 0.47 inch wide by 2.76 inches long and ends in a parabola. Interestingly enough, the forward spring clip groove is exactly 0.5 inch wide as it was in the Type 5 handguard, suggesting that it was made at Springfield.

The **Type 10** handguard was manufactured by Remington Arms for the M1903 rifle. The sight protector swell has a concave slope to the barrel band step, refer to Figure 2-40. The sight clearance groove is 0.59 inch wide by 2.5 inches long and has a square end, refer to Figure 2-41. The forward spring clip relief cut is longer at 0.9 inch. The clip is centered in the relief cut, leaving a gap of 0.2 inch on either side of the 0.5-inch-wide clip. This same handguard was also manufactured in quantity as a replacement handguard.

The **Type 11** handguard was manufactured by Remington Arms for the M1903 (Modified) rifle. It was 15.2 inches long. It differs from the Type 10 in that the sight protector swell has a slight convex slope. Like the Type 10 handguard, the sight line clearance groove is 0.59 inch wide, 2.5 inches long with a square end; the forward spring clip relief cut is 0.9 inch long with the clip centered in the relief cut leaving a gap of 0.2 inch on either side of the 0.5-inch-wide clip, see Figure 2-43. This same handguard was also manufactured in quantity as a re-

Model 1903 Springfield Rifle and Its Variations

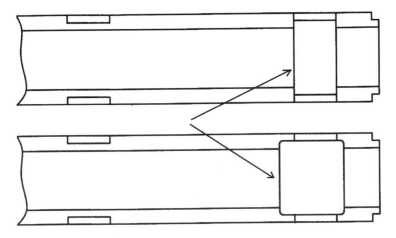

Fig. 2-43. Forward spring clip relief cut (arrows): top, pre-World War II; bottom, World War II.

placement handguard. The windage knob cut is semicircular and has a 0.3-0.4-inch radius.

NOTE: The forward spring clip relief cut on all World War II production handguards was 0.9 inch long. The pre-war forward spring clip relief cut was 0.6 inch long.

The **Type 12** handguard was manufactured for the United States Marine Corps M1903A1 Sniper Rifle. It was 15.2 inches long with a sight protector swell without a sight clearance groove and a very short concave forward slope. The apron leading to the barrel band step is flat and drilled through with a 1 inch by 0.5 inch oblong hole for the forward Unertl Telescopic Sight mounting block, see Figure 2-44. The hole may have rounded or squared ends. All appear to have been modified by hand. All had the elliptical windage knob cut.

The **Type 13** handguard, or barrel cover, was manufactured for the

Model 1903 Springfield Rifle and Its Variations

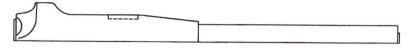

Fig. 2-44. Type 12 handguard for the USMC M1903A1 Sniper Rifle.

M1903A3 service rifle by Remington Arms and Smith Corona. It was also used on the M1903A4 sniper rifle. The M1903A3 did not have a sight protector swell. It was 1.68 inches wide at the rear, 1.13 inches wide at the front and 18.75 inches long. The top of the handguard formed a slight concave hump to the barrel band step. The area forward of the step was flat. The forward tenon was 0.36 inch wide and the rear 0.15 inch wide. The rear handguard clip was not set into a relief cut. The 0.5-inch-wide forward clip was set into a relief cut 0.65 inch long. Some, but not all, spring steel clips had a 0.05-inch-diameter hole in the center, see Figure 2-45.

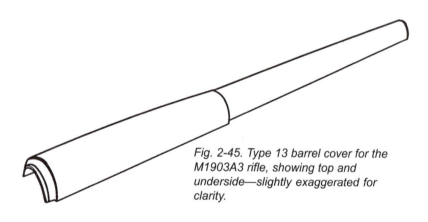

Fig. 2-45. Type 13 barrel cover for the M1903A3 rifle, showing top and underside—slightly exaggerated for clarity.

NOTE: A variety of inspection markings in the form of a letter(s) or number(s) will sometimes be found on the underside of any type of handguard. In theory, the same inspection initial(s) should be found inside the stock, forward of the magazine well as on the underside of the handguard in original M1903 rifles. In practice, they rarely are.

Model 1903 Springfield Rifle and Its Variations

Again, in theory, all Remington-manufactured handguards will be marked "R" and those that are not should be considered handguards made under the replacement-parts contracts of 1944 and 1945.

Smith Corona handguards were marked "X" or "E" but not consistently so.

Barrel Bands

Two barrel bands were used on the M1903 series of rifles. The upper band (except for the Type 1) doubled as the bayonet mount with a Krag-style stud and carried the stacking swivel. The lower band also held the forward sling swivel.

LOWER BARREL BAND
The lower barrel band encircled the stock at the midpoint and held the handguard in place. The bottom of the band was milled or stamped into an ear for the sling swivel. Five variations of the lower band were used. The lower band was 2.75 inches high (including the sling swivel stud), 1.45 inches across and 0.41 inch wide. Types 1-4 had a lightening groove milled around the circumference of the band 0.08 inch wide and 0.005 inch deep.

All lower barrel bands but the Type 5 were marked on the right side with the letter "U," indicating "UP" or toward the muzzle. This marking had been in use at Springfield (and Harpers Ferry) Arsenal since the M1861 Rifle Musket.

The **Type 1** lower band was used on the rod bayonet rifle and was a solid oval milled from bar stock with the sling swivel ear extending below, see Figure 2-46. It was used from the start of production to circa serial #200,000 (June 1906) and was manufactured at both Springfield and Rock Island. It was marked "U" with serifs and blued by dipping in a molten bath of potassium nitrate.

Model 1903 Springfield Rifle and Its Variations

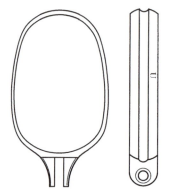

Fig. 2-46. Type 1 lower band, rod bayonet rifle.

The **Type 2** lower band was used on all service rifles from circa serial # 200,000 (June 1906) to the end of production in FY1927. Type 2 barrel bands were also milled from solid stock but split at the bottom between the sling swivel studs to enable the barrel band to be tightened, see Figure 2-47. The Type 2 band was marked "U" without serifs.

All replacement and spare parts lower bands manufactured by Springfield Armory and Rock Island are the Type 2. Type 2 lower barrel bands were also manufactured by Remington Arms for the M1903 and M1903 (Modified) service rifles until April 1942 when the Type 3 barrel band was approved and put into production. Two variations of the Type 2 lower barrel band were used.

Type 2A lower barrel bands were blued by dipping in a molten bath of potassium nitrate until circa serial 1917 when Parkerizing was approved but not introduced until 1919.

The **Type 2B** lower barrel bands were Parkerized starting in 1919 to the end of production by dipping into a solution of dilute phosphoric acid and powdered iron.

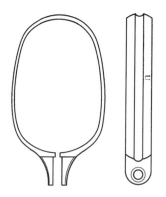

Fig. 2-47. Type 2 lower band, post-1906.

The **Type 3** lower barrel band was used on all M1922 stocks assembled to .22-caliber and .30-caliber target rifles with the short forend and no handguard, see Figure 2-48. These lower barrel bands

136

Model 1903 Springfield Rifle and Its Variations

are shaped to match the curve of the barrel and the shoulder of the stock. All were milled from bar stock and were Parkerized.

The **Type 4** lower barrel band was formed from the lower barrel band used on the U.S. Model 1917 Enfield rifle and assembled to the "Style T" and International target rifle. As none of these rifles were equipped with a handguard, the upper portion of the lower barrel

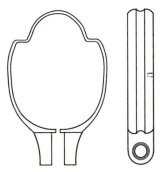

Fig. 2-48. Type 3 lower band for the M1922 stock.

band was reformed to match the contour of the barrel and the shoulder of the stock. The M1917's offset swivel was replaced with the standard Type 1 M1903 sling swivel. The Type 4 lower barrel band and swivel were Parkerized, see Figure 2-49.

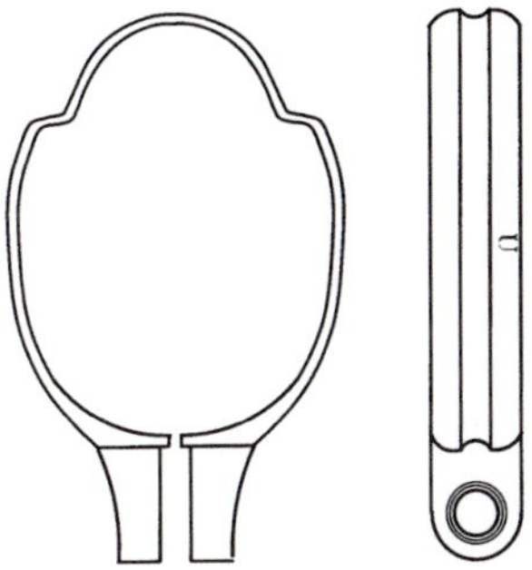

Variation 1 as used on the rifles noted in the paragraph immediately above had the circumferential lightening groove.

Fig. 2-49. Type 4 lower barrel band for the .30-caliber M1922 stock.

Variation 2 as used on the Match Springfield, Caliber .30, M1922 target rifles and the "Style T" heavy barrel rifles did not have the circumferential lightening groove.

The **Type 5** barrel band (Figure 2-50) was stamped from sheet steel to increase production. It was made by Remington for the M1903

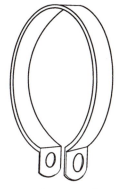

Fig. 2-50. Type 5 lower barrel band for the M1903A3.

Model 1903 Springfield Rifle and Its Variations

(Modified) and the M1903A3 from April 1942 to the end of production in 1944 and by Smith Corona for the M1903A3 in 1943-44. The Type 5 barrel band was blued.

SLING SWIVEL, LOWER BAND

Three types of sling swivels were installed on the upper band.

The **Type 1** lower band sling swivel was identical in shape to the sling swivel used on the M1892-1898 Krag Rifle but the diameters of the wire and hinge were slightly smaller. Like the Krag lower band swivel, it had a solid hinge. It was used on the M1903 rod bayonet rifle until

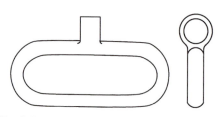

1905 when the M1905 knife bayonet was adopted and the rod bayonet rifles were converted to its use, see Figure 2-51.

The Type 1 solid hinge was used again after 1919 through

Fig. 2-51. Type 1 lower sling swivel.

the end of service rifle production in FY1927. Spare swivels for the lower band manufactured from 1929-1934 and 1937-1945 were also Type 1s with the solid hinge.

The **Type 2** swivel for the lower band had a split hinge and was in use from 1905 to 1917. Except for the split ear, it was identical to the Type 1, see Figure 2-52.

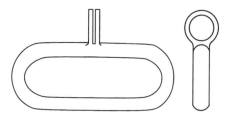

Fig. 2-52. Type 2 lower sling swivel.

Both the Type 1 and Type 2 sling swivels for the lower band were 1.7 inches wide by 0.7 inch high (not including the hinge) and made of steel wire 0.175 inch in diameter. The hinge was 0.2 inch wide by 0.370 inch high and had a hole

Model 1903 Springfield Rifle and Its Variations

0.188 inch in diameter drilled through it for the lower band swivel screw. Both types were blued using molten potassium nitrate.

NOTE: Split sling swivels were used on many of the USMC M1903A1 sniper rifles.

The **Type 3** sling swivel for the lower band was used on the M1903A3/ A4 rifles only. It was stamped from sheet steel and measured 1.73 inches wide by 0.69 inch high (not including the hinge) and 0.110 inch thick. The hinge was 0.25 inch wide by 0.460 inch high. The hinge was 0.1 inch thick and rolled over on itself to form a loop 0.195 inch in diameter, see Figure 2-53.

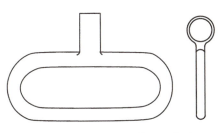

Fig. 2-53. Type 3 lower sling swivel.

NOTE: All lower band sling swivels are interchangeable. The Type 1 sling swivel will be found on very early M1903A3 transitional rifles as Type 3 sling swivels may be found on late M1903 (Modified) service rifles.

Sling Swivel, Lower Band Screw

Three types of screws were used to secure the sling swivel to the lower band.

The **Type 1** screw (Figure 2-54) was 0.790 inch long with a diameter of 0.180 inch. It was threaded for 0.280 inch and its tip was chamfered. Its fillister head was 0.270 inch in diameter and 0.1 inch thick at the edge. It was nearly identical to the lower band sling swivel screw used on the Krag M1892-1898 except that the Krag screw was 0.375 inch. The screws are interchangeable and, in fact, early M1903 rod bayonet rifles have been observed with this screw.

Fig. 2-54. Type 1 lower band screw.

Model 1903 Springfield Rifle and Its Variations

The **Type 2** screw was also 0.790 inch long with a diameter of 0.180 inch. It was threaded for 0.32 inch and had a cupped tip (flat tip that had been indented) to allow the assembler or armorer to prevent it from backing out by upsetting its tip, see Figure 2-55.

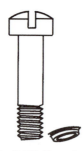

The Type 2 screw had a sharper "V" thread than did the Type 1 screw which had a rounded thread. This means that the Type 1 screw can be used in the Type 5 lower band (M1903A3/A4) but that the Type 2 lower band sling swivel screw should not be forced into the Type 2 lower band (M1903).

Fig. 2-55. Type 2 lower band screw.

Upper Barrel Band

The upper barrel band held the stock and handguard to the barrel. Two distinct kinds were used: one type for the rod bayonet rifle and the other for the knife bayonet rifle. All provided a mounting for the stacking swivel but only the last two provided a mounting for the M1905 knife bayonet.

The **Type 1** upper barrel band was milled from steel bar stock and was similar in appearance to the lower barrel band but was split between the stacking swivel ears, see Figure 2-56. The stacking swivel was hung from the upper band between two ears and held in place by a screw.

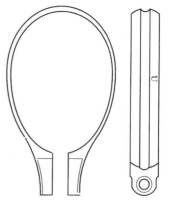

The **Type 2** upper barrel band was assembled to all M1903-type service rifles using the M1905 knife bayonet. It was made in two variations and milled from steel bar stock. The Type 2 barrel band was 1.910 inches long by

Fig. 2-56. Type 1 upper band.

Model 1903 Springfield Rifle and Its Variations

0.960 inch wide (at its widest point) and 1.820 inches high (from the bottom of the stacking swivel ear). The barrel band was drilled through for the barrel band screw 0.935 inch behind the front. The screw hole was 0.155 inch in diameter and threaded on the right side for the barrel band screw.

The Type 2 upper barrel band encircled the stock's forend with a solid band, see Figure 2-57. The rear top strap held the front of the handguard in place and the front top strap aligned the stock forend and handguard with the axis of the bar-

rel. The interior of the band was contoured to the barrel and shoulders of the forend.

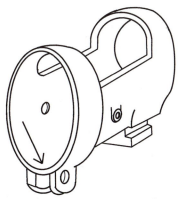

The Krag-style bayonet stud was located at the bottom front. It was rounded on the front end and squared at the rear. The stud was 0.656 inch long, 0.425 inch wide and 0.220 inch below the barrel band proper.

Fig. 2-57. Type 2 upper band.

The stacking swivel ears were located at the rear of the barrel band. Both left and right ears were "U"-shaped and drilled through for the stacking swivel screw. The ears were 0.420 inch long, 0.400 inch wide and 0.160 inch thick.

A cut 0.870 inch long was made between the two stacking swivel ears on rifles used for bayonet practice (arrow, Figure 2-57). This slot was first cut into the upper barrel bands installed on the Krag M1898 rifles. It allowed the upper barrel band to be snugged down on the stock so that it would not twist. Experiments performed by the author showed that tightening the barrel band against the stock and barrel could move the point of impact by as much as six inches at 100 yards.

Model 1903 Springfield Rifle and Its Variations

Two variations of the Type 2 upper barrel band were produced and are differentiated only by their finish. The **Type 1** barrel band was blued but not hardened; the **Type 2** barrel band was hardened and marked "H" on the lug and blued to late 1918, Parkerized after.

UPPER BARREL BAND SCREW

The upper barrel band screw was 1.275 inches long and 0.145 inch in diameter. Its head was 0.270 inch in diameter, slotted and 0.070 inch high at the edge, and the end of the screw was blunt. The screw was threaded at the head end. It was inserted from the right, through a hole in the upper band and a matching hole drilled through the stock. The blunt end of the screw entered the hole drilled in the left side of the upper barrel band.

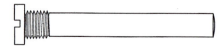

Fig. 2-58. Type 1 upper band screw.

Two types of upper barrel band screws were used. The **Type 1** screw was used for rifles equipped for the M1905 knife bayonet. This screw was threaded at the head end. It was blued in a molten solution of potassium nitrate and when new, had an iridescent appearance, see Figure 2-58.

The **Type 2** screw was Parkerized, was used only on the M1903A3 rifle (see Figure 2-59), and was properly known as the "bayonet lug band screw." It was threaded at the end of the shank.

Fig. 2-59. Type 2 upper band screw.

STACKING SWIVEL SCREW

Two types of stacking swivel screws were used on the Model 1903 Service Rifle and a third type on the M1903A3/A4 rifle.

Model 1903 Springfield Rifle and Its Variations

The **Type 1** screw was 0.690 inch long, 0.180 inch in diameter, was threaded for 0.20 inch and the tip was flat. The fillister head was 0.270 inch in diameter and 0.070 inch high at the edge. Two variations were used: **Variation 1** was blued in a molten potassium nitrate solution while **Variation 2** was Parkerized after it superceded bluing in 1919, refer to Figure 2-54.

The **Type 2** stacking swivel screw was used on the M1903A3/A4 rifle. It was 0.62 inch long and 0.185 inch in diameter, was threaded for 0.270 inch and had a cupped (indented) tip that allowed the assembler or armorer to upset the screw end to prevent it from backing out, refer to Figure 2-55. Its fillister head was 0.245 inch in diameter and 0.012 inch thick at the edge. The screw was blued.

The Type 1 (M1903) stacking swivel screw is interchangeable with the Type 2 stacking swivel screw used on the M1903A3/A4 stacking swivel band as it is 0.005 inch smaller in diameter. It was not used officially as its end could not be upset to prevent backing out. But a survey of original (appearing) M1903A3 rifles showed that they may have been used occasionally as field replacements.

BAYONET LUG BAND AND STACKING SWIVEL BAND — M1903A3/A4

The separate bayonet lug and stacking swivel band replaced the upper barrel band on the Model 1903A3/A4 rifles.

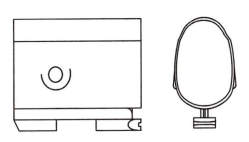

Fig. 2-60. M1903A3 bayonet lug band.

The bayonet lug band did not have the opening between the front and rear straps but was solid. It was stamped from sheet steel and welded together along the bottom, see Figure 2-60.

Model 1903 Springfield Rifle and Its Variations

The bayonet mounting was modified with a second stud. Both studs were welded to the bottom of the barrel band. The forward stud was 0.6 inch long; the rear stud was 0.4 inch long. Both are 0.435 inch wide and separated by 0.390 inch.

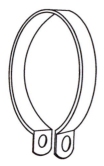

The exterior of the bayonet lug band was contoured to the barrel and shoulders of the forend and held in place with a screw that penetrated both sides of the band and the forend. It was 1.6 inches long, 1.145 inches wide and 1.605 inches high, including the bayonet lugs.

Instead of mounting the stacking swivel on the upper band, to make production more efficient the stacking swivel was placed on a separate barrel band similar to the lower band but smaller in diameter and height (1.845 inches high including the stacking swivel ears by 0.4 inch wide), see Figure 2-61.

Fig. 2-61. M1903A3 stacking swivel band.

Both the bayonet lug band and stacking swivel band were Parkerized.

Bayonet Lug Band Screw—M1903A3/A4

This screw is 1.280 inches long and 0.145 inch in diameter. It has a slotted fillister head 0.250 inch in diameter and 0.090 inch thick at the edge. The screw was threaded for 0.150 inch and had a cupped tip to allow it to be upset to prevent backing out. Original screws were blued; screws from refurbished guns were often Parkerized along with other parts. Refer to the Type 2 Barrel Band Screw, Figure 2-59.

Stacking Swivel

Four types of stacking swivels were developed and used for the M1903 service rifle and its variations. They are similar to the lower band sling swivel but with a section cut from the bottom. This allowed the swivels of three rifles to be interlinked to form a tripod to support the

Model 1903 Springfield Rifle and Its Variations

rifles in the field and keep them out of the dirt and wet.

The **Types 1** and **2** stacking swivels were only used on the M1903 rod bayonet rifle. Both had a flat area ground onto the outside of the hinge so that it would not contact the rod bayonet latch if pushed forward.

The Type 1 had a smaller-diameter hinge and when testing showed that it broke easily, the diameter of the hinge was enlarged to strengthen it, see Figure 2-62.

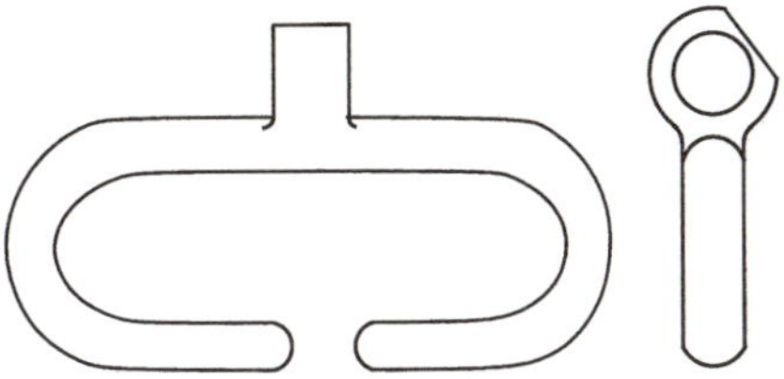

The Types 1 and 2 stacking swivels were 1.470 inches wide by 0.620 inch high and formed

Fig. 2-62. M1903 Types 1 and 2 stacking swivels.

from 0.220-inch-diameter steel wire. They were distinguished only by the diameter of the hinge which was 0.310 inch for the Type 1 and 0.340 inch for the Type 2.

The **Type 3** stacking swivel was used on all M1903-type service rifles equipped with the M1905 knife bayonet. The hinge was enlarged again to 0.385 inch to strengthen it and the flat surface was eliminated.

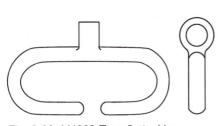

The Type 3 stacking swivel was 1.455 inches wide by 0.635 inch high and formed from 0.170-inch-diameter steel wire, see Figure 2-63.

Fig. 2-63. M1903 Type 3 stacking swivel.

The **Type 4** stacking swivel was used on all M1903A3 and A4 rifles. It was 1.75 inches wide by 0.655 inch high and stamped from sheet steel 0.10 inch thick, see Figure 2-64.

Model 1903 Springfield Rifle and Its Variations

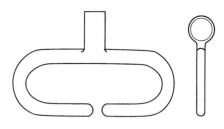

Fig. 2-64. M1903A3 Type 4 stacking swivel.

Stacking swivel Types 1, 2 and 3 were blued by dipping in molten potassium nitrate or Parkerized. Type 4 was blued.

RETAINING SPRING, BARREL BAND

The barrel band retaining spring was made of spring steel in the shape of an "L." The short leg of the "L" was round and was inserted in a hole drilled through the stock to anchor itself, see Figure 2-65. The long leg of the "L" lay in a groove cut in the right side of the forearm. A notch near its tip held the lower barrel band in place against the rifle's recoil. The retaining spring was 2.285 inches long by 0.130 inch wide.

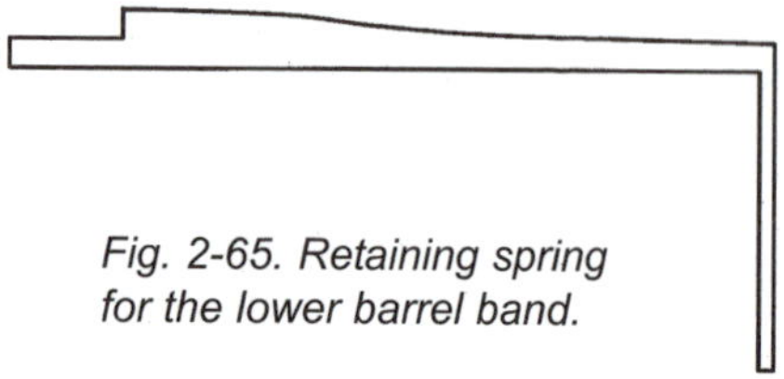

Fig. 2-65. Retaining spring for the lower barrel band.

Two types of retaining springs were used. The **Type 1** barrel band spring was installed in stocks intended for the M1903 service rifle and was blued in molten potassium nitrate whether or not the other metal parts were blued or Parkerized.

The **Type 2** barrel band spring was installed in stocks intended for the M1903A3/A4 rifles, 2.140 inches long and 0.145 inch wide. The retaining spring was stamped from sheet steel and blued.

REAR SLING SWIVEL ASSEMBLY

The rear sling swivel (butt swivel) assembly was very similar to that used on the M1873, M1884, M1888 and M1892/98 Rifles. It consisted of a metal plate inletted into the bottom of the stock which held the sling swivel itself, see Figure 2-66. The components of the assembly are, 1) butt swivel, 2) butt swivel plate, 3) butt swivel screws, 4) butt swivel pin. Three types of sling swivel assemblies were used.

The **Type 1** sling swivel assembly was blued; the **Type 2** swivel assembly was Parkerized. Both were 0.545 inch wide by 1.72 inches long. The swivel was 1.740 inches wide by 0.72 inch high and formed from steel wire 0.165 inch in diameter.

The **Type 3** swivel was formed from sheet metal; upper and lower plates were welded together and

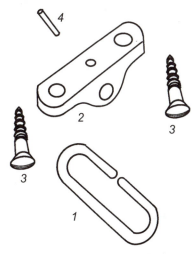

Fig. 2-66. Rear sling swivel assembly.

blued. Both plates were bent in the center to form a V-housing for the sling swivel. The swivel plate was 0.535 inch wide by 1.710 inches long. The swivel was 1.740 inches wide by 0.728 inch high and formed from steel wire 0.160 inch in diameter. Remington-made Type 3 plates were marked "R" or "RP"; Smith Corona-made plates were unmarked.

The Types 1, 2 and 3 rear sling swivel assemblies were interchangeable, although not officially, and they rarely were.

ROD BAYONET CATCH ASSEMBLY

The M1903 rifle was the seventh infantry weapon for which the Ordnance Department designed a rod bayonet. The objective was to decrease the soldier's weight load and decrease the loss rate of the separate bayonet. In all, the rod bayonet appeared on five separate models. The first and second arms to use a rod bayonet were the Model 1833 and 1836 Hall Carbines manufactured by Simeon North and at Harpers Ferry Arsenal—also the first newly manufactured percussion ignition arms. The bayonet was retained by a fixture welded to the barrel and moved backward into a hole in the forend. The 25.25-inch bayonet was triangular in shape with flutes on all three sides. The carbines were used to arm the 1st and 2nd Dragoons. The rod bayonet doubled as a cleaning rod.

The third arm was the Model 1880 .45-70 Rifle. Made as an experimental rifle, only 1,001 were manufactured. The bayonet was triangular in shape without flutes and again, was mounted on a fixture beneath the barrel. The fourth model was a hybrid rifle-carbine designated the Model 1882 Experimental Carbine. It was designed as a trial piece to test the concept of a rifle shorter that the issue Model 1873 Rifle and longer than the issue Model 1877 carbine that would serve both foot and mounted troops. Only 52 were manufactured before the

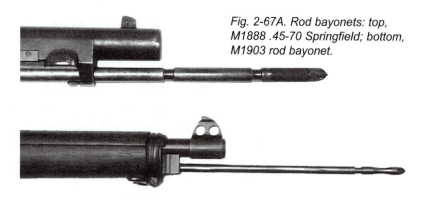

Fig. 2-67A. Rod bayonets: top, M1888 .45-70 Springfield; bottom, M1903 rod bayonet.

rod bayonet was discontinued. The fifth arm was the Model 1884 .45-70 Springfield rifle. It led to the sixth and most successful arm, the Model 1888 .45-70 Springfield rifle, of which 65,000 were manufactured. While several problems had cropped up with the rod bayonet concept, the Ordnance Department felt they had been overcome in the Model 1903 rifle. Accuracy was the major issue but by locating the catch assembly in the stock forend rather than welding it to the barrel, it was no longer considered an issue.

Model 1903 Springfield Rifle and Its Variations

The adoption of the metallic cartridge for breech loading and repeating rifles had gone a long way toward rendering the bayonet obsolete. By the 1890s, the bayonet was thought to be of use only for guarding prisoners and keeping civil order. But two new weapons that came into use in the series of wars that broke out between 1898 and 1905—quick-firing, breech-loading artillery and the machine gun—changed all that. Soldiers were driven into trenches and bunkers and marksmanship over extended ranges was thought to be the answer. But the Japanese developed a new battle tactic in their war with Russia (1903-1905). To end the stalemate of trench warfare, Japanese infantry raided Russian trenches at night. The bayonet proved a deadly weapon in these melees. President Theodore Roosevelt, who was a keen observer of the Russo-Japanese War and was even then maneuvering to bring both sides to the negotiating table, was well aware of the bayonet's newfound importance. Although President Roosevelt was an enthusiastic proponent of the M1903 rifle, he objected immediately and strenuously to the rod bayonet on the new Model 1903 rifle (Figure 2-67A). The rest is history.

The rod bayonet assembly (Figure 2-67B) consisted of three pieces, 1) the rod bayonet stud, 2) the rod bayonet catch and 3) the rod bayonet catch spring.

ROD BAYONET STUD
The rod bayonet stud was held in the forearm of the stock by a flange on its front end which slid over the stock nose and a lug at the rear which fitted into a slot in the stock. The top of the stud was curved so that when the barrel was mounted in the stock, it pressed it securely in place. The rod bayonet slid through holes in the rear lug and the front of the stud, refer to Figure 2-67B, 1.

ROD BAYONET CATCH
The rod bayonet catch was a cylindrical piece that tapered in the middle. A hole was drilled through its center with a locking shoulder immediately above. A projection on the front end, termed the "spur," fitted

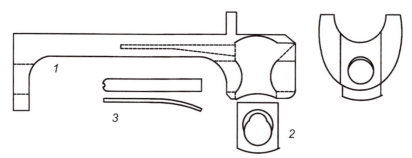

Fig. 2-67B. Rod bayonet catch assembly showing both top and side views of the rod bayonet catch spring.

into a slot in the rod bayonet stud to prevent it from turning. When the stud was pressed in, the locking shoulder moved up and out of contact with either the "rest groove" at the front, or the "action groove" midway along its length. When released, the locking shoulder dropped into either of the grooves to hold the bayonet in position, refer to Figure 2-67B, 2.

Rod Bayonet Catch Spring

This was a flat spring with a rounded and notched after end. It was bent down at a slight angle and bore against the rear notch in the rod bayonet catch to force it to lock the rod bayonet in the closed or extended position, refer to Figure 2-67B, 3.

Model 1903 Springfield Rifle and Its Variations

Barrels

The M1903 barrel was nominally 24 inches long. It was originally bored and rifled for a .30 caliber bullet (.308 dia.) and chambered for two .30-caliber cartridges in succession, the .30-M1903 and the .30-M1906, and later, for the .22-caliber rimfire cartridge. The barrel was manufactured in 1) the standard service rifle configuration (two variations, one for the M1903 and M1903A1 and other the M1903A3), 2) in a slightly heavier configuration for the .22-caliber rimfire cartridge (M1922, M1922M1 and M2), 3) one M1922 configuration for a .30-caliber barrel (NRA Sporter) and in 4) a heavy barrel configuration in .30 caliber with a straight taper from breech to muzzle for various national and international matches in the 1920s and 1930s. See Figure 2-68A.

Fig. 2-68A. Top, M1903 barrel; bottom, M1903A3 barrel.

NOTE: Private gunsmiths chambered and installed barrels in a variety of calibers and contours on surplus M1903 rifles for private individuals. These are not military firearms although some, by virtue of workmanship or the reputation of the gunsmith, may be collectible.

151

Model 1903 Springfield Rifle and Its Variations

MANUFACTURING TECHNIQUE

The M1903 barrel was manufactured from a carbon steel alloy known generically as "ordnance steel." Three types with slightly varying composition were used. The exact composition is of no real interest to collectors unless they have a degree in metallurgy. Nevertheless, if you are interested, the composition of all steels used to make barrels (and receivers and bolts) for the M1903 in all its variations can be found in *Hatcher's Notebook* (see Appendix I) starting on page 223 of the third edition. A brief description of the barrel-manufacturing procedure is given in Appendix B.

The M1903 barrel blank was made from bar stock which was heated and rolled through twelve sets of grooved rollers to produce a rough barrel varying in length from 24 to 25.5 inches. The rough barrels underwent a series of operations to form the final barrel. The barrel was then machined to final shape, rifled, and after World War I, stress relieved. A special cartridge producing 70,000 psi was used to proof M1903 service barrels.

The single exception to this process were the barrels manufactured by a subcontractor during World War I. The Avis Rifle Barrel Company used smaller-diameter round stock which they heated and upset at the breech end to the proper diameter. This practice, it was discovered in the 1920s, sometimes produced "burned," i.e., overheated, barrels which left them brittle. When the "brittle" barrel problem was discovered, the proof cartridge was increased to 75,000 psi and all remaining barrel blanks still in storage were retested.

M1903 SERVICE RIFLE BARRELS

A total of six types of service barrels were installed on the M1903/ M1903A3/M1903A4 rifle at the national armories and by subcontractors. Two of the variations were manufactured in .30-M1903 caliber and the remainder in .30-M1906. The service barrel is chiefly distinguished by the type of rear and front sight band used. All but one variation of the service rifle barrel had four grooves and lands while the exception had two lands and grooves.

Model 1903 Springfield Rifle and Its Variations

The M1903 .30-caliber service rifle barrel was 0.760 inch in diameter at the lower band position and 0.620 inch in diameter at the muzzle regardless of model or manufacturer.

The rifle barrel bore was nominally 0.30 inch in diameter. The M1903 barrel had four grooves 0.1767 inch wide by 0.004 inch deep. Groove diameter was 0.3075 inch and land diameter was 0.2995 inch. Later, a number of M1903A3 barrels were made with only two grooves 0.1767 inch wide by 0.004 inch deep. Groove diameter was relaxed to 0.3095 inch and land diameter to 0.3015 inch. All M1903 service barrel rifling was 1:10.5 inches.

Sight radius for the M1903 and M1903A1 was 22.14 inches. Sight radius for the M1903A3 varied from 27.8 inches (200 yards) to 28.4 inches (800 yards) as the aperture was moved back and forth for range.

Barrels accepted for service by Ordnance Department inspectors were marked with the name of the armory or manufacturer, the Ordnance Department escutcheon of a flaming bomb, and the month and year of manufacture (not the date of assembly). The marking was stacked vertically behind the front sight. Exceptions to the barrel-marking procedure are noted in the following paragraphs.

TYPE 1 M1903 BARREL

The **Type 1** barrel was chambered for the .30-M1903 cartridge in two variations distinguished by the type and manner in which the front and rear sight bases were attached. The rod bayonet barrel was 24.206 inches from muzzle to breech end and was manufactured between circa November 1903 to June 30, 1905, see Figure 2-68B.

Front Sight Attachment—The Type 1 barrel had the front sight mounted in a slot on a one-piece front sight stud which was a band that encircled the barrel. It was indexed by a cross-pin centered in the band so that it passed through a groove cut in the barrel 0.75 inch

Model 1903 Springfield Rifle and Its Variations

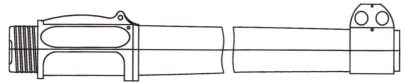

Fig. 2-68B. Rod bayonet barrel, original configuration.

behind the muzzle. The front sight blade fitted into a slot in the vertical part of the stud and was indexed by a lug or spline at the rear of the sight blade and held in place by a cross-pin. This front sight band can be identified by its one-piece construction and two lightening holes cut through the vertical part of the stud ahead and behind the indexing pins. See Figure 2-69.

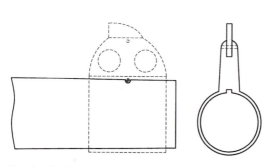

Fig. 2-69. Front sight mounting detail, original rod bayonet barrel.

NOTE: The Ordnance Department referred to the long, thin projection on top of the barrel that indexed the front sight as a "lug." A more correct definition would be a "spline."

Rear Sight Attachment—The rear sight was attached to the Type 1 barrel by a base with two bands that encircled the barrel, just ahead of the receiver face. A hole was drilled through the rear sight base at the top front end, just forward of, and below the base pin hole and a matching groove was cut crosswise in the top of the barrel. When the rear sight base was slipped over the barrel, it was located and indexed by the "base pin" which was inserted through the holes and the barrel groove, see Figure 2-70.

154

Model 1903 Springfield Rifle and Its Variations

When President Theodore Roosevelt objected to the use of the flimsy rod bayonet, the Ordnance Department adopted the M1905 knife bayonet. This required changes to the barrel and stock and provided the opportunity to make other changes as well.

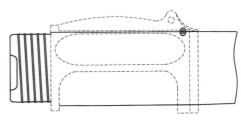

Fig. 2-70. Rear sight base mounting detail, original rod bayonet barrel.

Ferris and Beard (*The Springfield Model 1903 Service Rifle, Production and Alteration, 1905-1910,* see Bibliography, Appendix I) have done extensive and valuable research on the M1903 rod bayonet rifles and their alterations. They have identified five changes in the original configuration.

The **1st Variation** barrel was a Type 1 rod bayonet barrel that had already been manufactured. To prevent the loss of several hundred thousand dollars, these barrels were altered to accept the M1905 knife bayonet as approved April 3, 1905. This required that the front sight be set farther to the rear to allow the hole, or bore, in the bayonet's cross guard to slide over the muzzle. At the same time, the M1905 front and rear sights and their bases replaced the M1903 front and rear sights and bases.

They can be identified by the following: 1) The barrel was chambered for the .30-M1903 cartridge. 2) The M1905 front sight base was set back 0.75 inch farther from the muzzle than the M1903 front sight base. 3) The spline was not used to index the new front sight band so a hole 0.2 inch deep is visible at the rear. 4) The front sight base or band had a dovetail milled in the top to accept the front sight stud which held the front sight blade. 5) On the 1st Variation barrels, the front sight band is pinned at the front (see Figure 2-71, arrow). 6) The barrels were stamped with the armory/escutcheon/date behind the front sight.

Model 1903 Springfield Rifle and Its Variations

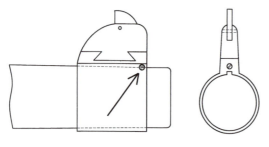

Fig. 2-71. M1905 front sight base and stud mounting detail on 1st alteration rod bayonet barrel.

All Springfield altered barrels will be dated "05" without the "Month." 7) The armory/escutcheon/date stamping on the barrel will show raised metal around the edges of the individual characters as they were die stamped after the barrel was finished (remember, rod bayonet barrels were not marked with the "armory/escutcheon/date"). 8) The rear sight base is pinned to the barrel at the bottom front, rather than the top front, see Figure 2-72, arrow 1. 9) The back of the rear sight base and the breech end of the barrel had a semicircular hole drilled at the 2 o'clock position to receive a round spline. This indexed the rear sight base band and prevented it from rotating left or right as had been a problem with the M1903 rear sight base band.

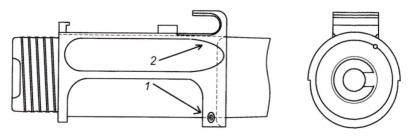

Fig. 2-72. M1905 rear sight base mounting detail on 1st alteration rod bayonet barrel.

NOTE: A small quantity of 2nd Variation barrels may show the rear sight band pinned at the top front. These will not have a groove on the bottom of the barrel.

Model 1903 Springfield Rifle and Its Variations

The **2nd Variation** barrel was manufactured at Rock Island Armory. At the time of manufacture it received the armory/ordnance escutcheon/month and year stamping. They are similar to the 1st Variation barrels made at Springfield except they will not show the front sight band pin hole at the front as they never had the M1903 front sight band installed.

Ferris and Beard postulate that an "unknown quantity of barrels was manufactured [between January and May 1905] in the original rod bayonet configuration [but without the Model 1903 front and rear sights installed]. These barrels would appear identical to [the 1st Variation barrels] except that an X-ray inspection would reveal no notch or hole where the original Model 1903 sights had been previously pinned. We further believe that most of these barrels had been stored 'in the white' in which case the barrels would not exhibit raised metal around the barrel stamping . . . [which] would have been dressed down with a file [during later finishing]."

Note: The shape of the lightening cuts on the M1905 rear sight band was changed to distinguish it from the rear sight band for the M1903 rear sight. The curved front end of the lightening cut was elongated toward the muzzle, refer to Figure 2-72, arrow 2.

On October 15, 1906, the decision to change from the M1903 (.30-M1903) cartridge to the shorter M1906 (.30-M1906) cartridge was approved. Type 1 barrels (those not already modified to 1st or 2nd Variation barrels) were converted to **3rd Variation** barrels. These were shortened by 0.2 inch to 24.0 inches and rechambered. This required that the rear sight mounting band be moved forward 0.2 inch, exposing the original crosscut indexing groove, see Figure 2-73, arrow. Please note that this procedure was only applied to Springfield-manufactured barrels that had undergone the 1st alteration to the M1905 knife bayonet and Model 1905 front and rear sights, and were now undergoing the 2nd alteration to the .30-Model 1906 cartridge. The

Model 1903 Springfield Rifle and Its Variations

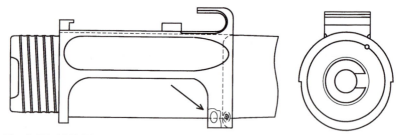

Fig. 2-73. M1905 rear sight base mounting detail on 1st alteration, 2nd variation rod bayonet barrel.

Model 1905 front sight was pinned at the rear where it would remain until the advent of the M1903A3, see Figure 2-74.

These barrels are believed not to have been blued or previously installed on receivers. They can be identified by the fact that

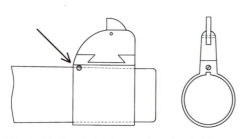

Fig. 2-74. Front sight mounting detail, M1905 front sight.

they did not have front sights mounted previously and will not show the spline for indexing the front sight 0.75 inch behind the muzzle (arrow). Rock Island barrels were stamped with "R.I.A./ ordnance escutcheon/ month-year" and Springfield Armory barrels with "S.A./escutcheon/1905." They will not show the raised metal around the stamping as they were polished smooth after die stamping and before being blued.

Type 2 Model 1903 Barrel

Beginning in 1906, the **Type 2** barrels were manufactured in .30-M1906 caliber and equipped for the M1905 Knife Bayonet, see Figure 2-75. The Type 2 barrels are 24.006 inches long from muzzle to breech end. Externally, they are identical to the Type 1, 2nd Variation barrel

158

Model 1903 Springfield Rifle and Its Variations

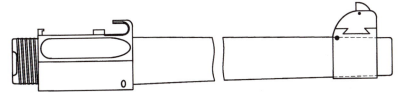

Fig. 2-75. Type 2 M1903 barrel.

with the exception of the addition of a spline to prevent the M1905 rear sight base from moving left or right. The addition of the spline required matching semicircular cuts to the rear interior (2 o'clock position) of the rear sight band and the barrel, see Figure 2-76, arrow. All Type 2 barrels will be chambered for the .30-M1906 cartridge and will show "armory/ordnance escutcheon/month-year" stamped behind the front sight. All will be equipped with the M1905 front and rear sight bases.

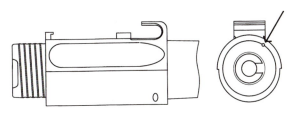

Fig. 2-76. Type 2 M1903 barrel showing the indexing spline.

The following variations of the Type 2 barrels are encountered. The **1st Variation** barrel was manufactured at Springfield Armory and was blued until circa serial #680,000 in mid-1919. Dates will be between "11-05" to circa "6-19."

The **2nd Variation** M1903 service barrel was Parkerized from circa serial #318,000 (RIA) or #1,103,000 (Springfield) through the end of spare parts production in 1941.

NOTE: The exact date of the changeover from bluing to Parkerizing is not known. Although approved in 1917, the change in procedure did not occur until mid-1919 and may have taken place over several weeks or months as equipment was installed and training completed.

Model 1903 Springfield Rifle and Its Variations

The **3rd Variation** service barrels were manufactured for the M1903 rifle at Rock Island Arsenal beginning in 1906. All RIA production M1903 barrels are blued. Dates will be between "4-04" to "7-13" and circa "6-17" to "6-19."

NOTE: The exact date when Rock Island Armory ceased manufacture of M1903 parts is not known. Assembled rifles have been noted with barrel dates as late as 1921. Whether these were original or replacement barrels is open to speculation.

The **4th Variation** barrels were manufactured by the Avis Company during World War I as replacement barrels for the M1903. Manufacture of replacement barrels continued after World War I under the name of the Avis Gun Barrel Company. Avis barrels are marked "AV/ordnance escutcheon/month-year."

Avis barrels were formed from steel rods by heating and upsetting one end to a diameter from which the breech end of the barrel could be machined, rather than machining down a steel rod 1.35 inch in diameter as did Springfield and RIA.

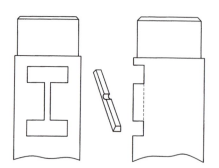

Fig. 2-77. Type 2 M1903 barrel showing the indexing spline.

This practice, it was discovered in the 1920s, sometimes produced "burned," i.e., overheated, barrels which left them brittle. When the "brittle" barrel problem was discovered, the proof cartridge was increased to 75,000 psi and all remaining barrels still in storage were retested.

The **5th Variation** barrels were manufactured for all Remington M1903 service rifles from circa serial #3,000,000 to 3,365,002 (November

Model 1903 Springfield Rifle and Its Variations

1941 through the end of 1942). They are identical to the Type 2, 3rd Variation barrels manufactured at Rock Island except they are marked "R A/ordnance escutcheon/month-year" and are Parkerized. The dates were between 11-41 to 3-42 as production was used up.

TYPE 3 M1903 BARREL

Type 3 barrels were manufactured for the Remington M1903 (Modified) between April and November 1942. Two major differences are apparent between the Type 3 and Type 2 barrels: 1) The new front sight band was indexed by a key held in a milled slot. The key was referred to as the "fixed stud key" and it replaced the spline that fixed the front sight band in place in the previous Type 2 barrels, see Figure 2-77. 2) The lightening cuts on either side of the M1905 rear sight barrel band were eliminated, see Figure 2-78, arrow. The barrels were Parkerized and the markings are "R A/ordnance escutcheon/ month-year." The barrel dates will fall between 4-42 and 10/11-42. These barrels are rifled 1:10.5 with four lands and grooves.

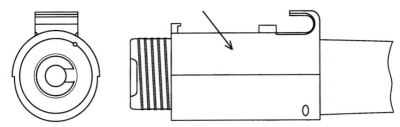

Fig. 2-78. Type 3 M1903 barrel and M1905 (Modified) rear sight base.

TYPE 4 MODEL 1903A3 REMINGTON BARREL

The **Type 4** barrels were manufactured by Remington Arms for the M1903A3 and M1903A4 service rifles. They were Parkerized and marked "R A/ordnance escutcheon/month-year." Barrel dates will fall between 10/12-42 and 3-44. Two variations were manufactured.

161

Model 1903 Springfield Rifle and Its Variations

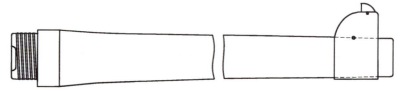

Fig. 2-79. Type 4 M1903A3 barrel.

All were 24.006 inches long and differed from Types 2 and 3 barrels in that they were not shaped for the M1905 rear sight base and lacked the transverse groove for the rear sight base indexing pin. Muzzles were counterbored and they had the milled slot for the fixed stud key for the front sight base as introduced in the Type 3 barrel, see Figure 2-79.

Type 4 barrels will often show a small transverse groove on the bottom of the barrel 4.2 inches from the muzzle for the bayonet lug band screw.

Type 4 barrels were not polished as were Types 1 and 2 barrels. Lathe cutting tool marks are visible as rings around the barrel.

Type 4 barrels are all Parkerized in a dark green-black color. Barrels that show a gray Parkerizing were refinished after World War II.

Type 4 barrels are marked on the bottom, 1.8 inches behind the front sight band with a "P" proof mark signifying that the barrel had been tested with the proof cartridge. Various inspector proof marks consisting of initials and symbols will be found stamped around the periphery of the barrel's breech end.

Almost all Type 4 barrels were rifled using the broaching method. Two broaches were pulled through the barrel, the first to make the first rough cut, the second to produce the finished rifling. The process was completed in less than three minutes per barrel.

Model 1903 Springfield Rifle and Its Variations

Type 4, **1st Variation** barrels were manufactured for the M1903A3 rifle and were fitted with front sights. They are rifled 1:10.5 with four lands and grooves.

The Type 4, **2nd Variation** barrels were manufactured for the M1903A4 sniper rifle and front sights were never fitted to these barrels. The fixed stud seat for the front sight was cut but remained empty. All barrels intended for the M1903A4 have a punch mark on the bottom. As each barrel was Parkerized *after* the front sight was assembled to it, if the fixed stud seat is bright or shows no evidence of Parkerizing, then the barrel is most probably one mounted on the M1903A3 receiver but which has had the front sight removed. These barrels are rifled 1:10.5 with four lands and grooves.

The Type 4, **3rd Variation** barrels were identical to the Type 4, 1st Variation barrels and were rifled 1:10.5 but with only two grooves. They were used as both original and replacement barrels . A note for shooters: Both British and American ordnance department testing of two-groove and four-groove barrels showed both to be equally accurate under military conditions.

Type 5 Model 1903A3 Smith Corona Barrel

The **Type 5** barrel was manufactured by High Standard Manufacturing Company, Inc., for the L.C. Smith Corona Company. They were identical to the Type 4, 1st Variation barrel manufactured by Remington with the exception of the markings. The markings were "SC/ordnance escutcheon/month-year." The barrels are Parkerized and barrel dates will fall between 10-42 and 3-44. High Standard did not manufacture two-groove barrels. Any two-groove barrel found installed on a Smith Corona receiver is a replacement.

NOTE: The Savage Arms Corporation produced a few 6-groove barrels for Smith Corona at the start of production. These barrel were marked "SC/ordnance escutcheon/month-year." As they were a temporary expedient, they have not been assigned as a *Type* in this text.

Model 1903 Springfield Rifle and Its Variations

All Type 5 barrels were rifled using the broaching method. Two broaches were pulled through the barrel, the first to make the first rough cut, the second to produce the finished rifling. The process was completed in less than three minutes per barrel.

NOTE: A large supplier of U.S. military parts some years ago re-rifled Type 4, 3rd Variation two-groove barrels to make 4-groove Type 4, 1st or 2nd Variation barrels. In many cases, the rework will be obvious on inspection of the bore—rough tool work and a difference in width and depth of the added grooves. On others, the bore will have to be slugged. To do so, obtain a .30-caliber lead bullet of at least 0.308 inch in diameter and force it through the barrel from the breech end. Measure the "raised" grooves on the slug with a micrometer. Original four-groove "grooves" will be 0.3094 inch in width. But "added grooves" will vary in width from 0.002 to 0.005 inch greater.

TYPE 6 MODEL 1903 REPLACEMENT BARRELS

Type 6 barrels were manufactured as replacement parts for the M1903 and M1903A1 service rifle by High Standard Manufacturing Company (marked HS) as distinct from those manufactured for Smith Corona (marked SC); by Johnson Automatics (marked JA); and Sedgley Manufacturing Company (marked S in a circle). With the exception of the Sedgley barrels, markings follow the usual practice of "manufacturer's initials/ordnance escutcheon/month-year of manufacture." Sedgley barrels were manufactured under contract to the U.S. Marine Corps and marked "USMC/month-year/S" in a circle. The year is usually 1944.

The Type 6 barrel was also manufactured as a replacement barrel by Springfield Armory in 1944 and 1945. They are marked behind the front sight: "SA /ordnance escutcheon/month year" without a hyphen. Dates will be in 1944 and 1945. These are the dates of manufacture and not of assembly. Four different barrel markings were used on Type 6 barrels, see Figure 2-80, l-r, Springfield Armory, Johnson

Model 1903 Springfield Rifle and Its Variations

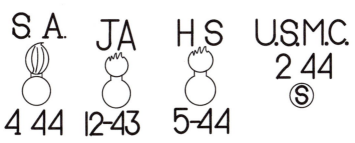

Fig. 2-80. Examples of replacement barrel factory marks behind the front sight band.

Automatics, High Standard for Smith Corona and as replacement barrels, and Sedgley Mfg. Co.

All Type 6 barrels were rifled using the broaching method. Two broaches were pulled through the barrel, the first to make the first rough cut, the second to produce the finished rifling. The process was completed in less than three minutes per barrel.

The muzzles of all Type 6 barrels were counterbored rather than crowned, see Figure 2-81.

STAR-GAUGED BARRELS
Beginning in 1905, an interior gauging system was installed at the Springfield Armory to provide precise measurements of the bore. Referred to as a "star gauge," it was a

Fig. 2-81. Muzzle crown (above) and counterbore cross-sections (below).

hollow tube with arms at one end that could be expanded by pushing a rod into it to force the arms against the lands or grooves. The amount of expansion was read at one-inch intervals directly from a dial indicator. A statistical sampling was made of service-rifle barrels during production runs to ensure that they did not exceed maximum and minimum standards. Beginning in 1921, barrels so gauged had a tiny eight-pointed star stamped on the crown at the six o'clock position, see Figure 2-82.

From the beginning in 1921, all barrels made for competition use were individually star gauged and so marked on the muzzle crown. The star-gauge record number was also stamped on the top of the barrel between the rear sight fixed base and the lower barrel band. The record number usually, but not always, consisted of

Fig. 2-82. Star-gauge marking found on the lip of barrel muzzles.

a letter above a number. Star-gauge numbers in 1921 and 1922 appeared to consist only of a four-digit number

M1903 rifles with barrels marked with the star-gauge eight-pointed star were installed on National Match, .30 caliber NRA Sporter rifles, .30 caliber International Match rifles and certain "Style T" rifles.

The manual star-gauge system was replaced in 1941 by the Precisionaire Gauge which was more accurate and easier to use.

USMC M1903A1 Sniper Rifle Barrels

The legend is that all barrels used on the Marine Corps famed sniper rifle were star-gauged National Match barrels. This is not so. While many of the rifles from which the sniper rifles were made were former National Match rifles, not all were, nor did the Marine Corps have enough National Match rifles to produce the 1,000 sniper rifles ordered for the two Marine raider battalions. Nor were they all M1903A1 rifles. All barrels used apparently had to meet star-gauge specifica-

Model 1903 Springfield Rifle and Its Variations

tions which the Marine armorers checked using their own star-gauging equipment. But they did not mark the barrels with the eight-pointed star as did Springfield Armory. A number of barrels on USMC M1903A1 sniper rifles that are replacements do not show the star-gauge mark.

L. Reynolds (see Appendix I, Bibliography) points out that a true USMC sniper rifle barrel will have a "punch mark at six o'clock, directly under the front scope block."

SUMMARY, M1903 SERVICE BARREL TYPES

Table 14 provides a summary of all barrel types used on M1903 Service Rifles.

Table 14 M1903 Barrels by Manufacturer, Type, Caliber, and Years of Use			
Manufacturer	**Type and Variation**	**Model and Caliber**	**Years of Original Installation**
Springfield Armory	1	M1903 rod bayonet, .30-M1903	1903-1905
	1-1	M1903 knife bayonet, .30-M1903	1905-1906
Rock Island	1-2	M1903, .30-M1903	1907-1910
Springfield Armory	1-3	M1903, .30-M1906	1907-1910
	2-1	M1903, .30-M1906	11-1905 to circa 6-1919
	2-2	M1903 & M1903A1, .30-M1906	Circa 11-1919 to 12-41
Rock Island	2-3	M1903, .30-M1906	4-1904 to 7-1913 and circa 6-1917 to 6-1919
Avis	2-4	M1903	1919-1920

Model 1903 Springfield Rifle and Its Variations

Table 14, cont. M1903 Barrels by Manufacturer, Type, Caliber, and Years of Use			
Manufacturer	**Type and Variation**	**Model and Caliber**	**Years of Original Installation**
Remington Arms	2-5	M1903	11-1941 to 12-1942
	3	M1903 (Modified)	4-1942 to 10/11-1942
	4-1 4-3	M1903A3	10/12-1942 to 3-1944
	4-2	M1903A4	1-1943 to 6-1944
Smith Corona	5	M1903A3	10-1942 to 3-1944
High Standard, Johnson Automatics, Sedgley Mfg. Co.	6	M1903, M1903A1	1942-1945
Springfield Armory	6	M1903, M1903A1	1944-1945
If barrel dates later than those given above are found on M1903, M1903A1 or M1903A3 rifles, they should be presumed to be replacement barrels.			

SPECIAL-PURPOSE M1903 BARRELS

Barrels manufactured for previous service rifles at the national armories were generally of two types, either rifle or carbine. Only during production of the .45-70 Springfield did the Ordnance Department experiment with specialized barrels for target shooting, and then only to a very limited extent. The advent of the National Matches in 1905 led to increasing interest in marksmanship. For the first time, civilians competed with military personnel in official matches. In their hands, service rifles which had undergone the attentions of custom gunsmiths began to give military shooters a real run for their money. This, coupled with increasing interest in marksmanship, led the Ordnance Department to sanction the development of competition rifles after World War I.

West Virginia shooting team at the National Matches, Camp Perry, Ohio, August 10, 1909. Ed Cote collection.

At the same time, the need to reduce the costs associated with marksmanship training in the cash-strapped post-WWI army led the Ordnance Department to develop rifles chambered for the .22-caliber rimfire cartridge to replace service rifles firing "gallery" or reduced-load cartridges. The use of the cheaper .22 cartridges allowed both the regular service as well as the reserves and National Guard to expand training at indoor ranges.

Special-purpose barrels of two kinds were therefore manufactured in the 1920s and 1930s for both competition rifles and .22 gallery rifles.

Model 1903 Springfield Rifle and Its Variations

All special-purpose barrels manufactured by Springfield were rifled using the hook cutter method.

BARREL COUNTOURS

Barrel contours depended on the purpose for which the barrel was manufactured, i.e., match, target and gallery rifles. The **M1922 .22-caliber barrel** was 1.20 inches in diameter at the breech end, 0.836 inch at the lower band position and 0.615 inch in diameter at the muzzle. Its contour was similar to the service rifle barrel contour but was larger in diameter throughout and had a convex curve from the front of the breech to the lower band position. The .30-caliber competition barrel had straight taper from breech to muzzle. Competition barrel diameters at the breech end were 1.310, 1.20 or 1.125 inches while the lower band position and muzzle diameters depended on the barrel's length. They were made in 24-, 26-, 28-, 30- and 32-inch lengths for various rifles. Table 15 below provides a list of all special-purpose barrels and their characteristics. Also, see Figure 2-83.

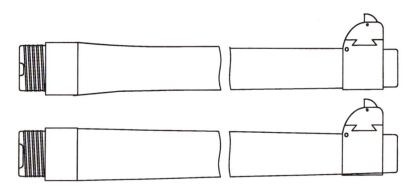

Fig. 2-83. Top: M1922 barrel contour; bottom: .30-caliber target or match barrel contour.

NRA SPORTER BARRELS

As difficult as it is now to believe, in the years immediately following World War I there were almost no sporting rifles chambered for the

Model 1903 Springfield Rifle and Its Variations

Table 15
M1903 Special-Purpose Barrel Types

Model	Years of Make	Caliber	Contour (1,2)	Length (inches)	Characteristics
National Match	1921-1936 1938-1940	.30-M1906	Service Rifle	20	Star-gauge marked
Special Target (3)	1921-1936 1938-1940	.30-M1906	Service Rifle	20	Most star-gauge marked
"Original Turning Bolt"	1919	.22	Service Rifle	20	
Model 1	1920	.22	Service Rifle	19.5	4 narrow grooves, 1:16 rifling
Model 2	1920	.30	Service Rifle	19.5	4 grooves and lands equal in width, dummy rear sight band, Lyman Long Slide rear sight
Rifle, Cal. .22, M1922 Gallery Rifle	1922	.22	.22-Caliber Barrel	24	May be drilled and tapped for scope on 7.5-inch centers, done on request only. Barrel diameter at breech 1.130, 0.836 at barrel band position and 0.615 at muzzle

Model 1903 Springfield Rifle and Its Variations

Table 15, cont.
M1903 Special-Purpose Barrel Types

Model	Years of Make	Caliber	Contour (1,2)	Length (inches)	Characteristics
International Match Rifle Type 1	1921	.30	Straight taper breech to muzzle	24	Barrel diameter at breech, 1.20 inches
International Match Type 2	1922	.30	Straight taper breech to muzzle	24, 28, and 30	Barrel diameter at breech, 1.20 inches
Match, Cal. .30, M1922	1922	.30	Straight taper breech to muzzle	24	Breech, 1.25 dia., 0.875 at muzzle, front sight stud integral with barrel, drilled and tapped for scope blocks on 6-inch centers
National Match Special	1925-1928	.30	Service Rifle	20	Star-gauge marked
International Match Rifle, 1924	1924	.30	Straight taper, breech to muzzle	30, 32	Commercial barrels from Remington Arms, Pope, and Winchester
International Match Rifle, Cal. .22, 1924	1924	.22	Straight taper, breech to muzzle	30	Breech 1.25 to 0.09 1.5 inches behind muzzle, step to 0.75 for B.A.R. front sight. Six grooves, 1:16 rifling

Model 1903 Springfield Rifle and Its Variations

Table 15, cont.
M1903 Special-Purpose Barrel Types

Model	Years of Make	Caliber	Contour (1,2)	Length (inches)	Characteristics
NRA Sporter	1924	.30	.22	20	Breech Diameter 1.20 inches
NRA Sporter	11/1924-33, 1938	.30	.22	20	Star-gauge marked after 11/1924. Breech diameter 1.20 inches
M1922M1 Cal. .22 Gallery Rifle	1925-1934	.22	.22	20	Drilled and tapped for scope blocks on 7.5-inch centers, front block only on barrel. Done on request only. Barrel dimensions same as M1922 .22-caliber Gallery Rifle
"Style T"	1925-1929	.30	Straight taper, breech to muzzle	26, 28 and 30	Breech diameter 1.310. Modified B.A.R. front sight stud, drilled and tapped for scope blocks on 7.2-inch centers, front block only on barrel
NBA Sporter	1926	.30	.22	20	Star-gauge marked. Breech diameter 1.20 inches

Model 1903 Springfield Rifle and Its Variations

Table 15, cont.
M1903 Special-Purpose Barrel Types

Model	Years of Make	Caliber	Contour (1,2)	Length (inches)	Characteristics
International Match Rifle, 1927	1927	.30	Straight taper, breech to muzzle	28	
Style A & B (300-meter Free Rifle)	1931	.30	Straight taper, breech to muzzle	28, 30	Fitted to rifles with Swiss Hammerli butt plates
M2, Cal. .22 Gallery Rifle	1934-1942+	.22	.22-caliber barrel	20	Not drilled and tapped for a scope at Springfield. Barrel dimensions same as for M1922 .22-caliber Gallery Rifle

1. Service rifle barrel was 0.760 inch in diameter at the lower band position.
2. .22-caliber barrel was 0.836 inch in diameter at the lower band position.
3. Designated "U.S. Rifle, Caliber .30, Model 1903, Special Target," they were reconditioned National Match rifles and many were sold through the DCM. After 1928, they were designated "U.S. Rifle, Caliber .30, M1903A1, Special Target."

Model 1903 Springfield Rifle and Its Variations

.30-M1906 cartridge. To encourage the development of shooting sports using the military cartridge, the Director of Civilian Marksmanship starting in 1924 sold the first of three types of .30-caliber barrels. The **NRA Type 1** .30-caliber Sporter barrel followed the contour of the M1922 .22-caliber barrel and its dimensions were the same. It was not star-gauge marked. In November of that year, the DCM announced that a complete Sporter rifle could be purchased by National Rifle Association members. The **NRA Type 2** Sporter barrel was produced which had the same contour as the M1922 .22-caliber barrel but was star-gauge marked on the muzzle crown.

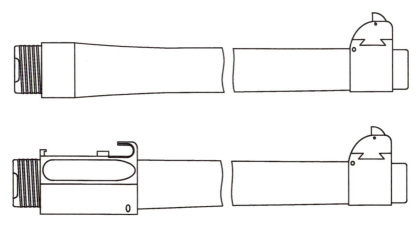

Fig. 2-84. Top: NRA Sporter, Type 1 barrel contour; bottom: NRA Sporter, Type 3 barrel contour.

In 1925, the **NRA Type 3** Sporter barrel was made available in the same contour as the service-rifle barrel for use in the service-rifle stock. The purchaser could chose to have the M1905 sight base installed or not, see Figure 2-84.

A **Type 4** Sporter barrel was manufactured for use in international match competition. It was contoured like the .22-caliber barrel, rifled and chambered for the .30-M1906 cartridge, star-gauge marked and 24 inches long.

MARKINGS—BARRELS

The standard barrel marking on the M1903 rifle and all derivative models was "Manufacturer/Ordnance escutcheon/month-year." This marking was applied to all barrels with two exceptions: 1) Barrels made in .30-M1903 caliber for the M1903 rod bayonet rifle were not marked with the Armory initials and date of manufacture at either Springfield or RIA. These markings were applied later when the barrels were altered to receive the M1905 knife bayonet. 2) M1903 and M1903A1 rifles rebarreled during World War II with barrels manufactured by Sedgley Manufacturing Company are marked "USMC/month-year/S within a circle." See Figure 2-84A.

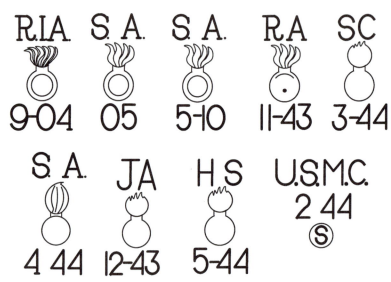

Fig. 2-84A. L-r, top row: Rock Island Arsenal (Types 2-3); Springfield Armory (Type 1-1); Springfield Armory (Types 1-3, 2 and 2-2); Remington Arms (Types 2-5, 4-1, 4-2 and 4-3); Smith Corona (Type 5); bottom row: Springfield Armory, Johnson Automatics, High Standard (for Smith Corona and replacements) and Sedgley Mfg. Co., all Type 6s.

Model 1903 Springfield Rifle and Its Variations

Proof-testing was performed on a statistically significant sample of barrels from each production batch and so not all barrels were proof-tested. Those that were received the "P" proof mark indicating that the barreled receiver had passed the proof-firing test with either the 70,000 psi (prior to the early 1920s) or 75,000 psi proof cartridge after. The mark is stamped on the underside of the barrel, either 1.5 or 11 inches behind the muzzle except for the Type 6 barrel on which it was stamped at 2.4 inches. See Appendix C for proof marks.

Inspectors' markings are found on all M1903, M1903A3 and M1903A4 barrels and consist of initials or numbers. They are most often found stamped around the periphery of the barrel at the breech end or in the vicinity of the "P" proof.

All barrel bores were tested with the star-gauge equipment to assure that dimensions were correct. Those service barrels that met dimensional standards for National Match barrels were stamped with the "star" mark on the muzzle and set aside for use on National Match, NRA Sporter, "Style T" and International Match rifles.

NOTE: "Manufacturer/ordnance escutcheon/month-year" markings were stamped on barrels during the manufacturing process and before assembly of the front sight to barrel, finishing and assembly to receiver.

TYPE 1 BARRELS—MARKINGS
With the exception of the original .30-M1903 barrels installed on the unaltered rod bayonet rifles which were unmarked, all other Springfield-made barrels were stamped with the armory/escutcheon/date behind the front sight.

Type 1, **1st Variation** .30-M1903 caliber barrels manufactured at the Springfield Armory and modified for the M1905 knife bayonet were marked "S.A./ordnance escutcheon" and dated "05" without the

Model 1903 Springfield Rifle and Its Variations

"month." If proof-tested, they were also stamped with the "P" proof mark 11 inches behind the muzzle on the bottom of the barrel.

All Type 1, **2nd Variation** barrels in .30-M1906 caliber were stamped with the armory/escutcheon/date behind the front sight—"S.A./escutcheon/month-year or R.I.A./escutcheon/month-year." If proof-tested, they were also stamped with the "P" proof mark 11 inches behind the muzzle on the bottom of the barrel. See Appendix D for proof marks.

Type 1, **3rd Variation** barrels manufactured at Springfield and Rock Island Armories were marked: "armory/ordnance escutcheon/month-year" behind the front sight band and if proof-tested, with the "P" proof mark 11 inches behind the muzzle on the bottom of the barrel.

TYPE 2 BARRELS—MARKINGS
All **Type 2** barrels were stamped with the armory/ordnance escutcheon/month-year behind the front sight. Other markings will be found stamped on the bottom of Type 2 barrels at the midpoint, including the proof mark "P" signifying that the barreled receiver had been fired with a proof cartridge and passed. Not all barrels were so proofed. Other markings include initials and numbers stamped by various inspectors during the manufacturing process. Marks observed include the letters, A, B, I, O, T, W and X. See Appendix D for proof marks.

Date markings on Type 2 barrels are: 1) 1st Variation: "11-05" to circa "6-19"; 2) 2nd Variation: circa "7-19 to 12-41"; and 3) 3rd Variation: "4-04 to 7-13" and circa "6-17 to 6-19."

TYPE 3 BARRELS—MARKINGS
Type 3, 1st, 2nd and 3rd Variation barrels were stamped with the armory/escutcheon/date behind the front sight—"S.A./escutcheon/month-year" or "R.I.A./escutcheon/month-year." If proof-tested, they were stamped with the "P" proof mark 11 inches behind the muzzle on the bottom of the barrel. Barrel dates are "4-42 to 10/11-42."

178

Model 1903 Springfield Rifle and Its Variations

TYPE 4 BARRELS—MARKINGS
All **Type 4**, manufactured by Remington Arms for the Remington Model 1903, were marked: "R A/ordnance escutcheon/month-year." Barrel dates will fall between "10 to 12-42" and "3-44." If proof-tested after assembly, they were also stamped with the "P" proof mark either 1.5 or 11 inches behind the muzzle on the bottom of the barrel.

TYPE 5 BARRELS—MARKINGS
All **Type 5** barrels were manufactured by High Standard for the Smith Corona M1903A3 rifles. They were marked "S C/escutcheon/month-year." Dates will range from 10-42 to 3-44. If proof-tested after assembly, they were also stamped with the "P" proof mark either 1.5 or 11 inches behind the muzzle on the bottom of the barrel.

Early Type 5 barrels (10-42 to 11-42) will be six-groove barrels and were manufactured by Savage under subcontract. Barrels marked between 12-42 and 1-43 will be a mix of six- and four-groove barrels. After 2-43, all Type 5 barrels will have four grooves. High Standard did not manufacture two-groove barrels. Therefore, any two-groove barrel on a Smith Corona rifle is a replacement.

NOTE: Very early (10 to 11-42) Type 5 barrels *will not* be marked "SC/escutcheon/month-year." Instead they will show the ordnance escutcheon 0.10 inch high above a punch mark. On the opposite side of the barrel the "P" proof was stamped. The muzzle is turned down (rebated) to 0.618 inch for the first 0.4 inch, instead of to 0.620 inch in diameter, for a distance of 0.166 inch ahead of the front sight band.

Type 5 barrels may show a rebated muzzle 0.618 inch in diameter for the first 0.45 inch.

TYPE 6 BARRELS—MARKINGS
These barrels were manufactured by High Standard (HS), Johnson Automatics (JA) and Sedgley (S within a circle) as replacement bar-

Model 1903 Springfield Rifle and Its Variations

rels. "HS" and "JA" marked barrels will show dates primarily for 1943 and 1944. Sedgley barrels will show a 1944 date. If proof-tested after assembly, they were also stamped with the "P" proof mark either 1.5 or 11 inches behind the muzzle on the bottom of the barrel.

Type 6 barrels manufactured by Springfield are marked "S A" in a circle/ordnance escutcheon/month-year. They will show the "P" proof mark on the bottom of the barrel 2.4 inches behind the muzzle if proof-tested.

NOTE: Sedgley barrels are marked "U.S.M.C." but they may have also been used to replace barrels on Army and Navy M1903A3 rifles after World War II.

SPECIAL-PURPOSE BARRELS
All barrels manufactured at Springfield Armory and installed on .22-caliber gallery or target rifles, .30-caliber target rifles and .30-caliber sporting rifles were stamped "S.A./ordnance escutcheon/month-year." All were star-gauge inspected as a matter of course but were only marked with the eight-pointed star on the crown of the muzzle if they were of the standard service configuration, refer to Figure 2-82.

INSPECTOR MARKINGS
During the manufacturing process, M1903 barrels of all contours and calibers underwent numerous quality-control inspections to assure that they met all specified dimensions. Markings ranged from a punch mark to a wide variety of single initials and numbers which stood for various factory and ordnance department inspectors. No comprehensive documentation has been found matching inspectors' names with initials and numbers and so most are unknown. Several researchers have tried to correlate initials and numbers with time periods and steel lots without success. It is a rare M1903 barrel which does not have at least one inspection mark. World War II barrels in particular which lack inspection markings may well be replacement barrels stored until disposal through the DCM program or sold as scrap.

Receivers

In spite of the changes made to the M1903 rifle during its 42 years of production, the receiver changed remarkably little. The primary alterations were to the size and location of the gas vent hole late in the production cycle and to markings and finish. Only in the case of the M1903A3 was a moderately significant change made when the receiver bridge was modified to accept a new rear sight.

GENERAL DESCRIPTION

The receiver is essentially a tube which holds the barrel at the forward end, the trigger mechanism below, the bolt release mechanism on the left side and the stock which is attached with two guard screws, see Figure 2-85. Springfield-manufactured receivers were made of Class C steel to circa serial # 1,275,767 (March 1927). Rock Island receivers were made of Class C steel to serial #319,921 (August 1918). After those respective serial numbers, both Springfield and Rock Island receivers were made of nickel steel. In the initial production of nickel steel receivers made at Springfield, partly finished receivers were included that had been left over when Rock Island stopped M1903 receiver production in 1919. Some of these receivers were marked Rock Island but had not been serial numbered and so received serial numbers in the Springfield series.

When Rock Island resumed production of new rifles in February 1917 they continued to use the single heat treatment method on receivers as with earlier production. Reports of both Springfield and RIA receiver failure began to accumulate as a result of heavy training use and wartime ammunition. The result was a formal investigation which identified the heat treatment method as the culprit. New rifle production was temporarily stopped at Springfield stopped between February and June 1917 at circa serial # 750,000 and Rock Island between January 30, 1918 at receiver serial #285,506 and May 11, 1918.

Model 1903 Springfield Rifle and Its Variations

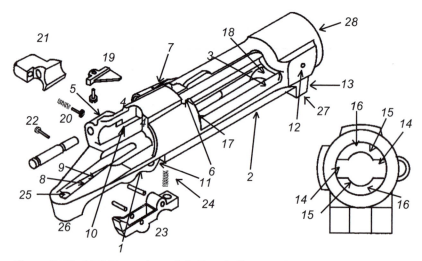

Figure 2-85. M1903 receiver: 1) bolt well, 2) magazine opening, 3) channel, 4) cutoff seat, 5) magazing cutoff thumbpiece recess, 6) clip slot, 7) ejector pin hole, 8) cocking piece groove, 9) sear nose slot, 10) extracting cam, 11) sear joint pin hole, 12) gas escape hole, 13) recoil lug, 14) bolt locking lug recesses, 15) locking cams, 16) locking shoulders, 17) safety shoulder, 18) cartridge ramp, 19) ejector and pin, 20) cutoff spindle and spring, 21) magazing cutoff thumbpiece, 22), cutoff spindle, screw and spring, 23) sear assembly including sear and trigger pins and 24) sear spring, 25) rear guard screw hole, 26) tang, 27) front guard screw hole and 28) barrel opening.

A new double heat treatment method was developed and tested along with the proper instrumentation for assuring that the proper temperatures were used. Springfield resumed production between serial #750-000-800,000 using the new heat treatment method, see Figure 2-86. At RIA, some 16,000 receivers between serial #s 269,506 to 285,507 which were in inventory were given the new double heat treating method. But out of this group, some 5,846 receivers had previously received the old single heat treatment and these were destroyed. The double heat treatment of new RIA receivers began at serial #285,507 (May 11, 1918).

Starting at serial #319,921, Rock Island Arsenal began to manufacture both receivers and bolts from nickel steel instead of the Springfield Class C steel which required the double heat treatment. Springfield did not switch to nickel steel for receivers and bolt parts until serial #1,275,767 on March 2, 1927.

Parkerizing was adopted first at Rock Island Arsenal on March 12, 1918 at circa serial #318,000. Springfield began Parkerizing in November 1918 at circa serial #1,030,000. The Parkerizing was applied to major parts only, including receivers, barrels, rear sight bases and mounts, bolts and trigger guards.

After the switch to nickel steel, the only other change made to the M1903 receiver was the change in the size and location of the gas port from the right side (0.125 inch in diameter) to the left side (0.20 inch in diameter) in 1936. In the earlier manufactured receivers returned for repairs to Springfield Armory, the second gas port was often added by drilling.

Fig. 2-86. Pyrometer used to measure the temperature inside a furnace.

NOTE: Nickel steel alloy receivers manufactured at Rock Island Arsenal after serial #319,921 were marked "NS" on the face of the receiver ring.

RECEIVER DIMENSIONS AND DIFFERENCES

The M1903 receiver (refer to Figure 2-85) is 8.6 inches long and 1.855 inches high at its highest point and 1.552 inches wide at its widest point. The receiver has 28 features: 1) the well through which the bolt passes, 2) magazine opening, 3) the channel in the left wall for the top bolt locking lug, 4) seat for the magazine cutoff thumbpiece, 5) magazine cutoff thumbpiece recess, 6) clip slot, 7) ejector pin hole, 8) cocking piece groove, 9) sear nose slot, 10) extractor cam, 11) sear "joint" pin hole, 12) gas escape or vent hole, 13) recoil lug with threaded hole for the front guard screw, 14) bolt locking lug recesses (two), 15) locking cams (two), 16) locking shoulders, 17) safety shoulder, 18) cartridge ramp, 19) ejector and pin, 20) cutoff spindle, screw and spring assembly, 21) magazine cutoff thumbpiece, 22) cutoff spindle, screw and spring, 23) sear assembly with sear, trigger pins, 24) sear spring, 25) rear guard screw threaded hole, 26) tang, 27) front guard screw threaded hole and 28) barrel opening.

The M1903 receiver has a single gas vent hole 0.125 inch in diameter on the front, right side of the receiver. At circa serial number 1,496,022 (1936), the right side gas vent hole was eliminated. Instead, a 0.20-inch-diameter gas vent was drilled on the left side of the receiver.

NOTE: Many older M1903 receivers will have gas vent holes on both left and right sides. If they were returned for repairs or refurbishing after 1936, a new left side gas vent hole was often drilled in the older receivers in compliance with current regulations.

Remington M1903 and Model 1903 (Modified) receivers made between November 1941 and January 1942 had gas vent holes on both sides of the receiver. By February 1942, the small 0.20-inch hole on the right had been eliminated. All M1903A3 receivers have a single 0.310-inch hole on the left side, see Figure 2-87, arrow.

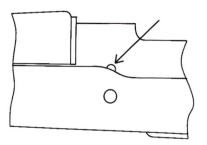

Fig. 2-87. M1903A3 receiver gas vent or hole.

The rear guard screw hole in the M1903 and Remington M1903 receiver tang was a blind and threaded hole, i.e., not drilled all the way

Model 1903 Springfield Rifle and Its Variations

through from below. Beginning in February 1942, the rear guard screw hole was drilled all the way through the tang on Remington-produced receivers.

The front guard screw hole in the M1903 and most of the Remington M1903 front recoil lugs were drilled 0.490 inch deep and threaded for the front guard screw (Type 1 or 2). Beginning in February 1942 with the last of the Remington M1903 production and on into the Remington M1903 (Modified) and M1903A3, the front guard screw hole was drilled to 0.590 inch in the recoil lug. The Types 1 and 2 front guard screws which were 1.20 inches long and used in the M1903 and M1903A1 tended to "strip" out of the deeper guard screw hole and so a slightly longer Type 3 (1.30 inches) front guard screw was developed. However, the longer Type 3 screw bottomed in the M1903 and M1903A1 front guard screw hole and prevented the barreled receiver from bedding properly in the stock, reportedly often causing severe accuracy problems.

Very early Smith Corona receivers lack the thumb relief cut on the left side of the receiver rail. It is not known at what serial number range Smith Corona added the thumb relief cut.

Receivers to circa serial #800,000 (July 1918) were highly polished and case-hardened in oil (carburized). After that, they were polished to a lesser extent, carburized, sandblasted, then Parkerized. After Parkerizing, service rifle receivers did not undergo additional polishing on interior surfaces—bolt ways, feed ramps and cam surfaces.

NOTE: Nickel steel receivers were not carburized but they were sandblasted and Parkerized.

The receivers used to assemble M1903 Mark I rifles to accept the Automatic Pistol, Caliber .30, Model 1918 (Pedersen Device), had an ejection port cut in the left side of the receiver wall, through the

Model 1903 Springfield Rifle and Its Variations

bolt channel. The ejection port is 1.325 inches long by 0.365 inch high with rounded ends, see Figure 2-88. These receivers were stamped "MARK I."

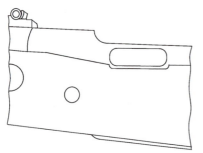

Fig. 2-88. The line of the stock as lowered for the Mark 1 ejection port.

NOTE: Mark 1 receivers were manufactured only by Springfield Armory.

The magazine cutoff housing on the left rear side flares out from the barrel of the receiver 0.4 inch, is 1.9 inches long and split in the middle for 0.56 inch. The inside of the housing is hollow and 0.2 inch wide. To receive the magazine cutoff spindle and cutoff a hole 0.2 inch in diameter is drilled and tapped for the ejector pin hole. In the M1903 receiver the rear of the housing has a vertical groove 0.1 inch wide and three notches. The groove guides the spring-loaded magazine cutoff spindle to each of the three notches: the bottom notch allows the bolt to be drawn back only far enough to insert a fresh cartridge by hand (OFF); the top notch allows it to be drawn back far enough to feed a cartridge from the magazine (ON) and the center notch allows the concave side of the cutoff to rotate into position to allow the bolt to be withdrawn from the receiver. In the M1903A3 receiver, there are the three notches but no guide groove.

National Match receivers received special finishing but were not marked nor did they differ externally from service rifle receivers. Feed ramps, bolt ways and cam surfaces were polished after Parkerizing. A very few late (post-1931) National Match rifles were drilled and tapped for the Lyman No. 48 receiver sight.

On receivers used to assemble NRA "Sporter" rifles, the front of the

Model 1903 Springfield Rifle and Its Variations

receiver ring is rounded slightly. The receivers used for the NRA "Sporter" model did not have their feed ramps, bolt ways and cam surfaces polished after Parkerizing. Some of these rifles that were rebuilt from National Match rifles may show smoother than normal feed ramps, bolt ways and cam surfaces but even so, they were usually sandblasted lightly before being refinished.

Receivers used for the "Style T" rifles were all drilled and tapped for the Lyman No. 48 receiver sight. The top of the receiver was also drilled and tapped for scope blocks on 7.2-inch centers with the front mounting on the barrel and the rear mounting hole located on the receiver ring.

NOTE: In the 1950s and early 1960s, complete M1903 and M1903A3 rifles were hard to find but parts had been sold on the surplus market. A California company manufactured cast receivers and added parts to make complete rifles. The receivers are marked "Santa Fe Ordnance" or "National Ordnance." These are not U.S. military rifles.

CLIP SLOT

With the advent of an effective bolt-action mechanism in the last two decades of the 19th century, arms designers turned their attention to developing a method for rapidly reloading the rifle. The Mauser clip-loading system was adopted early in the design stage. Developed first for the Belgian Model 1889 and refined through the Model 98 series, the system used a folded sheet metal charger with an interior slightly "S"-shaped spring. The rims of the charger were folded so that the cartridge rim was captured. The pressure of the spring held them tightly against the rim and upturned tabs at either end kept them from falling out. Five cartridges were held in each clip.

The front of the receiver bridge was milled to accept the clip—also called a charger—rims, see Figure 2-89, arrows. To load, the magazine cutoff was turned to the "on" position. The bolt was drawn back and one end of the clip was inserted into the clip guide. The

Model 1903 Springfield Rifle and Its Variations

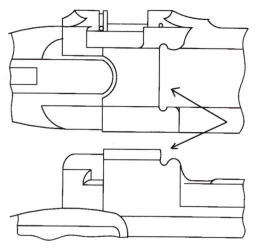

Fig. 2-89. Clip-loading slot on the M1903 receiver.

thumb was used to apply pressure at the base of the top cartridge and push them down into the magazine. When the bolt was closed to chamber a round, the clip was kicked out of the clip guide.

The system's advantages were it allowed the use of a closed magazine, eliminated the clip as a source of dirt and rust and provided the soldier with a full magazine in seconds. The clips were very inexpensive to make and added only a ounce to the soldier's burden.

MAGAZINE CUTOFF

The function of an ordnance department is not only to develop military equipment but to ensure it can be delivered when and where needed. Ammunition resupply is one of the greatest headaches of a combat arm, but was especially so in the 19th and early 20th century before the advent of reliable mechanical means to deliver equipment. Imagine, for example, how difficult it would have been to move 8.9 tons of ammunition several miles across a muddy, shell-cratered landscape. Yet that was a combat issue of 100 rounds of .30-M1903 cartridges per man for a 150-man company. The U.S. Ordnance Department was very concerned that soldiers given magazine-loading rifles would waste ammunition and increase the supply burden. This was the excuse given for not adopting the Spencer repeating rifle and carbine earlier during the Civil War.

The magazine cutoff was the answer. Its primary function was to control the movement of the bolt. When the magazine cutoff

Model 1903 Springfield Rifle and Its Variations

was in the "ON" position the bolt could be drawn back far enough to allow the next cartridge in the magazine to move up into the path of the bolt face. When it was in the "OFF" position the bolt was prevented from moving back far enough to allow the cartridge in the magazine to rise into the path of the bolt face, but far enough so that a fresh cartridge could be inserted into the chamber. This allowed the rifleman to keep his magazine full but continue to fire at the enemy by single-loading cartridges.

It was the job of the company or platoon officer to issue instructions for the use of the cutoff and the sergeant and corporals to see that they were carried out by the riflemen. To make it easier for them to do so without exposing themselves to enemy fire, the "OFF" side of the cutoff was blackened and the "ON" face was polished. The officer or non-com, in theory, could look down the line of riflemen under his command and tell at a glance if the magazine cutoff was engaged or not according to orders.

The second function of the magazine cutoff was to act as a bolt release. When turned to the middle position, it allowed the bolt to be withdrawn from the receiver.

The magazine cutoff was rectangular with grooved edges, see Figure 2-90. Five types of magazine cutoffs were used. The **Type 1** cutoff had serif-style letters and was in use to circa serial #590,000. The

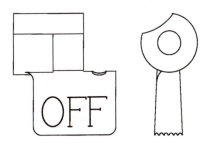

Fig. 2-90. M1903 magazine cutoff thumbpiece.

Type 1 cutoff was color case-hardened. The **Type 2** cutoff had sans serif letters and was used after circa serial #590,000. It was niter blued. The **Type 3** magazine cutoff was used in the M1903 Mk. I rifle. It had sans serif letters and a milled groove in the body to lock the Pedersen Device in place. It was niter blued. The **Type 4** magazine cutoff did not function as a cutoff but as a bolt release only. It was

Model 1903 Springfield Rifle and Its Variations

used on the M1922, M1922 M1 and M2 .22-caliber gallery rifles. Both faces were blank and polished. The **Type 5** was manufactured by Remington Arms and Smith Corona for the M1903A3. It had slightly sharper, squarer corners. Those manufactured by Remington were marked "R" or "R" in a circle and the lettering "ON" and "OFF" was in sans serif lettering. Those made by Smith Corona were unmarked or marked with a subcontractor's initial, and the lettering "ON" and "OFF" was in serif lettering. Most were niter blued. The **Type 6** magazine cutoff was manufactured by Springfield in 1944 and 1945. It resembles the Type 5 with sharper corners but has serif lettering. It is not marked with an inspector's or manufacturer's mark and was Parkerized.

NOTE: Pay close attention to the word "circa" in the previous paragraph. The Types 1 and 2 cutoffs were in use simultaneously for at least a year or more before all Type 1s were used up. Also, the cutoff was a frequently replaced part.

MAGAZINE CUTOFF SPINDLE

The magazine cutoff spindle served as the axis on which the cutoff

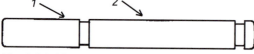

Fig. 2-91. Magazine cutoff spindle.

rotated, see Figure 2-91. It is 1.48 inches long and 0.205 inch in diameter. At 0.525 inch from the end is the cutoff spindle groove in which the magazine cutoff spindle screw rides (arrow 1). At the forward end is the dismounting groove by which the spindle can be pried from the receiver (arrow 2). To remove the spindle, unscrew the magazine cutoff spindle screw described below. Then draw it out with your fingernails or a tool edge.

Four types of magazine cutoff spindle were used. The **Type 1** spindle had a groove for the magazine cutoff spindle screw 0.1 inch wide and it was used in the M1903 rifle. It was in use to circa serial number

Model 1903 Springfield Rifle and Its Variations

590,000. After circa serial #590,000 the **Type 2** spindle was used and is identical to the Type 1 but was niter blued. The **Type 3** spindle had a groove only 0.05 inch wide and was used in the M1903A3 rifle. Neither type was marked and it was also niter blued. A **4th Type** was manufactured by Springfield from 1944 to 1945 as a replacement part. It was identical to the Types 1 and 2 but was Parkerized.

MAGAZINE CUTOFF SPINDLE SCREW

This screw is 0.6 inch long, 0.145 inch in diameter with a rounded end. It is inserted through the outer groove edge of the cutoff and rides in the groove in the magazine cutoff spindle to prevent the spindle from backing out, see Figure 2-92. Two types of spindle screws were used. The

Fig. 2-92. Magazine cutoff spindle screw.

Type 1 was manufactured by Springfield and Rock Island, had a slotted head end and was threaded for its entire length. The **Type 2** was manufactured by Remington and Smith Corona for the M1903A3. It was threaded for a little over half its length. The head end was slotted for 0.14 inch and spread apart. When screwed down into the cutoff, it served as a spring to hold the screw in place.

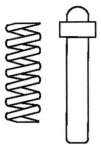

Fig. 2-93. Magazine cutoff spindle and spring.

MAGAZINE CUTOFF SPINDLE AND SPRING

The spring and spindle serves both as a guide and to hold the magazine cutoff in one of the three positions set by notches in the magazine cutoff housing on the left side of the receiver, see Figure 2-93. It guides in a shallow groove at the rear of the magazine cutoff housing to the three positions: the bottom notch positions the cutoff and bolt for single loading; the top notch is for loading from the magazine and the middle notch for withdrawing the bolt from the receiver.

Model 1903 Springfield Rifle and Its Variations

The spring is 0.140 inch in diameter and made from steel wire 0.026 inch in diameter and has six and one-half coils. Only one type was used throughout M1903 and M1903A3 production and no differences were noted between those manufactured for the M1903 and the M1903A3.

The spindle is 0.476 inch long and the spindle portion is 0.072 inch in diameter. Two types were used. The **Type 1** spindle was used in the M1903 and had a collar 0.148 inch in diameter and 0.075 inch high. The **Type 2** spindle was used in the M1903A3. Its collar was also 0.148 inch in diameter but only 0.050 inch thick.

EJECTOR

The ejector was shaped in the form of a right triangle with a boss at its base which was drilled through for the ejector pin. The pin serves as a pivot point for the ejector. When the bolt is drawn back, the ejector passes through the slot in the top locking lug and kicks the cartridge case out of the extractor, see Figure 2-94A.

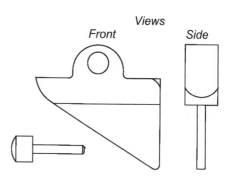

Views
Front　　　*Side*

Fig. 2-94A. M1903 ejector and ejector pin.

Three types of ejectors were used. The **Type 1** ejector was made of tool steel and unmarked. It was used throughout the production of the M1903 rifle. The **Type 2** ejector was made of nickel steel and marked "N." It was used from 1931 to the end of production, primarily in National Match rifles but also is seen in standard service rifles assembled in the mid-1930s on. The **Type 3** ejector was stamped from sheet metal and used in the M1903A3 rifle. Those manufactured by Remington are often marked "R" or "R" in a circle. Those manufactured by Smith Corona are unmarked.

Model 1903 Springfield Rifle and Its Variations

BOLT STOP

The bolt stop holds the bolt in the open position during inspection arms or when cleaning the rifle. It snaps into the receiver at the rear of the magazine well. Only one type was used, see Figure 2-94B.

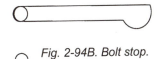

Fig. 2-94B. Bolt stop.

USMC SNIPER RIFLE RECEIVER

According to research conducted by L. Reynolds (See Appendix I, Bibliography) most USMC sniper rifle receivers fall into the serial range 900,000 to 1,532,000, almost the entire range of double heat treated receivers. All have the additional large gas hole on the left side, even if they have the smaller gas hole on the right. Rails were polished as on National Match rifles. The top of the receiver beneath the rear mount (aligned on top of the word "ARMORY") was ground down to bare metal and the two holes were drilled and tapped for the rear mounting block screws. The scope mount was centered and rested against the rear of the M1905 rear sight base.

MARKINGS

Receiver markings include the manufacturer's name and serial number. Also a variety of inspectors' initials and numbers will be found on the receiver, most on the bottom flat be-

Fig. 2-94C. Initials and codes of armory inspectors are marked on the bottom of Springfield and Rock Island receivers.

hind the recoil lug. Those observed include A, B, C, D, F, G, Q, R, S, T and various numbers from 1 through 10. See Figure 2-94C.

SPRINGFIELD RECEIVER MARKINGS

The top and right side of the Springfield M1903 receiver ring are marked as follows:

Model 1903 Springfield Rifle and Its Variations

U.S.
SPRINGFIELD
ARMORY
MODEL 1903.
385341

To circa serial #60,400, the letters in the address had serifs and were 0.90 inch high. Serial numbers also had serifs and were 0.2 inch high.

To circa serial #280,000, the letters had serifs and were 0.125 inch high. Serial numbers also had serifs and were 0.2 inch high.

To the end of production, sans serif (or block) letters were used that were 0.125 inch high. Serial numbers were sans serif and 0.2 inch high.

ROCK ISLAND RECEIVER MARKINGS

The top and right side of the Rock Island receiver ring are marked as follows:

U.S.
ROCK ISLAND
ARSENAL.
MODEL 1903.
134011

NOTE: The Rock Island markings have periods after "Arsenal" as well as "1903."

To circa serial #120,000, the lettering was 0.10 inch high and the letters had serifs. The numerals were 0.2 inch high with serifs.

Model 1903 Springfield Rifle and Its Variations

From serial #s 120,000 to 160,000, the lettering was increased in size to 0.12 inch. Numbers remained the same.

At circa serial #220,000, serial numbers were stamped in sans serif type and were 0.2 inch high. Lettering remained the same.

At circa serial #360,000, lettering was stamped in sans serif letters 0.12 inch high. Serial numbers remained unchanged.

Like the Springfield receiver, a variety of inspectors' initials are stamped on the RIA receiver, most on the bottom flat behind the recoil lug.

REMINGTON RECEIVER MARKINGS

Three types of receiver markings were used by Remington when they manufactured the M1903, M1903 (Modified) and the M1903A3/A4 rifles from 1941 to 1945 (including spare parts).

The first style of marking was stamped on the M1903 rifles manufactured from the start of the contract in 1941 to April 1942 on the top and right side of the receiver ring:

U.S.
REMINGTON
MODEL 1903
3001245

Lettering and serial numbers were in sans serif type. Lettering was 0.12 inch high and serial numbers were 0.14 inch high.

From April-May 1942 to the end of production, a second style of marking was stamped on the top and right side of the receiver ring:

Model 1903 Springfield Rifle and Its Variations

U.S.
REMINGTON
MODEL 03-A3
3892056

Lettering and serial numbers were in sans serif type. Lettering was 0.150 inch high. Serial numbers were 0.170 inch high.

The third style of marking was used only on the M1903A4 sniper rifle. It was identical to that used on the M1903A3 except that "U.S./Remington/Model 03-A3" was stamped on the left side of the breech and the serial number was stamped on the right side, see Figure 2-94D. This left the top clear for the attachment of the Redfield Jr. telescopic sight mount. This method complied with the long-standing Ord-

Fig. 2-94D. M1903A4 sniper rifle receiver marking.

nance Department directive that weapons markings never be obscured for both identification and safety reasons.

SMITH CORONA RECEIVER MARKINGS
The receiver is marked just behind the receiver ring:

U.S.
SMITH-CORONA
MODEL 03-A3
3671227

The "U.S." is 0.120 inch high, "Smith-Corona" is 0.110 inch high

Model 1903 Springfield Rifle and Its Variations

and the serial number is 0.175 inch high. All markings are sans serifs. There was only one style of Smith Corona receiver marking.

SPECIAL-PURPOSE RECEIVER MARKINGS
Three of the four .22-caliber "gallery" rifles carried different receiver markings than the .30-caliber receivers.

MODEL 1903 GALLERY PRACTICE RIFLE (HOFFER-THOMPSON)
The Hoffer-Thompson system made use of a standard M1903 rifle fitted with a .22-caliber barrel. The .22-caliber short cartridges were inserted into a Hoffer-Thompson cartridge holder which was then inserted into the magazine. Some, but not all of these rifles were stamped "22" transversely on the receiver bridge, the safety lug, the bayonet lug and the end of the forearm. Receiver markings then will be those used for the M1903 service rifle at that serial number range.

MODEL 1922, CALIBER .22

U.S.
SPRINGFIELD
ARMORY
MODEL OF 1922
CAL. .22
1375

MODEL 1922 MI, CALIBER .22
Two variations of markings have been identified:

U.S.
SPRINGFIELD
ARMORY
MODEL OF 1922
MI CAL. .22
8360

Model 1903 Springfield Rifle and Its Variations

```
U.S.
SPRINGFIELD
ARMORY
M1922 MI
CAL. .22
16546
```

M2, CALIBER .22

Four variations of markings have been identified.

```
U.S.
SPRINGFIELD
ARMORY
Cal. .22 M2
12635
```

Those converted to the M2 configuration from the original M1922 have an "A" stamped after the serial number.

```
U.S.
SPRINGFIELD
ARMORY
MODEL OF 1922MII
CAL. .22
1375A
```

Those converted from the M1922 MI and supplied with the adjustable headspace M2 bolt have a "B" stamped after the serial number. The die used to mark the second "I" in MII may have been a "1" or an "I" and it is usually stamped off center or crooked and may be larger or smaller than the original "I."

Model 1903 Springfield Rifle and Its Variations

U.S.
SPRINGFIELD
ARMORY
MODEL OF 1922I1
MI1 CAL. .22
9259B

U.S.
SPRINGFIELD
ARMORY
M1922 MII
CAL. .22
14265B

SHOOTING LOW-NUMBER M1903 RIFLES

In the early 1930s, opinion in the National Rifle Association's magazine, then entitled, "Arms and the Man," was evenly divided about whether or not to shoot "low-number" M1903s (Springfield serial #800,000 and Rock Island serial #285,507 and lower). One faction said absolutely not, the other said yes with the pre-M1 service load (172-grain bullet, 2,650 fps), or equivalent. In the early 1920s, then Major Julian Hatcher supervised testing of all "low-numbered" rifles in service. Those found acceptable were marked with one or more punch marks on the bottom of the receiver. Those that were not were withdrawn from service and the receivers were presumably removed and destroyed.

It is the author's opinion that safe is better than sorry and recommends that they not be fired with any ammunition. Better to preserve them for their value as historical artifacts. As a service to future generations, the author also recommends removing the striker from the end of the firing pin and storing it in the buttstock along with a note warning that the rifle is not to be shot and why. The rifle will not be able to fire a cartridge but the bolt will still work properly. Don't forget the note.

Bolts

Nine types of bolts were manufactured and used in the M1903 and M1903A3 series of service rifles. An additional four types were used in the .22-caliber "gallery" rifles. Table 16 (page 203) describes their distinguishing features and finishes. Tables 17 through 24 describe their markings (pages 231-237).

The service rifle bolt for the .30-caliber service rifle was 7.7 inches long (uncocked) from the tip of the front lug to the rear of the cocking piece. The diameter of the bolt body was 0.795 inch.

The M1903 bolt assembly was composed of twelve parts: 1) bolt body, 2) bolt sleeve, 3) cocking piece, 4) firing pin rod, 5) safety lock, 6) sleeve lock, 7) sleeve lock spring, 8) mainspring, 9) firing pin sleeve, 10) striker, 11) extractor, and 12) extractor collar. See Figure 2-95.

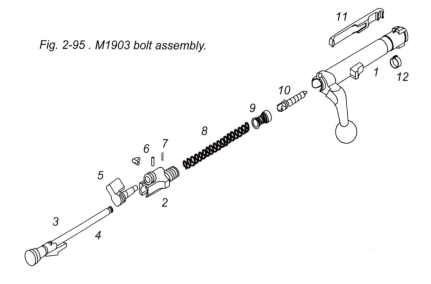

Fig. 2-95 . M1903 bolt assembly.

Model 1903 Springfield Rifle and Its Variations

NOTE: The bolt is considered to be in the closed, or "battery" position when the bolt handle is on the right, the split lug is on top and the locking lug is down.

BOLT BODY

The bolt body held all of the parts of the bolt assembly, see Figure 2-96. It was 5.80 inches long and 0.795 inch in diameter in the form of a hollow tube. The front end was drilled 0.08 inch in diameter for the striker tip. The rear was open in order to receive the firing pin/striker assembly.

The bolt body included a) the bolt handle, b) safety lug, c) top locking lug (split), d) bottom locking lug, e) extractor collar groove, f) extractor tongue groove, g) gas escape vent, h) firing pin hole, i) extracting cam, j) safety lock spindle notch, k) cocking cam, l) rim, m) cocking notch, n) bolt stop engaging notches—left side of safety lug—and o) sleeve lock notch.

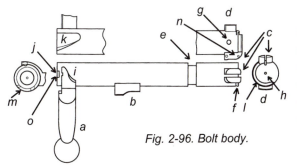

Fig. 2-96. Bolt body.

Inside, ahead of the bolt handle, the bolt body tube was threaded to match the threads on the bolt sleeve.

The bolt body has three points that lock it in place in the receiver against the recoil of the fired cartridge, two locking lugs (c) at the front and one safety lug (b) slightly past the midpoint. Eleven types of bolt bodies were used and are listed in Table 16, below.

The cocking cam (k) was the "V"-shaped cut at the rear of the bolt body, opposite the bolt handle. It served to force the cocking lug on the firing pin back as the bolt handle was raised. Two types of cocking cams were used on .30-caliber rifles: The cocking cam for the standard service rifle did not have a highly polished sear notch. The cocking cam used on some National Match, Sporting and "Style T" rifles had a highly polished sear notch. All .30-caliber cocking cams were 0.5 inch deep.

A third cocking cam was developed for the bolt bodies used on the .22-caliber M1922, M1 and M2 bolt bodies. It was 0.14 inch deep.

The bolt assembly used on the M1922, M1922 M1 and M1922 M2 was somewhat different in configuration and is discussed following the description of the .30-caliber bolt assemblies.

NOTE: In addition to markings described below, the difference between M1903 and M1903A3 bolt bodies can be easily distinguished.

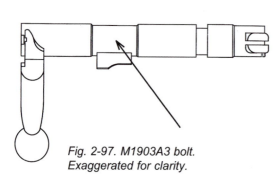

*Fig. 2-97. M1903A3 bolt.
Exaggerated for clarity.*

The finish on the M1903A3 bolt shows machine tool marks whereas few or none will be visible on the carefully machined M1903 bolt bodies made at Springfield and Rock Island. M1903A3 bodies show a definite narrowing in the area around the safety lug, see Figure 2-97, arrow. This area was simply cut away on a lathe to eliminate the time-consuming hand filing operations during wartime.

BOLT HANDLE

The bolt handle on the service rifle was 3.0 inches long. It extended from the right side of the bolt body for 0.5 inch before being turned down at a 23-degree angle. The bolt handle ended in a solid ball 0.772

Model 1903 Springfield Rifle and Its Variations

Table 16
Model 1903, Model 1903A1, and Model 1903A3 Bolt Body Types

Type	Bolt Handle	Gas Hole (inches)	Finish	Circa Serial #	Model	Comments
1	Straight	0.09	Bright	1-74,000 (Springfield) 1-40,000 (Rock Island)	rod bayonet	Bolt body not polished, handle dark heat-treated color
2	Straight	0.09	Blue	74,001-800,000 (Springfield) 40,001-240,000 Rock Island	Service	Bolt knob assembly color case-hardened to circa serial # 500,000. Bolt bodies and parts except spindle lock and mainspring blued
3	Bent	0.09	Blue	800,001-908,000	Service	Blue to mid-1918. Bolt handle swept back to rear
4	Bent	0.09	Parkerized	908,001-1,301,000	Service	Parkerized after mid-1918
5	Bent	0.09	Polished bright		National Match "Style T"	
6	Bent	0.09	Parkerized	1,301,001-1,496,021	Service	Nickel steel, stamped "NS" on bolt handle root

Model 1903 Springfield Rifle and Its Variations

Table 16, cont.
Model 1903, Model 1903A1, and Model 1903A3 Bolt Body Types

Type	Bolt Handle	Gas Hole (inches)	Finish	Circa Serial #	Model	Comments
7*	Bent	0.9 and 0.68	Parkerized	1,496,022 to end of production. Early bolt bodies may show the large gas holes added after manufacture	Service	2nd gas vent added in 1936
8	Straight	0.185	Parkerized	3,000,000 to 3,001,000	M1903	Used on earliest M1903A1 rifles manufactured by Remington Arms. May have been left over from original RIA production
9	Bent	0.185	Parkerized	3,000,000	M1903	Used on Remington Arms-manufactured bolts for the Remington M1903A1 and M1903 (Modified)
10	Bent	0.185	Parkerized	3,364,955	M1903 A3/A4	Narrowed waist around safety lug. If manufactured by Remington Arms, it will be marked "R" or "R" in circle, or a punch mark. If manufactured by Smith Corona it will be marked with an "X," punch mark, or "8" in any combination

Model 1903 Springfield Rifle and Its Variations

11	Re-curved	0.185	Parkerized	3,407,088 to 3,427,087; Z4,000,001 to Z4,002,920; 4,992,001 to 4,999,045	M1903A4	Bolt handle turned down and swept back up in a shallow, concave curve to clear the telescopic sight, when raised

* Types 6 and 7 bolts were used on the USMC 1903A1 Sniper Rifles. The majority of bolts were the Type 6 with the original gas vent enlarged. Bolt bodies were polished, numbered with the receiver serial number and blued. Because the Type 6 bolt body was nickel steel, the bluing came out a purplish or plum blue.

inch in diameter (M1903 and M1903A1) or 0.785 inch in diameter (M1903A3 and M1903A4). The bolt handle was square at the root and 0.455 inch wide.

Three variations of the bolt handle were used. From serial #1 to circa 800,000, the **1st Variation** bolt handle projected at a 90-degree angle from the right side of the bolt. The **2nd Variation** bolt handle was used circa serial # 750,001 to the end of production (both M1903 and M1903A1); the bolt handle was swept 10 degrees to the rear. See Figure 2-98 for a comparison of the three types of bolt handles. The **3rd Variation** bolt handle was used on the M1903A4 sniper rifle. The handle itself was bent slightly upward in an outward curve and excess metal was trimmed away to allow the bolt handle to

Fig. 2-98. M1903 bolt handle variations.

1st Variation

2nd Variation

3rd Variation

Model 1903 Springfield Rifle and Its Variations

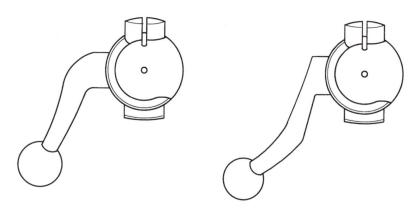

Fig. 2-99. Shape of bolt handles: left, standard service rifle; right, M1903A4 sniper rifle. Front end views.

fully open when the telescopic sight was mounted, see Figure 2-99.

Safety Lug

The safety lug (refer to Figure 2-96, b) is found 1.25 inches ahead of the bolt handle on the right side of the bolt body. It held the bolt in the receiver in the event that both locking lugs gave way as a cartridge ignited and pressure rose suddenly in the breech. The **Type 1** safety lug was 0.750 inch long, 0.398 inch wide, 0.187 inch high at the front and 0.3 inch high at the rear, and was scalloped on the top. There was a gap of 0.004 inch between the lug and the receiver when the bolt was in battery. The **Type 2** safety lug was introduced in 1944. It was square and without the scallop on the top.

Locking Lugs

The two locking lugs are located at the front of the bolt body, refer to Figure 2-96, c and d. The upper lug is 0.590 inch long, 0.395 inch wide and split into two parts to allow the extractor set to pass through. The lower lug is on the bottom of the bolt body at the front end. It is 0.385 inch long, 0.395 inch wide and 0.160 inch high at the back. Both lugs rotate into matching locking shoulders in the receiver.

Model 1903 Springfield Rifle and Its Variations

EXTRACTOR COLLAR GROOVE

The extractor collar groove (refer to Figure 2-96, e) provides a channel for the extractor collar which holds the extractor and allows it to turn as the bolt is opened and closed. The groove is located 1.280 inches behind the bolt face. It is 0.300 inch wide and 0.10 inch deep.

EXTRACTOR TONGUE GROOVE

The lip or tongue of the extractor (refer to Figure 2-96, f) rides in a guide groove cut into the front of the bolt body. The groove is 0.060 inch wide and 0.05 inch deep.

GAS ESCAPE VENT

The gas escape hole is found at the bottom front of the bolt, between the two locking lugs, refer to Figure 2-96, g. From serial #1 to circa serial # 3,000,000, the hole was 0.09 inch in diameter. From 3,000,001 (Remington and Smith Corona manufacture) the hole was 0.180 inch in diameter.

NOTE: From circa serial #1,491,532 to the end of production (including spare parts), a second gas vent hole was added to the bolt body, 0.20 inch in diameter. It was drilled behind the extractor collar groove in line with the original gas vent hole. This second gas vent hole was also added to bolt bodies that were returned to Springfield Armory or other major depots for repair or refurbishing and thus may be found at any serial number range.

FIRING PIN HOLE

The firing pin hole should more properly be called the "striker hole" as it is the striker tip that protrudes. Be that as it may, the hole is centered in the bolt face and is 0.08 inch in diameter, refer to Figure 2-96, h.

EXTRACTING CAM

The extracting cam is the curved surface milled into the bolt handle root, refer to Figure 2-96, i. When the bolt handle is raised it contacts the extracting cam inside the receiver bridge on the left and forces the bolt firing pin/striker assembly back just enough for the cocking cam to engage the sear, thus cocking the rifle.

SAFETY LOCK SPINDLE NOTCH

This is the semicircular notch cut into the rear of the bolt body below the sleeve lock notch that allows the spindle on the safety lock to turn when the bolt is in battery, refer to Figure 2-96, j.

COCKING CAM

The cocking cam is the V-shaped cut on the underside of the bolt at the rear (refer to Figure 2-96, k). When the bolt is in battery, the cocking cam nose rests in the cocking notch (m). When the bolt handle is raised, the extracting cam on the top of the bolt handle rides against the extracting cam in the receiver which moves the cocking piece and the firing pin/striker back. This action couples the bolt sleeve to the bolt body via the sleeve lock and holds the bolt sleeve in proper alignment until its left shoulder is again locked into the receiver.

RIM

The rim begins at the right edge of the split locking lug and surrounds a little more than half the circumference of the bolt face, refer to Figure 2-96, l. Its function is to center and hold the cartridge rim in place against the bolt face as the extractor lip snaps over it.

COCKING NOTCH

The cocking notch is a shallow groove filed into the back of the bolt body on the left side just above the start of the cocking cam, refer to Figure 2-96, m. When the bolt handle is raised to cock the firing pin/striker, the sear nose is guided by the cocking cam into the cock notch.

BOLT STOP NOTCHES

These are two circular indentations on the left side of the split lug against which the bolt stop nose rests when the bolt is open, refer to Figure 2-96, n. The bolt stop nose enters the forward notch when the magazine cutoff is off, the rear notch when it is on. It should be noted that these notches were not employed on the Remington M1903 or Remington or Smith Corona M1903A3 bolts. Nor were they used on Springfield-manufactured bolts made during World War II.

SLEEVE LOCK NOTCH
This is the square notch cut into the rear of the bolt handle root that engages the safety lock and holds the bolt sleeve in place after the bolt is opened, refer to Figure 2-96, o.

EXTRACTOR
The extractor is made of heat-treated Class B steel 3.355 inches long and 0.395 inch wide, see Figure 2-100. The forward end has a hook that clamps over the rim of the cartridge. Immediately behind the hook (a) is a tongue (b) which rides in a groove at the front of the bolt body. Behind it is the lug (c) which is undercut to receive the lugs on the extractor collar which rides in the extractor collar groove a quarter of the way back from the face. At the back end of the extractor is the back rest (d) which is shaped to fit the bolt curve. The extractor has a slight concave bend from the center lug to the rear which

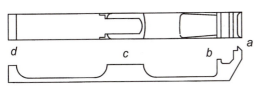

Fig. 2-100. M1903 extractor. Top and side views.

when in place, forces the front of the extractor and the lip downward, furnishing the spring pressure to grasp the cartridge rim.

The design of the extractor causes it to ride around the circumference of the bolt with the hook in constant contact with the cartridge. So, if the cartridge is not fully chambered and the bolt is withdrawn before locking shut, the cartridge comes back out with it. Many bolt-action hunting and some military bolt-action rifles do not have this feature and are prone to jams caused by double-feeding.

Three types of extractors were used. The **Type 1** extractor had a 0.10 gas escape hole at the tip. It was made in four variations: **1st Variation** was highly polished with a blued high gloss finish that may shade to purple. It was used primarily with the rod bayonet rifles but was replaced in 1906 with the **2nd Variation** extractor which was identical in size and shape but not as highly polished and with a niter blued finish. It was used to circa 1918. The **3rd Variation** extractor was the 2nd Variation extractor but polished to a high-gloss and left in the white. The **4th Variation** extractor was made of chrome-vanadium steel and highly polished. It was intended for use on National Match bolts from 1936 on. It was marked "C.V." at the top, rear.

The **Type 2** extractor was identical to the Type 1, 2nd Variation but did not have the gas escape hole. It was used from February 1942 to the end of production on the Remington Model 1903 (Modified) and the M1903A3/A4 rifles.

The **Type 3** extractor saw very limited use in ammunition test barrels. It had a claw 0.12 inch longer than the standard extractor. It was not used in service rifles.

BOLT SLEEVE

The bolt sleeve holds the firing pin rod/striker assembly and the safety lock assembly, Figure 2-101, and screws into the back of the bolt body. When the bolt handle is raised, the bolt sleeve is held in proper orientation by the spring-loaded safety lock spindle which snaps into the safety lock spindle notch on the bolt body. The spring-loaded safety lock spindle is held in a groove in the left side of the bolt sleeve by the pin.

The firing pin rod is inserted through the back of the bolt sleeve without its striker, collar or mainspring, refer to Figure 2-95. The spring slides over the firing pin followed by the collar and the striker. The assembled bolt sleeve then screws into the back of the bolt body.

The safety lock is mounted at the top of the bolt sleeve. Its shaft is inserted in the tunnel and is retained by a spring-loaded ball which rides in a groove and detent milled into the bolt sleeve.

Four different types of bolt sleeves were used on the M1903 and the M1903A3 bolts and are easy to identify. The **Type 1** was blued and used on the rod bayonet rifle without grooves and detents for the safety lock. The top of the tunnel is straight. The **Type 2** is similar to the Type 1 but with three grooves and detents for the safety lock. It was used on all service, gallery, match, and sporting rifles. The Type 2 was blued to 1918 and then Parkerized. Remington-type bolt sleeves were Parkerized. The **Type 3** bolt sleeve had a straight tunnel upper surface but with two grooves and detents. It was manufactured by Remington Arms,

Fig. 2-101. M1903 bolt sleeve. Top, Type 2; bottom, Type 4.

blued for the Remington M1903, M1903 (Modified) and M1903A3 and was marked "R" on the right shoulder. The **Type 4** bolt sleeve also had two grooves and detents and was made by Smith Corona for the M1903A3, and other WWII subcontractors as a replacement. The top, front of the tunnel angles downward and the sides are scalloped (refer to Figure 2-101). Subcontractor parts are marked "BP" or "G."

Smith Corona bolt sleeves are blued and unmarked. Subcontractor Type 4 bolt sleeves were Parkerized. Types 2, 3 and 4 are interchangeable. Bolt sleeves that are green in color have usually been refinished.

Safety Lock Spindle

The safety lock spindle has roughly the shape of the number "4." It is seated in the bolt sleeve in a hole drilled on the left side. A small spring with 11 coils applies outward pressure. The safety lock spindle

Model 1903 Springfield Rifle and Its Variations

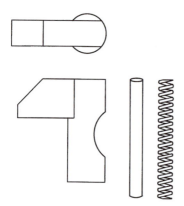

Fig. 2-102. Sleeve lock, spring and pin. Above, top and below, side views.

and spring are retained by a steel pin, see Figure 2-102.

The safety lock spindle serves to bind the bolt sleeve to the bolt body when the bolt is cocked. The lock sleeve is held in position by its right and left shoulders while the firing pin assembly is cammed back to bring the cocking piece lug into contact with the sear. When the bolt handle is lowered, the cocking piece is retained by the sear while the bolt body moves forward, guided by the cocking cam, and draws the bolt sleeve with it. As the front of the left shoulder enters the rear of the bolt well, the edge of the receiver wall depresses the safety lock spindle and allows it to slide into the safety lock spindle notch.

THE SAFETY LOCK

The M1903/M1903A3 uses a Mauser-style safety lock, see Figure 2-103. A paddle-shaped lever (a) with a forward protruding shaft is inserted into a tunnel at the top of the bolt sleeve. A cam on the end of the shaft under the thumbpiece rotates into one of two milled cuts on the cocking piece to block the firing pin from falling inadvertently (b). The safety lock is held in position by a spring-loaded spindle (c) in the inner side of the thumbpiece that presses down into a groove milled in the bolt sleeve. When the safety lock is in the off position, the cutaway section on

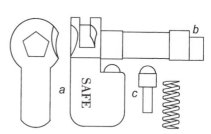

Fig. 2-103. Safety lever, spring and spindle. Left, end and right, top views.

212

Model 1903 Springfield Rifle and Its Variations

the base of the thumbpiece allows the firing pin to pass. When the safety lever is moved to the vertical or right position, its cams intersect grooves cut in the firing pin to prevent it from moving forward.

NOTE: To "safe" the rifle, the safety lever should always be turned fully to the right. If left in the vertical position, the firing pin may not be completely locked and may move forward when the safety lever is turned to the left, or "ready" position, causing an accidental discharge.

Five types of safety lock were used: three on service rifles, two on competitive rifles. The **Type 1** safety lock was almost identical to that used on the Argentine and Swedish Mauser rifles without a spring-loaded ball inserted into the thumbpiece which rode in a groove on the bolt sleeve. This type tended to rattle in the M1903 (but did not in the Argentine and Swedish Mausers) and so the spring-loaded spindle (refer to Figure 2-103, c) was added in 1904 to the **Type 2**. The surfaces are concave and unmarked. The outside corners of both the Types 1 and 2 safety lock thumbpieces are rounded. The **Type 3** safety lock was

manufactured by Remington (marked "R") and Smith Corona (unmarked) for the M1903A3. Functionally, the Type 3 is identical to the Type 2 and can be differentiated by the fact that the top or outside corners are square. Two variations were manufactured. In the

Fig. 2-103A. L-r, Type 3, 1st Variation and 2nd Variation safety lever.

1st Variation the safety lock axle was elliptical in cross section; in the **2nd Variation,** the axle was hemispherical, see Figure 2-103A above, arrows. Smith Corona used only the 2nd Variation.

The **Type 4** safety lock was the standard service rifle safety lock but reversed. Competition shooters using receiver sights like the Lyman 48 series held their faces closer to the bolt than did soldiers using the service rear sight. The recoil of the rifle often drove the safety lock into the shooter's cheek. The safety was reversed by milling the "cocking piece groove" on the right side rather than the left so that "ready" was to the right and thus did not injure the shooter.

The **Type 5** safety lock was similar to the standard service safety lock but was used on some late National Match rifles. Its locking cam surfaces were highly polished.

NOTE: The safety lock on the M1903A4 could not be turned all the way to the right when the Weaver 330C or M73B1 telescopic sight was mounted. It could be turned into the vertical position, however.

See the section on Bolt Assembly markings, below, for specific details of factory and inspection markings.

FIRING PIN/COCKING PIECE ASSEMBLY

This assembly is composed of four parts—1) cocking piece, 2) firing pin rod, 3) knob or bolt head and 4) cocking cam—and seven features—5) locking groove, 6) locking shoulder, 7) neck, 8) head, 9) nose, 10) cocking lug and (11) sear notch. The firing pin rod, cocking piece and head are assembled into one unit during manufacture. They cannot be separated and if one part needs replacing the entire unit must be replaced, see Figure 2-104.

The firing pin rod (2) is 5.8 inches long but enters the cocking piece (1) at 4.3 inches along its length. It is 0.290 inch in diameter. A groove was cut around the circumference of the pin at the front end 0.118 inch deep and 0.130 inch wide to form the neck (7). The tip of the firing pin is reduced in diameter to 0.246 inch to form the head (8). The notched end of the striker slips over the head and is held in place by the pressure of the mainspring on the firing pin sleeve.

Two types of firing pin were used for the .30-caliber service rifle and five for non-service .30- and .22-caliber rifles: the **Type 1** firing pin was manufactured by Springfield and Rock Island while the **Type 2**

Model 1903 Springfield Rifle and Its Variations

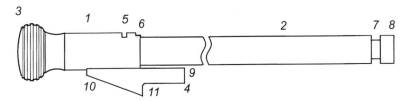

Fig. 2-104. Firing pin rod/cocking piece for the M1903 and M1903A1.

firing pin was manufactured by Remington and Smith Corona. Springfield and Rock Island firing pin assemblies were unmarked while the Remington and Smith Corona firing pin assemblies were marked "R" and "X" respectively, on the lug. Springfield- and Rock Island-made firing pin knobs (3) had six circumferential grooves with the rear three bands knurled. Remington and Smith Corona manufactured firing pin knobs which were knurled only. The two types are interchangeable.

The **Type 3** firing pin was fluted to reduce weight and provide faster lock time. It was used on the International Match rifles.

The **Type 4** firing pin was made of aluminum, again to reduce lock time. This was a commercial product.

The **Type 5** firing pin was designed by Sedgley to provide a smoother safety lever operation, again a commercial product.

NOTE: The .22-caliber firing pin/cocking pieces are described in detail in the section dealing with the .22 Bolt assembly, page 219.

The cocking piece is 1.2 inches long in the shape of a cylinder with a hole 0.290 inch in diameter drilled through it, refer to Figure 2-104, 1. The firing pin (2) screws into the cocking piece and is riveted in place. The cocking cam (4) with the lug (10) is welded to the bottom of the cocking piece. The cocking piece has two milled cuts at the front, the locking groove (5) and the locking shoulder (6). They receive the cam on the safety to place the rifle on "safe."

Model 1903 Springfield Rifle and Its Variations

Three types of cocking pieces were used, see Figure 2-105. The **Type 1** cocking piece (top) was 0.445 inch in diameter. The after end of the cocking piece (arrow A) was concave to make it easier to grasp the knob with the thumb and forefinger. These were used on all M1903 service rifles. The **Type 2** cocking piece (middle) used on the M1903A3 service rifle lacked the concave groove in front of the knob (arrow B). The **Type 3** cocking piece (bottom) lacked the flared knob but continued the diameter of the cocking piece to the after end. The Type 3 headless cocking piece was used on some National Match, Sporting and "Style T" rifles. It was made in two variations: the **1st Variation** was for the standard safety (right-SAFE, left-READY) and the **2nd Variation** was for the reversed safety (right-READY, left-SAFE).

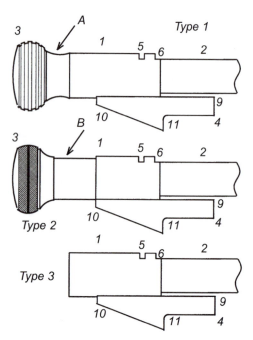

Fig. 2-105. Firing pin knob/cocking piece types: from the top, Types 1, 2 and 3.

The **cocking lug** (10) on the bottom of the cocking piece (1) engages the sear in the sear notch (11) when the bolt is cocked. Its nose (9) on the forward end is guided by the cocking cam on the bottom of the bolt body to move the firing pin back far enough for the lug's sear notch to engage the sear. Three types of cocking lugs were developed: the **Type 1** cocking lug had a ground and "smoothed" sear notch. The

Model 1903 Springfield Rifle and Its Variations

Type 2 cocking lug had a highly polished sear notch. The overall length of the Type 1 and 2 cocking notch was 1.380 inches long by 0.25 inch wide and 0.4 inch high to the top of lug.

The **knob** (refer to Figures 2-104, 3 and 2-105, 3) or bolt head is screwed into the end of the firing pin rod (2). The knob can be used to draw the firing pin assembly back to recock the rifle in the event of a misfire. Three types of knobs were used. The **Type 1** knob flared from 0.290 inch in diameter to 0.690 inch in diameter. The circumference had six grooves and five raised ridges running circumferentially around the knob. It was used on all M1903 and M1903A1 service rifles. The **Type 2** knob flared from 0.460 inch in diameter to 0.695 inch in diameter. It was knurled in a crosshatch pattern and lacked the grooves and ridges. It was used on the M1903A3 rifles. The **Type 3** knob was developed for the M1922 M2 .22-caliber Gallery Rifles and will be discussed in that section on page 219.

FIRING PIN SLEEVE

Sometimes referred to as the "collar," the firing pin sleeve covered the end of the striker where it slipped over the firing pin "head." It was 0.750 inch long by 0.410 inch in diameter and was hollow. The after end was concave in shape, see Figure 2-106.

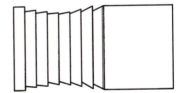

Fig. 2-106. Firing pin sleeve.

Two types of firing pin sleeve were made for the M1903 service rifle. Those manufactured by Springfield and Rock Island are unmarked, those by Remington are marked "R" and those by Smith Corona "X" or are unmarked. All were blued originally. Parkerizing indicates that the sleeve was refinished.

STRIKER

The striker is what many think of as the firing pin. It is 0.9 inch long. The forward end is 0.480 inch long and tapers from 0.261 inch in

Model 1903 Springfield Rifle and Its Variations

diameter to rounded point. The collar is 0.415 inch in diameter, 0.158 inch long and separates the striker portion from the rear socket which attaches it to the firing pin, see Figure 2-107. Three types of strikers were manufactured for the .30-caliber rifles and three for the M1922 and M1 .22-caliber rifles. These last are described in the section on the .22-caliber bolts on page 219.

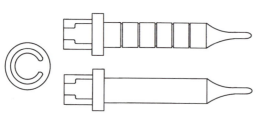

Fig. 2-107. Strikers: top, Type 1 used on the M1903, M1903A1 and the early M1903A3 rifles; below, Type 3 used on the late M1903A3 rifles.

The **Type 1** striker has six annular bands 0.2 inch wide separated by narrow grooves 0.015 inch wide that served to hold lubrication and accumulate dirt and grit that might cause the striker to jam inside the bolt body. The Type 1 striker as manufactured by Springfield and Rock Island was unmarked and used on all .30-caliber rifles produced at those two arsenals. All were blued originally.

The **Type 2** striker was identical in appearance to the Type 1 striker. It was manufactured in two variations. The **1st Variation** was made by Remington Arms for the Remington M1903, the M1903 (Modified), and the M1904A3/A4. It is marked with an "R." The **2nd Variation** was made by Smith Corona and is unmarked. Both were blued.

The **Type 3** striker was apparently manufactured during WWII for the M1903A3, according to Lt. Colonel Brophy. It is rarely encountered.

NOTE: a number of variations of the M1903 striker were produced by various commercial firms before and after World War II. They were intended either for use with target and hunting rifles or in service rifles as spare parts. The former are characterized by careful manufacture and attention to detail and dimension; the latter by rough work and finish. An example of the finely finished strikers manufactured for competition are those from Sedgley. The Sedgley striker was 0.2 inch longer than the service striker and was to be used with the Sedgley high-speed firing pin.

Mainspring
The mainspring drives the firing pin/striker assembly. It is a coil spring formed from piano wire 5.58 inches long by 0.045 inch in diameter, see Figure 2-108. Three types of springs were used. The **Type 1** mainspring was used in all .30-caliber M1903 rifles. It had a diameter of 0.395 inch and 34 coils. The **Type 2** mainspring was developed in 1936 and used on late National Match rifles. It had 30 coils which made the bolt faster and easier to cock without affecting ignition. The **Type 3** mainspring was used in the M1903A3 rifles. It had a diameter of 0.388 inch and 35 coils. The **Type 4** mainspring was developed for the M1922 and M1 .22-caliber gallery rifles. Although it had 33 coils of 0.45-inch piano wire, it was only 4.35 inches long. The spring was copper plated to distinguish it from the springs used in the .30-caliber rifles.

Fig. 2-108. M1903 mainspring.

.22-Caliber Bolt Assemblies
The .22-caliber bolt assembly used on the M1922, M1922 M1 and M1922 M2 .22-caliber rifles differs from that used in the .30-caliber rifles, see Figures 2-109 and 2-110. And the bolts used in the three .22-caliber rifles differ quite a bit from one another. To make it easier to understand the difference, each part of the three bolt models is described below in succeeding paragraphs.

Parts of the M1922 (Figure 2-109) and M1922M1 (Figure 2-110) bolts are:1) firing pin rod, 2) cocking piece, 3) cocking lug, 4) cocking cam, 5) nose, 6) sear notch, 7) locking shoulder, 8) locking groove,

Model 1903 Springfield Rifle and Its Variations

9) neck, 10) head, 11) firing pin sleeve, 12) firing pin rod cap, 13) safety lock assembly, 14) bolt sleeve, 15) bolt handle assembly, 16) bolt handle, 17) locking lug, 18) bolt head latch, 19) mainspring, 20) ejector, 21) bolt head, 22) striker, 23) striker spring plunger and 24) extractor.

Parts of the M2 .22-caliber bolt (see Figure 2-111) are: 1) the firing pin rod, 2) cocking piece, 3) cocking lug, 4) cocking cam, 5) nose, 6) sear notch, 7) locking shoulder, 8) locking groove, 9) striker, 10) safety lock assembly, 11) bolt sleeve, 12) bolt body, 13) bolt handle, 14) headspace adjusting screw (Type 2 only), 15) locking lug, 16) mainspring, 17) ejector, pin and spring, 18) bolt head, 19) extractor, 20) firing pin nut and 21) firing pin nut locking spring.

The M1922 and M1 simulated the bolt throw of the .30-caliber service rifle by using short extractors fixed on the bolt head that stopped the bolt throw when it encountered the bolt stop which was a modified "cutoff." By 1929, it was no longer thought necessary for the bolt throw to be the same as the service rifle. A new bolt assembly was designed by Captain G.A. Woody of the Ordnance Department that had a short throw more suited to the .22-caliber cartridge. Its ejector was longer so that it contacted the bolt stop sooner. In addition, a new firing pin assembly was developed to eliminate the separate striker. It used the .30-caliber service mainspring; a new, more positive extractor and a flared bolt head were added to protect the shooter's face and eyes by deflecting gas in case a cartridge ruptured.

NOTE: Each .22-caliber bolt for the M1922, M1 and M2 rifles was headspaced at Springfield. Bolts are not interchangeable between models and should not be interchanged between rifles of the same model. If it is necessary to do so, it should only be done by an experienced professional gunsmith familiar with the Springfield-made .22-caliber gallery rifles. Interestingly enough, the M1922 bolts were not serial numbered to the receiver but the M1922 M1 and M2 bolts were.

Model 1903 Springfield Rifle and Its Variations

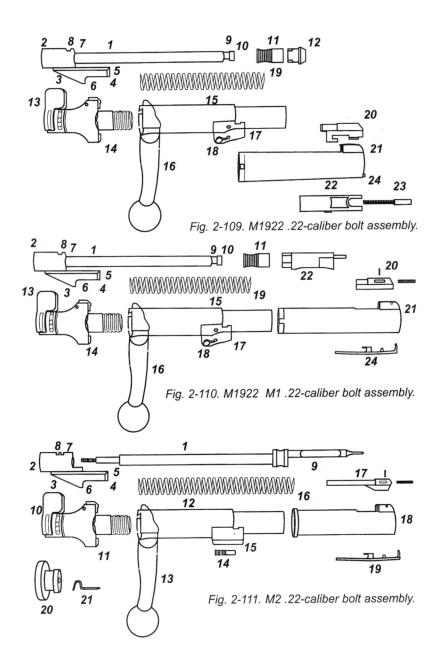

Fig. 2-109. M1922 .22-caliber bolt assembly.

Fig. 2-110. M1922 M1 .22-caliber bolt assembly.

Fig. 2-111. M2 .22-caliber bolt assembly.

Model 1903 Springfield Rifle and Its Variations

BOLT BODY

The .22-caliber bolt body used on the M1922, M1 and M2 rifles is shorter than the .30-caliber bolt at 3.5 inches. Like the .30-caliber bolt, the handle is swept slightly to the rear. The cocking cam has the same dimensions as the service rifle but the cocking cam is only 0.15 inch deep compared to 0.45 inch for the service rifle.

Fig. 2-112. The M2 bolt partially disassembled and showing the body and rebated end of the bolt head below the locking lug.

The bolt body's forward end is rebated to 0.548 inch for 1.220 inches. This rebated end slides into the bolt head. The bolt body is secured to the bolt head by a groove cut into the underside of the safety lug and by a raised lug on the back end of the bolt head, see Figure 2-112.

M1922 AND M1 BOLT BODIES

The safety locking lug on these two bolt bodies differs from that on the service rifle in that it contains a spring-loaded plunger similar to the sleeve lock on the .30-caliber bolt sleeve which serves to positively retain the separate bolt head, refer to Figures 2-109 and 2-110, 18.

M2 BOLT BODY

The M2 bolt differs in the arrangement for securing the bolt head and in its provisions for setting headspace. The M2 bolt head did not lock into the bolt body with a spring-loaded plunger mounted on the safety lug as in the M1922 and M1. Instead, a cut was milled on the forward inside edge of the safety lug. When the bolt handle was lowered and the bolt was in battery, a raised rim at the rear of the bolt head revolved into the cut and clamped the two parts together; see Figure 2-113 and refer to Figure 2-112.

222

Model 1903 Springfield Rifle and Its Variations

Two types of M2 bolt bodies were used. The **Type 1** bolt body was not adjustable for headspace on the first 3,800 M2 rifles. The safety lug resembles that used on the M1922 and M1922 M1 except for the cut for the bolt head rim. In an effort to improve accuracy, the M2 bolt system was designed so that its headspace could be adjusted

Fig. 2-113. The locking lug on the M2 bolt body slides over a matching lug on the bolt head.

when the bolt was fitted to the rifle. The **Type 2** bolt body therefore has an adjusting system consisting of an adjustment screw and set screw mounted in a threaded hole in the safety lug. The adjusting screw could be turned in or out to contact the receiver bridge, see Figure 2-114.

Fig. 2-114. Head space was adjusted on the M2 bolt with a screw which was set at the Armory and filled with a copper plug to prevent tampering.

Three variations of this adjustable headspace system were used. The **1st Variation** used an adjusting screw with a blunt tip and a screwdriver head. After the headspace was adjusted by turning the adjusting screw until it bottomed against the receiver bridge at the right measurement, a set screw in the underside of the lug was turned down to contact the head of the adjusting screw and secure it in place. The adjusting screw was designed so that its head was below the surface of the safety lug when properly adjusted. A lead seal was then inserted to prevent untrained personnel from attempting to readjust the headspace. As it turned out, the set screw did not prove capable of holding the adjusting screw in place against the receiver bridge.

Model 1903 Springfield Rifle and Its Variations

The **2nd Variation** bolt body used an adjusting screw with a slot in the tip and a heavily knurled section above the threads against which the set screw was tightened. Again, the set screw proved too delicate for the task and a **3rd Variation** of the bolt body used an unthreaded plug made of copper with a slotted head. The copper plug was turned down hard on the adjusting screw which forced it to conform to the thread pattern. Its tip was upset against the coarse knurling on the adjusting screw which held it securely. The head of the copper plug was cut off flush with the surface of the lug. It could only be removed by drilling it out. This system proved to be satisfactory.

NOTE: The lead seals on the 1st and 2nd Variation set screws as well as the copper plug on the 3rd Variation were embossed with the Ordnance escutcheon (flaming bomb). If this marking is absent, the headspace may have been readjusted at some later date by someone other than the Springfield Armory. If this is the case, the headspace should be checked by an experienced gunsmith.

BOLT HEAD
The bolt head is a separate cylinder with a single front locking lug, refer to Figures 2-109, 2-110 and 2-111. A channel is cut through the locking lug for the ejector. The firing pin hole is 0.09 inch in diameter. Behind the locking lug on the bolt head is a milled flat 0.51 inch long by 0.385 inch wide. The ejector is pinned into the lug and its afterend rides in the milled flat. The extractor is also contained within the bolt head. The bolt head face is rebated for the .22-caliber cartridge base. The bolt head is relieved on the bottom for 1.6 inch to allow the .22 cartridge to clear the magazine. The clearance cut is 0.38 inch wide and has a central rib 0.05 inch wide. The differences in the three bolt heads used for the M1922, M1 and M2 .22-caliber rifles are primarily in the number of firing pin holes and the internal arrangement of baffles for the firing pin assemblies. Even so, they are not interchangeable.

Model 1903 Springfield Rifle and Its Variations

M1922 Bolt Head—The M1922 bolt head has two holes on the bolt head face for the dual firing pin. The relief cut on the bottom of the bolt head for the cartridges is 0.08 inch deep.

M1 Bolt Head—The M1 bolt head is very similar to that used on the M1922. The M1 bolt head has only a single hole for the firing pin and the internal tunnel for the firing pin was wider. The relief cut on the bottom of the bolt head for the cartridges is 0.08 inch deep.

M2 Bolt Head—The M2 bolt head is similar to the M1 bolt head but has a smaller internal baffle for its one-piece firing pin. The relief cut on the M2 bolt head is 0.130 inch, 0.05 inch deeper than on the M1922 and M1 bolt head, to clear the new, higher magazine developed for the M2.

EJECTOR

The ejector on the .22-caliber M1922, M1 and M2 is mounted on the bolt head rather than in the receiver as with the .30-caliber rifles. It slides back and forth through a slot milled in the lug on the bolt head. Three types of ejectors were used: the **Type 1** on the M1922, the **Type 2** on the M1922 M1 and the **Type 3** on the M2. They are not interchangeable. Refer to Figures 2-109, 2-110 and 2-111.

The Type 1 ejector was 1.2 inches long and "hooked" over the safety lug. It was not spring-loaded. The Type 2 ejector was also 1.2 inches long but was secured to the safety lug by a pin. The hole in the ejector for the pin was elongated to allow the ejector to move back and forth. A small coil spring returned it to the "closed" position. The Type 3 ejector was 2.385 inches long. It was secured in the safety lug with a pin like the Type 2 and a spring returned it to the closed position.

The difference in length between the Types 1 and 2 and the Type 3 ejectors had to do with the bolt throw. The M1922 and M1 bolts were designed to simulate the full bolt throw of the .30-caliber service rifle.

Therefore the bolt had to be pulled all the way to the rear before the ejector encountered the bolt stop. But the M2 was built with a short bolt throw. The longer ejector encountered the bolt stop sooner and resulted in a shorter stroke.

EXTRACTOR

The extractor is 0.692 inch long and 0.215 inch wide. It fits into a channel cut into the side of the bolt head 0.216 inch above the magazine relief cut. Since the bolt head does not rotate, the extractor is fixed in the channel by a lug on the bottom of the extractor which slides into a matching hole in the channel. As the bolt is closed, the extractor rides up and over the rim of the .22 cartridge. The same extractor was used on the M1922M1 and M2 bolt heads but the extractor used on the M1922 bolt head was a spring-loaded rod housed in the bottom front of the bolt head, refer to Figure 2-109, 24.

NOTE: The extractors on the M1922M1 and M2 should only be removed for cleaning. To do so, carefully pry up the extractor lip and push the extractor forward while controlling its forward motion with the thumb of the other hand. To reseat, center the lug in the hole in the channel. Hold the front of the bolt head with the protruding extractor against a hard surface. Place your thumb on the extractor just ahead of the lug and push forward and down until it snaps into place.

BOLT SLEEVE

The bolt sleeve used on the M1922, M1 and M2 was the same bolt sleeve used on the M1903 .30-caliber service rifle. No changes were made to it, refer to Figures 2-109, 2-110 and 2-111.

SAFETY LEVER

The same safety lever assembly was used on the M1922, M1 and M2 .22-caliber rifles as on the .30-caliber service rifle. The lever was marked "SAFE" and "READY" in sans serif type 0.8 inch high.

Model 1903 Springfield Rifle and Its Variations

COCKING PIECE

The flared cocking piece was used only on the M2 Gallery Rifle and was a separate part from the firing pin rod. It slid over the firing pin rod which was threaded at the rear and was held in place by a separate knurled knob which screwed onto the firing pin rod. The knob was held in place by a spring.

It allowed the rifle to be cocked without opening the bolt and also served to deflect any gas that might escape from a ruptured cartridge, see Figure 2-115 and refer to Figure 2-111.

Fig. 2-115. The flared M2 cocking piece (arrow) deflected gas in case a cartridge ruptured. The cocking piece was fastened to the firing pin by the spring clip visible between the head and sleeve.

The flared cocking piece was 1.360 inches long. The lug was 1.170 inches long and the sear notch was 0.145 inch deep. The cocking piece was marked with its drawing number, C3995-1.

FIRING PIN

The .22-caliber firing pin was a modified .30-caliber service rifle firing pin shortened to 4.7 inches. Three different types were used in the M1922, M1 and M2 bolts.

The **Type 1** firing pin lacked a grasping knob and only protruded slightly from the rear of the bolt sleeve when the bolt was closed but not cocked. It had a groove and rebated front end similar to that used on the .30-caliber service rifle firing pin. Type 1 firing pins drove a striker to detonate the cartridge's priming compound. The Type 1 firing pin was used in the M1922, see Figure 2-116.

227

Model 1903 Springfield Rifle and Its Variations

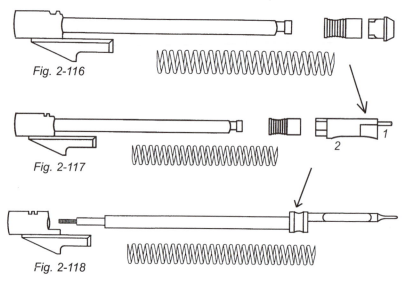

Fig. 2-116

Fig. 2-117

Fig. 2-118

Figs. 2-116-118. .22-caliber firing pins: top to bottom: Type 1, Type 2 and Type 3. Drawings not to scale.

With the **Type 2** firing pin, the designers at Springfield Armory provided a separate striker positioned to strike the rim of the .22-caliber cartridge case. It was attached to the firing pin rod with the same modified firing pin sleeve used in the M1922. The Type 2 firing pin assembly was installed in the M1922 M1 .22-caliber gallery rifle, see Figure 2-117, above.

The **Type 3** firing pin had an integral striker and was installed in the M2 .22-caliber gallery rifle. The front of the firing pin was a rod 0.9 inch in diameter and 0.37 inch long. It flared back to the body which was 0.226 inch in diameter and 1.68 inches long. It was ground flat on either side 0.72 inch. The front of the firing pin was 0.405 inch in diameter and 0.7 inch long. The new design was sturdy, striking the cartridge directly and firmly to solve the "cushioning" effect that occurred with the M1922M1 firing pin striker assembly, see Figure 2-118, above.

Firing Pin Sleeve (Collar)

The firing pin sleeve, or collar, was used only on the M1922 and M1 firing pins. It was similar to that used on the service rifle but slightly smaller at 0.725 inch long and 0.360 inch in diameter, refer to Figures 2-116 and 2-117.

Firing Pin Rod Cap

The firing pin rod cap was a truncated cap that attached to the shorter firing pin by a collar similar to that used on the .30-caliber service rifle. It was interposed between the firing pin and striker. It was used only in the M1922 bolt, refer to Figure 2-116.

Striker

Three types of strikers were used. The M1922 **Type 1** striker was double-headed. It struck the cartridge rim at the 12 and 6 o'clock positions. The firing pin had a firing pin cap held to the firing pin by a modified sleeve or collar. The firing pin cap struck the striker and drove it forward to

Fig. 2-119. Type 1 striker assembly for the M1922 gallery rifle.

detonate the priming compound in the cartridge rim, see Figure 2-119.

The **Type 2** striker was used in the M1 bolt, refer to Figure 2-117, arrow. It had a single rod which protruded through the bolt face (1). It was attached to the firing pin by a modified sleeve or collar (2). Because of the narrow diameter of the firing pin at 0.9 inch and the abrupt, 90-degree shoulder where the narrow pin joined the larger-diameter cylinder, breakage was a problem.

The **Type 3** striker was used in the M2 bolt. It was manufactured in a single piece using a standard service rifle firing pin rod to which was

229

Model 1903 Springfield Rifle and Its Variations

attached the striker on a drum guide, see Figure 2-118, arrow.

STRIKER SPRING AND PLUNGER

The striker spring and plunger were only used in the M1922 bolt. The plunger was spring driven. Its shaft fitted into a hole drilled in the face of the striker between the two striker pins. Its forward end bottomed against the inside of the bolt face. The spring kept the firing pin retracted at all times except when the mainspring drove it forward when the sear released the firing pin lug, refer to Figure 2-119.

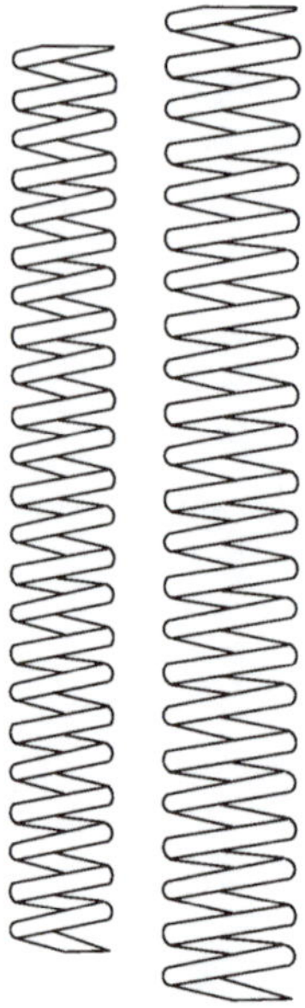

MAINSPRING

Two types of mainsprings were used in the M1922, M1 and M2 rifles, see Figure 2-120.

The **Type 1** mainspring was 0.4 inch in diameter. It had 24 coils and was copper-plated. It was used in the M1922 and M1 rifles. The **Type 2** mainspring was the standard .30-caliber mainspring. It was 0.395 inch in diameter and had 34 coils. It was not copper-plated.

Fig. 2-120. Types 1 and 2 mainsprings for the .22-caliber gallery rifles (not to scale).

MARKINGS – BOLT ASSEMBLY

All bolts will show inspection and other markings that will help identify them by manufacturer as shown in Tables 17-24.

SPRINGFIELD M1903 BOLT MARKINGS

Springfield bolts are not marked with the manufacturer's name or identification. That said, inspectors' markings, and in wartime, manufacturers' codes, can provide clues as to origin and period of manufacture. See Table 17.

Model 1903 Springfield Rifle and Its Variations

Table 17 Springfield Armory M1903 Bolt Markings	
Bolt Part	**Marking(s)**
Bolt Body	Early (straight bolt handle) bolt bodies are generally marked "S" on the safety lug. Other marks observed are "1M" and "1.5." Early bolts under serial #200,000 observed marked "1" on safety lug. Circa 1910-16, "2", "B" and "A". and other initials and numbers. Nickel-steel alloy bolts are marked "N.S." on the top of the bolt handle root. The receiver's serial number was engraved on National Match bolts with an electric pencil. Also observed are: "D1," "F1," "J4," "J5," "and J6" before and during the WWI period; "HO" for Hoover Ball and Bearing and "RE8620" (steel lot number). These last two were apparently used as replacement bolts by Springfield.
Extractor	Most are unmarked. Those made of chrome-vanadium steel in the late 1930s for National Match rifles were marked "CV."
Extractor Collar	Unmarked
Striker	Unmarked
Spring	Unmarked
Collar	Unmarked
Bolt Sleeve	Unmarked
Cocking Piece	Unmarked. Those made of chrome-vanadium steel in the late 1930s for National Match rifles were marked "CV."
Safety	SAFE on top; READY on underside; both with serifs circa serial #1-420,000; SAFE with serifs, READY sans serif to circa serial #420,000-550,000; after both use sans serif letters.

ROCK ISLAND ARSENAL BOLT MARKINGS

Rock Island Arsenal-manufactured bolts show no markings other than a punch mark on the bottom of the bolt handle root, see Table 18.

Model 1903 Springfield Rifle and Its Variations

Table 18 Rock Island Arsenal M1903 Bolt Markings	
Bolt Part	**Marking(s)**
Bolt Body	Punch mark on bolt handle root
Extractor	Unmarked
Extractor Collar	Unmarked
Striker	Unmarked
Spring	Unmarked
Collar	Unmarked
Bolt Sleeve	Unmarked
Cocking Piece	Unmarked
Safety	SAFE on top; READY on underside. Letters with serifs

REMINGTON M1903 BOLT MARKINGS

The M1903 bolt used on both the M1903 and M1903 (Modified) was manufactured by Remington Arms and resembles the bolts manufactured by Rock Island. Remington bolts were Parkerized an olive green (Rock Island Parkerizing was black); they have both the 0.1-inch gas vent and the 0.2-inch gas vent. See Table 19.

Table 19 Remington Arms M1903 Bolt Markings	
Bolt Part	**Marking(s)**
Bolt Body	Remington bolt bodies manufactured for the M1903 are marked "R" on the bottom of the bolt handle root and a punch mark and will show a hollow cross on the back of the bolt handle root. Other inspection markings will be found on the rear face of the bolt handle root consisting of various numbers and letters.

Model 1903 Springfield Rifle and Its Variations

Bolt Part	Marking(s)
Table 19, cont. **Remington Arms M1903 Bolt Markings**	
Bolt Part	**Marking(s)**
Extractor	"R" on underside
Extractor Collar	May be marked "R" on collar
Striker	"R"
Spring	Unmarked
Collar	Unmarked
Bolt Sleeve	"R"
Cocking Piece	"R"
Safety	SAFE on top (sans serif); READY on underside (serif), "R" on back

REMINGTON M1903A3 BOLT MARKINGS

Remington bolt bodies manufactured for the M1903A3 are marked "R" at various locations as shown in Table 20.

Bolt Part	Marking(s)
Table 20 **Remington Arms M1903A3 Bolt Markings**	
Bolt Part	**Marking(s)**
Bolt Body	Remington bolt bodies manufactured for the M1903A3 are marked "R" on the bottom of the bolt handle root and a punch mark. They will show an inspector's number or letter on top of the bolt handle root. Other inspection markings will be found on the rear face of the bolt handle root consisting of various numbers and letters. Some of the numbers will be boxed or circled. Subcontracted parts will be marked with their initials: 88 (Acros Co.); BF (Bonney Forge and Tool); BP (Brown Corp.); BS (Brown & Sharpe); CC (Chrysler Corp.); CCT (Commercial Controls Corp.); HO (Hoover Ball & Bearing Co.).

Model 1903 Springfield Rifle and Its Variations

Table 20, cont. Remington Arms M1903A3 Bolt Markings	
Bolt Part	**Marking(s)**
Extractor	"R" on underside
Extractor Collar	May be marked "R" or "R" in a circle
Striker	"R" on collar
Spring	Unmarked
Collar	Unmarked
Bolt Sleeve	"R" on right shoulder if Remington manufactured; BP (Brown Corp.); BF (Bonney Forge and Tool)
Cocking Piece	"R"
Safety	SAFE on top (sans serif); READY on underside (serif)

SMITH CORONA M1903A3 BOLT MARKINGS

Smith Corona bolt bodies are marked "X" on top of the bolt handle root and "7" and a punch mark on the underside. The punch marks are found on the bolt body 2.3 inches behind the front edge on the top and the right side of the split lug. The extractor is marked "S." The cocking piece shows a punch mark on the left side. See Table 21.

NOTE: Collectors may observe a greater number of replacement bolts in Smith Corona M1903A3s than in Remington M1903A3s. This is due in part to the side of the stock under the bolt handle being slightly too thick to allow the bolt handle to close completely. When the rifle was fired, the bolt handle jumped open. While not dangerous, it was disconcerting and many armorers either replaced the stock or the bolt until the problem disappeared. Naturally, it was easier to replace the bolt than the stock.

Model 1903 Springfield Rifle and Its Variations

Table 21 Smith Corona M1903A3 Bolt Markings	
Bolt Part	**Marking(s)**
Bolt Body	Smith Corona bolt bodies are marked "X" on top of the bolt handle root and "7" and a punch mark on the underside.
Extractor	"S" on underside or side of lug
Striker	Unmarked
Spring	Unmarked
Collar	Unmarked
Bolt Sleeve	Unmarked or with a "G"
Cocking Piece	Punch mark on left side
Safety	SAFE on top, READY on underside, both with serifs

.22 CALIBER GALLERY RIFLE BOLT MARKINGS

Hoffer-Thompson .22-Caliber gallery rifle bolt markings are identical to those used in service rifles. Bolt markings for the M1922, M1922 M1 and the M2 are described in Tables 22-24.

NOTE: From 1925 to the end of production in the late 1940s, all M1922, M1922M1 and M2 .22-caliber gallery rifles had the receiver serial number engraved with an electric pen on the bottom of the bolt body and bolt head. The serial number was often divided between the two parts.

Table 22 M1922 Bolt Markings	
Bolt Part	**Marking(s)**
Bolt Body	Unmarked to 1925; serial number engraved with electric pen from 1925 on.

Model 1903 Springfield Rifle and Its Variations

Table 22, cont. M1922 Bolt Markings	
Bolt Part	**Marking(s)**
Extractor	Unmarked
Striker	Unmarked
Spring	Unmarked
Collar	Unmarked
Bolt Sleeve	Unmarked
Cocking Piece	Unmarked
Safety	SAFE on top, READY on underside, both sans serifs

Table 23 M1922 M1 Bolt Markings	
Bolt Part	**Marking(s)**
Bolt Body	May be engaved "N.S." on bolt handle, serial number engraved with electric pen from 1925 on.
Extractor	Unmarked
Striker	Unmarked
Spring	Unmarked
Collar	Unmarked
Bolt Sleeve	Unmarked
Cocking Piece	Unmarked
Safety	SAFE on top, READY on underside, both sans serifs

Model 1903 Springfield Rifle and Its Variations

Table 24 M1922 M2 Bolt Markings	
Bolt Part	**Marking(s)**
Bolt Body	"NS/M2," serial number engraved with electric pen
Bolt Head	M2
Extractor	Unmarked
Ejector	C3998
Spring	Unmarked
Collar/Firing Pin	Punch mark
Bolt Sleeve	Unmarked
Cocking Piece	C3995 or C3995-1
Safety	SAFE on top, READY on underside, both sans serifs

Trigger Assembly

The trigger assembly of the M1903 rifle consists of: 1) the sear, 2) sear joint pin, 3) sear spring, 4) trigger pin, 5) trigger, 6) follower, 7) magazine spring, 8) floor plate and magazine box and 9-10) front and rear guard screws, 11) trigger guard and 12) floor plate, see Figure 2-121.

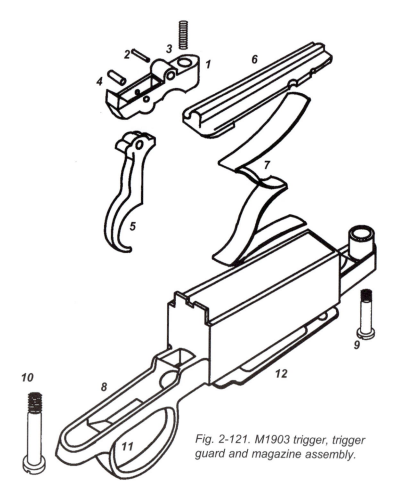

Fig. 2-121. M1903 trigger, trigger guard and magazine assembly.

Model 1903 Springfield Rifle and Its Variations

SEAR

The sear has five important points: 1) the sear nose projects above the top, rear of the sear body and releases the bolt when the trigger is pulled. The bearing on the top of the trigger pushes against the bottom of the sear, raising the

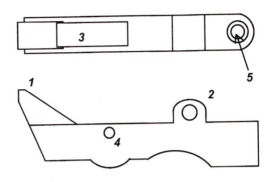

Fig. 2-122. Sear.

front and dropping the sear nose out of contact with the sear notch on the firing pin lug. 2) The sear joint pin hole receives the sear joint pin which permits the sear to rotate up and down, 3) the trigger slot, 4) the trigger pin hole and the 5) sear spring seat. See Figure 2-122.

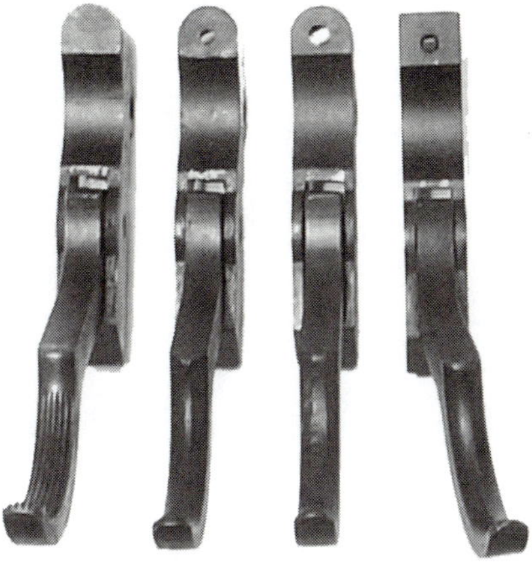

Eight different types of sears were used in the M1903 and M1903A3. Types 1-7 are characterized by a rounded face ahead of the sear spring seat while the Type 8 has a flat face, see Figure 2-123.

The **Type 1** sear can be identified by its lack of the round blind hole at the front to seat the sear spring, refer to Figure 2-122, 5.

Fig. 2-123. M1903 sears (L-R): Type 1, no hole beneath spring seat; Type 2, 0.060-inch hole; Type 6, Springfield-manufactured replacement sear with 0.120-inch-diameter hole; Type 8, M1903A3 sear with flat face.

Model 1903 Springfield Rifle and Its Variations

The **Type 2** sear is identical to the Type 1 but it did have a 0.060-inch-diameter blind hole at the bottom front for the sear spring, refer to Figure 2-123. This sear was used on all M1903 service rifles built by Springfield and Rock Island from 1914 to the end of rifle parts production in 1942.

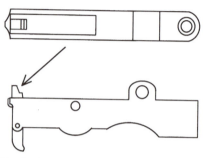

Fig. 2-124. Mk. I rifle sear.

The **Type 3** sear was used on the M1903 Mark I rifle. A trip lever that pivoted at the rear of the sear replaced the fixed sear nose, see Figure 2-124, arrow.

The **Type 4** sear was used in the National Match rifle, Sporting and "Style T" rifles. The sear nose was shortened slightly and polished to provide a trigger pull release weight of 3.5 to 4.5 lbs.

The **Type 5** sear was used from 1936 to the end of M1903 parts production at Springfield in 1939 in National Match, Sporting and "Style T" rifles. It was made of chrome-vanadium steel, had a slightly shortened and polished nose and was marked "CV" on the right side.

The **Type 6** sear was manufactured at Springfield in 1944 and 1945 as a spare part. It was identical to the prewar Type 2 sear except that the hole beneath the spring seat had been enlarged to 0.120 inch in diameter. It was marked "S" on the left side, refer to Figure 2-123.

The **Type 7** sear was similar to the Type 2 sear used in the Model 1903 except that it was Parkerized. It had the same 0.060-inch hole beneath the spring seat. Those manufactured by Remington (and subcontractors) were marked "R." They were used in the Remington M1903 and the M1903 (Modified).

Model 1903 Springfield Rifle and Its Variations

The **Type 8** sear was manufactured for the M1903A3 rifle. Its main point of difference was a flat face ahead of the sear spring seat, refer to Figure 2-123. Remington-made sears were marked "R" while those manufactured by Smith Corona were often marked "X."

NOTE: Sears and other trigger parts have been manufactured in the post-World War II years by a variety of private manufacturing concerns as aftermarket replacements. They are characterized by poor manufacturing techniques, rough finish and mold seams. These should never be installed in a rifle.

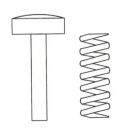

Fig. 2-125. Sear joint pin and sear spring.

SEAR JOINT PIN

The sear join pin has a head 0.30 inch in diameter and 0.129 inch thick at the edge. The pin is 0.128 inch in diameter and 0.480 inch long. It has a slightly domed end. It was unchanged throughout the production of the M1903 series of rifles. The sear join pin was unmarked, see Figure 2-125.

SEAR SPRING

This coil spring is 0.198 inch in diameter and has eight coils made of steel wire 0.045 inch in diameter. It was unchanged throughout the production of the M1903 series of rifles, refer to Figure 2-125.

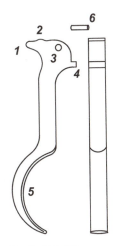

Fig. 2-126. Trigger.

TRIGGER

The trigger was 2.3 inches high and 0.2 inch wide at the center of the finger piece, see Figure 2-126. The curve of the finger piece was 1 inch high. It rotates forward and back in the sear slot on a pin. The trigger has five impor-

Model 1903 Springfield Rifle and Its Variations

tant areas: 1) heel, 2) bearing, 3) trigger pin hole, 4) stop, 5) finger piece and 6) trigger pin. With the firing pin cocked, the sear nose engages the firing pin lug and is held in place by the heel on the trigger. When the trigger is pulled to the rear, it rotates on the trigger pin and the heel moves out of contact with the sear, so that it drops down and pulls the sear nose out of contact with the firing pin lug, allowing it to move forward.

Five types of triggers were used. The **Type 1** trigger was similar to that used in the M1898 Krag rifle with a slender, smooth finger piece.

The Type 1 trigger was used from the start of production to circa serial #425,000 (1910).

The **Type 2** trigger had a slightly shallower curve (0.375 inch) and had six vertical grooves or serrations. The tip was knurled.

The Type 2 trigger was used from circa serial #s 425,000 to 760,000 (late 1917).

The **Type 3** trigger was identical to the Type 2 trigger but was not serrated. It was used from circa serial #760,001 (late 1917) to the end of production at Springfield.

NOTE: collectors may find Types 1, 2 and 3 triggers in use during the World War I period until supplies of the Types 1 and 2 ran out.

The **Type 4** trigger was used only on the M1903 Mark I. It had the same curve as the Type 2 but lacked the serrations or vertical grooves. It also had a shallow groove milled at the top back side of the trigger where the trigger lever on the Mark I sear made contact.

The **Type 5** trigger was used on National Match rifles. It was similar to the Type 2 trigger with six vertical grooves but the bearing surface on top of the trigger was highly polished. This trigger is found on all National Match, "Style T" and M1 and M2 .22-Caliber Gallery Rifles manufactured after 1930.

The **Type 6** trigger was manufactured by Remington Arms and used on the M1903 and M1903 (Modified) service rifles. It was identical to the Type 3 trigger (smooth finger piece) but was marked "R." These triggers can also be identified by the thicker tip on the finger piece. They were Parkerized.

The **Type 7** trigger was manufactured for the M1903A3/A4 rifle by both Remington Arms and Smith Corona and their subcontractors. It was stamped from sheet steel and marked "R" for Remington and "X" for Smith Corona. They have the thin tip on the finger piece like the earlier triggers.

Type 1 and Type 2 triggers manufactured through 1917 were blued. All later Type 2 and all Types 3 through 7 triggers were Parkerized.

TRIGGER PIN
The trigger pin is a case-hardened steel pin 0.30 inch in diameter by 0.3405 inch long. It acts as a pivot point for the trigger in the sear, refer to Figure 2-126, 6.

TRIGGER GUARD PLATE AND MAGAZINE
The trigger guard plate and magazine are a one-piece unit serving both as a protective guard for the trigger and as a container for cartridges, see Figure 2-127. The *Description and Rules for the Management of the Magazine Rifle, Model of 1903, Caliber .30* identified the following parts: 1) trigger guard bow, 2) front tang, 3) rear tang, 4) front guard screw stud, 5) magazine side walls, 6) rear magazine wall, 7) floor plate catch pin hole, 8) front guard screw hole, 9) trigger slot, 10) floor plate lug slot, 11) floor plate catch spring hole, 12) floor plate catch slot, 13) ramp and 14) lightening cuts.

Model 1903 Springfield Rifle and Its Variations

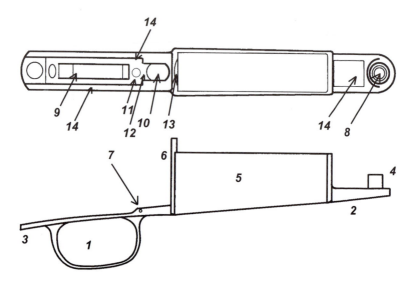

Fig. 2-127. Trigger plate and magazine box.

Five types of trigger guard plate were used. **Types 1-4** were milled from a steel billet and had the following dimensions in common: The trigger guard plate was 8.55 inches long by 1.09 inches wide at the widest point of the magazine. The rear of the plate was 0.655 inch wide and the front was 0.660 inch wide. The magazine well was 3.4 inches long by 0.935 inch wide at the rear and 0.785 inch wide at the front. The magazine walls were 1.3 inches high at the rear and 1.120 inches high at the front.

The **Types 5** through **7** were stamped from sheet steel and used on the M1903A3 rifle. Their dimensions were very similar to the Types 1-4 but the magazine well was slightly wider, see page 247.

The **Types 1 and 2** trigger slot openings were 1.0 inch long by 0.225 inch wide but the slot proved to be too long, see Figure 2-128. If the trigger was pushed forward when the rifle was cocked, it would re-

Model 1903 Springfield Rifle and Its Variations

Fig. 2-128. Type 2 M1903 trigger guard plate. Note the pin across the front of the trigger guard slot (1) and the "S" stamping (2) signifying it was modified at Springfield Armory.

lease the sear and fire the rifle. A pin was installed across the front of the trigger guard slot (**Type 2** trigger guard plate) to prevent the trigger from moving forward and allowed the Type 1 trigger guards to be reused (arrow 1). These trigger guard plates *only* were marked with a small "S" at the rear of the magazine box (arrow 2). The Types 1 and 2 trigger guard plates were used only on the rod bayonet rifle and its subsequent alterations.

The trigger slot in the **Type 3** trigger guard plate was 0.975 inch long and 0.225 inch wide and was used as the standard trigger guard plate for all M1903 production after 1905 and all M1903A1 production.

The floor plate catch slot is oval and is 0.540 inch long by 0.305 inch wide. The floor plate catch pin hole is 0.90 inch in diameter and passes through the width of the trigger guard plate.

The rear tang screw hole is 0.348 inch in diameter reduced to 0.255 inch in diameter and the front tang screw hole is 0.350 inch reduced to

Model 1903 Springfield Rifle and Its Variations

0.265 inch in diameter. The front tang screw hole passes through the front guard screw stud which is 0.510 inch in diameter and 0.470 inch high.

There are two lightening cuts in the trigger guard floor plate. The front cut is 0.640 inch long by 0.5 inch wide. The cut is concave in shape to a depth of 0.210 inch. The rear cut is 2.6 inches long by 0.5 inch wide and encompasses the trigger slot and the rear tang screw hole, refer to Figure 2-127, 14.

NOTE: The Type 3 trigger guard plates used on the USMC M1903A1 sniper rifles were modified slightly by the Marine Corps armorers assembling the sniper rifles. The front guard screw stud was nominally 0.450 inch high above the floor plate. Once the front guard screw was tightened, it brought the top of the screw stud and the bottom of the receiver into contact. The Marine armorers relieved the top of the front screw stud by 0.05 to 0.10 inch to prevent contact when the front guard screw was tightened. Often the screws were then staked into place when the assembly was completed.

Fig. 2-129. Trigger guard floor plates and magazine boxes for the M1922, M1922M1 and M2 .22-caliber gallery rifles. Jim Gronning collection.

The **Type 4** trigger guard plate and magazine was designed for use in the M1922, the M1 and M2 .22-caliber gallery rifles, see Figure 2-129. They are identical to the Type 3 trigger guard plate and magazine box but have a V-shaped relief cut machined in the top of the front magazine wall to clear the .22-caliber magazine.

Model 1903 Springfield Rifle and Its Variations

Fig. 2-130. The M1903 (left) trigger guard compared to the M1903A3 (right). The M1903A3 trigger guard plate was made from stamped and folded sheet steel while that used on the M1903 was milled from a forged steel billet.

The **Type 5** trigger guard plate and magazine was developed by Remington Arms for the M1903A3 rifle. It was stamped from sheet steel and the front and rear walls of the magazine were folded together to form the magazine box. The trigger bow was welded to the plate at the front and riveted at the rear with the rear guard screw lug, see Figure 2-130, arrow. The Type 5 did not have a separate floor plate or provisions for the floor plate catch. Remington trigger guard plates are stamped "R" or "R" in a circle on the back of the magazine box, usually on the right side. Type 5 trigger guard plates were blued; Parkerized plates have been refinished.

The Type 5 trigger guard plate was 8.55 inches long by 1.09 inches wide at the widest point of the magazine. The rear of the plate was 0.600 inch wide and the front was 0.655 inch wide. The magazine well was 3.4 inches long by 1.10 inches wide at the rear and 0.960 inch wide at the front. The magazine walls were 1.365 inches high at the rear and 1.165 inches high at the front.

Model 1903 Springfield Rifle and Its Variations

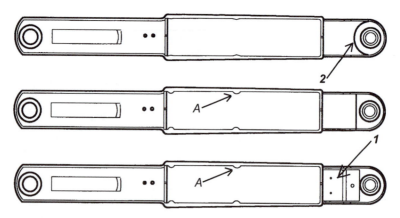

Fig. 2-130A. M1903A3 trigger guard plates top to bottom: Smith Corona (Type 7) and Remington Types 5 and 6.

The Type 5 (and 6) magazine boxes had two deeply impressed reinforcing ribs on the sides, see Figure 2-130A, arrow A. Looking at the magazine box from above, they appear as shallow "U"s. Just behind where the front guard screw post is riveted, the metal of the trigger guard plate forms a straight line as opposed to a curve in the Type 7.

Fig. 2-130B. Two Type 5 trigger guards. The one on the left has been shortened with a file, possibly by an armorer.

Two variations of the Type 5 trigger guard plate are encountered. The **1st Variation** had a front guard screw post 0.600 inch high and the Type 2 trigger guard. The **2nd Variation** had a front guard screw post only 0.590 inch high. The height of the front guard screw post may have been reduced by military armorers so that the shorter front guard screw could be used, see Figure 2-130B. It also had the Type 3 winter trigger guard.

Model 1903 Springfield Rifle and Its Variations

The **Type 6** trigger guard plate was manufactured by Remington Arms for the M1903A4 rifle, refer to Figure 2-130A (arrow 1) and also see Figure 2-130C. It was identical to the Type 5 trigger guard plate except for a "pad" between the front of the magazine box and the front guard screw (arrow 1). The pad was made of sheet steel and was folded into an inverted "U" to form a shelf or leaf that was tack welded to the trigger guard plate. The pad pressed against the wood in the area inletted for the trigger guard plate to stabilize it. The Type 6 trigger guard plate was blued and had the Type 3 trigger guard.

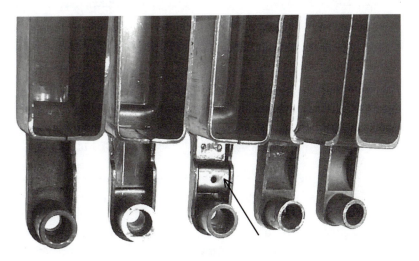

Fig. 2-130C. Trigger guard plates (r-l): Model 1903, Type 3; Caliber .22 gallery rifle, Type 4; Remington M1903A4, Type 6; Remington M1903A3, Type 5 and Smith Corona M1903A3, Type 7.

The **Type 7** trigger guard plate was manufactured by Smith Corona for the M1903A3 rifle. It was very similar to that made by Remington. They can be differentiated by the fact that the front guard screw on the Remington is separated from the magazine box by a straight line while the front guard screw on the Smith Corona trigger guard plate is surrounded by a curved line, refer to Figures 2-130A, arrow 2 and 2-130C.

Model 1903 Springfield Rifle and Its Variations

The Type 7 trigger guard plate reinforcing ribs on the sides of the magazine box are much narrower and when viewed from above, form shallow "V"s. The Smith Corona Type 7 had the Type 2 trigger guard and was Parkerized.

Smith Corona Type 7 trigger guard plates are usually not marked, although sometimes one with an "X" stamped on the rear of the magazine wall will be seen.

NOTE: The M1903 and M1903A3 trigger guard plates and magazine box are interchangeable with some slight fitting. But they were not interchanged as an Ordnance Department-approved practice.

TRIGGER GUARD PLATE AND MAGAZINE MARKINGS
Trigger guard plates and magazines manufactured at Springfield and Rock Island are unmarked with the single exception of the Type 2 trigger guard plate which has a small "S" stamped near the magazine catch to indicate that the trigger slot has been reduced in length.

The Type 5 trigger guard plate manufactured by Remington Arms is marked "R." The Remington "R" may be in a circle or freestanding and is usually stamped on the right rear panel of the magazine box. Smith Corona Type 7 trigger guards are usually unmarked although occasionally one stamped "X" on the back of the magazine box may be encountered.

TRIGGER GUARD
Three types of trigger guards were manufactured, see Figure 2-131. The **Type 1** M1903 trigger guard did not change from the start to the end of manufacture at either Springfield or Rock Island and was used on all service rifles, national match rifles, "Style T" rifles and .22-caliber gallery rifles. It was an integral part of the trigger guard plate.

The **Type 2** trigger guard was used on late Model 1903 (Modified)

Model 1903 Springfield Rifle and Its Variations

and M1903A3 rifles by Remington and Smith Corona. It was a separate piece stamped from sheet metal and welded to the trigger guard floor plate. The opening for the finger in the trigger guard was 1.8 inches long by 1.0 inch high.

The **Type 3** trigger guard was also used exclusively on the M1903A3 rifle. It had a larger opening for a shooter wearing gloves and is often referred to as the "Arctic" or "Winter" trigger guard. Although the trigger guard opening is 1.8 inches long by 1.1 inches high, only 0.1 inch higher than the Type 2, the difference in configuration is readily noticeable.

MAGAZINE FLOOR PLATE

The magazine floor plate was a separate piece that was held to the bottom of the magazine by a front

Fig. 2-131. Top, Type 1, M1903/1903A1 trigger guard; middle, Type 2 M1903A3 trigger guard and bottom, Type 3 M1903A3 winter trigger guard.

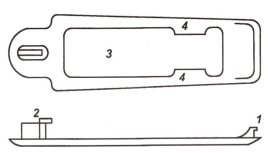

Fig. 2-132. M1903 rifle magazine floor plate.

lip and the floor plate catch at the rear. It was removable for cleaning and emptying the magazine. Three types of floor plates were used.

The **Type 1** floor plate was used on all Model 1903 rifles, see Figure

251

Model 1903 Springfield Rifle and Its Variations

2-132. It was 4.25 inches long by 1.0 inch wide at the front and 1.10 inches wide at the rear. It had a lip (1) milled into the front that hooked over the front edge of the magazine well and a lug (2) at the rear that was captured by the magazine floor plate catch. The interior of the floor plate was milled out to accommodate the magazine spring (3) which was captured at the forward end of the plate by twin lips (4).

Fig. 2-133. Left, M1903 floor plate; right, M1922, M1922M1 and M2 .22-caliber gallery rifle floor plate.

The **Type 2** floor plate was used on the M1922, M1 and M2 gallery rifles. It had the same dimensions as the Type 1 plate but had two openings cut through for the magazine and magazine catch as shown in Figure 2-133. These floor plates were specially made for the Gallery Rifles as they lacked the interior milling for the magazine spring. They were marked with the part number C4007.

NOTE: The M1903A4 did not have a separate removable floor plate.

The **Type 3** floor plate was used on the National Match, "Style T," Sporters and International Match rifles. The only difference between it and the Type 1 floor plate appears to be a deeper polish for a better finish.

Magazine Spring
The magazine spring is a repeating "Z" anchored to the floor plate. It pushes the follower and cartridges up, see Figure 2-134. Three types of magazine springs were developed and used. All were made from

spring steel. The top end of the spring was either rebated or tapered to slide between the fingers on the underside of the floor plate.

The **Type 1** magazine spring is characterized by rounded crimps at its bends and squared ends. The spring was 4.1 inches high when extended. It was used throughout M1903 production. Two variations are seen: the **1st Variation** had clipped corners at the bottom only. The top of the spring ends were

Fig. 2-134. Magazine springs for the M1903 rifle: left, Type 1; right, Type 2. Note the rolled and crimped bends in the Type 1 spring.

square. The **2nd Variation** had clipped corners at both ends. The clips were cut at a 45-degree angle.

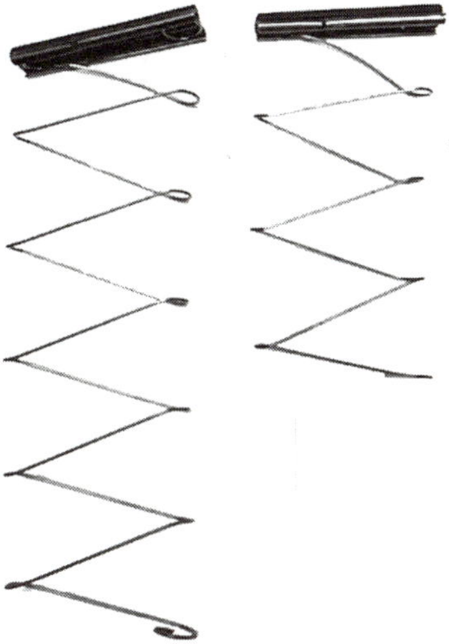

The **Type 2** magazine spring had "rounded" bends and round corners and was 5.2 inches high when extended. It was used in the Remington M1903, M1903 (Modified), and the M1903A3 and A4 rifles. Those manufactured by Remington are marked "R."

The **Type 3** magazine spring was made from steel wire 0.067 inch in diameter and was made for the so-called Air Service magazine, see Figure 2-135. Two variations were used: the 1st Variation had six "Z"

Fig. 2-135. Left, magazine coil spring for the Air Service magazine; right, coil spring for the sniper rifle extended magazine.

segments for the twenty-five-round magazine. The **2nd Variation** had four "Z" segments for the possible sniper rifle version. The top end of both springs was coiled at the rear to hold it in the Type 5 follower. It was not interchangeable with the Types 1-3 magazine springs or Types 1-4 followers. See Type 3 on page 261 for a more detailed explanation.

NOTE: Magazine springs show a blue color from the tempering process. In many cases, the blue is mottled with patches of red. This may have been due to impurities on the metal during the tempering process. It is not reflective either of serviceability or of period of manufacturing as the mottled coloring has been observed at all periods in both M1903 and M1903A3 manufacture. Springs with a Parkerized finish have been refinished.

NOTE: The M1903 Springfield and the M1917 Enfield used the same magazine spring interchangeably. The magazine spring used in the British Pattern 1914 Enfield has a longer upper arm and will not fit in the M1903 magazine but will fit in either the British Pattern 14 or American M1917 Enfield.

FOLLOWER

The follower forms the top of the magazine and rides up and down on the magazine spring to lift cartridges into the path of the bolt, see Figure 2-136. The top of the follower is divided by a rib (C) to the left of center that stacks the cartridges one atop of the other in the magazine. The bottom of the follower has two fingers (D) at the front end under which the magazine spring slides and a step (E) at the rear to prevent the spring from backing out. Five types were used.

The **Type 1** follower had square ends and was used in the M1903 rod bayonet rifle. Because it did not feed cartridges well, the **Type 2** was developed in 1905-06 with rounded corners at the front and rear and was used in the balance of M1903 service rifle production. Both the Type 1 and Type 2 were milled from bar stock.

Model 1903 Springfield Rifle and Its Variations

NOTE: The Type 2 follower was also used in the M1917 Enfield manufactured by Remington and Eddystone and marked "R" and "E" respectively. Winchester followers had a "hook" 0.715 inch long on the front underside, are marked "W" and are not interchangeable.

The **Type 3** follower was used in the National Match rifles and has been observed in some International Match rifles. The rib was highly polished to provide smoother feeding.

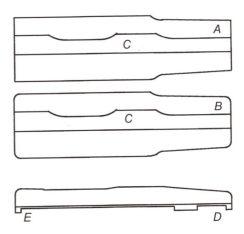

Fig. 2-136. M1903 magazine follower: Above and middle, top view of Types 1 and 2 followers showing square (A) and rounded ends (B) and ribs (C); bottom, view showing fingers (D) and step (E).

The **Type 4** follower was similar to the Type 2 except that it was made from stamped steel rather than milled from bar stock. The top of the follower with the rib and fingers was stamped first, then spot-welded to plates at the front and rear which provided stiffening. The front plate also prevented the spring from sliding forward while a raised tab on the rear plate prevented it from sliding backward. The Type 4 was used in the M1903A3 rifles. Those manufactured by Remington are marked "R"; those by Smith Corona are marked "X" or are unmarked.

The **Type 5** follower was manufactured for use in the Periscope rifle, and later, in the Air Service and Sniper rifles, see Figure 2-137. It was stamped from sheet steel but had guides on the underside to allow the Type 3 Magazine Spring to be captured and held. The followers are unmarked.

Model 1903 Springfield Rifle and Its Variations

Fig. 2-137. Magazine follower developed for the Periscope rifles and later used in the Air Service and Sniper rifle magazines.

GUARD SCREWS

The front and rear guard screws held the trigger guard and magazine in place in the stock, see Figure 2-138. The guard screws remained basically the same from the start of M1903 production through the end of M1903A3 production, with only the front guard screw being lengthened slightly to prevent stripping in the M1903A3.

REAR GUARD SCREWS

Two types of rear guard screws were used. The **Type 1** rear guard screw was 1.60 inches long, had a shank length of 1.450 inches and a head 0.08 inch thick at the rim. These screws were used on all Springfield M1903 and M1903A1 rifles and Rock Island M1903 rifles. See Table 25, page 259.

The Type 1 guard screw thread pattern followed the standard Springfield practice in use since the start of the Springfield Armory in 1794. It was based on the metric thread pattern used on the French Charleville muskets which had served as a pattern for the U.S. Model 1795 Musket. The top and bottom of each thread was rounded rather than left sharp.

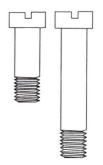

Fig. 2-138. Front and rear trigger guard screws.

The **Type 2** rear guard screw was also 1.60 inches long, had a shank length of 1.450 inches and a head thickness of 0.01 inch at the rim. These screws were used on all Remington Model 1903 (Modified) and M1903A3 rifles and Smith Corona M1903A3 rifles. Types 1 and 2 rear guard screws can be used interchangeably.

Model 1903 Springfield Rifle and Its Variations

The Type 2 screw, manufactured by Remington and Smith Corona and their subcontractors, followed the American Standard Form. It had a sharp "V" thread with sides forming a 60-degree angle. Even though it is called a sharp "V," the top and bottom of the thread have a slight flat. Even so, Types 1, 2 and 3 rear guard screws are able to be used interchangeably.

FRONT GUARD SCREWS

The **Type 1** guard screw threaded into a hole in the recoil lug. It was 1.20 inches long with a shank length of 0.800 inch. The hole for the front barrel guard screw in the recoil lug was blind and the screw did not bottom against it. It was manufactured by Springfield and Rock Island Armories for the M1903 and M1903A1 rifles and had the standard Springfield rounded "V" thread.

The **Type 2** front guard screw was also 1.20 inches long with a shank length of 0.800 inch. It was manufactured by Remington for the M1903, M1903 (Modified) and early M1903A3 rifles. It had the American Standard Form sharp "V" thread.

The **Type 3** front guard screw was 1.30 inches long with a shank length of 0.900 inch and had the American Standard Form thread. In the M1903A3 rifle, the guard screw hole in the recoil lug was drilled 0.1 inch deeper to eliminate the use of a bottoming tap. Both the 1.20-inch-long Types 1 and 2 screws supposedly did not penetrate far enough into the thread and were prone to "stripping" out. Accordingly, the Type 3 screw was lengthened 0.1 inch, which eliminated that problem. But when the Type 3 screw was used in the M1903 or M1903A1 receiver, it bottomed in the hole before it was fully turned in and prevented the barreled receiver from bedding properly in the stock. Unfortunately the problem was not immediately recognized and the three types of screws were not segregated. Nor did the 1943 or 1944 editions of the Technical Manual 9-1270 mention the change in length. Accuracy problems resulted when the longer Type 3 screw was used

Model 1903 Springfield Rifle and Its Variations

in receivers in which the front guard screw hole was only 0.490 inch deep.

NOTE: Do not install Type 3 front guard screws in M1903 or M1903A1 rifles or accuracy will be affected.

Type 1 front guard screw heads are 0.08 inch thick at the rim; Types 2 and 3 front guard screw heads are 0.1 inch thick at the rim.

Dimensions for the guard screws are presented in Table 25.

Rear Guard Screw Bushing

While not a part of the trigger guard and magazine, the rear guard screw bushing was associated closely with it and so is described here

again. It was a steel tube 1.10 inches long by 0.270 inch in diameter which was inserted into the stock at the back of the trigger guard plate inletting. The rear guard screw passed through the bushing which allowed it to be tightened without danger of crushing the wood and loosening the wood-to-metal fit, see Figure 2-139.

This guard screw bushing was used in all variations of the M1903 rifle including both the M1903A3 and M1903A4.

Fig. 2-139. Rear guard screw bushing.

The front guard screw passes directly through the trigger plate guard lug and into the recoil lug, eliminating the need for a bushing at that point.

Detachable Magazines

Five types of detachable magazines were developed, three for the .30-caliber rifles and two for .22-caliber Gallery rifles.

Model 1903 Springfield Rifle and Its Variations

Table 25 M1903 and M1903A3 Guard Screws, Rear and Front, Dimensions in Inches			
	Type 1	Type 2	Type 3
Rear Guard Screw			
Overall Length	1.600	1.600	N/A
Shank	1.450	1.450	N/A
Head Diameter	0.340	0.340	N/A
Head Thickness	0.080	0.100	N/A
Thread Length	0.680	0.680	N/A
Screw Tip	Flat	Flat	N/A
Front Guard Screw			
Overall Length	1.200	1.200	1.300
Shank	0.800	0.800	0.900
Head Diameter	0.340	0.340	0.345
Head Thickness	0.080	0.100	0.100
Thread Length	0.435	0.435	0.440
Screw Tip	Flat	Flat	Flat

All .30-caliber detachable magazines consisted of a magazine box (no separate floor plate), magazine spring and follower. The .22-caliber detachable magazines added a thumbpiece on the right slide which attached through a slot in the magazine wall to the follower. Using the thumbpiece, the follower could be depressed to aid in loading the magazine.

Model 1903 Springfield Rifle and Its Variations

NOTE: With the exception of the magazines for the .22-caliber gallery rifles, the magazines developed for the "Trench rifle," "Air Service rifle" and "Sniper rifle" are semidetachable at best. They formed the lower part of the internal magazine box and the floor plate attaching catch held them in place. While they could be detached in the field for cleaning, they were not meant to be removed to insert another loaded magazine in their place. Loading was accomplished through the top of the receiver using five-round clips or individual cartridges as with the standard service M1903 rifle.

The **Type 1** .30-caliber magazine was developed for the trench rifle with the pivoting stock and a "sitascope attachment" — a type of periscope that allowed a soldier to fire over the lip of a trench while remaining under cover. The magazine attached to the rifle in place of the standard floor plate. The magazine "extension," as it was termed, was also used with the M1910 "Air Service" rifles to be issued to aircraft and observation balloon crew. Although the rifles were never issued, a large quantity of the magazines were manufactured. It held twenty-five .30-M1906 cartridges and is shown in Figure 2-140.

Cover

Magazine

Follower and Spring

Fig. 2-140. Twenty-five-round Air Service rifle magazine. Craig Riesch collection.

The **Type 2** .30-caliber magazine was developed for the "U.S. Automatic Pistol, Cal. .30, Model of 1918" (Pedersen Device) for the M1903 Mark I rifle, see Figure 2-141. The magazine held 40 ".30 Auto-Pistol Ball Cartridges, Model of 1918" and weighed 1.07 lbs loaded and 0.34 lb empty. The

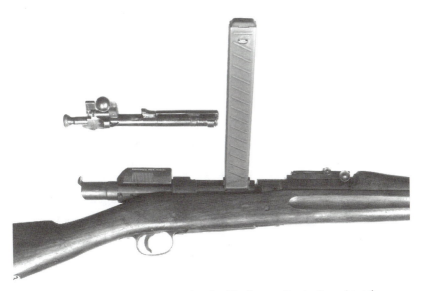

Fig. 2-141. Forty-round magazine for the "Pedersen Device"-equipped M1903 Mk. I rifle. Photo courtesy Remington Arms Corporation and Roy

magazine had ribs pressed into the surface of the sheet steel sides for reinforcement. On the rear face, visible to the shooter, were small numbered holes indicating the number of cartridges remaining.

The **Type 3** .30-caliber magazine (Figure 2-142) is thought to have been developed as an auxiliary fifteen-round

Fig. 2-142. Fifteen-round magazine for the M1903A4 sniper rifle. The magazine was apparently never issued for service. North Cape Publications collection.

Model 1903 Springfield Rifle and Its Variations

magazine for the M1903A4 or earlier sniper rifles. Locked into the M1903 trigger guard plate in place of the normal floor plate, it extends 2.81 inches below the stock and holds fifteen rounds of .30-M1906 ammunition. It was made by reducing the "Air Service" twenty-five-round magazine or else was newly constructed precisely as the Type 1 magazine for the Trench or Air Service rifle. No original documentation has yet been located.

 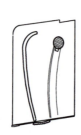 

Fig. 2-143. Left, M1922 magazine; middle, M1922M1 magazine and right, M2 magazine for the .22-caliber gallery rifles.

The **Type 4** magazine was developed for the .22-caliber Gallery rifles, Figure 2-143. Three variations were designed. The **1st Variation** was used for the M1922 .22-Caliber Gallery Rifle. It was 2.10 inches high and protruded below the bottom of the receiver. Its capacity was five rounds. The **2nd Variation** magazine was 1.910 inches high and flush with the bottom of the receiver. It was sometimes marked "M1" in the upper left corner. The **3rd Variation** was the

Fig. 2-144. .22-caliber gallery rifle magazines in trigger guards: rear, Type 4, 2nd Variation M1922 M1; front, Type 4, 3rd Variation M2. Note marking on the M2 magazine.

same as the 2nd variation but was longer (1.925 high by 1.325 wide and 0.360 thick) so that the top of the magazine was more in line with the chamber, see Fig. 2-144. It was marked "M2."

Model 1903 Springfield Rifle and Its Variations

CARTRIDGE HOLDER FOR THE HOFFER-THOMPSON RIFLE

The cartridge holder for the Hoffer-Thompson .22-caliber gallery rifle was made to simulate the .30-caliber cartridge with an extended neck which served as a chamber for the .22-caliber short cartridge, see Figure 2-145. The cartridge was inserted into the device. A spring-loaded firing pin with two strikers pushed the cartridge firmly into the neck, or chamber. The cartridge holder was then inserted into the

Fig. 2-145. Hoffer-Thompson .22-caliber cartridge holder. Phil Siess collection.

breech of the Hoffer-Thompson .22-caliber rifle and the bolt closed. When the trigger was pulled, the sear released the firing pin which struck the firing pin in the back of the cartridge holder and ignited the rimfire cartridge. The bullet passed through the chamber of the device into the .22-caliber bore of the barrel.

The cartridge holders could be inserted one at a time into the breech or slid into standard cartridge clips and loaded five at a time into the magazine. To eject the spent case, a separate tool was used. It was a steel or brass rod mounted in a screwdriver handle.

The cartridge holder was the weakest point of the system as it was difficult to keep clean and also corroded easily. Loading live rounds and unloading spent cases was time-consuming and hard on the fingers.

Model 1903 Springfield Rifle and Its Variations

SIGHTS

The sights used on the M1903 Springfield were the descendants of that designed by Lt. Col. R.A. Buffington, commanding officer of the National Armory at Springfield, MA, in 1884-1885 and developed for use on the M1884 .45-70 Springfield Rifle. The "Buffington" rear sight incorporated an adjustment for windage with greater precision than previously and the slide was designed to compensate for normal bullet drift (windless day) as it was raised to higher elevations.

By 1901, the original design had undergone many changes and improvements. It had also evolved into two variations: one that had built-in bullet drift compensation (Model 1901) and one that did not (Model 1902). This last was the final type of rear sight to be installed on the last Krag rifles manufactured or refurbished. In the 1902 rear sight (as in the M1898 rear sight) a tangent (curved) base replaced the stepped base that had evolved from that first used on the Model 1842 Rifle (Mississippi Rifle) through the Krag Model 1896 rear sight base. The tangent base allowed the rear sight to be used at extreme elevations without raising the sight leaf. Serrations along the left side held the slide securely against recoil when the binding knob was tightened and a peep sight for use at extreme elevations was also added. The M1902 sight was selected for use on the Model 1903 rifle and was installed on all rod bayonet rifles.

But the Board of officers, which convened in 1905 to evaluate the rear sight in view of the many complaints from the field, recommended a modification of the Model 1901 rear sight be used instead. The M1901 rear sight had a sloped base with a single step at the front, on which the slide rode to adjust the range. Instead of a "peep" the M1901 rear sight employed a sighting notch with a second notch at the top of the ladder plus a "peep" hole on the drift slide. The base was manufactured in two parts: the bottom was secured to the barrel via two screws and the upper part was secured to the bottom at front with a bolt which also served as an axis. Windage adjustments were made by loosening a binding lever on the front base and swiveling the upper

Model 1903 Springfield Rifle and Its Variations

part of the base to the right or left, see Figure 2-146.

The parts of the M1905 rear sight are: 1) fixed base spline, 2) fixed sight base, 3) fixed rear sight base pin, 4) windage knob, 5) windage spring, 6) windage screw collar, 7) windage screw, 8) joint pin, 9) rear sight moveable base, 10) base spring, 11) slide binding screw, 12) slide, 13) slide cap pin, 14) elevation leaf, 15) drift slide, 16) slide cap and 17) slide cap screw.

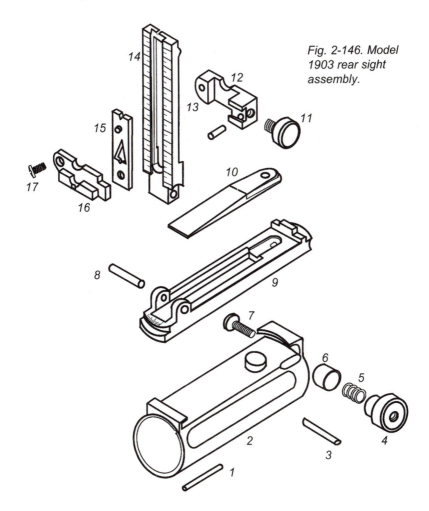

Fig. 2-146. Model 1903 rear sight assembly.

Model 1903 Springfield Rifle and Its Variations

Taking advantage of the pause in manufacturing to remodel the rifle for the Model 1905 knife bayonet, the M1901 rear sight was redesigned to make it more efficient. The binding lever was eliminated in favor of a side-mounted adjusting screw. The automatic wind-drift compensation of the M1901 rifle rear sight was retained, and the ladder was widened slightly. The slide was used almost exactly as designed for the M1901 rear sight. It was slightly wider, thicker and the left side was rounded. The new sight leaf was graduated for the M1903 cartridge with a 220-grain round-nose bullet. When the 150-grain spire point bullet was adopted in 1906, the graduations were changed to conform to the ballistics of the new cartridge.

When the new rear sight was adopted in 1905, the Ordnance Department took advantage of the manufacturing hiatus to also redesign the front sight. The original M1903 front sight was a band around the barrel into which the sight itself was dovetailed. This did not allow for sufficient lateral adjustment during targeting and so an inordinately high number of barrels were rejected. The redesign retained the band around the barrel and also included a moveable sight base in the dovetail. The sight was then pinned into the moveable sight base. The ability to adjust the base in the dovetail allowed for greater latitude in targeting and reduced the number of rejected barrels. When the M1906 cartridge was adopted, the new sight height was adjusted accordingly.

The process of developing the M1905 front and rear sight is described in the sections on the "United States Magazine Rifle, Caliber .30, Model of 1903 — 1st Alteration (.30-M1903)" and the "United States Magazine Rifle, Caliber .30, Model of 1903 — 2nd Alteration (.30-M1906)."

NOTE: The M1905 rear sight was designed so that when the leaf was in the down position and the slide was at its rearmost position, the battle sight was set automatically. With the 2,450 yard leaf and the .30-M1903 cartridge, the battle sight setting was 400 yards. With the 2,850 yard leaf and the .30-M1906 cartridge, the battle sight setting

Model 1903 Springfield Rifle and Its Variations

was 530 yards to 1911, 547 yards after. The battle sight setting meant that, all else being equal, the bullet would strike a human target when the rifle was aimed at any range between 100 and 547 yards with no further adjustment needed to the sight.

Experience during World War I conditions had shown that the open notch sight mounted far forward on the barrel was not the ideal rear sight for wartime conditions. Several proposals for developing an aperture or "peep" sight were put forth but all failed for lack of money and resources. When the M1 Garand was developed in the 1930s, it was equipped with an aperture sight mounted on the rear of the receiver very close to the eye. When Remington Arms began to produce the M1903 rifle in 1941, the Ordnance Department took the opportunity to develop an aperture sight. It is described in the paragraphs following the M1905 rear sight.

REAR SIGHT
FIXED REAR SIGHT BASE

The fixed rear sight base (M1905) is generally described as a steel band that encircled the barrel just ahead of the receiver face and was secured with a pin (1) at the front bottom and a spline (2) at the rear 1 o'clock position, see Figure 2-147. The pin prevented forward and rearward movement and the spline, left and right movement.

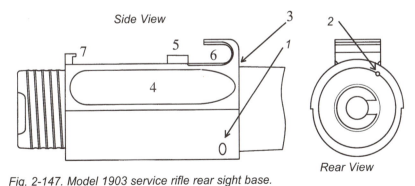

Fig. 2-147. Model 1903 service rifle rear sight base.

Model 1903 Springfield Rifle and Its Variations

The front of the fixed base was undercut (3) to secure the handguard rear tenon. The sides of the fixed base were relieved (4) to reduce the weight of the assembly. A round lug (5) projected above the flat top of the fixed base and acted as a pivot for the moveable base. There are two lips on the top of the fixed base: the forward lip (6) was undercut to accept the moveable base front lip and windage screw; the rear lip (7) was also undercut to accept the lip on the rear of the moveable base. The fixed base was assembled to the barrel using a special fixture, the setup inspected for accuracy and then holes drilled and reamed for the spline and pin.

Four types of fixed rear sight bases were used. The **Type 1** rear sight base was used with the M1903 rear sight, see Figure 2-148. Its platform was fixed in place and windage adjustments to the rear sight were made on the eyepiece. It was not a solid band like the later Types 3 and 4 but had two rings which encircled the barrel, leaving a gap between them. It was used on the original M1903 rod bayonet rifles. The Type 1 rear sight base was held in position by a base pin which was inserted through a hole in the top front of the band and passed through a groove in the barrel (arrow).

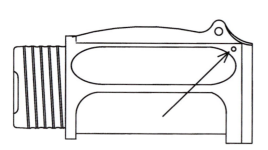

Fig. 2-148. Model 1903 rear sight base, Type 1.

The **Type 2** rear sight base was designed for the Model 1905 rear sight, see Figure 2-149. It had a pivot lug on which the rear sight assembly turned as it was adjusted for windage. The sight leaf traveled under an undercut lug (1) at the rear and a larger undercut at the front (2). When the sight was rotated past the lugs, it could be lifted off. The Type 2 rear sight base was similar to the Type 1 but the base pin hole was moved from the top front to the bottom front (3) of the rear sight base. The front curve of the lightening cut was also elongated toward the front of the base (4) as can be seen in the illustration.

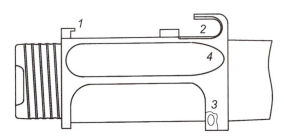

Fig. 2-149. Model 1903 rear sight base, Type 2.

Problems with "springing," or a tendency to twist on the barrel, led to the Type 2's replacement in October 1907 with the **Type 3** rear sight base. The base was changed to a solid steel band to eliminate the possibility of springing, see Figure 2-150, arrow. Otherwise, it was identical to the Type 2. And it remained unchanged to the end of production.

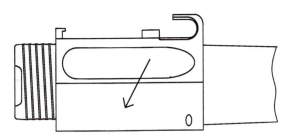

Fig. 2-150. Model 1903 rear sight base, Type 3.

The **Type 4** fixed sight base was manufactured by Remington and installed on the Remington M1903 and M1903 (Modified). It was identical to the Type 3 rear sight base.

The **Type 5** fixed sight base was also manufactured by Remington and was installed on M1903 (Modified) rifles. It lacked the lightening cuts on the sides below the sight, see Figure 2-151.

269

Model 1903 Springfield Rifle and Its Variations

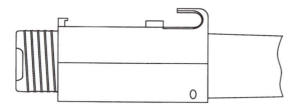

Fig. 2-151. Model 1905 rear sight base, Type 5.

SLIDE

The slide traveled up and down the leaf to set the elevation. It was secured at the desired elevation when the slide screw knob was tightened. When the leaf was flat on the base, the aperture on the slide was at the "battle sight" setting (530 yards to 1911, 547 yards after). The standard aperture width was 0.045 inch.

Seven types of slides were used. The slide moved along the leaf to raise it on the rails of the sloped base. A slide screw knob on the right side tightened the slide against the serrations on the left side of the leaf to hold it at the chosen elevation, see Figure 2-152.

The **Type 1** slide had seven parts: 1) slide, 2) sectioned view of the slide, 3) slide screw, 4) slide pin, 5) slide

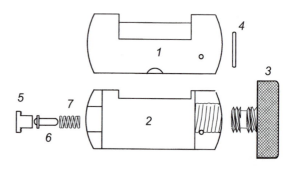

Fig. 2-152. Type 1, Model 1905 rear sight slide: above, slide cap; below, slide.

shoe, 6) slide spring plunger and 7) slide spring. It was used on the Model 1903 rear sight and when used lying flat in the battle sight setting, the range was 400 yards. The sight notch was 0.045 inch wide.

The **Type 2** slide was similar to the Type 1 but had a 0.125-inch-wide sight notch cut into the sight bar and was used with the Type 2, 2,450 yard leaf.

Model 1903 Springfield Rifle and Its Variations

The **Type 3** slide was developed for the Model 1905 rear sight, see Figure 2-153. It is composed of five parts: 1) the slide itself which contains a screw hole on the left side for the slide cap screw, an open sighting "U" notch, slide binding screw hole on the right and a smaller hole for the slide binding screw pin hole; 2)

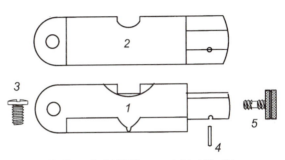

Fig. 2-153. Type 3, M1905 rear sight drift slide.

the slide cap which has an open "U" notch on its top, the screw hole for the slide cap screw on the left side, an open notch to allow the slide screw to pass, and a clearance cut for the open notch in the drift slide, 3) the slide cap screw, 4) the slide binding screw pin which prevents the accidental removal of the slide binding screw when it is loosened and 5) the slide screw. When used with the Type 3, 2,450 yard leaf of the M1905 sight and the .30-1903 cartridge, the battle sight setting with the leaf down and the slide in the rearmost position was 400 yards. When used with the Type 4, 2,850 yard leaf, the battle sight setting was

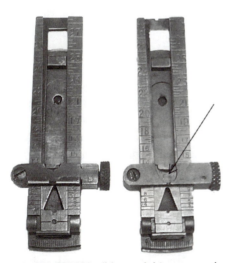

Fig. 2-154. M1939 slide on right compared to the M1905 on the left. Note the deeper and wider clearance cut for the sight notch (arrow). Craig Riesch collection.

Model 1903 Springfield Rifle and Its Variations

530 yards until 1911 when it was revised to 547 yards.

The **Type 4** slide was developed in 1939, see Figure 2-154. The only difference between it and the Type 3 slide was the shape of the clearance cut for the open notch. It was made deeper and wider to allow more light through the notch. It does not appear to have been widely issued and was not manufactured either by Remington or Springfield Armory during the 1944-45 contracts for replacement parts.

Right after World War I, the U.S. Marine Corps adopted a wider and higher sight blade for the M1903 rifle. This required a slide with a wider (0.10-inch) notch (**Type 5**) and a drift slide with a 0.10-inch aperture. The combination of the No. 10 front sight and the No. 10 drift slide provided a 250-yard battle sight. These slides were used primarily on M1903 and M1903A1 rifles rebuilt for use during World War II.

The **Type 6** slide was a World War II expediency. To shorten manufacturing time and eliminate precision machining, the slide cap was thickened which eliminated the need for the sight bar. The sight notch was cut through the thickened slide cap.

The rapid-fire course in the National Matches was fired with the battle sight. The **Type 7** slide was developed for use in the National Matches to allow the shooter a wider choice. The **1st Variation** had a sighting notch 0.035 inch wide and the **2nd Variation** had a notch 0.055 inch wide.

DRIFT SLIDE

The drift slide was only used on the M1905 rear sight, see Figure 2-155. It rides up and down on the leaf and is secured to the slide cap by the slide cap screw and the slide cap pin. Tightening the slide binding screw secures the drift slide in place. The drift slide has four sighting apertures:a) peep (circular hole), b) field view (open triangle), c-d)

Model 1903 Springfield Rifle and Its Variations

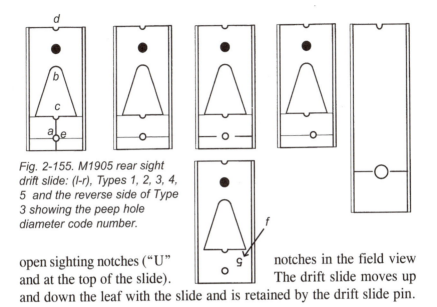

Fig. 2-155. M1905 rear sight drift slide: (l-r), Types 1, 2, 3, 4, 5 and the reverse side of Type 3 showing the peep hole diameter code number.

open sighting notches ("U" and at the top of the slide). notches in the field view The drift slide moves up and down the leaf with the slide and is retained by the drift slide pin.

The drift slide has two lines scribed across its width to allow the different apertures to be lined up with the desired distance on the leaf range scale (e). The top line extends outward from the lower edges of the field view triangle and the bottom line extends horizontally on either side of the peep.

The lower aperture or peep hole was 0.05 inch in diameter. The upper triangular-shaped aperture with a notch at the bottom was 0.26 inch wide by 0.300 inch high. The bottom sighting notch was 0.02 inch deep and scalloped on the side away from the shooter's eye.

NOTE: Until December 1907 (circa serial # 250,000) the size of the peep hole in the drift slide was 0.05 inch. After, slides with peep holes of 0.04 and 0.06 inch were also adopted and included as spare parts. Over the years other sizes were added — 0.07, 0.08 and 0.09 inch. All drift slides were numbered on the back to correspond: 0.05 inch = 5, 0.06 inch = 6 and so on (f).

273

Model 1903 Springfield Rifle and Its Variations

Five types of drift sides were used. The **Type 1** drift slide was used only for a short time — probably no more than a few months. In addition to the two horizontal lines, it had a third and vertical line filled with platinum scribed top to bottom through the lower peep sight. This was found to be unnecessary and was quickly discontinued. Most of these appear to have been used on the altered M1903 rifles.

The **Type 2** drift slide was almost identical to the Type 1 but lacked the platinum-filled vertical line through the lower peep sight.

The **Type 3** drift slide was introduced at circa serial #1,265,000. In the Types 1 and 2 drift slide, the horizontal line extending from the peep hole actually touched the edge of the peep. As the line was die stamped, it was feared that this might distort the peep hole. The line was shortened so that it did not touch the peep hole.

The **Type 4** drift slide was designed for use by National Match shooters. It had the peep hole offset to either the left or right to correct the wind gauge setting to zero. These drift slides were supposedly only available at the National Matches at Camp Perry.

The **Type 5** slide was designed by Col. D. C. McDougal, U.S.M.C., to provide a brighter sight picture and thus improve marksmanship in combat and on the target range. It was designated the "No. 10 Drift Slide." It had a lower aperture of 0.10 inch and was 2.75 times brighter than the standard 0.06-inch aperture. The upper aperture remained 0.26 inch wide by 0.300 inch high with a 0.02-inch sighting notch. It did not have the triangular field view.

SLIDE BINDING SCREW

The rear sight slide binding screw clamps the slide to the sight. It was 0.490 inch in diameter by 0.130 inch thick. Four types were used, see Figure 2-156.

Model 1903 Springfield Rifle and Its Variations

The **Type 1** slide screw was used on the M1903 rear sight slide. It was 0.5 inch in diameter and 0.16 inch thick. Its circumference was knurled. It was slotted with reliefs on either side like the Krag M1902, Type 4 slide screw.

The **Type 2** slide screw was used on the Model 1905 rear slight slide. It was 0.490 inch in diameter and 0.130 inch thick, was knurled about the circumference, had a central groove running around the circumference and its outer surface was dished with a central boss. It was used with both the 2,800 and 2,450 yard type leaf.

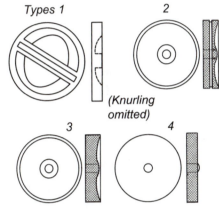

Fig. 2-156. Slide screws for the M1905 rear sight slide, Types 1, 2, 3 and 4.

The **Type 3** slide screw was also 0.490 inch in diameter and 0.130 inch thick. It was knurled but did not have the center groove about the circumference. It was used during WWI.

The **Type 4** slide screw lacked the dished outer surface and was flat. Otherwise, it was similar to the Type 3. The Type 4 was used only on slides manufactured late in World War I (circa serial number 1,130,100 in 1919) and for a short period thereafter. The Type 3 slide screw was used during all the rest of production. It was used in the interwar period.

The **Type 5** slide screw was manufactured by Remington Arms for the Remington Model 1903 and Model 1903 (Modified). It was identical to the Type 4. A few have been observed marked "R."

275

Model 1903 Springfield Rifle and Its Variations

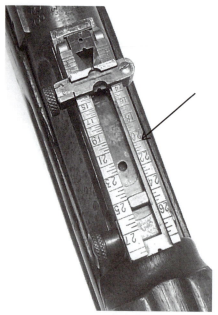

Fig. 2-157. M1905 rear sight leaf, Type 4.

REAR SIGHT LEAF

The rear sight leaf was 3.025 inches long by 0.705 inch wide. The base had a hole drilled through for the leaf pin and the top bar had a "U" notch for sighting at extreme ranges. The end of the spring bore against the round base to hold it in position. It had an opening through its center which varied from 0.275 inch wide at the bottom to 0.280 inch at the top and was 2.85 inches long. This allowed the drift slide to compensate for bullet drift up to 600 yards, see Figure 2-157.

The range scale was marked on the face of the leaf (arrow). Range gradations depended on the cartridge being used. Even-numbered gradations were scribed on the left side and odd numbered on the right. In all but one sight leaf, a "U" notch at the top extended the range by either 50 or 100 yards. Lines which extended across the leaf were at 100-yard intervals, lines extending halfway across the leaf were 50-yard intervals and the shortest lines extending one-quarter of the way were 25-yard intervals.

When the sight leaf was down, the sighting notch on the slide was set for the battle sight position. The Type 1 leaf battle sight setting was 400 yards; in 1908 the battle sight range was set 530 yards and in 1911, it was changed to 547 yards. When the leaf was raised vertically, the shooter had a choice of four additional sighting positions: 1) The 0.06-inch-diameter peep sight on bottom of the drift slide could be used at ranges from 100 to 2,350 yards by adjusting the slide up or

Model 1903 Springfield Rifle and Its Variations

down the leaf so that the scribed line bisecting the peep was in line with the chosen range. 2) The sighting notch at the bottom of the field view on the drift slide was also used at ranges between 100 and 2,450 yards. 3) The "U" notch on the top of the drift slide was used at ranges from 1,400 to 2,750 yards. 4) For the extreme range of 2,850 yards, the "U" notch at the leaf top was used.

Fig. 2-158. Type 1 Model 1903 rear sight installed on the rod bayonet rifle.

Eight types of sight leaves were designed and employed. All were blued except for the Types 5 and 7, which were Parkerized.

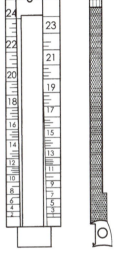

Fig. 2-159. M1905 Type 2 rear sight leaf, for the 1st Alteration Model 1903 rifle.

The **Type 1** sight leaf was of the tangent type and was used with the Model 1903 rear sight and the .30-M1903 cartridge. It was graduated to 2,400 yards for the .30-M1903 220-grain bullet and was blued. The "U" notch at the top of the leaf gave a range of 2,500 yards. Range gradations ran through the center of the solid leaf, see Figure 2-158.

The **Type 2** sight leaf for the 1st Alteration M1903 rifle in .30-M1903 caliber was graduated to 2,450 yards (2,300 yards on the right, 2,400 yards on the left and 2,450 using the "U" notch on the top of the leaf) and was the first to have the center opening. It did not have a rib on back of the top bar to prevent the slide from falling off. The sides

Model 1903 Springfield Rifle and Its Variations

were crosshatched to increase friction for the slide binding screw, see Figure 2-159. This sight was blued and was basically an alteration of the Model 1901 Krag rear sight with the adjustable windage screw added and the binding lever eliminated, see Figure 2-160

The **Type 3** sight leaf was the first to be used with the .30-M1906 cartridge. It was graduated to 2,850 yards as described above. See Figure 2-161 for variations of the sight leaf. A rib, half-round in cross-section, was added to the back of the top bar to act as a stop to prevent the slide from falling off the leaf. It was blued.

Fig. 2-160. Model 1901 Krag rear sight.

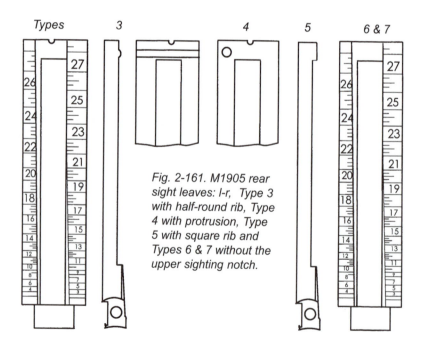

Fig. 2-161. M1905 rear sight leaves: l-r, Type 3 with half-round rib, Type 4 with protrusion, Type 5 with square rib and Types 6 & 7 without the upper sighting notch.

Model 1903 Springfield Rifle and Its Variations

The **Type 4** sight leaf was identical to the Type 3 but had a round protrusion, or stop, on the top back to prevent the slide from falling off. It was blued and the face was polished bright. It was used on the USMC M1903A1 rifles regardless of whether or not they had previously been National Match Rifles equipped with the Type 7 sight leaf.

The **Type 5** sight leaf was a spare-part replacement manufactured during World War II. It had a square rib across the top, back of the leaf to stop the slide from falling off. The slide was Parkerized and the face was not polished bright.

The **Type 6** sight leaf was similar to the Type 4 sight leaf but it was manufactured by Remington (marked, "R") or Smith Corona (usually unmarked). The leaf was blued but the face was not polished bright and the slide stop bar on the top, back of the leaf was rectangular. It did not have the 2,850-yard "U" sight notch at the top.

The **Type 7** sight leaf was based on the Type 3 but lacked the "U" notch on the top bar for the 2,850-yard range. These were used primarily on National Match Rifles. The leaf was Parkerized and the face polished bright.

NOTE: The Types 1, 2, 3, 4 and 7 sight leaves were polished after finishing. Only the Type 5 rear sight leaves was not polished bright. Only the Types 5 and 7 sight leaves were Parkerized. Any other type with a Parkerized finish has been refinished.

MOVEABLE BASE

The moveable base pivots right and left on the fixed base pivot. The degree of movement is controlled by turning the windage screw which acts on the worm gear machined into the lip on the front of the moveable base. The leaf is mounted on the moveable base. It is fastened between the ears by the joint pin. At the rear, a scale is scribed for windage. The scale has eleven divisions on each side, each of which corresponds to a lateral displacement of four minutes of an angle at 100 yards, or a total of 88 minutes, forty-four per side. The markings are approximate at best.

Only one type of moveable base was used for both the .30-1903 and .30-1906 cartridges. Those manufactured by Remington for the M1903 and M1903 (Modified) were marked "R." Smith Corona did not manufacture the moveable base.

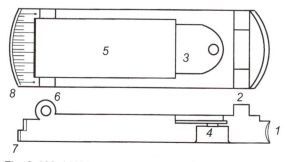

Fig. 2-162. M1905 rear sight moveable base.

The moveable base, see Figure 2-162, is 2.78 inches long by 0.720 inch wide. It has eight major parts or points: 1) the front lip is machined with worm gear teeth that allows lateral or windage adjustment, 2) shoulders on which the leaf rests in the down position, 3) a milled recess in which the spring is seated, 4) a blind hole in the bottom into which the pivot lug in the fixed rear base rests, 5) a rectangular open area for the spring, 6) the ears for the joint or hinge pin for the leaf, 7) the rear lip which rides under the rear lug on the fixed base and 8) the windage gradations.

The windage gradations are scribed into the metal and each point equals four inches of deviation from the center at 100 yards, or 4 minutes of angle.

The Windage Screw

The windage screw moves the moveable base right or left to adjust for windage, see Figure 2-163. The assembly consists of 1) the screw, 2)

Model 1903 Springfield Rifle and Its Variations

collar, 3) spring, 4) finger knob and 5) finger knob pin. The windage knob underwent four changes during the production of the M1903.

Fig. 163. Windage screw assembly.

The **Type 1** windage knob was 0.45 inch in diameter, was knurled about the circumference which was bisected with a narrow circular groove and had a concave outer surface with a central raised dimple. It was used to circa serial #360,000.

By 1909, the number of complaints about the difficulty of adjusting windage with the small knob had accumulated to such an extent that the knob was enlarged to 0.575 inch, see Figure 2-164 for illustrations of the various types of windage knobs. The **Type 2** windage knob retained the knurling and central groove and the concave outer surface with a raised central dimple. It was in use to circa serial #509,000.

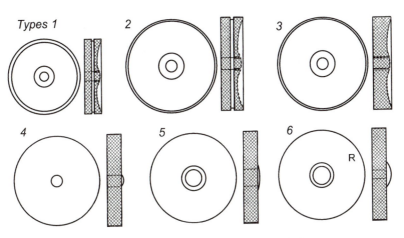

Fig. 2-164. Rear windage screw knobs, Types 1 through 6.

Model 1903 Springfield Rifle and Its Variations

The **Type 3** windage knob was also 0.575 inch in diameter, knurled around its diameter, but did not have the narrow circular groove and retained the concave outer surface with the raised central dimple. It was in use to circa serial #544,900.

The **Type 4** windage knob was 0.545 inch in diameter, knurled around its circumference without the narrow bisecting groove but had a flat outer surface without a raised central dimple. The new design was approved during World War I but does not appear to have been used until circa serial #1,130,100 in 1919, probably due to the number of the Type 2 and Type 3 knobs on hand.

NOTE: The Types 3, 4 and 5 windage knobs appear to have been used concurrently well into the 1920s.

The **Type 5** windage knob was 0.545 inch in diameter, knurled around its circumference without the narrow bisecting groove, had a flat face but did have a raised dimple in the center. It was in use from circa serial #1,130,101 to the end of production.

The **Type 6** windage knob was used on the Remington M1903 and M1903 (Modified) rifles. It was similar to the Type 5 except that the knob was riveted to the shaft of the windage screw. The knob was marked "R" for Remington.

BASE SPRING

The base spring fits into the moveable base and provides sufficient friction against the base of the leaf to hold it in either the upright or lowered positions. The spring has a lip at the front which fits an undercut in the spring seat of the moveable base, see Figure 2-165.

Two types of base springs were used in the Model 1903 rifle. The **Type 1** base spring was fitted to the Model 1903 rear sight. The **Type 2** spring was fitted to the Model 1905 rear sight. The Type 2 spring has a round hole at the front into which a drift pin or other implement

can be inserted to make
it easier to seat the base
spring in the moveable
base undercut.

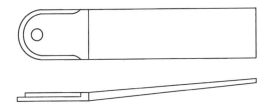

Both springs were
identical in size and
thickness. The M1903
spring was flat while

Fig. 2-165. Base spring, Type 2.

the Model 1905 spring was bent up slightly in order to apply pressure
to the leaf.

THE M1903A3 APERTURE REAR SIGHT

The aperture sight developed for the M1903A3 Rifle was a coopera-
tive effort between the U.S. Ordnance Department and Remington
Arms, see Figure 2-
166. It was mounted on
the receiver bridge,
rather than the barrel
and consisted of 1) a
U-shaped base which
held 2) the windage
yoke, 3) slide aperture,
4) spring and 5) wind-
age index knob.

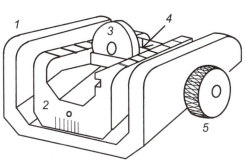

Fig. 2-166. Aperture rear sight for the
M1903A3 rifle.

The rear sight base was
made of sheet steel

0.125 inch thick. It is 1.0 inch wide by 0.910 inch long by 0.710 inch
high at the rear. The windage yoke and slide aperture were machined
from steel stock.

The left side of the windage yoke has twelve gradations or stops. The
range scale is on the right side and is marked in 100-yard increments.
Finger pressure moves the slide aperture up and down to select the

Model 1903 Springfield Rifle and Its Variations

desired range from 100 to 800 yards. The spring holds the slide aperture in place in the range gradation selected. The windage scale is scribed on the back of the windage yoke and the zero line at the center rear of the base. Each line on the windage yoke indicates a change of 4 minutes of angle at 100 yards. The total adjustment is 150 yards right and 150 yards left. Windage adjustments are made using the knurled windage index knob on the right.

Those rear sights manufactured by Remington Arms are marked "R" on the front elevation slide. Those manufactured by Smith Corona are generally unmarked. The base is Parkerized and the windage yoke and slide aperture are blued.

FRONT SIGHTS

The front sight blade on the M1903 rod bayonet rifle was fixed to a band around the muzzle. This allowed very little lateral movement to zero the rifle for windage which led to a high rate of barrel rejections for accuracy. A replacement was designed in 1905 that had a moveable stud dovetailed to the band. The front sight blade was pinned to the stud which could be moved left or right to obtain a windage zero.

By 1909, new barrel manufacturing methods, and the change from the older style "hook" cutters to "scrape" cutters that produced more consistent rifling, had so reduced the barrel rejection rate that front sights were set by bore sighting rather than by actually firing the rifle. In 1942 when the Model 1903A3 rifle was adopted, its front sight design and method of fixture (band, without a moveable stud, and spline) was quite similar to that originally installed on the M1903 rod bayonet rifle.

Four types of front sight assemblies were used on the M1903 rifle. The **Type 1** front sight assembly was designed for and used on the M1903 rod bayonet rifle, see Figure 2-167. The front sight stud (band) (1) which slid over the muzzle end of the barrel was indexed in place

284

Model 1903 Springfield Rifle and Its Variations

on a lug (2) machined into the top of the barrel which passed into a slot cut into the inside of the sight band. This prevented side-to-side

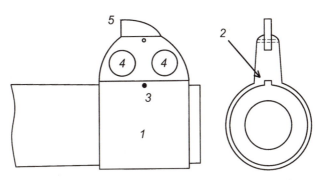

Fig. 2-167. Model 1903 front sight assembly (side and front views).

movement. It was then fixed in place with the front sight stud pin (3) that passed through the front sight stud from right to left in the center between the two lightening holes (4). This prevented fore-and-aft movement. The blade (5) was inserted into a slot at the top of the front sight band and pinned in place. This system, while sturdy and efficient, limited the amount of lateral adjustment that could be made when the rifle was sighted in and produced a high rate of rejection. The Type 1 sight was manufactured at Springfield and Rock Island and was blued.

The **Type 2** front sight assembly (Model 1905) was developed to allow more lateral adjustment during sighting in and reduced the rate of barrel rejection. The front sight base was modified to accept a moveable base which rested in a dovetail and could be moved left or right (no more than 0.025 inch) once the front sight base was indexed and fixed in place. The front sight base was slotted into the top of the moveable base, pinned in place and secured with a set screw (0.09-inch diameter) in the front of the base.

The M1905 front sight assembly consists of 1) a front sight stud (or sight band), 2) front sight moveable stud (or base) and 3) front sight (or front sight blade), 4) front sight stud pin, 5) front sight moveable stud screw, and 6) front sight pin, see Figure 2-168.

Model 1903 Springfield Rifle and Its Variations

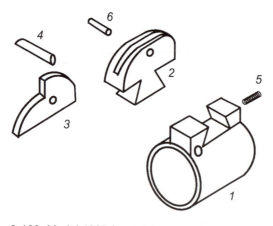

Fig. 2-168. Model 1905 front sight assembly.

Two variations were developed. The **1st Variation** was installed on barrels manufactured for rod bayonet rifles that had been rebuilt to accept the Model 1905 knife bayonet. These can be identified by the fact that: 1) the front sight base is pinned to the barrel at the front (Figure 2-169) and 2) there is a small, square hole about 0.2 inch long which can be seen at the rear where the band meets the barrel as the end of the spline is under the barrel band.

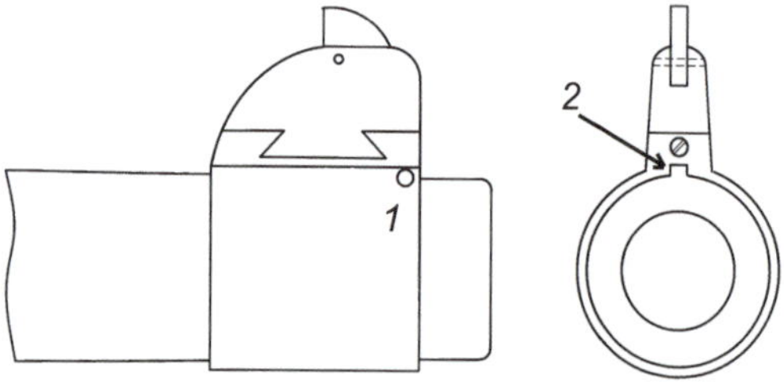

The **2nd Variation** was almost the same as the first except that the front sight base was

Fig. 2-169. Model 1905 front sight, Type 2, 1st Variation (side and rear views).

pinned at the back (see arrow in Figure 2-170) and no square hole is visible as the spline runs the full length of the front sight band It was used on barrels manufactured for the Model 1905 knife bayonet rifle to the end of M1903 production. Both variations of this front sight assembly were manufactured by Springfield and Rock Island and are blued or Parkerized according to the period of manufacture.

The **Type 3** front sight assembly is the same as the Type 2 but was

Model 1903 Springfield Rifle and Its Variations

manufactured by Remington Arms for the M1903 and M1903 (Modified) rifles. The blade and moveable base (marked "R") were blued while the front side stud was Parkerized.

The **Type 4** front sight assembly reverted partly to the original design. It consisted of the front sight stud or band which slid over the muzzle, and was indexed with a stud and key. The front sight blade was pinned into the front sight stud. It was stamped from sheet metal and installed on all M1903A3 rifles, see Figure 2-171.

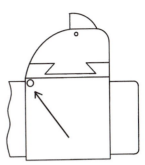

Fig. 2-170. Model 1905 front sight, Type 2, 2nd Variation.

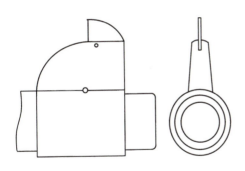

Fig. 2-171. Model 1903A3 front sight.

NOTE: Front sights were not installed on the M1903A4 sniper rifle. The end of the barrel is milled for the front sight key but it was never installed on original M1903A4 sniper rifles.

FRONT SIGHT BLADES
Three types of front sight blades were installed on M1903 series service rifles.

The **Type 1** front sight blade for the M1903 and M1903A1 was 0.05 inch wide. Five front sight heights from 0.477 to 0.537 inch were used to bring the rifle to zero elevation. Replacement blades will usually have their height marked on the right side, see Figure 2-172.

Model 1903 Springfield Rifle and Its Variations

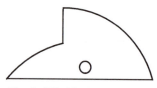
Fig. 2-172. Model 1905 front sight blade.

In 1919, the U.S. Marine Corps adopted a new "No. 10" front sight blade that was twice as wide at 0.10 inch (**Type 2**). It was designed to work with the new "No. 10" drift slide with a 0.10 aperture on the rear sight, also designed and adopted by the Corps, see Figure 2-173. The combination of No. 10 front sight and No. 10 drift slide provided a 250-yard battle sight. The blade height was determined by zeroing the rifle. These sights were installed only on M1903 service rifles used by the Marine Corps in World War II and to specialized target and sniper rifles between the wars. They were not applied to the M1903A3 rifle.

The **Type 3** front sight blade for the M1903A3 was 0.05 inch wide and var-ied in height like the Type 1. Front sight

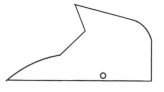
Fig. 2-173. USMC "No. 10" front sight blade.

blades were manufactured in the fol-lowing heights: 0.537, 0.522, 0.507, 0.492 and 0.477 inch. Extra high front sight blades were available and were marked "A," "B," and "C."

NOTE: If you intend to shoot your M1903 with the M1905 rear sight, you should understand that the markings on the sight ladder are as much "estimations" as anything else beyond two hundred yards. To establish ranges beyond two hundred yards, select the ammunition you will be shooting, set up your target at 300 yards and from a bench rest with the slide at 300 yards, fire a three-shot group to see where the bullets strike. It is almost guaranteed that you will have to adjust the slide until the group is centered. Mark the edge of the slide with a file and record the information. Repeat for each 100-yard additional distance as needed. You may also want to do the same for each inter-vening 50-yard distance.

Model 1903 Springfield Rifle and Its Variations

If you prefer not to mark your slide, you might search the gun shows and the Internet for the P.J. O'Hare Sight adjusting tool described in the following chapter on "Accessories."

When adjusting for windage, keep in mind that each gradation on the windage scale is "4 minutes of angle" or 4 inches at 100 yards, 8 inches at 200 yards, etc. You can interpolate between gradations if your eyes are good; if not, add a small magnifying glass to your shooting kit.

LYMAN MICROMETER WINDGAUGE RECEIVER SIGHT No. 48

In 1912, the Lyman Gun Sight Corporation began to market a new micrometer sight designated the "No. 48 Micrometer Windgauge Receiver Sight." It was unique in that the range and windage gradations did not relate to distance but to one minute of an angle which equals one inch at one hundred yards, two inches at two hundred yards, etc. This allowed the shooter to sight in his or her rifle at a known distance, record the elevation and windage settings and interpolate them quickly for further distances.

Fig. 2-174. The Lyman Micrometer Windgauge Receiver Sight No. 48C was mounted on the .22-caliber gallery rifles and .30-caliber sporting and target rifles, including the National Match rifles sold for commercial sale, after 1925.

The Lyman No. 48B rear sight with a slide length of 1.1875 inches, introduced in 1921, was chosen by the Ordnance Department to be installed on the M1922 .30- and .22-caliber

289

Model 1903 Springfield Rifle and Its Variations

rifles manufactured at Springfield Armory. The No. 48B allowed one minute of angle changes to elevation and windage (five clicks to one full turn of either knob). The windage scale was in front of the peep where it was covered when the aperture disk was used.

Experience on the range showed that one minute of angle changes were not exact enough and in 1925 the No. 48C was introduced which allowed one-half minute of angle changes to be made (ten clicks to one full revolution of either knob), see Figure 2-174. The windage scale was moved behind the peep where it remained visible when the aperture disk was used. The No. 48C was installed on all .22- and .30-caliber gallery and sporting rifles manufactured after 1925 including the M1922M1 and the M2 .22-caliber rifles.

All No. 48 sights had a screw-in rear aperture disk with a peep size that varied from 0.040 to 0.042 inch in diameter. Those installed at Springfield were relieved to allow clip loading; those sold commercially were usually not. The model designation is found stamped on the left side of the base facing the shooter. Since the parts of the sight were handfitted, each part has a fitting number and all should match. Unfortunately, when rifles were returned to Springfield Armory for repairs or upgrading, the sight was examined and any worn or defective parts were usually replaced, most without being renumbered with the original fitting number. All No. 48 parts were chemically blued with the exception of the slide which was polished bright. Sights that have been Parkerized or slides that have been blued or re-Parkerized have been refinished.

To fit the Lyman No. 48 sight to the rifle, the gunsmith used a number 33 drill to bore two mounting holes 0.600 inch apart on the right side of the receiver bridge 0.656 inch above the bottom of the receiver and 0.230 inch behind the clip guide. The holes were then threaded with a 6 x 48 tap. A square notch was cut in the right side of the stock to receive the sight.

The collector may encounter either .22- or .30-caliber rifles with a Lyman 48C sight that allows 15 clicks per full turn or one-third minute of angle changes. These sights were not supplied by Springfield Armory but are aftermarket additions. They were intended for

Model 1903 Springfield Rifle and Its Variations

use in international competition at 300 meters.

Another commercial Lyman Model 48 sight was the "S" model which is very similar to the "C" model except it has a peep sight that can be turned down and the windage scale is in front of the peep. This sight was introduced in 1939 for commercial sale by Lyman and was never installed by the Springfield Armory.

LYMAN NO. 17 SPECIAL FRONT SIGHT

The Lyman No. 17 Special front sight was a variation of the venerable No. 7 Windgauge Target Front Sight first introduced in 1889, but without the windage adjustment, see Figure 2-175. The No. 17 Special

Fig. 2-175. Lyman Model 17 Special front sight with "pin and ball" fixed insert.

tube was mounted on a dovetail that fit the front sight dovetail on the Model 1903 rifle. It was almost always mounted on the .22-caliber gallery and .30-caliber sporting and target rifles, including the National Match rifles which had the Lyman No. 48 sight. The sight post was a hollow circle mounted on a post which Lyman referred to as the "pin and ball" reticle.

After 1939, the Model 17A front sight was installed which had interchangeable inserts.

Chapter 3
Accessories

This chapter describes the items of equipment and ammunition that were "general issue" only for the individual soldier, sailor or marine, and certain items of equipment that were part of the combat infantryman's equipment.

The Model 1903 rifle and its variations and component parts were in production from 1903 to 1945 and in service well into the 1950s. The USMC M1903A1 sniper rifle saw service during the Korean War and the M1903A4 sniper rifle during both the Korean War and the war in Vietnam. Literally hundreds of accessories and appendages were developed for the rifle, both by the ordnance department and by commercial manufacturers. A complete review of all of them is obviously beyond the purview of this book. The author suggests that those interested consult *The Springfield 1903 Rifles*, by Lt. Colonel William S. Brophy, USAR, ret. (see Appendix I).

OILER AND THONG CASE

The buttstock of the M1903 rifle had two holes drilled, one above another. They were 6.2 inches deep by 0.785 inch in diameter and 4.7 inches deep by 1.2 inches in diameter, respectively. The bottom hole was drilled to lighten the stock and the upper hole was drilled to hold the oiler and thong case or the spare parts container.

The Oiler and Thong Case was 6 inches long by 0.75 inch in diameter and was stored in the top hole. It was a tube divided into two sections. Both ends had screw caps. The upper section was filled with lubricating oil (sperm oil was officially used until 1941, although other light lubricating oils were substituted as sperm oil became unavailable) and its screw top had a wire dripper long enough to reach to the bottom of the section. The soldier used the wire dripper to apply oil to the working parts a drop at a time. Soldiers were taught not to overlubricate their weapons to avoid attracting dust and dirt. The oiler cap had a leather washer to prevent leakage. Its end cap was fitted with a leather pad to prevent the tube from making noise as it moved back and forth in the buttstock compartment. The padded cap was always placed next to the butt plate cap. The lower section contained the thong and brush used for cleaning the bore.

Fig. 3-1. (Above) Type 1 Oiler and Thong case, (middle) Type 2 and below, Type 4. Notice the bevel in the Type 2 case (arrow).

Two types of Oiler and Thong Cases were used and both were made of nickel-plated brass. The upper end of the **Type 1** oiler cap was flat and leaked under field conditions. The oiler end of the **Type 2** case was beveled to produce a smaller flat and thus a better seal, see Figure 3-1, arrow. The **Type 3** Oiler and Thong Case was identical to the Type 2 except that it had a small arrow pointing to the leather-padded oiler cap. This reminded the soldier to turn the padded end up against the metal butt plate cap. Both the Types 2 and 3 were issued to the end of 1942 when the **Type 4** clear plastic oiler and thong case replaced them. The Type 4 conserved scarce brass and was cheaper to produce, plus it allowed the soldier to see the level of oil in the container.

Thong and Bore Brush

The pull-through thong and bore brush consisted of two brass ends, a threaded brush and a "weight" to drop down the bore, see Figure 3-2. The two ends were connected by waxed or varnished twine 2.5 to 3

Model 1903 Springfield Rifle and Its Variations

Fig. 3-2. Thong and bore brush.

feet long. The slotted patch holder was 0.220 inch in diameter by 1.20 to 1.30 inches long. In 1908, the two brass pieces (weight and brush tip) were threaded together and the twine was wrapped around them, then inserted in the second compartment of the oiler tube, with the brush. In mid-1942, iron replaced the brass parts. The earliest iron parts were blued, but later were Parkerized.

The **Type 1** brush tip had a brass body and the bristles were originally blackened pig bristles. The brush was changed from a brass to an iron body in mid-1942, but with non-metal bristles (**Type 2**). Later, during the war, a mix of brass and nonmetal bristle bore brushes were issued.

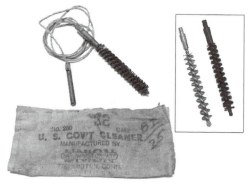

Fig. 3-3. Thong, brush and original burlap packing bag. Inset, brass and bristle brushes. Craig Riesch collection.

The brush was 3.0 ± 0.125 inches long and 0.40 inch in diameter when the bristles were new, see Figure 3-3.

NOTE: The Oiler and Thong Case and the Pull-Through and Bore Brush were also issued for the M1 Garand and the Browning Automatic Rifle.

294

Model 1903 Springfield Rifle and Its Variations

SPARE PARTS CONTAINER

Between 1911 and 1924, every other rifle was issued with a spare parts container in place of the Oiler and Thong Case. The spare parts container was a wooden tube drilled and inletted to hold a spare firing pin rod and striker and extractor. These were the parts considered the most likely to break under combat conditions. By sharing these parts between two rifle-men, a soldier

Fig. 3-4. Spare parts container. Craig Riesch collection.

could repair his rifle quickly. The container was made of maple according to specifications but every container observed by the author and reported by others appears to be made of walnut. See Figure 3-4.

The lug on the cocking piece protruded beyond the diameter of the spare parts container case and so a square channel was milled in the bottom of the upper pocket from 1911 on. Many stocks made previously had the channel added during repairs or refurbishment.

NOTE: The collector should be aware that reproductions of the spare parts container have been made for several years. Since the last spare parts container was supposedly made in 1924, beware of "new" appearing and smelling spare parts containers. If it doesn't look and smell old, it probably isn't.

FRONT SIGHT AND MUZZLE COVER

The front sight and muzzle cover was made from sheet steel and covered the muzzle and front sight blade to protect both from damage if the rifle should be dropped on its muzzle or strike an obstruction. Five types of front sight cover were used.

Model 1903 Springfield Rifle and Its Variations

The **Type 1** muzzle cover was made for the rod bayonet rifle. It is a blued sheet metal cap that completely covered both the muzzle and

front sight. The cap was case-hardened to add "spring" to the steel so that a dimple pressed into each side would hold it in place. It was blackish in color from the case-hardening process and unmarked. See Figure 3-5.

Fig. 3-5. Model 1903 muzzle cover cover for the rod bayonet rifle. North Cape Publications

When the M1905 front sight was adopted, the muzzle cover was discontinued in favor of a front sight cover. The **Type 2** front sight cover served only to protect the front sight. It was designed to be attached to the rifle on a semipermanent basis, being removed only for cleaning. Like its predecessor, it was made of case-hardened sheet steel and clipped over the barrel, see Figure 3-6. It was blue or blackish in color from the case-hardening process. Most sight covers were marked on the left side "US/ordnance escutcheon."

Fig. 3-6. Type 2 front sight cover for the M1903 service rifle.

The metal thickness of the Type 2 front sight cover varied somewhat over the years.

A **Type 3** muzzle cover was developed and issued in 1921 for the National Match rifle only. It resembled the original Type 1 muzzle cover. It was longer and like the Type 1 was slightly oversized so that it could be slipped on and off without disturbing the layer of carbon black often applied by match shooters to the front sight to eliminate glare. See Figure 3-7.

Model 1903 Springfield Rifle and Its Variations

The **Type 4** front sight cover was manufactured for use with the USMC No. 10 front sight which was higher and larger in diameter than the standard M1905 front sight, but was otherwise identical.

The **Type 5** front sight cover was identical to the Type 2 front sight cover but was Parkerized. Most of these are associated with World War II. They were made by Remington, Smith Corona, Sedgley

Fig. 3-7. M1921 muzzle cover for the National Match Rifle. North Cape Publications collection.

and various other contractors. All are marked on the left side "US/ ordnance escutcheon" and on the right with the initial of the maker, i.e., "S" for Springfield Armory; "R" or "R" in a circle for Remington.

Smith Corona front sight covers were not marked with the company's initials. Sedgley-made covers were marked with an "S" in a circle on the left side but not the "US/ordnance escutcheon," see Figure 3-8.

Fig. 3-8. Front sight cover manufactured by Remington Arms for the Model 1903A3.

SCREWDRIVER

The screwdriver was designed to fit every screw in the M1903 rifle and make it easier to take the rifle down without damaging screw heads. It was issued one per rifle company squad and to one in eight soldiers in other units. It had three screwdriver blades and a pin to drift out the pins in butt plate cap, ejector,

Model 1903 Springfield Rifle and Its Variations

floor plate catch and sear. Several types are found: **Type 1,** hollow rivet, marked "U.S.," case-hardened black. **Type 2**, solid rivet, marked "U.S.," case-hardened black. **Type 3**, solid rivet, marked "U.S.," case-hardened black, marked with the Ordnance Department code. **Type 4**, manufactured by outside contractors such as SECo. These are marked with the manufacturer's initials and part number "B147065" on the narrow blade, "U.S." and part number "B147064" on the wide blade, and are Parkerized black, see Figure 3-9.

Types 1 through 3 were machined from steel bar stock while Type 4s were stamped from sheet steel.

Fig. 3-9. Screwdrivers for the M1903 rifle: (l-r), Type 1, Type 2 and Type 4 showing front and rear views. North Cape Publications collection.

CLEANING RODS

Cleaning rods for the Model 1903 rifle came in two styles. Until 1916, the "barracks" cleaning rod was made in one piece. In 1913, a jointed rod was introduced for field use.

The **Type 1** M1903 cleaning rod was formed from brass rod 0.25 inch in diameter. The handle end was formed into a circle and the working end was upset and ground to a button tip. The rod was nominally 32 inches long, see Figure 3-10.

Model 1903 Springfield Rifle and Its Variations

The **Type 2** cleaning rod, introduced in 1906 (Model 1906), was also made of brass rod 0.25 inch in diameter with the working end

Fig. 3-10. Type 1 Model 1903 cleaning rod.

ground to a button tip. The handle was now an ellipse of cast brass, attached to the rod with a steel collar, and swivelled as the rod was pulled through the rifling, see Figure 3-11.

(Photographed to show both ends)

Fig. 3-11. Type 2, Model 1906 cleaning rod.

The Type 2 rod was augmented by the **Type 3** rod introduced in 1910 and intended for field use. It consisted of three long sections and one short section of brass rod 0.25 inch in diameter and was 32 inches long when assembled. The short end had a button tip that allowed a fifth section to be screwed to the rod. This fifth section was drilled and tapped to accept the bore brush. The handle was an aluminum disk rounded on the top edges for comfort. Two variations of this rod were issued: the **1st Variation** had an unmarked top while the **2nd Variation** was marked "1913." The Type 3 rod was issued in a canvas case.

In 1916, two new cleaning rods (**Type 4**) were introduced and were referred to as the Model of 1916 Barrack Rod and the Model of 1916 Cleaning Rod. The Barrack rod (**1st Variation**) had a football-shaped aluminum handle, steel collar and brass sleeve. The rod itself was made of brass 0.25 inch in diameter and 32 inches long and ended in

Model 1903 Springfield Rifle and Its Variations

a button tip. The field rod (**2nd Variation**) was also made of 0.25-inch-diameter brass rod but was made in four sections and had the aluminum football handle. The short, end section had a button tip that was tapped and drilled for the bore brush. Both variations had swivelling handles. The Type 4, 2nd Variation rod was issued in a canvas case, see Figure 3-12.

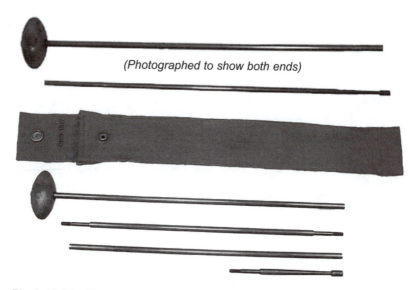

(Photographed to show both ends)

Fig. 3-12. The Type 4 Model 1916 cleaning rod: top to bottom: one-piece barrack cleaning rod; field rod with canvas carrying case. Craig Riesch collection.

In 1932, the **Type 5** cleaning rod was issued. Like the Model 1916, the M1 and M2 rods were issued in one piece for barracks use (M2) and jointed for field use (M1). The rods on both were made of steel with an aluminum "T"-shaped handle that swivelled. The M2 rod was 0.26 inch in diameter and 32 inches long, and drilled and tapped for a slotted cleaning jag and a one-piece bore brush. The M1 jointed rod consisted of four sections, and like the M2, the last section was drilled and tapped for a cleaning jag and bore brush, see Fig. 3-13.

For the .22-caliber gallery rifles, the **Type 6** M1922M1 cleaning rod was issued one per rifle. It used the oval handle of the M1906 Type 2. The rod itself was made of steel and was 0.2 inch in diameter by 38 inches long.

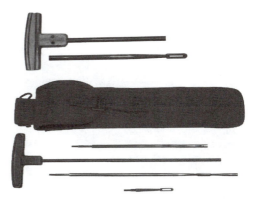

Fig. 3-13. M1 and M2 barracks and field cleaning rods. Top, M2 barracks rod showing handle and end; bottom, M1 field rod.

The end was ground to a double button tip, see Figure 3-14. The handles were probably removed from obsolete Model 1906 cleaning rods as they are identical.

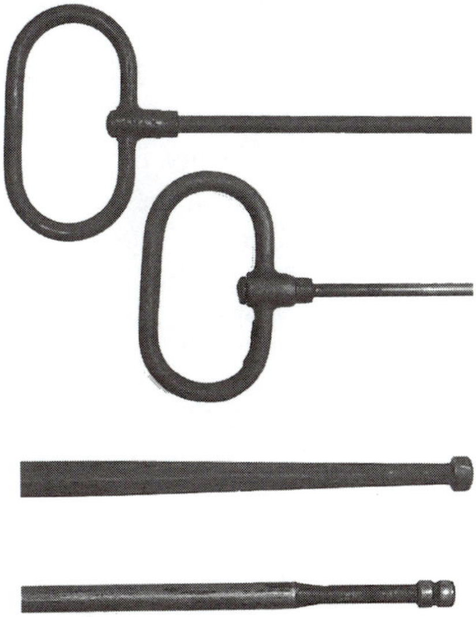

M1903 RIFLE SLINGS

Eight different slings were authorized for use with the Model 1903 series of rifles.

MODEL 1903 RIFLE SLING

The Model 1903 sling was used with the Krag and the Model 1903. It made from a single piece of leather 68.5 inches long by 1.25 inches wide, with a double brass hook at one end and a slit for a button at the other and two keepers or slid-

Fig. 3-14. Type 6 Model 1922 cleaning rod (bottom) compared to the Type 2 Model 1906 barrack rod (top). Ed Cote collection.

Model 1903 Springfield Rifle and Its Variations

Fig. 3-15. M1903 rifle sling.

ing loops, see Figure 3-15. The sling had twenty sets of double holes on the upper end and three on the lower end. The hook end of the sling was passed through the upper sling swivel toward the rear of the rifle with the smooth side against the stock. The first keeper was passed over the hook end. Both ends of the sling were then pulled down to the lower sling swivel. The end with the slit was passed through the lower sling swivel, smooth side against the stock. It was pulled through and the button inserted to hold it in place. The end with the hook was passed through the second keeper, then drawn down and hooked into any of the three sets of holes on the lower end, depending on the degree of tautness desired. The second keeper was pushed down against the lower sling swivel.

MODEL 1904 RIFLE SLING

The sling was the Model 1904 developed for both the Krag and the M1903 rifle. The 48-inch-long version was used with the Krag and the 50-inch-long version for the M1903 rifle. The sling was made of a single piece of leather 1.25 inches wide with a double brass hook at one end, two loops and 1 button. The Krag sling had three sets of holes at the end opposite the hook while the M1903 sling had only two. It was used in the same manner as the M1903 sling.

Model 1903 Springfield Rifle and Its Variations

MODEL 1906 RIFLE SLING

The Model 1906 sling was very similar to the Model 1904 but did not have the two sets of adjusting holes in the lower end of the sling. Instead, the twenty sets of holes in the upper end had all been shifted downward. This sling did not prove satisfactory and was quickly replaced.

MODEL 1907 RIFLE SLING

The Model 1907 rifle sling is probably the best known of all American military slings. It is still in use nearly 100 years later by both military and civilian shooters and hunters. It is probably the most versatile sling for either carrying or holding a rifle steady while shooting from any position, see Figure 3-16.

The M1907 **Variation 1** sling was made from two 1.25-inch-wide

Fig. 3-16. M1907 rifle sling.

leather straps connected with a "D" ring. The sling had two leather keepers. The upper strap was 49 inches long with a brass claw at one end and twenty-six pairs of holes punched two-thirds of its length. The lower strap was 24.7 inches long with sixteen pairs of holes, a brass claw at one end and the "D" ring sewn into a flap at the other. All hardware was brass which was chemically blackened to provide a "gunmetal" gray appearance. The slings were marked with the manufacturer's name or code and date of manufacture near one or both claws. After 100 years no better sling for precision shooting has been invented.

The Model 1907 **Variation 2** sling was identical to the Type 1 with the exception of the metal hardware which was Parkerized steel. The Type 2 sling was adopted in early 1942 after brass was declared a war-critical commodity.

MODEL 1917 KERR ADJUSTABLE SLING

The Kerr sling was manufactured from cotton webbing. It was made of two pieces of khaki web, 1-1/4 inch wide, each of which was fitted with a square loop on one end and a snap-hook affair on the other. The fittings were steel and were stamped "NobuckL," which was a commercial brand name used by the Kerr Adjustable Strap Company. The lower part of the sling was 15 inches long, while the upper portion was 39 inches long and had an extra square loop fitting held in place by a 1/2-inch-wide steel sliding band. While approved for the M1903 rifle, the M1917 Kerr sling was primarily used with the M1917 Enfield rifle. See Figure 3-17.

Fig. 3-17. M1917 Kerr sling.

Model 1903 Springfield Rifle and Its Variations

Model 1923 Sling

The Model 1923 sling was a canvas web, two-piece sling with two large buckles 1.30 inches wide. It was quite difficult to install and as a consequence was never very popular. The 46-inch-long strap had a buckle on one end and a metal cap on the other. The 28-inch strap had a "D" ring sewn on at one end and a metal cap on the other. A sliding lock on the long strap positioned the sling and the short strap had a

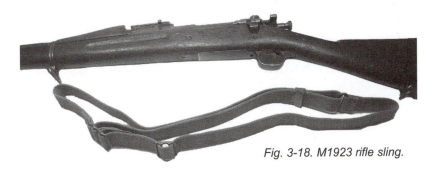

Fig. 3-18. M1923 rifle sling.

sliding buckle for adjustments, see Figure 3-18. The **1st Variation** M1923 sling was khaki in color and marked with the manufacturer's name and dated in ink. The **2nd Variation** sling was the same except that the color was changed from khaki to olive drab in mid-1943. Some Model 1923 slings observed have brass hardware finished to appear gunmetal gray while others had Parkerized steel fittings.

M1 Sling

The M1 sling was a single cotton webbing strap 46 inches long and 1.28 inches wide. A buckle was sewn on at one end and a metal cap was crimped onto the other. The butt end of the sling had a flat metal snap hook to attach to the butt swivel of the stock. The other end had a sliding lock which secured the sling in position, see Figure 3-19. The M1 sling was developed for use with the M1 Garand, the M1903 rifle, the M1 Thompson submachine gun and the M3 submachine gun. Little more than a simple strap, it was a very efficient sling.

305

Model 1903 Springfield Rifle and Its Variations

Fig. 3-19. M1 rifle sling.

The **1st Variation** of the M1 sling was khaki-colored with a narrow buckle measuring 0.85 inch wide, a small slide with a flat bottom surface, and was 0.45 inch thick. The hardware was Parkerized steel, although some end caps appear to have been blued. This 1st Variation was made in the first part of 1943 and was marked with the manufacturer's name and date in ink.

The **2nd Variation** M1 sling was the same as the 1st Variation except that the canvas webbing was olive drab. Made from mid-1943 to 1945.

The **3rd Variation** of the M1 sling was the same as the 2nd Variation except that the sliding lock was redesigned to hold the sling tighter and not cut into the webbing. The new slide lock was 0.65 inch thick and had a ridge pressed into the bottom to accommodate a thicker locking tab. Made from 1945 to the mid-1950s.

The **4th Variation** of the M1 sling was the same as the 3rd Variation except that the buckle was wider, measuring 1.3 inches wide. Some of the 1950s period slings appear to have blackened brass hardware. Slings made in the late 1950s and early 1960s have more green in the webbing. Made from the mid-1950s to approximately 1970.

The **5th Variation** of the M1 sling was the same as the 4th Variation except that the strap material was changed from canvas to nylon. The hardware was a greenish chemical-filmed steel. The nylon strap was made in brown or green. Some end caps were painted black. These slings were not marked.

NOTE: The 3rd and 4th Variations of the M1 sling may have been used with the M1903A4 sniper rifle or the USMC M1903A1 sniper rifle during either the Korean or Vietnam Wars. It is doubtful that 5th Variation ever saw use on either rifle as they were withdrawn from service before the time of the sling's manufacture.

AMMUNITION CLIPS

The clip held five cartridges. The clip was a metal strip with the sides folded up to form rims. The cartridge rims slipped under the folded clip rims. A flat spring pushed the cartridges outward against the rim while a tab at either end of the clip kept them from sliding out, see Figure 3-20. Two reinforcing ridges were pressed into the body to stiffen the clip. The first clips did not have the tabs on the springs to hold the cartridges in place. Semicircular cuts were made in the clip body and pressed upward to engage similar locking shoulders on the spring. One clip body style had oval locking shoulder holes. Clips made for the Ashworth spring had small square cuts made in each end. A die-cut tab on either end of the Ashworth spring locked into the square end cuts. Finally, two small tabs on either side of all clip bodies were pressed outward. These tabs held the clip under tension in the clip guide.

Fig. 3-20. M1903 rifle ammunition clip at top; steel (left) and brass (right) clips below.

Model 1903 Springfield Rifle and Its Variations

*Eight ty*pes of service clips have been identified and six types of dummy clips. Identifying features are described in Table 26, opposite, and Figure 3-21 on page 310.

Clips used with the service rifle had rounded ends (except the very earliest type) and thin vertical tabs on their springs. The rounded ends made them easier to load into the rifle; the tabs kept the cartridges from falling out of the clips when carried in the cartridge pouch and handled roughly during field or combat use.

Dummy cartridges and clips were used away from the firing range to teach soldiers to handle the clips and load them quickly into the rifle. They had square ends and no tabs which made them easier to reload with fresh cartridges. Service clips were rarely reloaded and were inexpensive enough that they were often left where they lay when ejected from the rifle. Eight types of service clips have been identified and six types of dummy clips. Identifying features are described in Table 26, opposite, and Figure 3-21 overleaf.

Seven types of flat spring were used in the service clips, all with end tabs. The **1st Variation** spring was flat and wavy, i.e., had three slight bends which forced the spring outward to hold the cartridges in place. It was 2.035 inches long and did not have a center hole. The **2nd Variation** was also made of brass although during World War II they were also made of steel. It was 2.035 inches long and did have a 0.10-inch hole in the center to help align it in the clip. The **3rd Variation** spring was also flat and wavy and had two semicircular cuts about one-third of the way in from the end. The metal was bent down to form a locking shoulder that engaged a similar cut in the clip body to hold the spring place. It was 2.035 inches wide and had a 0.20-inch hole in the center. The **4th Variation** was similar to the 3rd Variation but was 2.2 inches long with a locking tab at the end. The **5th Variation** spring had three raised ridges on the spring, two on either side and one shorter ridge in the center. The spring was 2.2 inches long and shaped in the form of a shallow trough with the sides turned up to

Model 1903 Springfield Rifle and Its Variations

Table 26 Ammunition Clips for the M1903 Rifle (inches)						
Clip Type	Spring Type		Spring			Clip Length
	Spring/Clip	Variation	Hole	End Shape	End Locking Tab	
Service Rifle						
1	Brass/Brass	1	No	Square	No	2.035
2	Brass/Brass	2	0.10	Round	No	2.035
3	Brass/Brass	3	0.20	Round	No	2.035
4*	Brass/Brass	4	0.20	Round	Yes	2.200
5	Brass/Brass	5	None	Round	Yes	2.200
6	Steel/Brass	6	0.20	Round	Yes	2.200
7	Steel/Steel	6	0.20	Round	Yes	2.200
8	Steel/Brass	7	No	Round	Yes	2.200
Practice or Dummy						
1	Brass/Brass	1	No	Square	No	2.035
2*	Brass/Brass	2	0.10	Round	No	2.035
3*	Bronze/Brass	2	0.10	Round	No	2.035
4	Brass/Brass	4	0.20	Square	No	2.200
5	Brass/Brass	6	No	Square	No	2.200
6	Steel/Steel	7	No	Square	No	2.200
* Patent dates stamped on clip body: Sept. 20-1904, Feb. 14-1905 and Jan. 16-1906.						

Model 1903 Springfield Rifle and Its Variations

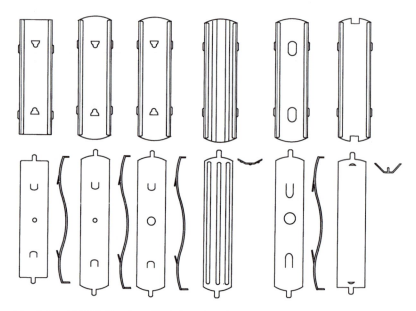

Fig. 3-21. M1903 Service clip (above) and spring (below) variations: (l-r), Type 1 with 1st Variation spring, Type 2 with 2nd Variation spring, Types 3/4 with 3rd and 4th Variation spring, Type 5 with 5th Variation spring, Types 6/7 with the 6th Variation spring and Type 8 with 7th Variation spring.

slide under the rim of the clip. Shallow tabs were cut and turned down into matching cuts in the clip body to hold the spring in place. The **6th Variation** was developed by William D. Ashworth who was foreman of the Double Action Press Shop, Frankford Arsenal, in 1925. The **7th Variation** was developed and used during World War II and was in the form of a deep trough with a central ridge.

The springs were made of three materials: brass, bronze and steel. Bronze springs were used in only one type of service and dummy clip. The springs used in the dummy clips were similar to those used in the service clips but without tabs and with square ends.

Two clips were carried in each cartridge belt pocket, separated by a tab of cloth. When needed, the soldier opened the bolt of his rifle, drew out a clip, inserted the bottom end of the clip into the clip guides at the front of the receiver bridge and pushed down on the base of the top cartridge with his thumb, pushing each cartridge down below the lips of the magazine. When the bolt was closed, the clip was pushed up and out of the clip guide and fell to the ground. With practice, a M1903 rifle could be reloaded in seconds. The clips were inexpensive enough that they could be left lying where they fell.

CARTRIDGE POUCH

The McKeever cartridge box was developed by 1st Lieutenant Samuel McKeever and adopted by the U.S. Army in 1874, see Figure 3-22. The bridle leather cartridge box opened like a clam shell and cartridges were held in loops riveted to the back of the box. They had two straps on the back that allowed them to be worn on the garrison belt. Eight "patterns" of the McKeever cartridge box were made for the .50-70, .45-70, .30-40 and .03-03/.30-06 cartridges. The .30-06 McKeever cartridge box was worn until the 1st World War period whenever web cartridge belts were not authorized. They were worn as part of the uniform at the U.S. Military Academy at West Point, New York, until the late 1930s.

Fig. 3-22. McKeever cartridge box for the .30-06 cartridge. Mike Metzgar collection.

311

Model 1903 Springfield Rifle and Its Variations

CARTRIDGE BELTS

Soldiers armed with the .45-70 Springfield and Krag rifles carried their ammunition in leather pouches on garrison duty or in web cartridge belts when on field duty. The web belts were generally known as "Mills" belts after (Brevet) General Anson Mills in spite of the fact that they were also manufactured by other companies, such as Hulbert, Spaulding, Plant, Chase and Russell. Mills' patent web gear was preferred by the soldier. Mills had patented a weaving machine that manufactured webbing items in one piece. For instance, the cartridge loops on the belt were woven together rather than assembled by sewing separate pieces together. They lasted longer and did not fray or separate as quickly. The Mills' patent ammunition belts, and later dozens of other military accouterments from haversacks to suspenders, were so successful that by the eve of World War II, the armies of dozens of nations around the world wore "Mills" equipment.

The most widely produced Mills' ammunition belt prior to the development of the M1903 rifle was the well-known blue webbing belt with two rows of forty cartridge loops for the .30-40 Krag rifle, see Figure 3-23. But the top-loading magazine of the M1898 Mauser and the M1903 rifle required the use of a cartridge clip holding five cartridges. The cartridge clip in turn required a new way for the soldier to carry clipped ammunition.

Fig. 3-23. Krag cartridge belt, 25th Infantry. North Cape Publications collection.

Model 1903 Springfield Rifle and Its Variations

The answer was a belt with pockets rather than single cartridge loops. The Mills company and others quickly furnished a variety of patterns to the U.S. Army for testing. The belts were worn about the waist and could be supported with Mills woven suspenders if desired. The pockets held ten cartridges each in two clips with the clips separated by a tab of cloth. Belt closures were wire hook and "T," pockets were closed by eagle buttons (unrimmed to mid-1914, rimmed to February 1917) and Lift-the-Dot fasteners after March 1917. Belt colors varied from khaki to dark green: from 1904 to 1909, they were usually khaki; from 1909 to 1914, dark green; from 1914 to 1916, pea green; and after 1916, khaki again until 1943.

Cartridge belts for U.S. military forces are an entire study by themselves. The salient features of the most widely used cartridge belts designed for use with the M1903 rifles are described in Table 27, with Figures 3-24 a-o on the following pages. Also, consult the bibliography for additional references (Appendix I).

BANDOLIERS

Two major types of bandoliers were used by the U.S. Army. The **Type 1** was an over-the-shoulder belt with separate pockets for one clip of ammunition. The **1st Variation** was the Model 1912 Cav-

Fig. 3-25. M1912 Cavalry Bandolier, close-up view above, overall below. Craig Riesch collection.

alry Bandolier, Figure 3-25. It was made of heavy canvas webbing material, and had twelve flat-bottomed pockets for .30-06 rifle cartridges in clips and three pockets for loose revolver or pistol car-

Model 1903 Springfield Rifle and Its Variations

Table 27, Cartridge Belts Issued with the Model 1903 Springfield
(Craig Riesch collection)

Fig. 3-24, a. M1903 Cavalry Belt, 1st Variation with saber chape, nine pockets and rimless eagle snaps.

Fig. 3-24, b. M1903 Infantry Belt, 2nd Variation without the saber chape and with nine pockets and rimless eagle snaps.

Fig. 3-24, c. M1903 Infantry Belt, 3rd Variation without saber chape, nine pockets and rimless eagle snaps. The first M1903 belt by Mills, circa 1907.

Fig. 3-24, d. M1909 Cavalry Belt with four pistol ammunition pockets for the M1909 .45-caliber revolver and nine rifle pockets with rimless eagle snaps.

Model 1903 Springfield Rifle and Its Variations

Fig. 3-24, e. M1910 Mounted Belt, 1st Variation. Four pistol ammunition pockets for the M1909 .45-caliber revolver and eight rifle pockets with rimless eagle snaps. Belt by Mills, dated 1913.

Fig. 3-24, f. M1910 Dismounted Belt with ten rifle pockets, rimmed eagle snaps. Belt by Mills, dated 1916.

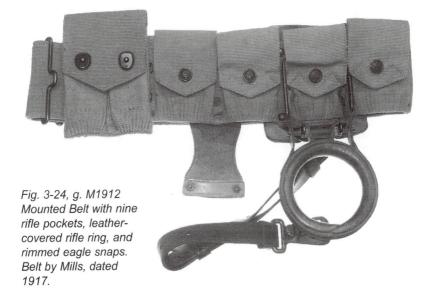

Fig. 3-24, g. M1912 Mounted Belt with nine rifle pockets, leather-covered rifle ring, and rimmed eagle snaps. Belt by Mills, dated 1917.

Model 1903 Springfield Rifle and Its Variations

Fig. 3-24, h. M1910 Mounted Belt, 2nd Variation (circa 1914), with nine rifle pockets and rimmed eagle snaps. Belt by Mills, dated 1917.

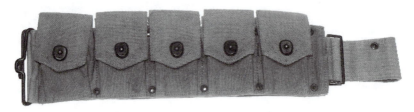

Fig. 3-24, i. M1910 Dismounted Belt. Sewn construction, ten rifle pockets, "lift-the-dot" snaps. Belt by Long, dated 6-18.

Fig. 3-24, j. M1918 Second Assistant, Browning/Colt Automatic Rifle Gunner's Belt. Four pockets for BAR magazines, four rifle pockets. Belt by P. B. & Co., dated 6-18.

Model 1903 Springfield Rifle and Its Variations

Fig. 3-24, k. M1923 Dismounted Belt. Ten rifle pockets, "lift-the-dot" snaps. Belt by Boyt, dated 1944.

Fig. 3-24, l. M1923 Mounted Belt. Nine rifle pockets, "lift-the-dot" snaps. Belt by Burlington Mills, Inc., dated 1941.

Fig. 3-24, m. M1910 Garrison Belt (enlisted). Two pockets holding one clip of .30-06 cartridges each, rimmed eagle snaps. Belt by Mills, dated 1916.

Fig. 3-24, n. M1917 Garrison Belt. Two pockets holding one clip of .30-06 cartridges each, "lift-the-dot" snaps. Belts are unmarked.

Model 1903 Springfield Rifle and Its Variations

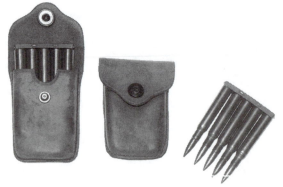

Fig. 3-24, o. M1910 Leather Garrison Belt Pouches. Rimmed eagle snaps, holds one clip of .30-06 cartridges each. Pouches by Rock Island Arsenal, dated 1915.

tridges. The pockets were fastened closed with Lift-the-Dot snap fasteners. The bandolier was sewn so that it conformed to the soldier's body and worn so that the buckle was over the shoulder and the pistol cartridge pockets under the arm. The bandolier was issued only to cavalry troops. The **2nd Variation** of the Model 1912 Cavalry Bandolier was similar to the 1st Variation, Model 1912, but was not contoured to the body, see Figure 3-26.

The **Type 2** bandolier was made of cotton duck in O.D. color; the cloth bandolier had six pockets to hold sixty cartridges in twelve clips of five cartridges. Two

Fig. 3-26. M1912, 2nd Variation Cavalry Bandolier. Notice its straight rather than curved lines. Michael Metzgar collection.

variations were used. The **1st Variation** was the Pattern 1904. It had six pockets holding two loaded clips. A cloth strap went over the neck and shoulder; a safety pin on the strap allowed the bandolier to be adjusted for length, see Figure 3-27. The **2nd Variation** was used during World War II. It was made from lighter cloth with a close weave and was light brown or greenish in color. The pockets were slightly wider to hold two clips of five cartridges (60 cartridges total). They were issued to riflemen carrying the M1903 or M1903A3 rifle in forward combat areas.

Fig. 3-27. Pattern 1904 (Type 2, 1st Variation) cloth bandolier for the M1903 rifle. Michael Metzgar collection.

Before 1940, bandoliers were packed twenty to a zinc-lined M1917 ammunition case which weighed eighty pounds. After, they were packed four to an M8 ammunition can which weighed seventeen pounds. Under combat conditions, an infantryman was expected to carry one or two M8 cans to the front line to serve both rifleman and machine gunners. See Figure 3-28. The Type 2 bandolier was issued to all riflemen.

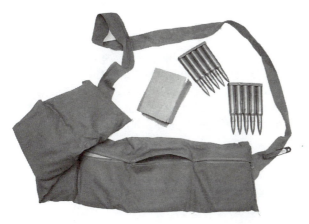

Fig. 3-28. World War II variation of the M1904 bandolier. Cloth is lighter and greener in color. Ammunition is headstamped "DEN 43" packed in Type 8 clips. North Cape Publications collection.

MUZZLE COVER

The muzzle cover (Figure 3-29) was adopted in mid-1943 and was designed to fit over the muzzle of the M1903, M1903A1, M1903A3 and M1903A4, the M1 Garand and M1 Carbine. They were made of

Model 1903 Springfield Rifle and Its Variations

Fig. 3-29. Muzzle cover for the M1903 series rifles. This example is marked "P.L. 1944." North Cape Publications collection.

khaki-colored canvas and most examples are dated 1944. The strap circled the barrel and was held in place by snaps.

BAYONETS

Four basic types of bayonet, with several variations in each, were used with the M1903 rifle and its variations. Bayonets were supplied with each service rifle.

MODEL 1903 BAYONET

The Model 1903 rod bayonet was used with the original incarnation of the M1903 rifle until 1906. It was 23.5 inches long and 0.281 inch in diameter. The bayonet was pointed and had three flutes in the tip. Unlike the rod bayonet used on the previous M1881, M1884 and M1888 rod bayonet rifles, the M1903 rod bayonet was not designed to be used as a cleaning (wiping) rod, see Figure 3-30.

Fig. 3-30. Rod bayonet for the M1888 .45-70 Springfield Rifle. North Cape Publications collection.

The M1903 rod bayonet was not attached to the barrel but was contained entirely within the stock. It was controlled by a rod bayonet stud (described in the chapter on Parts under the section, Rod Bayonet Catch Assembly) and two grooves in the bayonet. The forward groove 1.5 inches behind the point held the bayonet in the "rest" position in the stock with only the bayonet tip showing under the barrel. The second groove was 11.75 inches behind the point and it held the bayonet in the extended position, ten inches beyond the muzzle. The spring-driven bayonet catch rode up and down in the rod bayonet stud. It had a hole drilled through the center with a lip that entered the grooves to hold the bayonet in the chosen position, see Figure 3-31.

Fig. 3-31. M1903 rod bayonet. M1903 rod bayonet rifle courtesy of Gary James.

President Theodore Roosevelt was not pleased with the rod bayonet on the new rifle and Secretary of War William Howard Taft ordered a board convened to test and select a new bayonet.

M1905 BAYONET
The new detachable blade bayonet was approved on April 3, 1905 and consequently, was designated the M1905 Bayonet. The blade was 16 inches long with a stopped fuller on each side 12.35 inches long. A false edge on the top front of the blade was 5.56 inches long. The bayonet ended in a spear point. The bayonet had two catches, one for the scabbard and the other to lock the bayonet on the rifle barrel via a Krag-style lug. Wooden grips or scales were bolted to the hilt. Numerous variations of the bayonet were made and a complete description would constitute a book by itself. We will discuss only the major

changes in the following paragraphs. The reader is referred to the Bibliography in Appendix I for further reading.

M1905 bayonets were manufactured by Springfield Armory and Rock Island Arsenal. All M1905 bayonets made by Springfield were marked on the left side with the initials of the Armory or factory of manufacture, ordnance department escutcheon and the year of manufacture. On the right it was marked "U.S." and a serial number. All M1905 bayonets manufactured by Rock Island were marked in the same manner except that in the year 1906, they were not serial numbered, see Figure 3-32.

Fig. 3-32. M1905 Type 1 bayonet and scabbard. Woody Travis collection.

The M1905 bayonets were manufactured in several variations including one intended for the M1 but also used on the M1903 Springfield during World War II. They are described below.

The **Type 1, 1st Variation** M1905 bayonet had a grip screw hole 0.2 inch in diameter. The hook on the bayonet catch was 0.20 inch long and the opening in the top of the pommel for the catch was 0.25 by 0.22 inch long. The catch proved to be defective and broke easily when the bayonet was mounted to the barrel. Also, the swivel hole in the catch was too small and easily broken. Grips were oil-finished smooth walnut. All were recalled and modified as described below.

The **2nd Variation** M1905 bayonet was the Variation 1 with the following modifications. The bayonet catch was enlarged to 0.35 inch and the hole for swivel in the catch was enlarged and changed from a circle to an oval. The boss for the grip screw was enlarged to 0.3 inch. The hole in the bayonet pommel top was enlarged to 0.38 inch long. All altered bayonets were stamped "A" on the pommel.

The **3rd Variation** bayonet was new production identical in all respects to the Type 2. The bayonet pommel, hilt, guard, catch and ricasso were blued to about 0.25 inch beyond the guard. The blade was polished bright. The grips were left rough after the milling operation to provide a more secure handhold. The Variation 3 bayonet was manufactured to 1917.

The **4th Variation** M1905 bayonet was manufactured during World War I. Its blade was blued to the tip. The collector should note that all 2nd and 3rd Variation bayonets returned for repair or refurbishing between 1917 and the end of 1918 were blued as well.

The **5th Variation** M1905 bayonet from November 1918 to the end of production was Parkerized. All previous variations of M1905 bayonets sent for repair or refurbishing were also Parkerized.

After an estimated 1,002,000 M1905 Type 1, Variations 1 through 5, bayonets were manufactured, production ended in 1922. Rock Island had manufactured an estimated 429,900 Variations 1 through 5 bayonets from 1906 to 1912 and from 1917 to 1919. No Type 1 M1905 bayonets were manufactured by commercial subcontractors.

The **Type 2 Model 1905** bayonet was manufactured from late 1942 to May 1943 by six commercial companies. They are quite similar to the Model 1905 Type 1 bayonet except for a rougher finish, lack of serial number, commercial factory initials on the ricasso and dates of 1942 and 1943, see Figure 3-33. The grips were also changed from wood to black or reddish Bakelite with narrow vertical grooves. The bayonet blade and associated steel parts were Parkerized. All were marked on

Fig. 3-33. Type 2 M1905 bayonet manufactured during World War II. Woody Travis collection.

the ricasso with the initials of the company over the initials "US" separated by the ordnance department escutcheon, over the year of manufacture.

The manufacturing companies were: Union Fork & Hoe Company; Oneida, Ltd.; Utica Cutlery Company; Pal Blade and Tool Company; American Fork and Hoe Company; and Wilde Tool and Drop Forge Company.

M1 BAYONET

In mid-1943, a new bayonet was ordered with a shorter blade to be used with the M1903, M1903A1, M1903A3 and M1 Garand. The Bayonet, M1 was identical to the Model 1905 Type 2 except for the shorter blade and the markings, see Figure 3-34. The blade was 10 inches long with a fuller on each side 5.75 inches long, beginning 3 inches from the point. The blade tip ended in a spear point. The grips were Bakelite, either black or brown. The same companies which made the M1905, Type 2 bayonet—with the exception of Wilde Tool—manufactured the Bayonet, M1. The blades were marked on the obverse "company initials/ordnance escutcheon/U.S." On the reverse, the earliest were dated "1943." Those made in 1944 and later were not dated.

Fig. 3-34. M1 bayonet, North Cape Publications collection.

Model 1903 Springfield Rifle and Its Variations

MODEL 1905E1 BAYONET

In 1944-45, the Ordnance Department reduced the blade length of many 16-inch M1905 Types 1 and 2 bayonets to 10 inches by cutting off the tips. The ends were then reground to either a spear or clip point. They can easily be distinguished by the fact that the blood groove runs out past the tip. The wood grips were exchanged for black or reddish Bakelite grips. The modified bayonets were Parkerized and stamped with the code of the contractor doing the work on either the blade or handle, see Figure 3-35. The M1905E1 can have any Model 1905 Type 1 or Type 2 date or manufacturer. They were later reclassified as the Bayonet, M1.

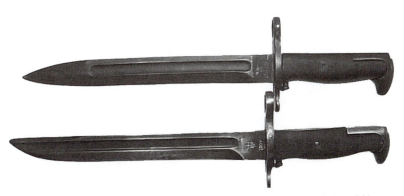

Fig. 3-35. The Bayonet, M1 and M1905E1 bayonet compared: top, M1; bottom, M1905E1. North Cape Publications collection.

SCABBARDS

Although there were relatively few changes to the Model 1905 and M1 bayonet, their scabbards underwent a positively confusing number of revisions.

MODEL 1905 SCABBARD

The original scabbard for the M1905 bayonet had a body made of wood and covered with russet (reddish brown) leather and a steel belt

Model 1903 Springfield Rifle and Its Variations

loop identical to that used on the Krag bayonet scabbard, see Figure 3-36.

The leather cover was sewn on the right side and the manufacturer's name, ordnance inspector's mark and date of manufacture were stamped into the leather on the back. A metal throat piece was held to the scabbard by three rivets front and back. Metal parts were blued. Two hooks on either side of the mouth engaged the scabbard catch on the bayonet to hold it securely.

Model 1905 scabbards were made (or remade) in three types. The **Type 1** scabbard had the Krag metal belt attachment that clipped over the cartridge belt and was attached to the metal throat by a swivel, see Figure 3-37. All Type 1 scabbards had a small drain hole on the

Fig. 3-36. Type 1 Model 1905 bayonet and scabbard. Woody Travis collection.

back 0.625 inch above the tip in the form of a metal eyelet.

Three variations of the Type 1 Model 1905 scabbard were made. The **1st Variation** had a metal throat 1.5 inches high. The wooden body of the scabbard can be seen by looking down on the throat. The **2nd Variation** had a metal throat 2.875 inches high, see Fig-

Fig. 3-37. Close-up of the Type 1 M1905 bayonet scabbard belt attachment.

ure 3-38. The **3rd Variation** had an aluminum body which can be seen by looking down on the throat from the top. These are believed to have been manufactured in limited numbers for field trials only.

Fig. 3-38. Type 1, 1st (top) and 2nd (bottom) Variation M1905 scabbards. Woody Travis collection.

The **Type 2** scabbards were equipped with a wire double belt loop. These were referred to by the ordnance department as the Model 1905-Modified Scabbard, see Figure 3-39. Three variations were made. The **1st Variation** had a leather collar 2.25 inches high into which the wire double belt loop was sewn, attached to the scabbard body by two rivets. The **2nd Variation** had the leather collar attached by five brass rivets. One-half inch of the metal throat shows above the collar. The **3rd Variation** had the collar attached by six rivets and no part of the throat can be seen. The rivet ends are on the outside and are peened over brass washers.

Fig. 3-39. M1905-Modified Scabbards, left, 1st Variation; right, 3rd Variation. Woody Travis collection.

MODEL 1910 SCABBARD

The Model 1910 scabbard replaced the russet leather body with a rawhide body covered with a web sheath. A leather tip was sewn to the bottom of the web. A drain hole was drilled in the wooden body of the scabbard and

Model 1903 Springfield Rifle and Its Variations

in the leather tip on the reverse side at the bottom. The web sheath could be removed for cleaning. A total of eight variations of the M1910 scabbard have been observed, see Figure 3-40. The **1st Variation** had a seamless woven sheath with a web tab for the belt hanger sewn to the

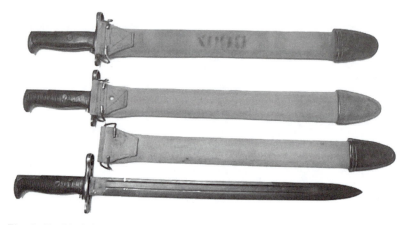

Fig. 3-40. Model 1910 bayonet scabbards: top to bottom, 2nd Variation, 4th Variation and 7th Variation with M1905 bayonet. Woody Travis Collection.

back. The belt hanger ran through a metal tube which was enclosed by the tab, see Figure 3-41. The sheath was khaki and the tip was brown leather. The **2nd Variation** was identical but without the metal tube. The sheath was khaki and the tip was brown leather. The **3rd Variation** had a leather tab enclosing the belt hook sewn to the back of the tube. The sheath was khaki and the tip was brown leather. The **4th Variation** had a web tab sewn to the back and reinforced with a single brass rivet. The sheath was khaki and the tip was brown leather. The **5th Variation** was made during WWI. It was similar to the 2nd Variation but had a finer web weave and was marked on the back with the maker's name and often a date. The **6th Variation** was made of canvas and sewn together. The khaki tip was brown leather. The canvas tab was sewn to the back of the tube. The **7th Variation** was similar to the 5th Variation. The sheath was khaki but with a black tip. The **8th**

Variation was made of canvas and was similar to the 5th and 7th Variations except that it was covered with white canvas and had a black leather tip.

Markings on scabbards are inconsistent at best. Some tips will show manufacturer's name and date and often an inspector's mark; others will not. Colors will vary as with the cartridge belts. From 1904 to 1909, the color was khaki; from 1909 to 1914, it was dark green; from 1914 to 1916 it was pea green and after 1916 was khaki again. But colors in the M1910 scabbard are complicated by the fact that soldiers washed the sheaths so often that the colors faded. They also bleached them to achieve a uniform color with other pieces of web equipment. For parade, inspections and other specialized duty, scabbards were often rubbed with a white clay called blanco to make them very white. Other scabbards were painted white or other colors and the leather tips were painted black, both in the service and by those outside like honor guards, drill teams and so on. Brass and steel belt hooks were also used, sometimes within the same variation, especially in those made during World War I.

Fig. 3-41. 1st Variation M1910 scabbard; note the metal tube (arrow). Craig Riesch collection.

MODEL 1917 SCABBARD

The scabbard made for the U.S. Model 1917 Enfield rifle bayonet was authorized in 1920 as a substitute standard for the Model 1910 scabbard. The M1917 scabbard body is made of sole leather, rough side out, stitched up the back and dyed green or dark brown. A stamped steel tip, or chape, and a steel neck are fitted to the scabbard. The M1917 scabbard is fitted with double-hook wire hangers for attachment to the cartridge belt, see Figure 3-42. Four variations of U.S. Model 1917 scabbards were manufactured, two with leather bodies and two with plastic bodies.

Fig. 3-42. M1917 scabbard.

The **1st Variation** body is identical to the British P-1907 scabbard but is painted green or olive. The steel neck has a 2.0-inch-wide leather loop hanger riveted to it, and the double-hook hanger is attached to the loop.

The **2nd Variation** has the double-hook hanger attached directly to a rolled lip on the scabbard throat. The body is identical to that of the 1st Variation scabbard. The 1st and 2nd Variations are shown in Figure 3-43.

The **3rd Variation** was manufactured 1943-44, see Figure 3-44. The body was made of cloth-reinforced olive drab phenolic resin. The steel neck has a gray-green Parkerized finish. This scabbard

Fig. 3-43. M1917 Scabbards: left; 2nd Variation scabbard; right; 1st Variation. Woody Travis collection.

should not be confused with the M3 scabbard. They are similar in appearance, but the body of the M1917 scabbard is longer (17.5 inches

Model 1903 Springfield Rifle and Its Variations

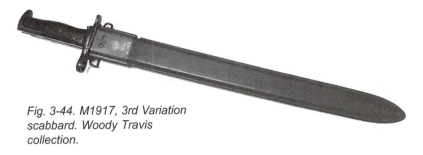

Fig. 3-44. M1917, 3rd Variation scabbard. Woody Travis collection.

vs 16.8 inches for the M3) and the steel neck is stamped "U.S. M1917." The metal neck of the 3rd Variation scabbard is longer and is held to the body with two rivets. Also, mouthpieces on the two scabbards are configured differently. The words, "U.S.–1917/B.M. Co." (Beckwith Manufacturing Company) are molded into the back of the 3rd Variation of the M1917 scabbard. The metal throat is not marked. As an aside, the M1917 bayonet will not fit in the M3 scabbard made during World War II.

The **4th Variation** M1917 scabbard was manufactured during the Vietnam War for newly manufactured M1917 bayonets to be used on various combat shotguns then in the U.S. military inventory. These Vietnam-era scabbards are made of fiberglass rather than phenolic resin and have a grommet-reinforced tie-down hole at the tip. They are marked with the U.S. Defense Department eagle symbol enclosed in a box, rather than the Ordnance Department's "flaming bomb" symbol.

M3 SCABBARD

The M3 scabbard was manufactured of phenolic resin reinforced with duck cloth by both the Detroit Gasket and Manufacturing Company and by Beckwith Manufacturing Company in 1942, see Figure 3-45. A metal throat piece with the double belt loop and bayonet catch hooks was crimped to the scabbard body. A small drain hole was drilled at the bottom of the reverse side. In June 1942 four internal ribs were added to prevent the blade from rattling in the scabbard. Contract

Model 1903 Springfield Rifle and Its Variations

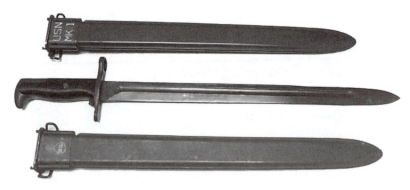

Fig. 3-45. M3 Scabbards manufactured during WWII: U.S. Navy Mk 1 above, Beckwith-manufactured M3 below. Michael Metzgar collection.

totals for both companies were 450,000 and 500,000 respectively. The scabbard body was olive green and the metal parts were Parkerized a dark grey color. The metal throat is marked "U.S." over the Ordnance Department's flaming bomb escutcheon. Those made for the U.S. Navy were marked "U.S.N./Mk 1."

Two types of M3 scabbards were made. The **1st Variation** made only in 1942 had a smooth interior. Because the bayonet rattled when in the scabbard, internal ribs were molded into the walls of the **2nd Variation** to hold the blade tightly.

A white duck cover was used with M3 scabbards obtained by the U.S. Marine Corps, similar to those used for the M1910 bayonet scabbards. A tab at the top was folded over to form into a belt loop. Snaps on the tab allowed the belt loop to be adjusted for garrison belts, dress or cartridge belts.

M7 SCABBARD

The M7 fiberglass scabbards were made for the M1 and the M1905E1 bayonets. They were made of olive-green fiberglass with metal throats, see Figure 3-46.

Model 1903 Springfield Rifle and Its Variations

Two variations of the M7 scabbards were used. The **1st Variation** was made from the M3 scabbard. The metal throat piece was removed and slit up the sides 0.187 inch. The scabbard body was shortened and retouched on both sides and the metal top replaced and crimped into the notches. The notches are not visible on the sides of the M7, 1st Variation scabbard.

The **2nd Variation** M7 scabbards were newly manufactured in 1944 and 1945. They were identical to the 1st Variation with the exception of the markings and the style of crimp. They were marked on the front of the throat "U.S." inside a circle. The back will often show a mold code or the letters "VP" and a code number. The crimp was made into notches in the plastic scabbard body (arrow in Figure 3-46) as with the original full-length M3 scabbards.

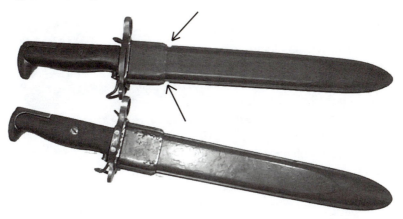

Fig. 3-46. M7 scabbards manufactured during WWII: 2nd Variation above, 1st Variation below. North Cape Publications collection.

BREECH COVER

The M1917 breech cover was made of canvas, originally for the M1917 Enfield rifle but could be made to fit the M1903 Rifle. A thong on the forward end tied the breech cover to the lower band sling swivel and

Model 1903 Springfield Rifle and Its Variations

four Carr snaps fastened it around the rifle breech, see Figure 3-47. One breech cover was issued per rifle.

Fig. 3-47. M1917 breech cover. North Cape Publications collection.

NATIONAL MATCH ACCESSORIES

The three main accessories used with the National Match Rifle by many target shooters were the front and rear sight cover and a sight-adjusting micrometer. One of the most popular manufacturers of these accessories before World War II was the P.J. O'Hare Company of South Orange, New Jersey.

Several types of front sight cover were in use by match shooters during the 1920s and 1930s. Those shooters who wanted more protection than that afforded by the M1921 National Match Sight Protector often purchased the sight protector designed by a Major J.E. Session and sold through P.J. O'Hare. It was a brass cylinder with hood for the front sight. The sight protector slipped over the front sight and rotated closed, see Figure 3-48.

Fig. 3-48. P.J. O'Hare "Session" front sight cover. Craig Riesch collection.

In the days before chemical blackening solutions, target shooters often coated rifle sights with carbon black using a small miner's carbide lamp. The carbon black left a thin, non-reflecting coating on the sights which made them easier to see in bright sunlight. When the shooter left the line, he or she had to take particular care not to smear the coating on the front and rear sights. Not only was it messy, but if smudged, the lamp had to be fired up again and the process repeated.

The solution was a cover for the rear sight. Again, P.J. O'Hare furnished the most popular item. Developed also by Major J.E. Ses-

Model 1903 Springfield Rifle and Its Variations

Fig. 3-50. P.J. O'Hare rear sight micrometer. North Cape Publications collection.

sion, and called variously the Session, Convoy and O'Hare sight protector, it slipped over the top of the sight leaf and covered the sight bar, see Figure 3-49.

Adjusting the sights of the Model 1903 rifle for minute of angle changes was difficult under the best of conditions and close to impossible under the tension of a match. Several types of micrometers were developed to allow minute adjustments to be made easily to the rear sight. Again the most popular was one sold through the P.J. O'Hare Company, see Figure 3-50. It was made of brass and allowed changes of one-half minute of angle to be made with precision. To use, the slide screw was tightened and the claw at the bottom of the micrometer was placed under the sight bar. The adjusting knob at the top of the sight micrometer was turned until the flat at the top of the scale (arrow) rested on the top of the sight leaf.

The shooter then fired a three- or five-shot group and measured the distance from the center of the group to the center of the bull. If the group was centered 2 inches below at 200 yards, he placed the sight micrometer on the sight with the claw hooked under the sight bar, loosened the slide screw and turned the adjusting knob on the top of the micrometer eight clicks up and reset the

Fig. 3-49. P.J. O'Hare rear sight cover. North Cape Publications collection.

slide screw. The micrometer claw raised the sight bar to bring the center of the group up 2 inches to the center of the bull.

Chapter 4
Telescopic Sights for the Model 1903, Model 1903A1 and Model 1903A4 Rifles

TELESCOPIC SIGHTS

Twelve different telescopic sights were mounted on the M1903 Springfield and its variations in an effort to provide a sniper rifle. They were the Warner & Swasey Models of 1908 and 1913 (see Figure 4-1); the Winchester A5 and Lyman 5A, the Weaver 330C and its military version the M73B1, the Lyman Alaskan, Lyman Alaskan M73E1, M81, M82 and M84 and the Unertl USMC telescopic sight.

Fig. 4-1. Model 1903 rifle with the Warner & Swasey sniper scope mounted, adjusting wrench and carrying case. North Cape Publications collection.

TELESCOPIC MUSKET SIGHT, MODEL 1908

The Telescopic Musket Sight, M1908 was manufactured by Warner & Swasey. The sight consisted of three parts: 1) telescope, 2) the lever or arm on which the telescope was mounted and 3) the mount or slide which was affixed to the rifle's receiver with three screws, see Figure 4-2.

The Warner & Swasey prismatic sight had a short focal length of 7 inches. The focal length, combined with the 20 mm objective lens, provided a magnification of 6X with an eye relief of 1.5 inches.

Model 1903 Springfield Rifle and Its Variations

PLATE II.

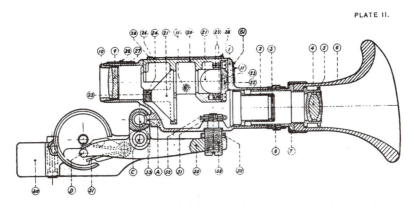

Fig. 4-2. Schematic of the M1908 Warner & Swasey prismatic telescopic sight taken from the Description of Telescope Musket Sights Models of 1908 and 1913, *published in 1917.*

The small lens limited the amount of light reaching the eye and the short eye relief required the use of a rubber eyecup. The rubber cup often fit so snugly that three holes had to be punched in it to relieve the vacuum created when the rubber cup was shoved back against the shooter's face by recoil.

The reticle, etched on a glass insert, consisted of vertical and horizontal lines and three stadia lines that provided a man-sized target 5 feet 8 inches high at 1,000, 1,500 and 2,000 yards. A Poro prism was used to provide an erect image but it also further reduced the amount of light reaching the shooter's eye and the prism was easily knocked out of alignment in its mount. The eyepiece was a Steinheil achromatic lens mounted in a long neck which was screwed in and out to focus and was locked in place by a focusing lock nut. The inside of the sight was painted flat black but the paint tended to chip off and stick to the reticle. Range and drift tables were fastened to the top of the telescopic sight with a range plate for the three stadia attached to the rear of the prism housing, see Figure 4-3.

The telescopic sight was attached to a mounting arm mated with a bracket bolted to the left side of the M1903 rifle's receiver. The bracket had two 0.8-inch locking notches spaced one inch apart. The

337

Model 1903 Springfield Rifle and Its Variations

Fig. 4-3. Range and drift tables etched on metal plates and attached to the top of the Warner & Swasey telescopic sight.

dovetail on the arm slid over a matching dovetail on the bracket and a plunger engaged the chosen notch but did not lock into place. A disk at the front of the arm provided the elevation adjustment which acted against a spring at the rear of the bracket to tilt the scope. A windage screw on the arm pressed against the bracket to move the scope left or right as needed. Elevation adjustments could be made in theory to 3,000 yards but at ranges beyond 400 yards, play in the mounting system introduced accuracy errors. The detachable mount was made of steel and the scope housing of brass and bronze. The entire assembly was painted with a glossy black enamel. The field of view was quite good at 7 yards wide per 100 yards of distance. The complete assembly weighed 2 lbs.

Model 1903 rifles were selected for the sniper role by star gauging. The eight-pointed star was not marked on the rifle's muzzle as this practice was not initiated until 1921. Senich reports that 2,075 M1908 Warner & Swasey sights were sold to the U.S. Government between 1908 and 1912 but Brophy estimates that only 1,550 were mounted on M1903 rifles.

All M1908 Warner & Swasey telescopic sights mounted on rifles were marked with the rifle's serial number—"FOR RIFLE No. XXXX" on the inside of the arm where it mated to the bracket. Each Warner & Swasey telescopic sight was serial numbered in its own

338

Model 1903 Springfield Rifle and Its Variations

sequence. The Model 1908 sight was issued in consecutive serial numbers but not attached to consecutively serial numbered rifles.

Extensive work performed by W. P. Eyeberg and communicated to the author shows that the M1903 rifle serial numbers with the M1908 scope ran generally between 312,000 and 410,000. Two rifles were noted with serial numbers of 116 and 298 and these may have been still in the rod-bayonet state when they were fitted. Telescope numbers ran generally from 2 through 1,720. The reader should note that 1,720 was the highest number observed at the time of the study and not the highest number produced. It is believed that both the M1908 and the later M1913 Warner & Swasey series of scopes were numbered consecutively. The lowest M1913 scope serial number noted in the study was 2,008.

Telescopic Musket Sight, Model of 1913

In 1913, the Warner & Swasey scope was slightly redesigned, see Figure 4-4. The magnification was lowered to 5.2X which increased the image brightness, but the sight still could not be used much later than early dusk and not at all at night. A clamping screw was added to

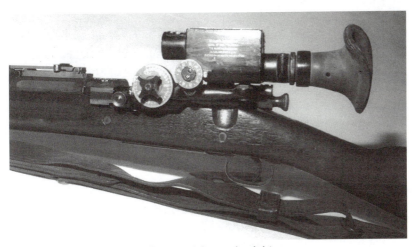

Fig. 4-4. M1913 Warner & Swasey telescopic sight.

secure the eyepiece adjustment and a cruciform elevation screw replaced the older knurled wheel. The sight still weighed 2 lbs and the sight line remained high enough above the stock that the shooter could not hold the stock comb securely against his cheek. Soldiers complained of aching necks after long practice sessions. The M1913's mounting arm was not marked with the rifle's receiver serial number.

On the range, the Telescopic Sight, Model of 1913 performed acceptably, but under field conditions, it was finicky, delicate, heavy and difficult to use. During World War I, an unknown number of rifles equipped with the Warner & Swasey sight were sent to Europe with the American Expeditionary Force.

A total of 5,041 M1913 Warner & Swasey sights are thought to have been acquired by the Ordnance Department and an estimated 4,000 were installed on M1903 rifles. Combined with the total reported by Senich for the M1908 (2,075), it appears that 7,116 Warner & Swasey M1908 and M1913 scopes were purchased, plus a small number of scopes bought in 1906 for preliminary testing. W.P. Eyeberg's study of observed Warner & Swasey telescopic sight and rifle serial numbers suggests that the number is closer to 10,000 total, but gaps in the rifle serial number sequence may be the result of sales to the Canadian and British armies, both of which used the Warner & Swasey M1913 to a limited extent. Serial numbers observed in the M1913 series ranged from 2,000 to 7,900 and were attached to rifles in the serial number range from 580,000 to 938,000. Also, an unknown number of sights with three-digit serial numbers (M1908) were mounted on the Automatic Machine Rifle, Caliber .30 (Benet-Mercie). Markings on the Warner & Swasey sight are as follows:

Model of 1908

> TELESCOPIC MUSKET SIGHT
> MODEL OF 1908 NO. XXX
> THE WARNER & SWASEY CO.
> CLEVELAND OHIO U.S.A.
> PAT . FEB. 13-06 MAY 22-06

Model 1903 Springfield Rifle and Its Variations

Model of 1913

The Warner & Swasey scope was carried in a rectangular leather case when not mounted on the rifle. The case had a pocket on the outside (a few had the pocket inside) for the adjusting wrench. An over-the-shoulder carrying strap was attached.

WINCHESTER A5

The Winchester A5 telescopic sight was first manufactured in 1910 by the Winchester Repeating Arms Company of New Haven, Connecticut, as a commercial sight and proved quite popular with target shooters. The body was made from a solid steel tube bored through and lathe-turned to the proper outside diameter which made it very strong. The tube was 15.875 inches long and 0.75 inch in diameter, see Figure 4-5.

Elevation and windage micrometer dials allowed adjustments in one minute of angle increments by bearing against the left side and

Fig. 4-5. Winchester A5 Telescopic Sight mounted on an M1922 M1 .22-Caliber rifle. Ed Cote collection.

Model 1903 Springfield Rifle and Its Variations

Fig. 4-6. The elevation and windage markings on the Winchester A5 commercial scopes were red but were white on military contract scopes. Ed Cote collection.

top of the tube. The division markings were painted red on commercial scopes but were changed to white on scopes purchased by the Army and Marine Corps, see Figure 4-6.

Several different reticle patterns were available but the most popular was the standard vertical and horizontal crosshairs. The tube was 15.875 inches long and 0.75 inch in diameter. It provided a 5X magnification with a narrow 3-degree field of view at 100 yards and an eye relief of 2 inches.

The mounts were made of nickel steel. The front mount was designed so that it would not dent the tube. A plunger projecting from the bottom of the mount engaged a groove in the bottom of the tube (see Figure 4-7) to keep it from rotating but allowed it to move forward as the rifle recoiled. The shooter then pulled it back into position. The rear mount had a spring-loaded plunger in the left side to hold the tube against the windage adjusting plunger and a "grasshopper" spring (a coil spring with extended arms) pushed it up against the elevation adjusting plunger.

The A5 scopes were marked:

Model 1903 Springfield Rifle and Its Variations

MANUFACTURED BY THE WINCHESTER REPEATING ARMS CO.– A5
NEW HAVEN, CONN. U.S.A. PATENTED FEBRUARY 9, 1909

No U.S. Army or Marine Corps markings were applied to the scopes or mounts.

The Winchester A5 scope was tested by the U.S. Army's School of Musketry between 1912 and 1915 and ultimately rejected. But as it was the best commercial scope then available in the United States (and Great Britain and Canada), the British and Canadian military adopted it and so did the U.S. Army when the United States entered the war in 1917. Some 500 scopes were purchased by the Army but it is doubtful if more than a few were sent to France. It appears that most were used in training. The Marine Corps, on the other hand, adopted the A5 as its standard sniper scope, designating it "The Winchester Telescopic Sight, Model

Fig. 4-7. The plunger on the front mount prevented the scope from rolling.

A5." It was used with a Mann-type rear mount in which the mount and its recess were wedge shaped so that recoil seated the scope ever more firmly. It was thought that this type of mount would help to maintain zero if the scope was removed and replaced.

The rights to manufacture the A5 scope were purchased in 1928 by the Lyman Gun Sight Corporation which continued to market it as the Lyman Model A5 Telescopic Sight. Both the Army and Marine Corps continued to use the Winchester A5 and Lyman 5A scopes on target rifles and USMC sniper training rifles until World War II.

Model 1903 Springfield Rifle and Its Variations

The Winchester A5 was also mounted on the .22 gallery and sporting rifles purchased through the Director, Civilian Marksmanship Program during the 1920s and 1930s.

LYMAN 5A TELESCOPIC SIGHT

When the Lyman Gunsight Corporation purchased the rights to the Winchester A5 telescopic sight, they made a few improvements in the design. These included larger and stronger lens mountings and a reversal of the screws holding the internal parts together. The Winchester design had the screws passing through the tube from the inside to prevent tampering but Lyman reversed them and added spring washers to strengthen the assembly. Lyman 5A scopes replaced Winchester A5 scopes as needed until 1941.

Bases used for both the Winchester and Lyman 5A scope mounts were color case-hardened steel. Front mounts were 0.5 inch wide by 1.355 inches long by 0.3 inch high and rear mounts were 0.5 inch wide by 1.342 inches long by 0.2 inch high.

THE UNERTL TELESCOPIC SIGHT

At the start of World War II, the U.S. Marine Corps still retained a few Model 1903 rifles equipped with either the Winchester A5 or Lyman 5A scopes. A few of these were used on the Marines' first major offensive combat engagement at Guadalcanal in late 1942. A Marine Corps Equipment Board recommended that sniper equipment be improved and standardized. They recommended a scope of about 8 to 10 power and that the Winchester 70 rifle be procured as a standard sniper rifle but when tests were run against the Springfield M1903 rifle, there proved to be little difference in accuracy.

In 1941, the Marine Corps initiated sniper rifle training with M1922, M1922 M1 and M2 .22-caliber gallery rifles equipped with Winchester and Lyman 5As, as well as the Lyman M48C rear receiver and Lyman 17A aperture front sights. A testing program to develop a new sniper rifle was also started with the small number of commercial telescopic sights then available. John Unertl, owner of the

Model 1903 Springfield Rifle and Its Variations

Fig. 4-8. USMC M1903A1 Sniper Rifle. Larry Reynolds collection.

Unertl Company, offered one of his target telescopes for testing. At the conclusion, approval was given on January 6, 1943 to build 1,000 Model 1903A1 .30-caliber Springfield Rifles equipped with the new Unertl 8X telescope and mounts, see Figure 4-8. The Lyman 5A scope was to be retained for the time being.

The intention was to allocate nine of the new sniper rifles to each rifle company and four per headquarters company in the 1st and 2nd Marine Raider Battalions. The rifles were assembled from parts on hand at the Marine Corps' Philadelphia Armory.

The Unertl telescopic sight selected by the Marine Corps was the Target Scope model without the recoil return spring, see Figure 4-9. The spring was replaced by a ring attached to the tube before the front mount and served to hold the tube in place. Its magnification was nominally 8X (actually, it was 7.8X). It had a 1.25-inch objective lens and a tube 24 inches long. Adjustment was in 1/4 minute of angle clicks although a few with 1/2 minute of angle clicks have been observed by the author and others. The reticle was a crosshair with a center dot. Its eye relief was short, only 2.25 to 2.75 inches, and its field of view was eleven feet at one hundred yards. The tube body was 0.75 inch in diameter. The scopes were serial numbered in their own series and not to the rifle. Serial numbers seem to run between 1,000 and 2,800. The mounts were made of duraluminum with case-hard-

Model 1903 Springfield Rifle and Its Variations

Fig. 4-9. The Unertl Target Model telescopic sight was used by the U.S. Marine Corps on the M1903A1 sniper rifle. The sight was marked USMC-- SNIPER. North Cape Publications collection.

ened steel bases and mounting screws. The rear base mounted on the receiver ring immediately behind the standard 1905 rear sight and base (which was left intact) and the front base was mounted on the barrel 7.2 inches ahead of the rear base, see Figure 4-10. The rear mount allowed adjustments to be made for range and windage in increments of one-quarter minute of an angle. A Micarta carrying case was supplied with each scope and while effective at protecting the scope, they were rarely carried in combat because of their length and bulk. The Marine Corps also produced a metal can with a wooden disk in the bottom to secure the objective lens. Estimates of Unertl scopes purchased by the Marine Corps range from 1,800 to 6,000 units, including spares for replacement.

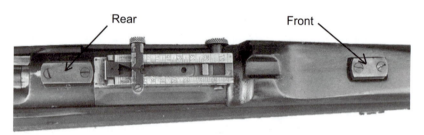

Fig. 4-10. USMC M1903A1 sniper rifle front and rear bases. Larry Reynolds collection.

Most but not all USMC sniper rifles used the "C" stock configuration. The handguard was the Type 9, 1st Variation replacement handguard modified to remove the front part of the convex swell lead-

346

Model 1903 Springfield Rifle and Its Variations

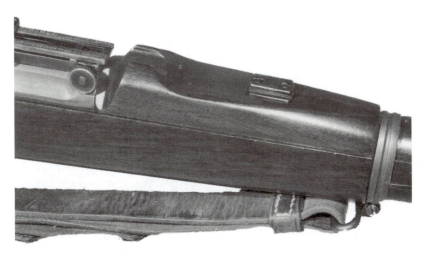

Fig. 4-11. The handguard was planed down forward of the rear sight protector hump and a hole with rounded ends cut through for the front mount. Larry Reynolds collection.

ing to the barrel band groove, see Figure 4-11. This design was first used on USMC rifles equipped with the Winchester A5 telescopic sight during World War I. A hole with rounded ends was then drilled

Fig. 4-12. Rear mount on the USMC M1903 sniper rifle for the Unertl scope. Larry Reynolds collection.

and chiseled through the handguard for the front base which was attached to the barrel with two screws. The rear base (Figure 4-12) was also attached to the receiver bridge with two screws. The large 0.20 gas port was drilled through the

Model 1903 Springfield Rifle and Its Variations

left side of the receiver ring. While a large number of National Match rifles that had been used by Marine Corps shooting teams before the war were used to make up the sniper rifles, not all USMC sniper rifles were National Match rifles. Those that were not had many of the National Match rifles' features. Almost all had polished rails and bolts, the latter of which was numbered with the receiver's serial number using an electric pen. Barrels were all star gauged but not all were marked as such on the muzzle. Those made up from National Match rifles that had been assembled at Springfield Armory and which retained their original National Match barrel were, if manufactured after 1921. See Chapter 1, Model 1903A1 (Sniper) USMC and appropriate parts sections in Chapter 2 for a complete description of the rifle.

The Unertl telescopic sights furnished under contract to the Marine Corps were marked:

J. UNERTL

USMC–SNIPER

XXX

Their first combat use came with the Raider Battalions in the jungles of New Georgia. But after-action reports disparaged the delicate scopes and mounts and pointed out that scoped rifles were of little use in that kind of terrain. The Commandant, who had previously supported the sniper rifle concept, concurred and in February 1944, the acquisition of further Unertl scopes was ended. At least one hundred of the sniper rifles were transferred to the Navy for use in minesweeping.

In the spring of 1945, a review was undertaken of the Unertl-equipped sniper rifles. The outcome was more favorable and they were authorized for issue once again in August of that year. It was noted that when the supply of M1903A1 sniper rifles became exhausted, they would be replaced with the M1C Garand sniper rifle. The M1903A1 USMC sniper rifles were to see action once again during the Korean War before being declared obsolete and eliminated from inventory.

Model 1903 Springfield Rifle and Its Variations

Those few USMC M1943A1 sniper rifles that survived World War II and the Korean Conflict, along with surplus and now obsolete USMC M1903s, M1903A1s and M1903A3s, appear to have all been sold in 1954 to members of the Corps for $25.00 through Organic Sales at various Marine Corps installations. The author has not been able to find any indication that the sniper rifles were sold complete with scopes and accessories, although it is likely that a few were. Most appear to have been stripped and sold as standard infantry rifles, although surviving documentation shows that some were sold with mounting blocks still attached.

MODEL 1903A4 SNIPER RIFLE

America's first large-scale offensive combat action in World War II at Guadalcanal in late 1942 showed that a well-handled sniper rifle could play a significant role. Accordingly, based on tests conducted by the Infantry Board and the Ordnance Department, Headquarters, U.S. Army Ground Forces approved the adoption of a sniper rifle based on the M1903 Springfield and the Weaver 330C telescopic sight. The Weaver scope was chosen only because it met minimum standards while offering one great advantage—it was readily available. Adopted

Fig. 4-13. M1903A4 sniper rifle with M73B1 telescopic sight in a "C" stock. First contract. North Cape Publications collection.

in December 1942, the new sniper rifle (see Figure 4-13) was characterized as follows: 1) The rifle was the M1903A1, changed to the M1903A4 before production actually began. 2) The scope was the 2.5X Weaver 330C, replaced in early 1943 by the militarized version, the M73B1. 3) It was mounted on the rifle using the Redfield Jr. one-

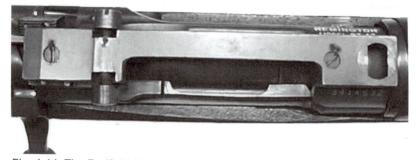

Fig. 4-14. The Redfield Jr. one-piece mount was attached to the receiver ring at the front and receiver bridge at the rear. Note the positioning of the manufacturer's name, model number and serial number.

piece mount with 3/4-inch rings, 4) bolted to the top of the receiver bridge (rear) and the receiver ring (front), Figure 4-14, with 5) the manufacturer's name, model number and serial number split between the left and right sides so that they would not be covered by the mount. Further, 6) a new concave bolt handle was developed that cleared the scope when the bolt handle was raised. The barreled action was to be mounted in 7) a pistol grip stock when available or the straight-grip "S" style stock when not (later the scant-grip stock was approved as a

Fig. 4-15. M1903A4 sniper rifle in a scant-grip stock by Keystone. North Cape Publications collection.

substitute standard), see Figure 4-15. The rifle was to have 8) neither front nor rear sights and in fact the front mounting point for the front sight was left empty. Finally, 10) the barrel could be rifled with either four or two grooves depending on availability. The rifle, scope and Model 1907 sling but without ammunition or bayonet weighed 9.125 lbs.

There was no apparent attempt to select either barrels or finished rifles for accuracy, a practice borne out by the fact that the model designation stamped on the receiver ring remained "M1903A3." If the rifle did not meet acceptable accuracy standards as a sniper rifle it could be returned to service as an M1903 rifle. Remington Arms received the responsibility for manufacturing the M1903A4 sniper rifle. None were manufactured by Smith Corona.

MODEL 1903A4 TELESCOPIC SIGHT

The Weaver 330C as well as its successor militarized version, the M73B1, had a 0.75-inch outside diameter and was 10.875 inches long, see Figure 4-16. It was set at zero windage and 100 yards elevation at the factory. The Redfield Jr. mount was attached to the rifle with two

Fig. 4-16. The M73B1 telescopic sight was based on the Weaver 330C commercial sight. North Cape Publications collection.

screws, one in the receiver ring and the other in the receiver bridge. The telescopic sight was attached to the mount by means of a lug on the front ring. The lug was placed into the mounting recess which was at right angles to the bore. The scope was then turned 90 degrees to the left to bring the rear lug into position over the rear mount. The rear lug was held in position by two adjusting crews with overlarge heads that threaded laterally into the rear mount. The heads bore against the rear lug and held the scope firmly in place.

Model 1903 Springfield Rifle and Its Variations

The telescopic sight was mounted in split rings which were clamped about the scope body by two screws in the forward ring and one screw in the rear ring. The scope was assembled to the rear mounting ring by passing the telescope tube through the ring until it was stopped by the adjusting plate. The clamping screw was turned down lightly to hold the tube. The front mount (two clamping screws) was passed over the tube and positioned about 3.35 inches ahead of the rear ring. It was also lightly tightened down about the tube. Once mounted on the rifle, the front mounting screws were loosened enough to allow the tube to move forward or back to bring the rear mount into position over its lug. The right and left mounting screws were then inserted and tightened loosely. With the rifle in a secure rest, the armorer positioned the reticle so that the windage crosshair was perfectly vertical.

The scope was targeted by bore sighting. The assembled rifle and telescope was placed in a secure rest and adjusted until the target was centered in the rifle's bore at 100 yards. The armorer then adjusted the crosshairs using the windage and elevation knobs until they were centered on the target, or at least as close as he could bring them.

To establish an elevation zero, if the horizontal crosshair (elevation) was higher than the target, the mount was shimmed at the rear to raise it the proper distance. If the horizontal crosshair was below the target, the shim was placed beneath the front of the mount. The armorer used a set of shims (Part No. A153174, A, B, C and D) which ranged in thickness from 0.005 ± 0.001 inch to 0.020 ± 0.001 inch to bring the elevation crosshair on target, or to elevation zero.

To establish the windage zero, with the elevation crosshair still centered on the target, the armorer turned in the left screw until it made contact with the rear mount and moved the vertical (windage) crosshair on target. He then turned the right screw in until it encountered the rear mount. With the elevation zero established, the left windage screw was staked in place.

The telescopic sight was adjusted for parallax at the factory by focusing the scope at twenty-five yards, then moving the reticle forward or back until the crosshair was in sharp focus. An armorer tested for parallax in the field by locking the rifle in a secure mount and sighting on a target 100 yards or more distant. If, when sighting through the eyepiece, he moved his head from side to side and detected any apparent movement between the crosshairs and the target, he knew that parallax had to be reset. If parallax had to be readjusted in the field, the armorer loosened the screws holding the adjusting plate and moved it back or forward as necessary until the crosshairs were again in sharp focus at twenty-five yards and beyond.

When assembling the scope to the rings, the ring clamp screws were left slightly loose so that the tube could be rotated to bring the crosshairs into perfect alignment. The windage adjustment knob (marked "L") was then on the left and the elevation knob (marked "UP") was on top, see Figure 4-19. All subsequent tele-

Fig. 4-19. Close-up of the M73B1 elevation (top) and windage (left) knobs.

scopic sights used on the M1903A4 sniper rifle went through much the same mounting and aligning procedure.

An unknown number of M73B1 scopes were also manufactured at the Frankford Arsenal in an effort to alleviate the shortage of scopes, see Figure 4-20.

The French M73B2

In late 1944, the Ordnance Department, in an effort to improve the M73B1, worked with the newly liberated French company, Optique et Precision de Levallois, to develop an improved telescopic sight that would retain the exterior features of the M73B1 and still fit the 3/4-

inch rings. A much-needed sunshade was mounted on the scope body and a range-scale reticle was substituted for the crosshairs. The projecting elevation and windage adjusting knobs were eliminated in favor of ring adjustments.

A modified mount was developed by Redfield which replaced the weak right and left cap screws with a threaded shaft that ran through the base. A projecting lug captured a recess in the underside of the rear ring. Zero was set by a jam nut and a threaded sleeved knob which was both stronger and easier to adjust.

Fig. 4-20. The Frankford Arsenal-manufactured M73B1 telescopic sight for the M1903A4 rifle. Larry Reynolds collection and photograph.

An unknown but rather small number of the French scopes, designated Telescope M73B2, were produced and used in the European Theater as the M1903A4 had already been reduced to "Limited Standard."

At least five different markings have been noted on the M1903A4 series of telescopic sights used during World War II:

MODEL 330
PATS PEND.
W.R. WEAVER CO.
EL PASO, TEX. USA

330 SCOPE–M8
PATENTS PENDING
W.R, WEAVER CO.
EL PASO, TEXAS

TELESCOPE M73B1
PAT'D–PATS. PEND.
W.R. WEAVER CO.
EL PASO, TEX. USA

TELESCOPE M73B1
FRANKFORD ARSENAL
SERIAL NO. XXX

TELESCOPE M73 B2
NO. XXXXX
O.P.L. FRANCE

The exterior metal parts of the Weaver, M73B1 and M73B2 scopes were polished and blued. A Parkerized finish indicates that the scope was refinished.

SNIPER RIFLE PRODUCTION

Three blocks of serial numbers were allocated to Remington Arms for the M1903A4 (Smith Corona did not build M1903A4s). The first block of 19,999 ran from serial numbers 3,407,088 to 3,427,087. They were stocked with the Springfield-made "C" and "scant-grip" stocks marked "S" and "K" (for Keystone) in the magazine cutoff recess. A survey of sniper rifles in this series (admittedly small at 13) suggests that most manufactured before May 1942 were equipped with four-groove rifle barrels.

Many of the early M1903A4s in this first block were equipped with Weaver 330C commercial 2.5X telescopic sights and the remainder with the "Telescope, M73B1." This military version of the 330C

Model 1903 Springfield Rifle and Its Variations

was adjustable for 1/4 minute angle changes in elevation and windage. The scope was officially designated "Sight, Telescopic, M73B1." The commercial 330 scopes had either a crosshair or tapered post reticle while the M73B1s had a crosshair only.

Fig. 4-21. A "Z" prefix was added to the first 2,920 M1903A4 rifle serial numbers in the second contract block because of an overrun in M1903A3 production. North Cape Publications collection.

A second block of 14,999 serial numbers was assigned in June 1943, running from 4,000,001 to 4,015,000. M1903A3 production, running ahead of schedule by two days, ran into this block and duplicate serial numbers were inadvertently produced. Only 2,920 from this block of M1903A4s were built and they had a "Z" stamped before the serial number, see Figure 4-21. These "Z" prefixed M1903A4 rifles have either 2- or 4-groove barrels, are equipped with the M73B1 telescopic sight and are stocked with either "S" or "Scant-Grip" stocks.

The third and final block of 7,044 serial numbers issued for the M1903A4 ran from 4,992,001 to 4,999,045. They were equipped very much like the Block 2 M1903A4s. But only an estimated total of 6,300 M1903A4s were made in this block before production of the M1903A3 ended in the early summer of 1944. The last M1903A4 rifles left the Remington Arms production line in June 1944, making it the last M1903 rifle of any variation to be produced.

The actual number of M1903A4s produced is not known. Campbell suggests a total of 28,365, Brophy 29,964.

Model 1903 Springfield Rifle and Its Variations

WORLD WAR II

The M1903A4 sniper rifle was widely distributed to combat troops from mid-1943 on. The first units to receive them were Airborne and Infantry units taking part in the North African campaign. Army units in the Pacific received them a bit later in keeping with the "European Theater First" strategy but by mid-1944, virtually every front-line combat unit had received at least a part of their quota. French Army B (later the French First Army) units were even equipped with the M1903A4 sniper rifle during Operation Dragoon, the invasion of Southern France which began on August 15, 1944. When the USMC M1903A1 sniper rifle was withdrawn from service in 1944, it was replaced with the M1903A4.

In spite of its extensive service, the M1903A4 was far from the ideal sniper rifle. Soldiers complained that the scope was too delicate and that the windage screws, if broken or lost, were nearly impossible to replace. The scope itself did not do well in the humid environment of the South Pacific and China-Burma-India theaters. It leaked moisture and the lenses misted over and mildew and mold crawled up the sides of tube and onto the crosshairs.

The small sight knobs and the minute markings were hard to make out in the field. The light-gathering power of the small-diameter objective lens was too low to make it of use in low-light situations— heavily overcast days, dawn or twilight. The low 2.5-magnification might have been a bit more acceptable if the light-gathering power of the scope had been greater. The mount was not sturdy enough to withstand the rough handling of soldiers in combat; drop the rifle and the chances were that if the scope were not broken, it was at least knocked out of alignment. Finally, in spite of what the technical manuals said, the scope did not maintain its zero when removed and then replaced. As a consequence, soldiers left the scope on at all times which only increased the chances of damaging it. Beyond the scope, the rifle itself was not especially suited to the role.

The initial testing that resulted in the selection of the M1903A3 as the sniper rifle had been conducted using the M1903A1, which from the standpoint of manufacture and fitting, was an altogether different rifle. The M1903A1 was built much like a fine sporting rifle. A great deal of attention was paid to drilling and rifling the barrel and fitting the barreled receiver into the stock. It is almost certain that the Infantry Board had the National Match version of the M1903 in mind when it made its decision to base the new sniper rifle on the M1903. But the M1903 was no longer being made by the time the sniper rifle entered production. The emphasis was on numbers produced and dependability and in the process accuracy was paid little more than lip service, especially after the end of 1943. The M1903A3 stocks had been "opened up" so that no handfitting was needed to assemble the barreled action to the stock. The author once owned an M1903A4 which appeared original in all respects and which had seen little or no action. Even with the stock bolts snugged up, the barreled action rattled in the stock. To make it shoot accurately, the receiver had to be shimmed all around with cardboard.

Even so, the M1903A4 equipped with the M73B1 scope stood the Army and Marines in fairly good stead to the end of the war, and if not all that popular, was at least useful.

Post-World War II

Not quite five years after the end of the deadliest war in the history of mankind, the U.S. military found itself again engaged in combat on the edge of the Asian landmass. The Chinese deployed an amazing number of snipers equipped with their copy of the venerable Mosin-Nagant M1891/30 sniper rifle. In keeping with the traditions and practices adopted from the Soviet Red Army, snipers were an integral part of their front-line units.

The M1C Garand had completed development just as World War II was winding down but it saw wide distribution during the Korean War. The M1903A4, which had been relegated to the status of limited standard, was also shipped in large numbers to Korea. There, some of the M1903A4s were reequipped with the somewhat sturdier Lyman Gun Sight-manufactured Alaskan telescope, either the com-

Model 1903 Springfield Rifle and Its Variations

Fig. 4-22. Four of the twelve different telescopic sights used on the M1903A4, top to bottom: M73B1, Lyman Alaskan M73E1, M81 (without its sunshield) and the M84. North Cape Publications collection.

mercial variant, or those acquired by the Ordnance Department during and after World War II. It appears that Lyman was unable to fulfill its agreement to provide Alaskan scopes to Remington Arms for the M1903A4 Sniper Program during World War II. Those it did deliver to the Ordnance Department went to the M1C Garand Program.

Four variations of the "military" Alaskan are observed: 1) The M73E1 with just the part number "7634671" stamped on the windage and elevation adjustment mounts, "7674029" on the scope tube or body and "7634670"on the eyepiece. 2) The M81 in two variations, one with the commercial markings but stamped "M81" and 3) the M81 and 4) the M82 variations without commercial markings. New 7/8-inch rings had to be purchased from the Lyman Gun Sight Corporation, see Figures 4-22 and 4-23. Virtually all of the Lyman scopes mounted on the M1903A4 appear to have been done so at the Army depot level.

The M1903A4 did not prove popular with the troops who used it in Korea, as complaints about its accuracy and durability were

Model 1903 Springfield Rifle and Its Variations

Fig. 4-23. The M1903A4 with the Lyman Alaskan M73E1 military contract scope. The scope body, windage and elevation housing and eyepiece show part numbers. North Cape Publications collection.

rife. But a good deal of that may have been due to inadequate, or, in many cases, a complete lack of training for those who used the rifle. One anecdote is illustrative and was told to the author by a friend who served as a Navy medical corpsman with the Marines in Korea.

"We had both a Model 1903A4 with the M73B1 sight and an M1C with the post sight (M82). For over a month we were entrenched along the top of a ridge line overlooking a wide valley. On the other side were the Chinese troops. Both rifles were propped on sandbags and were there for anyone to use who wanted to try his luck. Our company did not have a designated sniper."

Fig. 4-24. A few M1903A4s were fitted with the M84 telescopic sight in the late 1950s and saw use in Vietnam in 1964-1965. North Cape Publications collection.

In the late 1950s and early 1960s, many of the M1903A4s that remained in service were once again reconditioned. A small number were reequipped with the M84 telescopic sight which had been developed for the M1D Garand sniper rifle.

The M1903A4's swan song came early in the Vietnam conflict. A small number of rifles equipped with the M84 scope were sent to both American and South Vietnamese forces in 1964-65 but saw limited use. They were later withdrawn and the M1903A4 was declared obsolete, see Figure 4-24.

Markings on the commercial Lyman Alaskan, military-acquired M73E1 Alaskan, M81, M82 and M84 telescopic sights areas follow. All exterior metal parts were blued or finished with black oxide. Parkerization indicates refinishing. All scopes mounted on the M1903A4 with the Redfield Jr.mounts used Lyman 7/8-inch rings.

Commercial Lyman Alaskan:

THE LYMAN GUN SIGHT CORP.
MADE IN U.S.A. MIDDLEFIELD, CONN ALASKAN
U.S. PATENT NO. 2078858

    Reticle Pattern: Post
    Sunshade/Rubber eyecup
    Magnification: 2.5X

Military Lyman Alaskan (M73E1):
THE LYMAN GUN SIGHT CORP.
MADE IN U.S.A. MIDDLEFIELD, CONN ALASKAN
U.S. PATENT NO. 2078858
    Windage and Elevation mounts marked: 7634671
    Windage and Elevation caps marked: A7575180
    Eyepiece marked: 7634670
    Scope body marked: 7674029
    Reticle Pattern: Post
    Sunshade/Rubber eyecup
    Magnification: 2.5X

Model 1903 Springfield Rifle and Its Variations

M81

THE LYMAN GUN SIGHT CORP.
ALASKAN
MADE IN U.S.A. MIDDLEFIELD, CONN
U.S. PATENT NO. 2078858
TELESCOPE M81
SERIAL NO. XXXXX
STOCK NO. 64373

Windage and Elevation mounts marked: 7634671
Windage and Elevation caps marked: 7575180
Eyepiece marked: 7634670
Scope body marked: 7674029
Reticle Pattern: Crosshairs
Sunshade/Rubber eyecup
Magnification: 2.5X

TELESCOPE M81
SERIAL NO. XXXX
STOCK NO. 84373

Windage and Elevation mounts marked: 7634671
Windage and Elevation caps marked: 7575180
Eyepiece marked: 7634670
Scope body marked: 7674029
Reticle Pattern: Crosshairs
Sunshade/Rubber eyecup
Magnification: 2.5X

Model 1903 Springfield Rifle and Its Variations

M82 (Prior to 1948)

TELESCOPE M82
SERIAL NO. XXXX
STOCK NO. 84374

Windage and Elevation mounts marked: 7634671
Windage and Elevation caps marked: 7575180
Eyepiece marked: 7634670
Scope body marked: 7674029
Reticle Pattern: Post
Sunshade/Rubber eyecup
Magnification: 2.5X

M82 (1948 and after)

TELESCOPE M82
SERIAL NO. XXXX
STOCK NO. F001-0084888

Windage and Elevation mounts marked: 7634671
Windage and Elevation caps marked: 7575180
Eyepiece marked: 7634670
Scope body marked: 7674029
Reticle Pattern: Post
Sunshade/Rubber eyecup
Magnification: 2.5X

M84

TELESCOPE
M84
SERIAL NO. XXXXX

Reticle Pattern: Post and elevation crosshair
Sunshade/Rubber eyecup
Magnification: 2.2X

Model 1903 Rifle Serial Numbers

PRODUCTION RANGE—SPRINGFIELD ARMORY

The first complete M1903 Springfield Rifle was produced in 1903 and serial numbered "1" in the Rod Bayonet configuration. Surprisingly enough, it was not sent to the Springfield Museum but was issued. It was discovered in 1917 in France after having gone through the change from rod bayonet to knife bayonet to .30-06 caliber, then restocked in 1917 and reissued again to Frank C. Lynaugh, Company E, 49th Infantry Regiment, American Expeditionary Force. When Company E's Springfields were withdrawn and exchanged for M1917 Enfields, Private Lynaugh protested the loss of his unique rifle. His complaint came to the attention of his company officer, who, recognizing its value, arranged to have it sent to the Springfield Armory Museum.

Production of the M1903 service rifle ended at Springfield in 1927 although non-service rifles such as the U.S. Rifle, Caliber .22, M2 continued to be assembled into 1942. Spare-parts production continued to 1939 (including receivers) and assembly of rifles continued for two more years before Remington Arms Company began production. The last complete M1903 rifle is thought to have been serial number 1,532,878, built in October 1939. But higher-serial-numbered receivers have been noted: 1,534,854 was formerly in the collection of the late Lt. Col. William S. Brophy; 1,547,989 was listed in the Director of Civilian Marksmanship (now the Civilian Marksmanship Program) records and 1,592,563 was recorded at the Frankford Arsenal, although it is possible that the number was a transcribing error.

Serial number 1,532,878 was identified as the highest serial number by the late Major General Julian Hatcher. But current thinking is that he was reporting the last rifle completed and not the last receiver produced. Springfield Armory manufactured spare parts including barrels as late as 1944. The usual manufacturing practice was to produce "extra" units to be used in the future as spare parts. If these were produced as unfinished receivers, they may well have not been serial numbered or hardened until needed. This practice could account for receivers above General Hatcher's reported serial number 1,532,878.

It is also conceivable that Springfield continued to manufacture receivers as replacement parts after 1939, possibly as high as the 1,592,563 serial number reported from Frankford Arsenal.

Either practice would not be uncommon. Instances of serial numbers and dated receivers higher than the last year of rifle production (1925) and serial numbers beyond the last reported (517,277) are relatively common in the m/96 rifle receivers manufactured for the Swedish Army at the Carl Gustafs stad Gevärsfaktori in Sweden, many of whose practices paralleled those of the Springfield Armory. See *The Swedish Mauser Rifles* by Steve Kehaya and Joe Poyer.

Fig. A-1. U.S. Magazine Rifle, Caliber .30, Model 1903 (rod bayonet), serial number 1, Rock Island Arsenal. Inset shows the rifle's 1905-dated Conrad Nelson cartouche. Photographs courtesy of Rock Island Arsenal Museum and Chris Gayman Leinickem, Director.

PRODUCTION RANGE—ROCK ISLAND ARSENAL

Rock Island Arsenal's serial number "1" fared better than Springfield's serial number "1." It was immediately sent to the Rock Island Arsenal where it remained in its original form. It is one of the very, very few original M1903 (rod bayonet) rifles to have survived, see Figure A-1.

Model 1903 Springfield Rifle and Its Variations

The RIA receiver serial number range is broken into two sections, 1905-1913 and 1917-1919, although assembly of previously manufactured parts apparently continued to at least 1921. The total produced is estimated at between 430,742 and 451,133. The last figure may include spare receivers.

Production Range—Remington Arms Company

The Remington Arms Company was approached in 1940 by the British government to manufacture a variation of the M1903 rifle. Before the contracts could be finalized, the U.S. Army issued a new contract to the company on September 17, 1941 that superceded the British contract. Remington first manufactured an almost exact copy of the Rock Island M1903 using surplus RIA tools, fixtures and jigs that had been in storage for twenty years. As the contract progressed, simplified methods of production were introduced that led, over a one-year period from the M1903 through the M1903 (Modified) to the M1903A3 rifle and its sniper version, the M1903A4. Production of the M1903 variation ended in June 1944 with the final rifles being produced in the M1903A4 configuration.

As noted above, the total number of receivers manufactured at both Springfield and Rock Island is in dispute. The picture is hardly clearer when it comes to Remington and Smith Corona. Record keeping had improved by the 1940s and there was less time to dispose of old records before such researchers as Lt. Col. William S. Brophy and Clark S. Campbell gained access.

Even so, there are differences of opinion. A report prepared by the Public Relations Division, Remington Arms Corporation, Inc., Bridgeport, CT, and dated May 9, 1945, sets the figure for combined production of all Remington variations of the M1903 rifle from November 1941 through June 1944 at 1,084,079. Campbell appears to have used these numbers as well. Brophy provides a total for all Remington production of the Model 1903 variations during the same period as 1,178,761. This amounts to a difference of 94,682–approximately 1.5 month's peak production.

Model 1903 Springfield Rifle and Its Variations

Production Range—Smith Corona

The L.C. Smith Corona Typewriters Company was provided with a letter contract for 100,000 M1903 (Modified) rifles on February 24, 1942, little more than a month after the contract was first proposed to the High Standard Manufacturing Company. High Standard agreed but only if they could use L.C. Smith Corona as a subcontractor for all parts except the barrels which they would manufacture. It was then decided that Smith Corona should be the prime contractor and High Standard the subcontractor. Production began in November 1942 with 5,540 rifles completed by the end of December. These included some barrels with six grooves manufactured by Savage. Stocks were subcontracted to American Bowling & Billiard Corporation and were the "S" configuration without the pistol grip or scant grip. Smith Corona did not produce any M1903A4 sniper rifles.

The total rifles built by Smith Corona is not clear. Campbell provides two figures, 233,998 and 234,580 rifles (*The '03 Era*, pages 116 and 129), and Brophy, 236,831 ending in February 1944.

Total Number of M1903 Rifles and Variations Produced

It is incorrect to speak of total "rifles" produced. Rather, the focus should be on the total number of *receivers* produced. For instance, we know that 49,000 to 62,000 rod bayonet rifles manufactured at Rock Island were altered to accept the M1905 knife bayonet while still remaining in .30-M1903 caliber. A further 62,540 were then altered again to the .30-M1906 caliber. There are no records of new receivers being made for these rifles and so it is assumed that existing receivers were simply reused. The same situation occurred at Springfield Armory but the numbers were greater: 209,183 rod bayonet rifles altered to accept the M1905 knife bayonet and 207,446 later altered to .30-M1906 caliber. Again, the original receivers were used.

Model 1903 Springfield Rifle and Its Variations

It is not known to what extent, if any, Remington Arms and Smith Corona produced spare receivers. So, if we stick with figures we know and take the low and high estimates, we have a low of 3,282,279 and a high of 3,459,288 Model 1903 and variation receivers/rifles manufactured. This provides us with a variance of 177,009 during a production period totaling forty-one years.

NOTABLE SERIAL NUMBERS

49,628. First Springfield production rifle in the M1905 alteration series completed and was taken directly from Assembly to the Museum. It has a 1-06 dated barrel.

285,507. New double heat treatment of receivers was begun at Rock Island Arsenal on May 11, 1918.

319,921. Point at which M1903 receivers made of nickel steel alloy were begun to be manufactured at Rock Island Arsenal (August 1918).

346,779. Believed to be the last complete M1903 rifle manufactured at Rock Island Arsenal. A total of 445,000 receivers were believed to have been manufactured, including rifles assembled after 1919 and spare receivers. Several hundred or more receivers beyond #346,779 were manufactured as spares, several hundred of which were used by Springfield in 1928 during the switch to nickel steel receivers.

800,000. New double heat treatment of receivers was begun at Springfield Armory in mid-1917.

1,275,767. Point at which M1903 receivers made of nickel steel alloy were begun to be phased in at Springfield Armory (March 1927).

1,532,878. Believed to be the last complete M1903 rifle manufactured at Springfield Armory in October 1939. It is possible that as many as 60,000 additional receivers may have been manufactured as spare parts between the official end of production in 1939 and the actual end of all

M1903 spare parts production in 1944.

3,000,000. First M1903A1 manufactured by Remington Arms on Rock Island Arsenal tooling and delivered in September 1941.

3,133,445 (circa). First M1903 (Modified) manufactured by Remington Arms and delivered in March-April, 1942.

3,364,955 (circa). First M1903A3 rifle manufactured by Remington Arms and delivered in December 1942.

3,407,088. First M1903A4 sniper rifle manufactured by Remington Arms and delivered in April 1943.

3,608,000. First M1903A3 rifle manufactured by Smith Corona, November 1942 and delivered in December 1942.

DUPLICATE SERIAL NUMBERS—M1903A3/A4

On August 11, 1942, William C. Morin, Captain, Ordnance Department, Army Inspector of Ordnance, Contracting Officer's Representative, wrote to W.T. Wood, Remington Arms Co., Inc., Ilion, NY, regarding duplicate serial numbers. The letter was uncovered in the Remington Arms Company files by Clark S. Campbell.

To that point, Remington had been marking any duplicate serial numbers that were turned up with the letter "A" before the serial number on its second use. Captain Morin instructed Remington Arms to use the letter "Z" instead, noting that it had been "used for similar purposes in other facilities."

He also noted in his letter that approval had been granted to set up the serial number stamping machine so that a given serial number could only be used once. This eliminated the need to keep records of serial numbers of scrapped receivers in the future.

The fact that "Z"- marked receivers appear after August 1942 suggests that a considerable stockpile of scrapped and/or duplicate

Model 1903 Springfield Rifle and Its Variations

receivers existed that were subsequently made available for assembly into finished rifles at a later date, including the author's own Z-prefix M1903A4 sniper rifle.

SERIAL NUMBER LISTING

Think the annual serial numbering ranges of the M1903 and its various models are straightforward and well known? Think again. There are at least three sets of annual serial numbers that are accepted by collectors as valid but in truth, none are. All are based on various production records and annual reports from the four manufacturers: Springfield Armory, Rock Island Arsenal, Remington Arms and Smith Corona. None take into account rifles in the inspection process when the counts were made, receivers transferred into inventory for spare parts, receivers discarded for various reasons and clerical and other transcription errors between reports.

The serial number ranges for Springfield in Table A1 were compiled by Lt. Col. Brophy from several sources to which he added the "extra receivers manufactured to finished rifles reported for the years 1935 and after . . ." The author has revised a few serial number ranges where direct observation of original rifles with later end-of-year serial numbers has occurred. The serial numbers for Rock Island Arsenal are based on "Expenditures at Rock Island Arsenal, Fiscal Years 1905-1914," as amended by C.S. Ferris in *Rock Island Rifle, Model 1903*, see Appendix I, Bibliography.

In the case of the Remington Arms and Smith Corona M1903A3 rifles, the annual serial number ranges are based on estimates made by the author from reports of monthly production and observation of serial numbers and barrel dates. The author emphasizes that they are, at best, estimates. No outraged phone calls, letters or e-mails, please.

But we would be pleased to accept any and all e-mails containing December or January barrel dates *and* serial numbers from any Springfield Model 1903 or M1903A1, Rock Island M1903, Remington Arms Model 1903, Model 1903 (Modified), Model 1903A3, or Model 1903A4 rifles or Smith Corona Model 1903A3 rifles.

370

Model 1903 Springfield Rifle and Its Variations

Table A1 Model 1903 Receiver Serial Numbers		
Year	Springfield Armory[1] (Calendar Year)	Rock Island Arsenal[2] (Fiscal Year)
1903	1-30,503	Tooling Up
1904	45,905	Tooling Up
1905	100,000[3]	18,000[4]
1906	192,321	54,375
1907	269,563	87,840
1908	337,862[5]	120,954
1909	358,085	141,070
1910	398,276	168,882
1911	456,376	191,324
1912	502,123	211,665
1913	531,561	231,378
1914	559,109[7]	234,753
1915	580,601	No Production
1916	620,176	No Production
1917	632,826	238,000[8,9]
1918	761,758[10]	289,900[9]
1919	1,055,092	322,747[9]
1920	1,162,525	430,742[9]
1921	1,211,300	No Production
1922	1,239,641	

Model 1903 Springfield Rifle and Its Variations

	Table A1, cont. Model 1903 Receiver Serial Numbers	
Year	**Springfield Armory[1] (Calendar Year)**	**Rock Island Arsenal[2] (Fiscal Year)**
1923	1,252,387	
1924	1,262,492	
1925	1,267,101	
1926	1,270,301	
1927	1,274,765	
1928	1,285,289	
1929	1,305,901	
1930	1,338,406	
1931	1,369,761	No Production
1932	1,404,026	
1933	1,425,934	
1934	1,441,812	
1935	1,491,532	
1936	1,505,411	
1937	1,510,017	
1938	1,511,037	
1939	1,530,144	
1940 January to December	1,538,594 - 1,548,621[11]	**Remington Arms (Calendar Year)**
1941	None	3,000,001-3,003,001

Model 1903 Springfield Rifle and Its Variations

Table A1, cont. Model 1903 Receiver Serial Numbers		
Year	Remington Arms (Estimated[11])	Smith Corona (Estimated[11])
1942	3,003,001-3,352,995	3,608,000-3,613,540
1943	3,352,996 -4,998,300	3,613,540-3,707,000 4,708,000-4,828,435
1944	4,998,301-5,004,801 to 5,005,345	4,828,436-4,845,831

1. Annual Ordnance Reports.
2. Dependable production serial numbers for Rock Island Arsenal (1905-1914) are not available. The source used here for the period 1905-1914 are the Expenditures at Rock Island reports as interpreted by C.S. Ferris (*Rock Island Rifle, Model 1903*). He points out a probable error in the FY 1909 totals. When corrected, the total production figure of 234,753 results which agrees closely with the total found in the Chief of Ordnance Reports to the Secretary of War, and others, during this period. The figures are for completed rifles which are not the same as receivers produced. Ferris estimates an additional 1%, or 2,347, receivers were produced as spares.
3. Turned into storage as rod bayonet rifles.
4. Turned into storage as unassembled rod bayonet rifles.
5. Full production of M1903 (.30-06) begun.
6. Production of completed rifles ceased in November 1913. Receiver production may have ended earlier. Last receiver serial number as reported by Col. G. W. Burr, Commanding Officer, RIA, to Chief of Ordnance in a telegram dated April 30, 1917 was 237,533. This *may not* have been a completed rifle but a receiver manufactured for use as a replacement part.
7. There appears to be a typographical error in the list of serial numbers compiled by Brophy in that his entry for 1914 is 20,960 lower than for 1913 (page 425). The correct number should probably be 55,906 with a corresponding increase the following year.
8. Production of the M1903 rifle resumed at RIA on February 25, 1917.
9. Ferris states that RIA production resumed officially on February 25, 1917 but that rifle barrels dated 12-16 have been observed. He also states that production resumed with serial #238,000. If so, then based on monthly inspection and acceptance reports, the serial number ranges for 1917 to May 1919 are offered with the proviso that they do not include spare parts receivers placed in inventory nor the unknown number of rifles assembled after production ended in May 1919.
10. New heat treatment introduced at Springfield Armory circa serial number 750,001-800,000, and at Rock Island Arsenal at #285,507, as standard procedure.
11. Serial number ranges by calendar year for Remington Arms and Smith Corona production are estimates only. Serial numbers shown for the beginning of each year are in the range verified by observation.

APPENDIX **B**
M1903 Manufacturing Procedures and Finishes

BARREL MANUFACTURING TECHNIQUE

The M1903 barrel blank was made from bar stock which was heated and rolled through twelve sets of grooved rollers to produce a rough barrel varying in length from 24 to 25.5 inches. The rough barrels underwent a series of operations which included: heating, rolling to near-final shape, straightening while hot with a drop hammer, cutting to rough length and cooling to form the final barrel.

The barrel was straightened a second time and then rifled. Rifling was accomplished by "scrape cutting," a slow but precise process applied to all barrels manufactured by Rock Island Arsenal and by the Springfield Armory before World War II. The four grooves were cut to 0.1767 inch wide and a depth of 0.004 inch with a tool drawn through the bore. It took 46 minutes to cut the four grooves in a single barrel but the cutting method produced extremely smooth surfaces. When the star gauge was later introduced to measure barrel diameters, it was found that most barrels did not vary more than 0.0001 inch in diameter from one end of the bore to the other!

Because of the method of manufacture and the numerous machining operations performed on the blank, severe stresses were set up in the metal. Barrels made during and before World War I often showed evidence of such stress by very large changes in point of impact as the barrel heated during rapid fire. To reduce manufacturing stresses, a separate procedure was added to the manufacturing process after the war. The barrels were heated to a set temperature and cooled at a specific rate to relieve the stresses.

When the rifling was completed, the chamber was cut to 0.004 inch short of the final dimension. This allowed the assembler to properly headspace the barrel by hand with a finishing reamer after it was assembled to the receiver and fitted with a bolt. Soldiers in the pre-World War II army were warned in the most dire terms that bolts should not be swapped between rifles except by an armorer who could recheck or adjust the headspace. An excellent warning for modern-day 1903 riflemen: always have the headspace of a M1903 rifle checked with the proper headspace gauges.

RECEIVER MANUFACTURING TECHNIQUE

Springfield-manufactured receivers were made of Class C steel to circa serial #1,275,767 (1927). Rock Island receivers were made of Class C steel to serial #319,921 (August 1918). After those respective serial numbers, both Springfield and Rock Island receivers were made of nickel steel. In the initial production of nickel steel receivers made at Springfield, partly finished receivers were included that had been left over when Rock Island stopped M1903 receiver production in 1919. Some of these receivers were marked Rock Island but were not serial numbered and so received serial numbers in the Springfield series.

The biggest controversy surrounding the Model 1903 rifle has always concerned pre-World War I receivers and how they were heat-treated. Major General Julian Hatcher provides a through explanation of the problem and how it was resolved in his *Hatcher's Notebook*. But to summarize quickly, receivers were given a case-hardened surface which provided excellent resistance to wear, by heating to a specified temperature and then cooling rapidly in oil. The workmen at both Springfield and Rock Island, all old hands with many years of experience, did not use instruments to determine the temperature but rather judged it visually by inspecting the color of the heated metal. Unfortunately, changes in ambient light affected the color they saw in the furnace and a certain percentage of receivers were hardened to the point that they became brittle.

When Rock Island resumed production of new rifles in February 1917 they continued to use the single heat treatment method on receivers as with earlier production. Reports of both Springfield and RIA receiver failure began to accumulate as a result of heavy training use and wartime ammunition. An investigation identified the combination of poor ammunition with soft heads and the current heat treatment method as the culprit. Springfield stopped new rifle production between February and June 1917 at circa serial #750,000-800,000. Rock Island also halted production of receivers and bolts on January 30, 1918 at receiver serial #285,506.

A new double heat treatment method was developed and tested along with the proper instrumentation for assuring that the proper temperatures were used. Springfield resumed production at circa serial #750,001 and the new heat treatment method was phased in between then and circa serial #800,000. Hatcher notes that some earlier single-heat-treated receivers that had been set aside, were put back onto the assembly line right after #800,000. How many exactly is apparently not known.

At Rock Island, some 16,000 receivers between serial #s 269,506 to 285,507 already in inventory were given the new double heat treating method. But out of this group, some 5,846 receivers had previously received the old single heat treatment and these were destroyed. The double heat treatment of new Rock Island receivers began as standard procedure at serial #285,507 (May 11, 1918).

Starting at serial #319,921, Rock Island Arsenal began to manufacture both receivers and bolts from nickel steel instead of the Springfield Class C steel which eliminated whatever problem remained. Springfield switched to nickel steel receivers and bolt parts at serial #1,275,767 on March 2, 1927.

Parkerizing was adopted first at Rock Island Arsenal on March 12, 1918 at circa serial #318,000. Springfield began Parkerizing in November 1918 at circa serial #1,103,000. The Parkerizing was applied to major parts only, including receivers, barrels, rear sight bases and mounts, bolts and trigger guards.

FINISHES

Model 1903 parts were blued from the start of production to November 1918 when the new finish called Parkerizing was applied. **Bluing**

Model 1903 Springfield Rifle and Its Variations

(called browning by the Ordnance Department) was accomplished by dipping the cleaned and degreased steel parts in a heated solution of salts which quickly oxidized the surface and produced a characteristic blue-black finish. The degree of shine to the finish was directly proportional to the amount of polishing the metal surface was given. Bluing did not necessarily protect the metal from rusting; rather, it eliminated light reflections.

Bluing was a time-consuming process and was accomplished in the following manner. If the part was the barrel, the bore was coated with cosmoline and the ends plugged to make them watertight. The part was boiled in lime water for 20 minutes to remove all traces of grease and oil, cooled and wiped clean of lime. The part was then coated with the browning solution and allowed to stand for 15 minutes, followed by another coat of browning solution. It was then placed in a steam-heated cabinet for sixteen hours. The fine coat of rust thus produced was carded (brushed) off with a fine wire wheel. More browning mixture was applied and the barrels (and all other parts being blued) were returned to the steam-heated cabinet. After three hours they were removed, carded, and swabbed with the browning solution and allowed to stand in the steam cabinet overnight. The rust was carded off a final time and the barrel (or other part) was cleaned and oiled.

Smaller steel parts such as screws, pins, knobs and so on were **niter blued** (also called heat blue) by dipping them in a solution of molten potassium nitrate for up to twenty minutes. As the steel part heated it took on the characteristic color of the temperature range. An iridescent blue color is obtained at between 600 and 650^0 F. It was a quick and efficient way of coloring small parts but could not easily be applied to larger parts.

In March 1918 at Rock Island and November 1918 at Springfield, a new finishing method known as **Parkerizing** replaced the bluing method. It was quicker and provided greater protection against rust and corrosion. The part was degreased, then boiled in the Parkerizing solution for 30 minutes. The Parkerizing solution contained a proprietary mixture of dilute phosphoric acid and finely powdered iron which produced a thin but tough layer of iron phosphate on the steel. The M1903 Parkerized parts were then dipped in an oil containing a black dye to produce the black, non-glare finish found on all M1903 service rifles produced after World War I.

A process called **carburizing** was used to harden the surface of the part. Any color produced was the by-product of the process. Carburizing is similar to case-hardening in that a very hard surface to a depth of a few thousandths of an inch results. The hard surface resists wearing yet the interior of the steel retains a certain plasticity that allows it to resist shock. Carburizing was applied to receivers, butt plates and bolt parts. In the carburizing process, the part was heated in an atmosphere containing a large percentage of carbon which reacted with the surface metal to produce a high content of carbon in the steel, and therefore a harder steel.

In the **case-hardening** process, the steel part was a placed into a metal box filled with bone meal and scrap leather. The box was placed into a furnace and heated to around 1200^0 F and held at the temperature for a specified period of time. The longer the part was heated, the deeper the case or surface hardness. The box was removed from the furnace and the part quickly dropped into a coolant. If a blackish finish was required, the part was dropped into light oil to cool. If a mottled red-blue-yellow finish was required, it was dropped into water. To increase the color intensity, air was sometimes bubbled through the water tank.

APPENDIX C

Marking Procedures
for the Model 1903 Rifle and Its Variants

Proofing and marking methods for the M1903 Springfield series of rifles remained remarkably consistent from start to finish of production. When the rifle was assembled from new parts or a rifle was given a new receiver and/or barrel, it underwent proof firing. Two procedures were used, "A" for new rifles or those receiving new receivers and/or barrels and "B" for rifles rebuilt from components which had previously been proof-tested. See the "Markings" sections under "Barrels" and "Receivers" in Chapter 2 for specific markings by model.

PROCEDURE A

The head space was checked to measure the linear distance between the bolt face and the chamber shoulder with the bolt closed and locked to assure that it was between 1.940 and 1.943 inches. The rifle was then locked into a cradle. Until 1927, one high-pressure proof cartridge (called a "blue pill") producing 68,000 psi was loaded into the chamber over an empty magazine. A metal shield was lowered over the rifle and the test cartridge was fired remotely. Five service rounds (52,000 psi each) were then loaded into the magazine and fired. From 1927 on, a second high-test cartridge was also fired over an empty magazine.

The head space was rechecked to make certain it remained within the original specifications or as close to them as possible, not exceeding 1.946 inches under any circumstances.

PROCEDURE B

Procedure B, added in 1927, was identical to the original Procedure A but without the second proof cartridge.

Model 1903 Springfield Rifle and Its Variations

PROOF MARKS

Proof-marking procedures varied in minor detail during the production life of the Model 1903 rifle and its variants. Barrels, bolts and receivers were proofed by firing a proof cartridge exceeding by half that developed by a normal cartridge. To show that the part or assembled rifle had been proofed, the following markings were applied.

Barrel: Until 1923, a small punch mark was made on the lip of the muzzle of all barrels proofed; after, the punch mark was centered in the Flaming Bomb of the Ordnance Escutcheon near the muzzle.

If the barrel was proofed separately from the finished rifle, it was marked with a "P" on the underside of the barrel about midway between the rear sight band and muzzle. The "P" was 0.19 inch high and sans serif.

Receiver: At various times, the receiver was marked with a sharp-pointed punch, either on the bottom flat or on the shoulder flat below the serial number.

Bolt: The bolt was punch marked on the bottom of the bolt handle root.

Stock: When the rifle was proofed, the Armory inspector or his designate stamped a "P" inside a circle on the stock just behind the trigger guard plate. From 1903 to 1905, the "P" had serifs. From 1906 on it was replaced by a stamp design that did not have serifs, although the "P" with serifs saw occasional use into the early 1920s. The "P" was 0.31 inch high.

New proofing rules were issued in 1923 and required that the receiver, barrel and bolt always be marked with a punch to show that each part had been proof-tested. This was done as stocks were often changed and those replaced in the field, if new, did not have the "P" proof stamped behind the trigger guard.

Although proof rules issued in 1933 stated that a rifle proofed for a second time should have a second "P" stamped behind the trigger guard, no examples have been observed. It seems that this ruling was ignored, or if followed, was done to a very small number of rifles.

Accuracy: The 1923 Ordnance Field Bulletin required one rifle in 100 to be fired at 200 and 500 yards for accuracy and one rifle in 5,000 to be fired 6,000 times for endurance.

FINAL INSPECTION PROOF MARK

After the rifle had been completely assembled and proof-tested, it was inspected a final time by the armory inspector or his designate and marked with a stamp on the left side below and slightly behind the cutoff recess. During the manufacture of the .45-70 Springfield rifle and carbine and the Krag rifle and carbine, the stamp had taken on the form of a rectangle with clipped corners containing the initial of the armory inspector and the year date it was applied in a graceful script. As production increased, more inspectors were required and the script stamps gave way to stamps with sans serif letters and the year and finally to rectangles without clipped corners and block or sans serif letters and no year date. As late as 1917, the regulations still called for initials and date but by 1906, the date was fast disappearing. The last instance of it being used was at Rock Island Arsenal by W.M. Halferty (WMH 1918).

Many of the M1903A1 rifles produced just before World War II are marked with the inspector's initials without a rectangle and certainly without a date.

Late World War II and postwar rebuilds are marked with the Armory initials over the inspector's initials: example, S.A./G.A.W. (Springfield Armory/George A. Woody) inside a box with rounded corners.

Model 1903 Springfield Rifle and Its Variations

The non-service rifles produced by Springfield Armory were proof marked differently:

1. The M1903 .22-caliber Hoffer-Thompson rifles were marked on the stock with the inspector's mark but barrels were not proof marked.

2. M1922, M1922M1 and M2 .22-caliber gallery rifles did not show either the inspector's proof on the stock or the barrel proof mark.

3. The .30-caliber non-service rifles usually were not marked with the inspector's proof on the stock but usually did show barrel proof marks. The word "usually" means just that.

REMINGTON ARMS/SMITH CORONA PRODUCTION

The M1903, M1903 (Modified) and M1903A3 rifles built by both Remington Arms and Smith Corona were to be marked in accordance with the standard practice described in the 1933 regulations. The rifles' parts were further to be marked to identify the manufacturing concern who actually produced them. Remington Arms and its subcontractors followed the marking procedure faithfully, Smith Corona less so. The standard Model 1903A3 will show the following markings:

Barrel: "RA/ordnance escutcheon/month year" or "SC/Ordnance escutcheon/month and year." Also HS for High Standard on replacement barrels. A punch prick proof mark will be applied in the middle of the ordnance bomb in the escutcheon to show that barrel was proofed. Also a small "P" with serifs on the bottom of the barrel, two inches below the front sight. Various factory stamps will be found at the breech end of the barrel.

Receiver: "U.S./Remington/Model 03-A3/Serial number" or "U.S./Smith-Corona/Model 03-A3/Serial number" over the chamber. Various factory inspector markings will be found on the flat between the recoil lug and the magazine well. Also on either side of the receiver below the shoulders.

Model 1903 Springfield Rifle and Its Variations

Bolt: A punch mark will show on the bottom of the bolt handle root to indicate that the bolt has been proofed. All parts of Remington-made bolts are marked "R" or "R" in a circle with the exception of the mainspring, firing pin sleeve, sleeve lock and the various pins and springs. Smith Corona bolts are marked "X" on the bolt handle root and occassionally on other major parts.

Stock: Various factory markings are found on original M1903A3 stocks. On the outside bottom ahead of the magazine well, stocks were marked with the manufacturer's and Ordnance Department inspector's proofs as single initials alone, inside boxes, circles, or triangles. Smith Corona also used a "2" or "6" in a diamond.

Some other initials that differentiate the stocks are: "7," "9," "12," and "23" in a circle; plus "8" in a box and "18" alone appear to be unique to Smith Corona. Any letter or number in a diamond is probably stamped on a Smith Corona stock as the author has never identified any Remington-inspected stock using a diamond.

The author's observations are that Remington Arms used the following letters and numbers in a circle: "4," "6," "13," "16," "17," "21," "22," "26," "28," "39," and "72." Also in a circle were the letters "B," "D," and "F." The letters "B" and "L" were used in a box as were the numbers "0," "2," "18," "34," "59" and "72." Enclosed in a triangle were the letters and numbers "D," "J," "L," "T," "5," "38," "75," and "89." The letter "Z," the numbers "0," "8" and the "+" symbol were stamped without an enclosure.

Stocks were also marked with the Ordnance Department inspector's initials. For the Rochester Ordnance District, which included both Remington Arms and Smith Corona, they were "RLB" or "END" inside a rectangle (Roy L. Bowlin or E.N. Dewey). Either of these two cartouches were stamped on Remington M1903 and M1903 (Modified) rifles to circa serial #3,280,000. After, the initials F.J.A. for Frank J. Atwood were used. His initials were also stamped on all Smith Corona M1903A3 rifles. The Ordnance Department escutcheon (crossed cannon) was stamped to the right.

Model 1903 Springfield Rifle and Its Variations

Procedure called for the initials of the manufacturer to be placed before the Ordnance escutcheon but only Remington complied by marking "R.A." on the stock, and not all the time.

The initials of the actual stock manufacturer are often found in the magazine cutoff relief or on the stock forend tip: "R" for Remington, "K" for Keystone, "A" for American Bowling and Billiard Corporation and "S" for Springfield. "E" for Smith Corona was often stamped on the forend tip as well as in the barrel channel.

The proof mark "P" in a circle was stamped on the stock wrist below the trigger guard plate. Remington used a cartouche stamp with a circle 0.380 inch in diameter; the letter "P" was 0.25 inch high. Smith Corona used a cartouche stamp 0.50 inch in diameter and the letter "P" was 0.31 inch high.

Original M1903A3 stocks can often be differentiated by the number or initial stamped behind the trigger guard: Remington stamped the letter "R" or "42," "43," or "44." Smith Corona stamped "F," "M," or "O."

Remington or Smith Corona stocks that do not have inspectors' stamps ahead of the trigger guard and the Ordnance Department inspection cartouche on the stock wrist are probably replacement stocks.

Many of the parts for the M1903A3 rifle were subcontracted to smaller companies between 1941 and 1944. Subcontractors were required to mark their parts for later identification in case problems with a particular part arose This requirement was applied to all small arms produced during World War II but it seems that only the Ordnance Officers overseeing the M1 Carbine manufacturing project faithfully enforced the rule.

Remington-made and subcontracted parts are almost always marked to identify a part as made by Remington ("R" or "R" in a circle) but Smith Corona proved to be more lax. Smith Corona parts, when they are marked, show an "X" or "E" or a subcontractor's marking. Table C1 provides a list of some subcontractors and their markings by part.

Model 1903 Springfield Rifle and Its Variations

See the part-by-part description in Chapter 2 for markings on specific parts.

Table C1		
Some M1903A3 Subcontractor Markings by Part		
Marking	Company	Part
88	Acros Company	Bolt
BF	Bonney Forge & Tool Works	Bolt
BP	Brown Corporation	Bolt Sleeve
BS	Brown & Sharp	Bolt
CC	Chrysler Corporation	Bolt and Ejector
CCT	Commercial Controls Corporation	Bolt
HO	Hoover Ball & Bearing Company	Bolt
RW	Rhodes Metaline Company, Inc.	Sight parts
RP	Rochester Products Division, GMC	Swivels
RS	Roller Smith Company	Swivels
HS	High Standard Manufacturing Company	Barrels

THE QUESTION OF REBUILT RIFLES

Almost from the beginning of M1903 production, rifles were returned to the Springfield Armory or other depots for repairs and rebuilding; military service, even in peacetime, being very hard on small arms.

Until 1940, it appears that rebuilt rifles were not marked in any special way, in spite of a 1927 Ordnance Field Bulletin requiring them to be marked with the final inspector's initials and the initials of the establishment at which they were rebuilt. A few M1903s have

Model 1903 Springfield Rifle and Its Variations

been observed with the marking S.A.D.A.L or S.A.-D.A.L on the left side of the stock without a rectangle, indicating that the rifle was repaired (and restocked) at Springfield Armory and inspected by David A. Lyle who was an Armory inspector from 1916 to at least 1942. However, it has not been possible to determine when the rifles so marked were actually rebuilt. Suffice it to say that most rebuilt rifles with both rebuild facility and inspectors' initials appear to have been marked between 1940 and 1945.

Table C2 shows other Springfield Armory rebuild markings. All are contained within a square box with sharp corners.

The M1903 series of rifles were also repaired and rebuilt at Rock Island Arsenal, most commonly in the periods right after World Wars I and II. Rebuild markings were applied to the left side of the stock as at Springfield. Table C3 shows the rebuild markings used.

The M1903 series of rifles were also repaired and rebuilt at other arsenals and depots around the country. Table C4 provides a list of those depots and their markings. All are post-World War II.

See Appendix D for a list of all known armory inspectors between 1903 and 1952.

Table C2 Springfield Armory Rebuild Markings	
Arsenal/Inspector's Initials	**Period of Use**
S.A.D.A.L. (S.A.-D.A.L.)	Pre-World War II Rebuilds
S.A./S.P.G.	1936 to October 1940
S.A./G.H.S.	October 1940 to July 1942
S.A./E.McF.	July 1942 to August 1943
S.A./G.A.W.	August 1943 to October 1944

Model 1903 Springfield Rifle and Its Variations

Table C2, cont. Springfield Armory Rebuild Markings	
Arsenal/Inspector's Initials	**Period of Use**
S.A./N.F.R.	October 1944 to October 1945
S.A./S.H.M.	Post-World War II
S.A./J.L.G.	Post-World War II
S.A./J.F.C.	Post-World War II
S.A./S.P.G.	Post-World War II
S.A./B., also C, F, K, R, S, T, and W	Post-World War II

Table C3 Rock Island Arsenal Rebuild Markings	
Arsenal/Inspector's Initials	**Period of Use**
F L W /RIA	Post-World War I
J.C.C./RIA	Post-World War I
R I A/E.O.	Post-World War I
R I A/I.C.C.	Post-World War I
R I A/L.A.A.	Post-World War I
R I A/F.L.W.	Post-World War I
R I A/E.A.A.	Post-World War II
R I A/F.Z.	Post-World War I
R I A/A.H.B.	Post-World War I
R I A/F K	Post-World War II

Model 1903 Springfield Rifle and Its Variations

<table>
<tr><td colspan="2" align="center">Table C3, cont.
Rock Island Arsenal Rebuild Markings</td></tr>
<tr><td align="center">Arsenal/Inspector's Initials</td><td align="center">Period of Use</td></tr>
<tr><td>R I A/FK2</td><td>Post-World War II</td></tr>
<tr><td>R I A/FK3</td><td>Post-World War II</td></tr>
<tr><td>R I A/EB</td><td>Post-World War II</td></tr>
</table>

Table C4 Arsenal and Depot Rebuild Markings--Post-World War II In Rectangle (cartouche)		
Arsenal	**Inspector's Initials**	**Period of Use**
Anniston Arsenal	AN	Post-World War II
Augusta Arsenal	AAB, AAHO, AAHI, AAL, AAP, AAR, AAS	Post-World War II
Benicia Arsenal	B.A./J.L., B.A./J.S., B.A./WK, B.A./W.L., BA/WL	Post-World War II
Ogden Arsenal	O.G.E.K. (in rectangle) O.G.E.K. (not in rectangle)	Post-World War II
Raritan Arsenal	RA or RA-P	Post-World War II
Red River Arsenal	R.R.A. or RRAD in rectangle	Post-World War II
San Antonio Arsenal	C.S.A.A. or C-S.A.A. on either left or right side; H-S.A.A., L-SAA, SSA-1, or S.S.A.A.	Post-World War II

Model 1903 Springfield Rifle and Its Variations

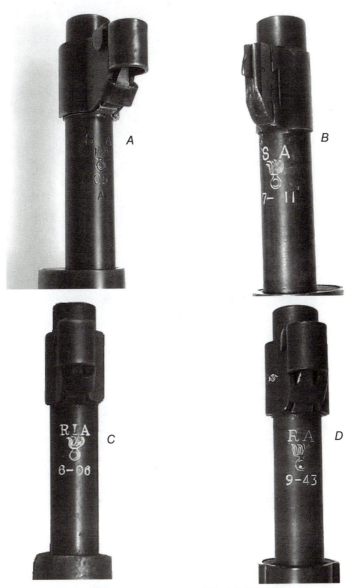

*Figs. C-1, A thru D showing four types of Model 1903 barrel markings: A)
Springfield Armory M1903 rod bayonet rifle, 2nd Alteration and B) M1903
Springfield Armory rifle; C) Rock Island rod bayonet, 2nd Alteration and D)
Remington M1903A3.*

Model 1903 Springfield Rifle and Its Variations

Figs. C-5 thru 7, M1903 receiver markings. Top down: Springfield M1903 rod bayonet, Rock Island M1903, 2nd Alteration and M1903 Springfield.

Model 1903 Springfield Rifle and Its Variations

Figs. C-8 thru 11. M1903 receivers, top down: Springfield M1903 Mk. I for the Pedersen Device, Remington M1903A3 and cast commercial receiver by National Ordnance, made in the 1950s. This last is not a military M1903 rifle receiver.

Model 1903 Springfield Rifle and Its Variations

Fig. C-12. J.S. Adams/ 1904 cartouche, M1903 rod bayonet rifle, Springfield. Courtesy, Gary James.

Fig. C-13. K.S. Morse cartouche, M1903 2nd Alteration, Springfield. Craig Riesch collection.

Fig. C-14. C. Nelson/ 1909 cartouche, RIA, M1903 rifle. Craig Riesch collection.

Model 1903 Springfield Rifle and Its Variations

Fig. C-15. J.S. Adams sans serif cartouche, M1903 rifle, Springfield. Compare with Fig. C-12. Craig Riesch collection.

Fig. C-16. David A. Lyle cartouche, Model 1903A1 National Match rifle, Springfield. North Cape Publications collection.

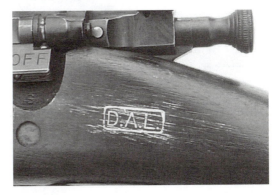

Fig. C-17. Frank J. Atwood cartouche with Ordnance Department escutcheon and Remington Arms marking, M1903A4 sniper rifle. North Cape Publications collection.

Model 1903 Springfield Rifle and Its Variations

	Appendix D		
	Inspection Markings Found on the Model 1903 Series of Rifles		
Initials	**Name**	**Time Period**	**Armory, Arsenal or Factory**
AAHI	? Rebuild	?	Augusta Arsenal
AAJ	?	1918	Springfield Armory
AAL	? Rebuild	Post-World War II	Augusta Arsenal
AAP	? Rebuild	Post-World War II	Augusta Arsenal
AAR	? Rebuild	Post-World War II	Augusta Arsenal
AAS	? Rebuild	Post-World War II	Augusta Arsenal
AAW	A.A. White	1905-1906	Springfield Armory
AFK	?	1916-1918	Springfield Armory
AFW	?	1917	Springfield Armory
AHA	?	1940-1942	Springfield Armory
AHB	?	1917-19?	Springfield Armory
AHG	A.H. Lewis	1905-1906	Springfield Armory
AHGL	A.H.G. Lewis	1905-1906	Rock Island Asenal
AHW	?	?	Springfield Armory
AJH	A.J. Hall	1904	Springfield Armory
AMC	A.M. Cooley	1901-1910	Springfield Armory
AWH	A.W. Hatch	1902-1903	Springfield Armory
BA-JL or JS	?	Post-World War II	Benicia Arsenal

Model 1903 Springfield Rifle and Its Variations

	Appendix D, cont. Inspection Markings Found on the Model 1903 Series of Rifles		
Initials	**Name**	**Time Period**	**Armory, Arsenal or Factory**
BCM-K	?	Post-World War II	Benecia Arsenal
BFJ	B.F. James	1904-1906	Springfield Armory
BFL	B.F. Lougharan	1905-1906	Springfield Armory
BHM	?	1908-1915	Springfield Armory
CAW	C.A. White	1904-1905	Springfield Armory
CCH	C.C. Hubbard	1905-1906	Springfield Armory
CCV	C.C. Valentine	1906-1908	Springfield Armory
CD	C. Davis	1905-1906	Springfield Armory
CD	C. Drommer	1898-1910	Springfield Armory
CEE	C.E. Evans	1905-1906	Springfield Armory
CJB	?	1918-1920	Springfield Armory
CLB	C. L. Bartlett	1904-1906	Springfield Armory
CMB	C.M. Boyington	1901-1910	Springfield Armory
CN	C. Nelson	1905-1913	Rock Island Arsenal
CPL	C.P. Lynn	1905-1906	Springfield Armory
DAL	?	1916-1942	Springfield Armory
DAT	D.A. Turner	1914-1915	Springfield Armory
DJD	D.J. Davis	1904-1906	Springfield Armory
DWM	D.W. Massey	1908-1909	Springfield Armory

Model 1903 Springfield Rifle and Its Variations

	Appendix D, cont. Inspection Markings Found on the Model 1903 Series of Rifles		
Initials	**Name**	**Time Period**	**Armory, Arsenal or Factory**
EAA	?	Post-World War II	Rock Island Arsenal
EAE	E.A. Elliott	1894-1910	Springfield Armory
EAG	E.A. Gowrie	1902-1909	Springfield Armory
EAK	E.A. Kingsbury	1904-1906	Springfield Armory
EB	? (RIA/EB)	Post-World War II	Rock Island Arsenal
EH	Ethan Hancock	1917-1918	Springfield Armory
EHD	Elbert H. Dewey	1918-1920	Springfield Armory
EJK	E.J. Kernan	1909-1910	Springfield Armory
EJS	E.J. Schoch	1904-1906	Springfield Armory
ELH	?	1904-1906	Springfield Armory
ELV	Edgar Vannier	1913-1919	Rock Island Armory
EMcF	Earl McFarland	1942-1943	Springfield Armory
EML	E.M. Lovering	1908-1909	Springfield Armory
END	E.N. Dewey	1941-1945	Remington Arms
EO	?	1913-1919	Rock Island Arsenal
ETS	E.T. Stevens	1890-1920	Springfield Armory
EW	?	1917	Springfield Armory
FA	Frank Adams	1904-1906	Springfield Armory

Model 1903 Springfield Rifle and Its Variations

	Appendix D, cont.		
	Inspection Markings Found on the Model 1903 Series of Rifles		
Initials	Name	Time Period	Armory, Arsenal or Factory
FA	Frank B. Austin	1918-1919	Springfield Armory
FAM	F.A. Massey	1903-1906	Springfield Armory
FAR	?	1906	Springfield Armory
FAT	Felo Threats	1941-1942	Springfield Armory
FBA	Francis B Austin (?)	1918-1919	Springfield Armory
FER	F.E. Randall	1905-1906	Springfield Armory
FEW	F.E. Wilson	1901-1920	Springfield Armory
FFH	F.F. Hull	1905-1906	Springfield Armory
FHE	F.H. Elwell	1894-1910	Springfield Armory
FJA	Frank J. Atwood	1942-1944	Remington Arms Smith Corona
FK	F. Krack (RIA/FK)	1940-1951	Rock Island Arsenal
FK2	F. Krack 2 (RIA/FK2)	1940-1951	Rock Island Arsenal
FK3	F. Krack 3 (RIA/FK3)	1940-1951	Rock Island Arsenal
FLW	Francis L. Ward	1917	Rock Island Arsenal
FMK	F. M. Kelsey	1904-1906	Springfield Armory
FWA	F. W. Adams	1904-1906	Springfield Armory
FWM	F.W. Macher	1905-1906	Springfield Armory
FZ	?	1917-19?	Rock Island Arsenal

Model 1903 Springfield Rifle and Its Variations

	Appendix D, cont.		
	Inspection Markings Found on the Model 1903 Series of Rifles		
Initials	Name	Time Period	Armory, Arsenal or Factory
GAS	G.A. Spooner	1899-1910	Springfield Armory
GAW	G.A. Woody	1943-1944	Springfield Armory
GBA	G.B. Allen	1894-1920	Springfield Armory
GCS	G.C. Schnell	1904-1905	Springfield Armory
GEM	G.E. Miller	1905-1906	Springfield Armory
GEW	G.E. Worden	1905-1920	Springfield Armory
GFG	G.F. Gray	1902-1920	Springfield Armory
GRG	G.R. Goring	1908-1910	Springfield Armory
GZ	G. Zauche	1905-1906	Springfield Armory
HAC	H.A. Colvin	1904-1920	Springfield Armory
HCW	H.C. Washburn	1904-1906	Springfield Armory
HEW	H.E. Wallenberg	1905-1906	Springfield Armory
HHD	H.H. Denny	1918-?	Springfield Armory
HLK	H.L. Keyes	1890-1920	Springfield Armory
HMB	H.M. Brooks	1902-1920	Springfield Armory
HWH	H.W. Hunt	1899-?	Springfield Armory
ICC	?	1917-?	Rock Island Arsenal
ILA	?	1903-?	Springfield Armory

Model 1903 Springfield Rifle and Its Variations

	Appendix D, cont. Inspection Markings Found on the Model 1903 Series of Rifles		
Initials	**Name**	**Time Period**	**Armory, Arsenal or Factory**
IR	I. Randall	1904-1906	Springfield Armory
IS	?	Post-World War II	San Antonio Arsenal
JAW	J.A. Woodward	1905-1906	Springfield Armory
JBL	?	1942-1944	Remington Arms
JBT	J.B. Tyler	1899-1902	Springfield Armory
JC	J. Clancy	1905-1907	Springfield Armory
JC	? (RIA/JC)	?	Rock Island Arsenal
JCP	J.C. Parker	1905-1906	Springfield Armory
JEC	J. E. Craig	1898-1906	Springfield Armory
JES	?	1918	Rock Island Arsenal
JFC	J.F. Coyle	1906-1908	Springfield Armory
JFG	?	1908-?	Springfield Armory
JFS	J.F. Sullivan	1898-1908	Springfield Armory
JHB	J.H. Boyer	1896-1920	Springfield Armory
JHC	J.H. Clayton	1890-1920	Springfield Armory
JHF	J.H. Fletcher	1908-1909	Springfield Armory
JHH	J.H. Howarth	1899-1910	Springfield Armory
JKB	J.K. Burbank	1901-1910	Springfield Armory

Model 1903 Springfield Rifle and Its Variations

	Appendix D, cont.		
	Inspection Markings Found on the Model 1903 Series of Rifles		
Initials	**Name**	**Time Period**	**Armory, Arsenal or Factory**
JLG	James L. Guion	1950-1953	Springfield Armory
JLH	J.L. Hansen	1917/1918?	Rock Island Arsenal
JMC	J.M. Crighton	1894-1910	Springfield Armory
JNB	J.N. Boyer	1905-1906	Springfield Armory
JNH	J.N. Hemenway	1906-1907	Springfield Armory
JPO	J.P. O'Neil	1904-1910	Springfield Armory
JR	J. Reid	1904-1920	Springfield Armory
JRD	J.R. Dearborn	1901-1920	Springfield Armory
JS	?	1932-1937	Rock Island Arsenal
JSA	J.S. Adams	1890-1920	Springfield Armory
JWA	J.W. Alden	1905-1906	Springfield Armory
JWE	J.W. Ewig	1898-1910	Springfield Armory
JWM	J.W. McCoy	1927-1929	Springfield Armory
K	?	1920s	Springfield Armory
KSM	K.S. Morse	1898-1915	Springfield Armory
LAA	?	1917-1919	Rock Island Arsenal
LLK	L.L. Kuralt	1905-1910	Springfield Armory
LM	L.M. Menz	1908-1909	Springfield Armory
LOH	L.O. Hale	1902-1906	Springfield Armory

Model 1903 Springfield Rifle and Its Variations

<table>
<tr><td colspan="4">Appendix D, cont.
Inspection Markings Found on the Model 1903 Series of Rifles</td></tr>
<tr><td>Initials</td><td>Name</td><td>Time Period</td><td>Armory, Arsenal or Factory</td></tr>
<tr><td>LSAA</td><td>?</td><td>Post-World War II</td><td>San Antonio Arsenal</td></tr>
<tr><td>LTT</td><td>?</td><td>1940-1942</td><td>Springfield Armory</td></tr>
<tr><td>MMC</td><td>M.M. Custer</td><td>1906-1910</td><td>Springfield Armory</td></tr>
<tr><td>MPB</td><td>M.P. Benjamin</td><td>1899-1910</td><td>Springfield Armory</td></tr>
<tr><td>MR</td><td>?</td><td>Post-World War II</td><td>Mt. Rainier Ordnance Depot</td></tr>
<tr><td>MW</td><td>M. Witkop</td><td>1908-1909</td><td>Springfield Armory</td></tr>
<tr><td>NL</td><td>N. LeClair</td><td>1905-1906</td><td>Springfield Armory</td></tr>
<tr><td>NLB</td><td>N.L. Benoit</td><td>1900-1904</td><td>Springfield Armory</td></tr>
<tr><td>NRA</td><td>National Rifle Association</td><td>1913-1917</td><td>Springfield Armory</td></tr>
<tr><td>O</td><td>?</td><td>World War II Period</td><td>Springfield Armory (on parts)</td></tr>
<tr><td>OAT</td><td>O.A. Thornton</td><td>1907-1910</td><td>Springfield Armory</td></tr>
<tr><td>OEL</td><td>Ora E. Lindsey</td><td>1919</td><td>Rock Island Arsenal</td></tr>
<tr><td>OG</td><td>Indicates repair or refurbishment at Ogden Arsenal</td><td>Post-World War II</td><td>Ogden Arsenal</td></tr>
<tr><td>OGEK (boxed)</td><td>Elmer Keith</td><td>1949-1956</td><td>Ogden Arsenal</td></tr>
<tr><td>OGEK (unboxed)</td><td>E. Klouser</td><td>Post-World War II</td><td>Ogden Arsenal</td></tr>
<tr><td>OHA</td><td>Otto H. Armstrong</td><td>1918-1919</td><td>Rock Island Arsenal</td></tr>
<tr><td>P</td><td>Firing proof on barrels and stocks</td><td>1903-1944</td><td>Springfield Armory, Rock Island Arsenal, Remington Arms, Smith Corona</td></tr>
</table>

Model 1903 Springfield Rifle and Its Variations

	Appendix D, cont.		
	Inspection Markings Found on the Model 1903 Series of Rifles		
Initials	Name	Time Period	Armory, Arsenal or Factory
PJK	P.J. Kiley	1901-1906	Springfield Armory
PK	P. Keller	1904-1906	Springfield Armory
PHMB	P.H.M. Brooks	1909-1910	Springfield Armory
RA	Remington Arms	1942-1944	Remington Arms
RA-P	Raritan Arsenal	Post-World War II	Raritan Arsenal
RAC	R.A. Carr	1899-1920	Springfield Armory
RBC	R.B. Chamberlain	1905-1906	Springfield Armory
RDD	R.D. Draper	1905-1906	Springfield Armory
RIA	Rock Island Arsenal	1904-1960s	Rock Island Arsenal
RIA/EB	E. Blind	1917-19?	Rock Island Arsenal
RIA/F	Frank Krack	Post-World War II	Rock Island Arsenal
RIA/FK	Frank Krack	Post-World War II	Rock Island Arsenal
RIA/F2	Frank Krack	Post-World War II	Rock Island Arsenal
RIA/F3	Frank Krack	Post-World War II	Rock Island Arsenal
RLB	Roy L. Bowlin	1941-1942	Remington Arms
RM	R. Matthews	1905-1906	Springfield Armory
RMD	R.M. Dennon	1895-1920	Springfield Armory

Model 1903 Springfield Rifle and Its Variations

	Appendix D, cont.		
	Inspection Markings Found on the Model 1903 Series of Rifles		
Initials	**Name**	**Time Period**	**Armory, Arsenal or Factory**
RNS	R.N. Stannard	1905-1906	Springfield Armory
SA/C	?	Post-World War II	Springfield Armory
SA-DAL	(Also, S.A.D.A.L)	1930-1940s	Springfield Armory
SA/EMcF	Earl McFarland	1942-1943	Springfield Armory
SA/GAW	G.A. Woody	1943-1944	Springfield Armory
SA/GHS	G.H. Stewart	1940-1942	Springfield Armory
SA/JLG	James L. Guion	1950-1953	Springfield Armory
SA/NFR	Norman F. Ramsey	1944-1945	Springfield Armory
SA/P	?	Post-World War II	Springfield Armory
SA/R	?	Post-World War II	Springfield Armory
SA/SD	?	Post-World War II	Springfield Armory
SA/SHM	Stephen H. McGregor	1945-1947	Springfield Armory
SA/SPG	Samuel P. Green	1936-1950	Springfield Armory
SC	Smith Corona	1942-1944	Smith Corona
S-C	Smith Corona	1942-1944	Smith Corona
SD	?	Post-World War II	Springfield Armory
SEB	S.E. Bugbee	1901-1910	Springfield Armory

Model 1903 Springfield Rifle and Its Variations

	Appendix D, cont.		
	Inspection Markings Found on the Model 1903 Series of Rifles		
Initials	**Name**	**Time Period**	**Armory, Arsenal or Factory**
SHB	S.H. Broughton	1890-1920	Springfield Armory
SLT	S.L. Tuttle	1894-1920	Springfield Armory
SP	S. Priestly	1904-1906	Springfield Armory
SPS	Sidney P. Spaulding	1940-1941	Springfield Armory
SS	Samuel O. Sangler	1919	Rock Island Arsenal
SSAA	?	Post-World War II	San Antonio Arsenal
TCC	?	1904-1918	Rock Island Arsenal (leather scabbards)
THM	T.H. Mills	1900-1921	Springfield Armory
TJL	T.J. Lovett	1904-1906	Springfield Armory
USMC	Marking on replacement M1903 barrels supplied by Sedgely	1942-1944	Any repair or ordnance depot
WAW	W.A. Walker, Jr.	1905-1906	Springfield Armory
WCA	?	World War I	Springfield Armory
WCF	W.C. Fielding	1898-1920	Springfield Armory
WEB	W.E. Boynton	1902-1910	Springfield Armory
WEH	W.E. Hosmer	1905-1915	Springfield Armory
WES	W.E. Strong	1916-1918	Springfield Armory
WFB	W.F. Bradbury	1898-1902	Springfield Armory
WFF	W.F. Fennyery	1904-1906	Springfield Armory

Model 1903 Springfield Rifle and Its Variations

Appendix D, cont. Inspection Markings Found on the Model 1903 Series of Rifles			
Initials	**Name**	**Time Period**	**Armory, Arsenal or Factory**
WFW	W.F. Wilbur	1905-1906	Springfield Armory
WHH	W.H. Hayden	1901-1906	Springfield Armory
WJC	W.J. Carr	1890-1920	Springfield Armory
WJH	W.J. Hines	1904-1910	Springfield Armory
WJO	W.J. Ober	1904-1906	Springfield Armory
WJS	?	1909	Rock Island Arsenal
WJS	?	1919	Springfield Armory
WK	?	1919	Rock Island Arsenal
WMH	W.M. Halferty	1917-1918	Rock Island Arsenal
WS	W. Syrett	1904-1905	Springfield Armory

APPENDIX **E**

The Model 1903 National Match Rifle

From the turn of the 20th century to 1980, the U.S. Army has established specifications for the National Match version of the current service rifle, starting with the Model 1892 Krag Rifle and Carbine and continuing through the M1903, M1903A1, M1903A3, M1 Garand and M14 rifles. Complete specifications for a discrete National Match rifle—as distinct from service rifles selected for accuracy—began in 1921. After discussions were held by participants in the previous year's matches, military armorers and production experts at the National Armory at Springfield and the Executive Officer of the National Matches issued what came to be known as an "X.O." letter which contained specifications for the "Rifle, U.S. Caliber .30, Model 1903, National Match Rifle (1921)," the first of the purpose-built National Match Rifles. They are summarized in the following table.

The specifications were continually refined until by 1939, the year the last National Match 1903A1 was built, the Springfield Armory and Rock Island Arsenal (1919) had turned out a total of 31,900 National Match rifles (28,907 from Springfield and 3,000 from Rock Island).

After World War II, when National Match Competition resumed, an attempt was made to develop a National Match version of the Model 1903A3. But it never made it to the firing line and it was quickly replaced by the M1 Garand. Between February 1946 when the Marines used the Garand for the first time in the Pacific Division Rifle Matches held in Hawaii and 1963 when the last National Match M1 Garand was built, a complete set of specifications and build instructions were developed for that rifle.

The M14 rifle underwent the same process until it was unseated at the National Matches at Camp Perry in 1998 by the M16. The specifications developed for each rifle were the "bible" for five

Model 1903 Springfield Rifle and Its Variations

generations of military and civilian gunsmiths. But no more. None of the services have, at this writing, published specifications for a National Match M16 rifle.

Table E1 Model 1903/1921 Springfield National Match Rifle Specifications (inches)	
Barrel	
Bore	0.3005 ± 0.0001
Grooves	0.3085 ± 0.0001
Star Gauged	"Star" mark stamped on lip of muzzle
Bolt	
Headspace	1.940 to 1.944
Mainspring	Service mainspring reduced to minimum size and diameter consistent with reliable release and safety
Receiver	All runways and cams polished smooth and left bright
Sear	Nose shortened consistent with reliable release and safety
Sight Cover	National Match Model of 1921
Sights	Placed in a jig and filed smooth and flat on top and sides. Peep sight aperture exactly 0.06 inch. Two extra furnished at 0.06 and 0.07 inch in diameter.
Stock	American black walnut without visible figure. The configuration was the standard service "S" type without pistol grip. Stock immersed four times in warmed linseed oil. Barrel bands hand tightened only.
Striker	Minimum length consistent with reliable ignition
Trigger Pull	Two stage, 3 1/2 to 4 1/4 pounds. No creep allowed

APPENDIX F

The Pedersen Device

On October 8, 1917, eight months after the United States had entered the "Great War" in Europe, a lone civilian trudged to the firing line at the Congress Heights Rifle Range at Washington, DC. Behind him were three-high-ranking Ordnance Department officers including General Crozier, Chief of Ordnance.

The civilian was J.D. Pedersen, an independent small-arms designer who worked closely with the Remington Arms Company. In fact, Remington thought so highly of Mr. Pedersen that they had, since 1907, provided him with his own workshop and a machinist to assist him. Their trust was not misplaced. He had developed several money-making shotguns and a semiautomatic pistol for the company.

On this crisp autumn day, Mr. Pedersen took from his case what appeared to be a standard Springfield Model 1903 rifle. He pressed a clip of cartridges into the magazine, nodded for the officers to cover their ears and fired five shots at the distant target.

Then he did something unexpected. He flipped the bolt release to the center position and pulled out the rifle's bolt. From a metal pouch attached to his belt, he pulled a block-like object which he pushed into the bolt race and locked in position with the rifle's cutoff switch. He then took a long stick of metal from the rifle case and snapped it onto the right side of the rifle so that it protruded at a 45-degree angle. Without pause, he shouldered the rifle and fired forty rounds as fast as he could pull the trigger. When the rifle clicked empty, he snatched a new magazine from the case, unlatched the used magazine, snapped the new one in place and emptied it as well.

Turning to the surprised Ordnance officers, he offered the rifle for inspection, pointing out that he had replaced the bolt with a blowback device that fired a smaller, lighter cartridge from the forty-round protruding magazine, see Figures F-1, F-2 and F-3.

Model 1903 Springfield Rifle and Its Variations

Figs. F-1 and F-2 show an unidentified employee of the Remington-UMC Company demonstrating the Pedersen Device. These two photographs have never before been published. Photographs F-1, F-2 and F-3 courtesy of firearms historians Burt Kellerstedt and Roy Marcot.

Model 1903 Springfield Rifle and Its Variations

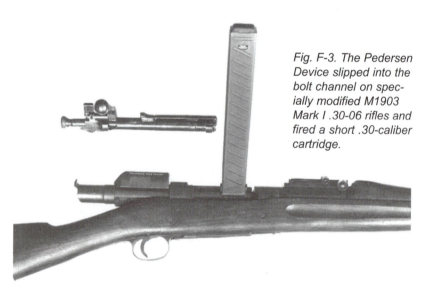

Fig. F-3. The Pedersen Device slipped into the bolt channel on specially modified M1903 Mark I .30-06 rifles and fired a short .30-caliber cartridge.

Model 1903 Springfield Rifle and Its Variations

"Imagine, gentlemen," he is certain to have said, "the effect of eighty shots fired at an enemy in less than a minute by an entire of company of soldiers, or a regiment or even a division!"

The Ordnance Department has always had a deep streak of the "NIH" syndrome (not invented here) but the importance of what they had just seen was so obvious that they rushed back to the War Department. Within days, both Mr. Pedersen and an ordnance officer were aboard a fast Navy destroyer on their way to France to explain the new invention to General John Pershing, commander-in-chief of the American Expeditionary Force then assembling. He could not have come at a better time.

The failure of the 1917 Allied offensives with their consequent huge loss of life prompted General Pershing to listen hard to what the young officer was telling him. If, in fact, the new device would really do under battle conditions what it had demonstrated at Congress Heights, he would be very interested indeed.

By early December of that year, several prototype devices had been manufactured and engineering and manufacturing drawings were being drawn up as well as plans for production. All of this work, as well as extensive testing, went on under conditions of the strictest secrecy. Rather than refer to it as the "Pedersen Device," it was decided to call it the "Automatic Pistol, Caliber .30, Model of 1918."

The new "automatic pistol" was a simple blowback device that fired a slightly souped-up pistol cartridge with an 80-grain gilding metal jacketed bullet placed over 3.5 grains of powder which produced a muzzle velocity of 1300 feet per second. Contrast this with the 150-grain bullet over 45 grains of powder and a muzzle velocity of 2,700 feet of the World War I .30-Model 1906 cartridge. The service bullet fired from the M1903 rifle would penetrate 60 inches of pine (a measure of performance then in use) while the little .30-M1918 bullet would only penetrate 8 inches. But at ranges of up to 350 yards, that was thought to be more than sufficient to kill an enemy soldier.

The device looked very much like the slide of a semiautomtic pistol. It contained a firing pin assembly which was released when a

Model 1903 Springfield Rifle and Its Variations

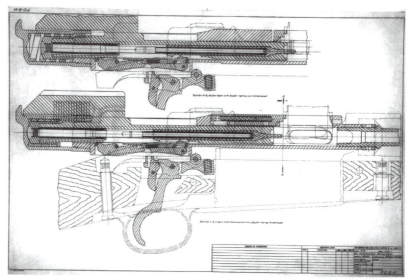

Fig. F-4. This photograph of an original Remington Arms Company engineering drawing shows the interaction of the M1903 modified sear and the firing pin release lever in the Pedersen Device. Photograph courtesy of Remington Arms Company and Roy Marcot.

"flipper" on the modified sear in the Model 1903 Mark I rifle in contact with a release lever in the Pedersen Device was tipped forward as the trigger was pulled. The firing pin was driven forward by its spring to strike the cartridge primer in its chamber. The resulting recoil was imparted to a counterweight riding in a track on the top of the device to extract and eject the fired cartridge and insert a new one ready for the next shot, see Figures F-4 and F-5.

So what was there about a puny little pistol cartridge that would stand the entire Ordnance Department on their collective ear and so excite an old warhorse like General Pershing who had seen and done most everything a soldier could expect to see and do?

By the end of 1917, the opposing lines had been so fixed in place for three years on the battlefield they might as well have been cast in concrete—and some positions were. Literally millions of men

412

Model 1903 Springfield Rifle and Its Variations

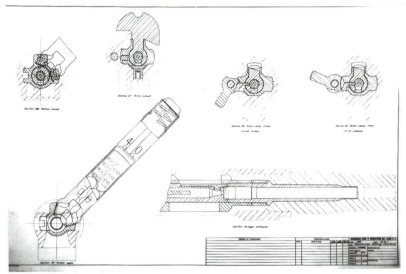

Fig. F-5. This photograph of an original Remington Arms engineering drawing shows the 40-round magazine and its method of attachment. Photograph courtesy of the Remington Arms Company and Roy Marcot.

on both sides had lost their lives in futile attacks on each other's trenches which stretched in nearly unbroken lines from the Swiss-French to the Belgian-Dutch borders. Each side had three main trench lines opposed at distances ranging from 100 to 1,000 meters. The trenches were dug deep and fortified with barbed wire. The bottoms were lined in places with duckboards—slatted platforms—and every fifty meters or so was a bunker in which the troops could sleep, eat and rest. And shelter from artillery fire.

The trenches were muddy and the water level varied with the season. The vast amounts of particulate particles released in the gunsmoke acted as core particles for moisture and increased the amount of precipitation that fell summer and winter. Soldiers had to be rotated out of the line every seven to ten days not only to preserve their sanity but to dry out. Artillery fire killed and wounded the majority of sol-

Model 1903 Springfield Rifle and Its Variations

diers but trench foot caused by constant immersion in water, flu and pneumonia killed or incapacitated almost as many.

The summer of 1917 had seen almost continuous attacks—offensives, they were called—by both sides on the Western front even as fighting was winding down on the Eastern front after the fall of the Kerensky government in St. Petersburg. Entire divisions of German troops were preparing to move west. More men had died and been wounded in the offensives of that year than in the two preceding years of war and American troops had gotten their first taste of what trench warfare was all about.

An offensive had developed into a stylized movement of troops as familiar to either side as a ballet. Weeks of intense artillery bombardment building to a nonstop crescendo in the final three to five days were intended to wear down the defenders, although by 1917, they had learned to move back to reserve trenches beyond the immediate target area. The offensive usually began shortly after dawn. The artillery bombardment ceased abruptly. Whistles blew in the trenches of the attackers and the first wave of troops on a one, two, three or more division front clambered "over the top" burdened with packs, rifles, shovels, canteens, ammunition and knives and slogged across the shell-cratered, barbed wire-encrusted thousand or so meters of mud between the opposing forces. For the first part of their journey, their own machine guns raked the enemy trench line. But soon that ceased as the line of attackers crossed their own line of fire.

Within minutes, the defenders' own artillery began to whistle in, targeting the expanse of no-man's-land and the trenches and supporting trenches the attackers had just left. With the high explosive came gas shells. The attackers, already wearing gas masks, fought for every breath as they slogged through the mud and mire.

As soon as the supporting machine guns fell silent, the defending machine guns opened up. Years of experience had taught both sides the best way to place the heavy Maxim, Spandau, Hotchkiss, Vickers—and by 1918—the American Browning machine guns for the greatest killing effect. The defending infantry had by now scurried

414

back into their forward trenches to meet the attackers and they poured rifle fire at the advancing infantry as well.

Through this sleet of steel and lead, the attackers struggled on. Burdened as they were, after a hundred or so paces, they were reduced to a slow trudge through the mud, heads down, bodies hunched to provide the smallest target.

As the first wave, or at least those that were left, approached the coils of barbed wire lining the approaches to the enemy trench, the second wave climbed over the top and followed through the hail or artillery, gas, machine gun and rifle bullets. As they reached the barbed wire and opened up the passages that the first wave had managed to cut, the third wave was flowing across no-man's-land after them. Few of the first wave would ever survive to engage in hand-to-hand combat with the enemy. That was the job of the second and third waves. But with the defenders' artillery creating an inferno between the trench lines and hampering the movement of fresh attackers, the defenders were able to pour in reinforcements relatively unhampered.

This had been the scenario since early 1915 when the trench lines had stabilized. Neither side had been able to muster sufficient numbers of attackers to overwhelm the defenders and beat them back to the point where they could hold sections of the enemy's trench long enough to consolidate their position. Even the new tanks that had been introduced that summer had not brought the long-sought breakthrough. They had been squandered in the mud and shell holes piecemeal.

On December 8, 1917 at Langres, France, headquarters of the American Expeditionary Force, Captain J. C. Beatty of the Ordnance Department met with a board of officers consisting of a brigadier general, two colonels and a major to demonstrate the new secret weapon that had so excited General Pershing in October. Captain Beatty had brought with him from the Remington plant in Bridgeport, Connecticut, a preproduction model of the Automatic Pistol, Caliber .30, Model of 1918. He explained the "pistol device" was fitted to the Model 1906 Springfield. Then during one long day, Beatty ran the new system through a series of tests for penetration, accuracy, rapid-

Model 1903 Springfield Rifle and Its Variations

ity of fire and fire for endurance and demonstrated how the rifle was converted from a bolt action to a semiautomatic rifle until his hands were sore.

The Board was so impressed that they made their report one day later, recommending that the Pedersen attachment be adopted as soon as possible and that an initial order for 100,000 rifles and Pedersen Devices, plus 5,000 rounds of ammunition per unit, be manufactured and shipped to the AEF. They further recommended that the device be "kept as secret as possible." Only two copies of the report were prepared and they destroyed all other records pertaining to the testing.

General Pershing, and everyone else involved in the project, was convinced that they had in the Pedersen Device the perfect offensive and defensive weapon for trench warfare. On the offensive side, 50,000 American troops climbing out of their trenches as soon as the artillery bombardment ceased, all walking across no-man's-land and firing their Pedersen Device-equipped rifles from the hip would prevent the enemy's machine gunners and riflemen from firing at them. And because each soldier would carry 400 rounds of ammunition, they would have plenty left to defend themselves once they had captured a portion of the enemy's trenches. Then, because the killing machine guns would have been silenced from the start, the second and third waves would arrive quickly to reinforce those of the first wave that had survived artillery and gas bombardment. Spreading out from the point of penetration, they would break through and overrun the second and third trenches and push out behind the enemy lines.

When used in a defensive posture, each soldier would have 400 rounds of ammunition to fire at the attacking enemy, thus supplementing their heavy machine guns with "light machine guns in the hands of every soldier."

The Board's recommendations were accepted and orders were given immediately to begin production of an initial 500,000 units which would be delivered to the AEF in France in time for the spring offensive of 1919.

Fortunately, in October 1918, the great breakthrough came as

416

Model 1903 Springfield Rifle and Its Variations

American, British and French troops smashed through the German lines and raced to the Rhine. A demoralized government in Berlin called for an Armistice a month later and the last shot of World War I was fired on November 11, 1918.

It is interesting to speculate about what would have happened if the October breakthrough had not occurred and if the Pedersen Devices had arrived as planned. Would the spectacle of three divisions' worth of American troops climbing out of their trenches and pumping millions of rounds of ammunition at the German defenders as they trudged across no-man's-land have been sufficient to bring the long-sought breakthrough?

Probably not. The American planners did not seem to have taken into account the effect of artillery bombardment on the attackers nor the hampering effects of gas shells. The Russians had long used massed infantry charges in an effort to overwhelm an entrenched enemy with indifferent success. Not until World War II when a high proportion of Red Army soldiers were armed with submachine guns did the tactic work, and then only when the opposing Nazi forces were caught by surprise or did not have sufficient artillery and machine guns to support the positions they were defending.

The submachine gun had already been introduced into the German army in 1918, see Figure F-6. In the hands of special storm troop units, they had come close to achieving a breakthrough in British lines, and not in massed attacks but in small unit operations. Planning for larger scale offensives was already underway for operations in 1919 in which the storm troopers would mount surprise attacks to clear the way for the infantry which would incorporate their own submachine gun squads. The German High Command fully expected that sufficient submachine guns would be available from the Bergman factories in Gaggenau and Suhl by early 1919.

But on the defense, the Pedersen Device probably would have accomplished much of what was expected of it. With virtually unlimited rifle fire added to artillery and machine gun fire, the trenches would have become well-nigh impregnable. There would have been virtually no chance that the Germans could have achieved a break-through, even with dozens of divisions recalled from the Eastern front.

When World War I ended on November 11, 1918, 65,000 Pedersen Devices had been manufactured. The secrecy lid was loosened somewhat in December 1919 when their classification was downgraded to Confidential and they were placed in storage along with the 101,775 or so M1903 Mark I rifles built for them.

As the planners and analysts began to take stock of the events of the Great War, they became convinced that trench warfare was finished. Steady improvements in the internal combustion engine and the development of the tank,

Fig. F-6. The M.P. 18, I submachine gun was designed by Hugo Schmeisser. It was expected to be produced in sufficient quantities during 1918 to furnish each German Army infantry company on the Western front with six submachine guns in a special storm trooper squad.

truck and airplane would make the next war one of movement, as Germany would again demonstrate some twenty years later.

Further testing in the 1920s revealed some defects of the Pedersen Device that had not been considered in the rush to get them to the front. One was the lower power and subsequent high trajectory of the small cartridge. Beyond 350 yards, it was considered ineffectual. And if aimed at 350 yards, its trajectory would have taken it over the heads of most troops at 100 yards. Another factor that had not been considered before was the additional 13.51 lb burden of equipment that would have been added to each soldier's load when the

Model 1903 Springfield Rifle and Its Variations

device (1.782 lbs), scabbard (0.535 lb), magazine pouch (0.459 lb) and ten loaded magazines (1.073 lbs each) were used.

Testing had also shown that unless the soldier had to attach the device before "going over the top"; otherwise, if he stopped in no-man's-land to change the bolt for the device he would probably lose the rifle bolt in the noise, confusion and fear of the attack, leaving him without a long-range infantry rifle. But if he attached the device before leaving his trench, he could not fire effectively at the enemy for the greater part of the attack.

And another minor consideration also cropped up. It was noticed during rifle practice with the device that troops working the target butts kept their heads well down when .30-Model 1906 ammunition was being used, but often raised their heads to see what was going on when the .30-Model 1918 ammunition was being fired. The reason was traced to the absence of the crack of a passing bullet. The .30-Model 1918 ammunition did not travel fast enough to break the sound barrier much beyond a hundred yards from the muzzle as the .30-06 bullet did. It was judged that this would have a deleterious effect in combat by not causing enemy soldiers to keep their heads down.

The 65,000 Pedersen Devices remained in classified storage until March 23, 1931 when the secret classification was removed. They were offered to the Marine Corps and Navy but were rejected as having no practical use. In April of that year, all devices in storage were destroyed by melting them in a furnace. The few dozen or less that have survived are eagerly sought by collectors.

As an interesting footnote, despite the rigorous security measures taken to protect the existence of the Pedersen device during and after World War I, Army Ordnance Intelligence discovered a complete M1903 Mark I rifle with Pedersen Device in the reference collection of the Rheinisch Westfallian Sprengstoff, A.G. in Nurnberg, Germany, in the summer of 1945. It had been in the collection for twenty-five years.

The Pedersen Device was tested not only on the M1903 rifle but the M1917 Enfield (M1917 Enfield Mark II) and the Mosin-Nagant

Model 1903 Springfield Rifle and Its Variations

(Model 1918 Mosin-Nagant) as well. But it was only produced in quantity for the M1903. Those M1903 rifles set up for the "Pedersen Device" have an oval ejection port milled into the left side of the receiver through the bolt channel. The ejection port was 1.325 inches long by 0.365 inch high with rounded ends. These receivers were stamped "MARK I" on the right side of the receiver ring, between "MODEL 1903." and the serial number.

Fig. F-7. M1903 Mark I receiver marking. Mike Metzgar collection.

A special (Type 3) magazine cutoff was used in the M1903 Mark I rifle. It had a milled groove in the body to lock the Pedersen Device into the bolt channel. The magazine cutoff held the device in place when turned down, or to the "ON" position. Its spindle was replaced by a spring-loaded plunger that held the ejector in place so that it would not flop forward and block the removal of the device.

The device had a short, stubby barrel with a slightly oversized bore that was rifled with 12 shallow grooves. The grooves started the bullet spinning but did not engrave the bullet as it passed through the device barrel and entered the service rifle's bore.

Markings on the Pedersen Device on the right and left side:

REMINGTON-BRIDGEPORT
PEDERSEN'S PAT'S PENDING

U.S.A. 1918—Mark I
XXXX

The rifle's receiver was marked as shown in Figure F-7.

The standard "S" stock (Type 2F) was installed on the Model

Model 1903 Springfield Rifle and Its Variations

1903 Mark 1 used with the Pedersen Device. The ejection port in the left side of the receiver was lower than the line of the stock and a cut was made in the stock wood on the left side about 1.5 inches long and 0.1 inch deep starting where the stock line dips behind the receiver ring. When the Pedersen Device was withdrawn from service, the rifles were refurbished and overhauled but the stocks were not changed.

Accessories manufactured for the Model 1903 Mark I and the Pedersen Device consisted of a rectangular magazine pouch holding five loaded magazines, the magazine itself capable of holding forty rounds, as well as a metal scabbard with a standard cartridge belt attachment for carrying the device when not attached to the rifle and an adjusting wrench, see Fig. F-8.

The special .30-caliber ammunition was manufactured by Remington Arms-UMC Company in Bridgeport, CT, and Hoboken, NJ. Those manufactured at Bridgeport were headstamped RA 18 and RA 19 while those made at Hoboken were headstamped RA H 18 and RA H 19. The cartridges were packed in forty-round boxes, enough to fill one magazine. Five boxes were packed in one carton.

M1903 Mark I rifles were manufactured and assembled from early 1918 to 1920. The first M1903 Mark I rifle was serial #1,034,502 as reported by Lt. Col. L.D. Hubbel, Commanding Officer for the Ordnance Department to the Office of the Chief of Ordnance in a summary dated November 20, 1918. Serial number and barrel dates as late as 1921 have been reported but not observed by the author. The earliest observed barrel date was March 1918 and the latest was May 1920. The latest serial number known to be reported as of this writing is 1,197,834.

Records indicate that 101,775 M1903 Mark I rifles were manufactured between 1919 and early 1921 while the Army decided what to do with the weapon system. How many more were manufactured earlier in 1918 and 1919 is not known but Brophy estimated a total of 145,000 Mark I rifles produced.

On the following pages is reproduced the confidential report of the Board of Officers, AEF Headquarters, Langres, France, December 9, 1917, which reviewed and approved the Pedersen Device

Model 1903 Springfield Rifle and Its Variations

Fig. F-8. L-r: Ammunition pouch holding five magazines, magazine and .30-Model 1918 ammunition, Pedersen Device and metal scabbard with cartridge belt attachment. Photograph courtesy of Remington Arms Company and Roy Marcot.

and recommended its manufacture and use to General Pershing. To the author's knowledge, the report has never been published before. It is reproduced from the single typed, carbon copy of the report brought back to the United States by Captain J.C. Beatty of the Ordnance Department and discovered 81 years later in the Remington files by firearms historian Roy Marcot.

Model 1903 Springfield Rifle and Its Variations

Proceedings of a Board of Officers convened at Langres, France on the 9th of December, 1917, pursuant to the following orders:

Headquarters American Expeditionary Forces
December 8, 1917

Special Orders No. 181.

23.   A Board of Officers to consist of

Brigadier General James W. MacAndrew, National Army
Colonel J. H. Parker, Infantry, National Army
Colonel Leroy Eltings, General Staff
Major A. E. Phillips, Ordnance Department
Captain J. C. Beatty, Ordnance Department

is appointed to meet at Langres at the call of the President thereof to test and report upon the suitability for the military service of a certain device mentioned in letter from the Chief of Ordnance, U.S. Army, dated October 12, 1917 (O.O. 4764.1.179). The work and report of the board will be expedited.

Such journeys as may be required by the members of the board from their stations to the place of meeting of the board and return are necessary in the military service.

BY COMMAND OF GENERAL PERSHING:
(Signed) James G. Harbord,
Brigadier General,
Chief of Staff

Model 1903 Springfield Rifle and Its Variations

Official:

(Signed) Robert C. Davis

Adjutant General

Langres, France 9 December, 1917

The board met 10:30 A.M. pursuant to the foregoing order. Present, all members.

After repeated tests for penetration, accuracy, rapidity of fire, and fire for endurance, the board submits the following report:

1. That the attachment permits the service rifle to be changed from a high powered, quick firing rifle to a semi-automatic rifle firing a smaller cartridge of the same caliber.

2. That it permits the soldier to carry at least four hundred rounds (400) of ammunition, capable of being effective over the shorter ranges in addition to a regular supply of service cartridges to be used over the longer ranges.

3. That the change from the service bolt to the attachment, or the reverse, can be made in about fifteen (15) seconds, and in no way injures or incapacitates the rifle for the service cartridge or any of its functions.

4. That tactically the device is of Special importance for the following purposes;

(a) In an attack from trenches at ranges up to 350 yards, the attachment enables the assaulting troops to overwhelm the defensive with fire.

(b) In the defense of trenches or of a position that attachment enables a preponderance of fire to be delivered at short ranges.

(c) During an advance, when the artillery and machine gun barrage "lifts", the assaulting infantry can protect its immediate front by creating a so-called barrage of fire to the enemy trenches.

(d) In the trenches it provides the soldier with a semiautomatic rifle and a magazine holding forty (40) cartridges.

(e) Just previous to and during the consolidation of the captured positions counterattacks are to be guarded against; the supply of ammunition in the hands of troops is generally low and replenishment usually impossible owing to the enemy barrage; the automatic bolt and two hundred (200) rounds of ammunition per man should be with the troops during this critical period.

(f) The device will very greatly simplify the supply of ammunition.

(g) Its greatest value will be in surprise effect.

5.   The board therefore recommends that the Pedersen attachment for the rifle be adopted as soon as possible, and that an initial order for one hundred thousand (100,000) of these attachments be placed at once. The board also recommends that this device be kept as secret as possible, and that it not be issued for use until at least fifty thousand (50,000) are ready to be placed in the hand of troops. The board is of the opinion that the initial supply of ammunition should be about five thousand (5,000) rounds per gun, with a daily supply of about one hundred (100) rounds per gun.

6.   A copy of the record of tests made is attached, from which it will be seen that the board has made a few minor suggestions to the inventor with a view of meeting practical requirements.

7.   The board directed that only two copies of its proceedings be prepared, and that all other records should be destroyed.

Having no further business before it, the board then adjourned *sine die*.

> (Signed) J. W. MacAndrew
>   Brigadier General, National Army
>   President
>
> (Signed) John H. Parker
>   Colonel, Infantry, National Army
>   Member
>
> (Signed) Leroy Eltings
>   Colonel, General Staff
>   Member
>
> (Signed) Albert E. Phillips
>   Major, Ordnance Department
>   Member
>
> (Signed) John C. Beatty
>   Captain, Ordnance Department
>   Recorder

APPENDIX **G**

Attaching the Model 1907 Leather Sling

Following are simplified instructions for mounting the M1907 sling on your M1903 Springfield.

Lay down the rifle, sights down and muzzle pointing to the right.

Lay out the two pieces of the sling, short piece on the left, long piece on the right, both with the smooth side pointing to the bottom of the rifle.

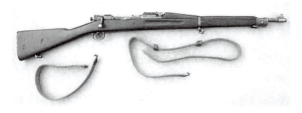

Pick up one keeper and slide it over the free end of the long piece to about five inches from the hook.

Slide the D-ring on the short piece over the free end of the long piece, then take the free end of the long piece and feed it back through the keeper so that it forms a loop with the D-ring in its bight.

Slide the second keeper over the free end (called the feed end), then slide the free end through the forward sling swivel,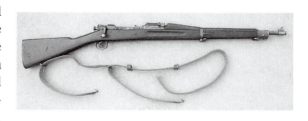

then back through the second keeper so that it forms a second loop with the sling swivel at its bight.

Model 1903 Springfield Rifle and Its Variations

Hook the clawed end of the long piece into the ninth set of holes on the feed end.

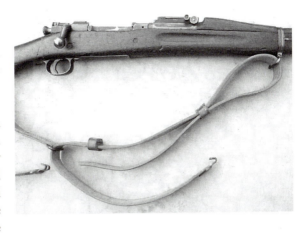

Slide the hooks on the short end through the rear sling swivel and pull it tight and hook it into the feed end as close to the long end's claw as needed.

To use the sling as a shooting support, unhook the short end claw and let it dangle loose.

Slide your hand between the inside strap and the feed end, then twist

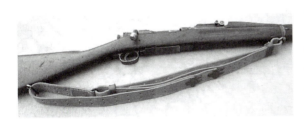

your wrist over the top of the inside strap and to the left so that the sling lies against the back of your hand. If the sling is adjusted properly, the butt-stock should wedge tightly against your shoulder. If your arms are longer or shorter than average, adjust the claw in the feed end up or down until you achieve a tight "wedge" fit.

Appendix **H**
Ammunition

Four basic types of ammunition were developed for the M1903 Spring-field rifle and its variants. The first cartridge was the .30-Model 1903, followed by the .30-Model 1906, then the .30-Model M1 and finally the .30-Model M2 cartridge. Listed below are some specifications for cartridges intended for rifle use only. As the cartridges for the Model 1906 rifle are a study in themselves, the author suggests consulting several of the authorities listed in the bibliography for more detailed information than is possible to include here.

Cartridge, .30-Model 1903
U.S. Caliber .30 Ball Cartridge (1903)
> 220-grain round-nose bullet, cupronickel jacket
> Boxer primer composition of tersulphide of antimony, potassium chlorate, sulphur and ground glass
> Powder weight (mean) 42 grains depending on the powder lot used
> Cartridge weight is 450 grains depending on the weight of the powder charge used
> Muzzle velocity: 2,200 fps
> Overall length: 3.330 inches
> Approved: 1903

Blank Cartridge, Model of 1903
> Hollow paper bullet with 5 grains of E.C. smokeless powder to assure bullet disintegration after leaving the muzzle
> Tinned case
> Propelling charge: 10 grains
> Overall Length: 3.22 inches to prevent machine assembling of a ball cartridge in a clip

Model 1903 Springfield Rifle and Its Variations

Guard Cartridge
> Two 42-grain balls held in the case neck by cannelure and
> crimp
> Propelling charge was 43.5 grains

Guard Cartridge
> 177-grain round-nose unjacketed bullet
> Propelling charge is that required to provide a velocity
> of 1,150 fps

Gallery Practice Cartridge
> 107-grain round-nose lead bullet
> Propelling charge is 3 grains of .38-caliber (pistol) ball
> powder
> Range not to exceed 100 feet.

Dummy Cartridge
> 220-grain round-nose bullet, cupronickel jacket
> Tinned case with six longitudinal corrugations and three holes
> around the perimeter of the case
> Primer has no charge
> Early variations (1903) had no holes in the case and
> corrugations ran into shoulder
> 1904 variations had four 0.13-inch holes drilled around the
> case behind corrugations
> 1905 variations had three 0.13-inch holes drilled in alterna-
> tion corrugations

Cartridge, .30-Model 1906
U.S. Caliber .30 Ball Cartridge (1906)
> 150-grain spire pointed bullet, cupronickel jacket copper color
> Boxer primer composition of tersulphide of antimony,
> potassium chlorate, sulphur and ground glass
> Powder weight varies from 47 to 50 grains depending on
> powder lot used

Model 1903 Springfield Rifle and Its Variations

Cartridge Weight is 392 grains, depending on composition of
powder charge

Muzzle velocity: 2,700 fps

Overall length: 3.315 inches

Approved: 1906

Blank Cartridge, Model of 1906

Hollow paper bullet with 6 grains of E.C. smokeless powder
to assure bullet disintegration after leaving the muzzle

Tinned case

Propelling charge: 10 grains

Overall Length: 3.22 inches to prevent machine assembling
of a ball cartridge in a clip

Blank Cartridge, Model of 1909

Tinned case

Case mouth closed with shellacked paper cup

Propelling charge: 12 grains

Overall length: 2.489 to 2.494 inches

Dummy Cartridge

Tinned case with six longitudinal corrugations and three holes
around the perimeter of the case

150-grain spire point bullet

Primer has no charge

Guard Cartridge

150-grain spire point bullet, copper color. Slightly imperfect
bullets were used

Cartridge case has five cannelures encircling the body

Propelling charge is 9.1 grains of Bullseye or 16.7 grains of
Du Pont Rifle Smokeless No. 1

Muzzle velocity: 1,200 fps

Guard Cartridge

150-grain spire point bullet, copper color. Slightly imperfect
bullets were used

Cartridge case had six short cannelures 0.19 inch long pressed
into the case shoulder

Model 1903 Springfield Rifle and Its Variations

Propelling charge is 9.1 grains of Bullseye or 16.7 grains of
Du Pont Rifle Smokeless No. 1

Muzzle velocity: 1,200 fps

Cartridge, Armor Piercing, Caliber .30, M1917

Steel core 0.910 inch long inside lead shell surrounded by
cupronickel jacket open at the tip

Germany objected to the cartridge as a "dum dum" bullet and
they were withdrawn

Cartridge, Ball, Caliber .30 M1

U.S. Caliber .30 M1 Ball Cartridge

150-grain boattail M1 bullet, gilding metal jacket

Boxer primer composition of tersulphide of antimony,
potassium chlorate, sulphur and ground glass

Powder weight varies from 47 to 50 grains depending on
powder lot used

Cartridge Weight is 392 garins, depending on composition
of powder charge

Muzzle velocity: 2,647 fps

Overall length: 3.315 inches

Approved: 1925

Cartridge, Ball, Caliber .30 M2

U.S. Caliber .30 M2 Ball Cartridge

150-grain spire pointed bullet; boxer primed; gilding metal
jacket

Muzzle velocity: 2,805 fps

Approved in 1939

Cartridge, Armor Piercing, .30 Caliber, M2

168.5-grain tungsten chromium or manganese molybdenum
steel boattail, black tip

Muzzle velocity: 2,775 fps

APPENDIX I
Bibliography

Books

Ball, Robert W. D., *Springfield Armory, Shoulder Weapons, 1795-1968,* Antique Trader Books, Dubuque, IA 52004, 1997.

Barnes, Frank, *Cartridges of the World*, DBI Books Inc., 4092 Commercial Ave., Northbrook, IL 60062, 5th Edition, 1985.

Beach, 1st Lieutenant S.H., *History of Small Arms Procurement, 1939-1945, Ordnance Department, U.S. Army*, reprinted by Springfield Research Service, PO Box 4181, Silver Spring, MD 20914.

Brophy, Lt. Col. William S., *The Springfield 1903 Rifles,* Stackpole Books, Harrisburg, PA 17105, 1985.

Brophy, Lieutenant Colonel William S., *The Springfield Armory 1890-1948*, Andrew Mowbray Publishers, PO Box 460, Lincoln, RI 02865, 1991.

Campbell, Clark S., *The '03 Era: When Smokeless Revolutionized U.S. Riflery*, Collector Grade Publications, Inc., Coburg, Ontario, Canada, 1994.

Cole, M.H., *U.S. Military Knives, Bayonets and Machetes: Book III*, M.H. Cole, 501 Ridge Road, Birmingham, AL 35206, 1979.

Crossman, Captain Edward C., *The Book of the Springfield*, Small Arms Technical Publishing Company, Marines, NC, 1932.

Dorsey, Stephen, *U.S. Martial Web Belts and Bandoliers: 1903-1981,* Collectors' Library, Eugene, OR 97440, 1993.

Ezell, Edward C., *Small Arms of the World*, Stackpole Books, Harrisburg, PA 17105, 12th Edition, 1983.

Model 1903 Springfield Rifle and Its Variations

Ferris, C.S., *Rock Island Rifle, Model 1903,* Scott Duff Publications, Export, PA. 15632, 2001.

Ferris, C.S., and John Beard, *Springfield Model 1903 Service Rifle, Production and Alteration, 1905-1910*, C.S. Ferris, Arvada, CO 80001-0420, 1995.

Fuller, Stephen L., *United States Martial and Collectors Arms,* Military Research Service, San Jose, CA 95159, 2nd Edition, 1982.

Green, Constance McLaughlin, Harry C. Thomson and Peter C. Roots, *The United States Army in World War II; Technical Services—The Ordnance Department: Planning Munitions for War.* Washington, DC, 1955.

Harrison, Jesse C., *U.S. Military Markings, 1900-1965*, The Arms Chest, Oklahoma City, OK 73150, 1993.

Hatcher, Julian S., *Hatcher's Notebook*, Stackpole Books, Harrisburg, PA, 1947, rev. ed., 1966.

Hogg, Ian V. and John Weeks, *Military Small Arms of the 20th Century*, DBI Books, Northfield, IL 60093, 4th Edition, 1981.

Janzen, Jerry L., *Bayonets from Janzen's Notebook*, PO Box 2863, Tulsa, OK 74107, 1984.

Madis, George, *U.S. Military Arms, Dates of Manufacture from 1795*, Art & Reference House, Brownsboro, TX 75756, 1989.

Mallory, Franklin B., *Summary of D.C.M. Rifle Sales, 1922-1942*, Springfield Research Service, Silver Spring, MD 20914, 1976.

Mallory, Franklin B. and Ludwig Olson, *The Krag Rifle Story,* Springfield Research Service, Silver Spring, MD 20914, 2nd Edition, 2001.

___, *Mills Woven Military Equipments*, Mills Woven Cartridge Belt Company, Worcester, MA, 1912.

Model 1903 Springfield Rifle and Its Variations

Morse, D.R. and D.T. Morse, *Production Statistics: U.S. Arms Makers,* Firing Pin Enterprises, Phoenix, AZ 85060-0696, 1997.

Senich, Peter S., *The Complete Book of U.S. Sniping*, Paladin Press, Boulder, CO, 1988.

Shaffer, James B., Lee A. Rutledge and R. Stephen Dorsey, *Gun Tools: Their History and Identification*, Collectors' Library, PO Box 263, Eugene, OR 97440, 1992.

Smith, W.H.B. and Joseph E. Smith, *The Book of Rifles,* The Telegraph Press, Harrisburg, PA, 3rd Edition, 1963.

Tantum, William H., IV, *Sniper Rifles of Two World Wars*, Museum Restoration Service, Bloomfield, Ontario, 1967.

Magazine Articles

American Rifleman Reprint, *Model 1903 Springfield Rifles,* National Rifle Association, Fairfax, VA 22030-9400, Revised Edition, 4th Printing, 2000.

Byrd, Larry, "The U.S. Remington Model 03-A3 Reference Standard Rifles," *U.S. Martial Arms Collector,* Springfield Research Service, Number 88, Falls Church, VA 22040, April 1999.

Campbell, Clark S., "Remington '03 Rifle Production," *U.S. Martial Arms Collector,* Springfield Research Service, Number 90, Falls Church, VA 22040, October 1999.

Canfield, Bruce N., "The First '03s," *American Rifleman,* The National Rifle Association, November 2001.

____, "Donald F. Carpenter Notebook, Remington Arms Period–World War II," *U.S. Martial Arms Collector,* Springfield Research Service, Number 92, Falls Church, VA 22040, April 2000.

Ewalt, Fred and Bill Hansen, "Model 1903 Rifle Handguard Variations," *U.S. Martial Arms Collector,* Springfield Research Service, Number 90, Falls Church, VA 22040, October 1999.

Model 1903 Springfield Rifle and Its Variations

Furler, Ed, Jr., "Time Capsule Springfield," *Gun Journal*, December 1990.

Gagner, Wayne P., "The Elusive Bushmaster Carbine," *U.S. Martial Arms Collector,* Springfield Research Service, Number 91, Falls Church, VA 22040, January 2000.

Hansen, Bill, "The Red Star Remington '03 Rifles," *U.S. Martial Arms Collector,* Springfield Research Service, Number 89, Falls Church, VA 22040, July 1999.

Hatcher, Maj. Julian S., "The Pedersen Device," *The American Rifleman,* The National Rifle Association, May 1932.

Horn, Captain R.O., "Fire Discipline, Control and Direction," *Infantry Journal,* January-February 1913.

Phillips, William G., "The Evolution of the Pocket-Type Rifle Cartridge Belt in the United States Service," *Military Collector and Historian,* Spring 1970.

Reynolds, Larry, "U.S.M.C. 1903A1/Unertl Sniper Rifle," *U.S. Martial Arms Collector*, Springfield Research Service, Number 94, Falls Church, VA 22040, October 1999.

Correspondence
D.F. Carpenter, Director of Manufacture, Remington Arms Co., to W.E. Leigh, British Purchasing Commission, May 28, 1941, production of Springfield and Enfield Rifles.

Charles Walker to S. M. Alvis, Manager, Ilion Research Division, Remington Arms Co. February 9 and 14, 1970. Pedersen Device.

Randall C. Wilks to L.K. Goodstall, Remington Arms Co. February 2, 1973. Pedersen Device.

Walbridge P. Eyeberg to Joe Poyer, July 3, 1983, Warner & Swasey and M1903 Mark I serial numbers.
E.F. Furler to Joe Poyer, May 2, 1993. Air Service Rifle Magazines.

Model 1903 Springfield Rifle and Its Variations

Reports
"Production of the Rifle, U.S. Caliber .30, M1903 and M1903-A3 at the Ilion, N.Y. Works of the Remington Arms Company, Inc.: A Summary Report." Prepared by the Public Relations Division, Remington Arms Company, Inc. Bridgeport, Connecticut, May 9, 1945.

Manuals
Ammunition Inspection Guide, TM 9-1904, War Department Technical Manual, 2 March 1944.

Basic Field Manual: U.S. Rifle, Caliber .30, Model of 1903, FM 23-10, Government Printing Office, Washington, DC, March 12, 1924.

Basic Field Manual: U.S. Rifle, Caliber .30, Model of 1903, FM 23-10, Government Printing Office, Washington, DC, January 2, 1940.

Basic Field Manual: U.S. Rifle, Caliber .30, Model of 1903, FM 23-10, Government Printing Office, Washington, DC, September 30, 1943.

Description of the Infantry Equipment, Model 1910, March 11, 1912, revised July 2, 1914, Washington, Government Printing Office, No. 1718, 1917.

Description and Rules for the Management of the U.S. Magazine Rifle, Model of 1903, Caliber .30, Department of the Army, March 3, 1904. Washington, Government Printing Office.

Description and Rules for the Management of the U.S. Magazine Rifle, Model of 1903, Caliber .30, Department of the Army, March 3, 1904, revised April 18, 1906. Washington, Government Printing Office.

Description and Rules for the Management of the U.S. Magazine Rifle, Model of 1903, Caliber .30, Department of the Army, March 3, 1904, revised April 18, 1906, revised February 14, 1908. Washington, Government Printing Office.

Description and Rules for the Management of the U.S. Magazine Rifle, Model of 1903, Caliber .30, Department of the Army, March 3, 1904, revised

Model 1903 Springfield Rifle and Its Variations

April 18, 1906, revised February 14, 1908, revised 1909. Washington, Government Printing Office.

Description of Telescopic Musket Sights, Models of 1908 and 1913, Department of the Army, December 14, 1908, revised July 22, 1912, revised November 18, 1915. Washington, Government Printing Office. 1917.

Handbook for the Rifle, United States Rifle, Caliber .30, Model of 1903, Ordnance Document 1923, War Department Document No. 987, Office of the Adjutant General, Washington, DC, October 1919.

Horse Equipments and Equipments for Officers and Enlisted Men, May 10, 1905, revised July 3, 1908, Washington, Government Printing Office, No. 1719, 1917.

Training Regulations, Weapons, United States Rifle, Caliber .30, Model of 1903, Accessories and Appendages, Government Printing Office, Washington, DC, 1940.
>   Changes No. 1, September 10, 1940
>   Changes No. 2, November 15, 1941
>   Changes No. 3, August 4, 1942
>   Changes No. 4, November 6, 1942
>   Changes No. 5, December 17, 1942

U.S. Rifles, Cal. .30, M1903, M1903A1, M1903A3 and M1903A4, TM9-1270, Department of the Army, Washington, DC, May 19, 1942.

U.S. Rifle, Cal. .30, M1903A4 (Sniper's), Characteristics and Operation and Use of Telescopic Sight, TM 9-1270, War Department Technical Manual, War Department, 28 September 1943.

Weapons: United States Rifle, Caliber .30, Model of 1903, Accessories and Appendages, TR 32–10, War Department, Washington, DC, March 12, 1924.

Model 1903 Springfield Rifle and Its Variations

Fig. I-1. Proposed British version of the Model 1903 Springfield Rifle.

Fig. I-2. Remington Model 1903 Springfield Rifle.

Fig. I-3. Remington Model 1903A3 Rifle.

Fig. I-4. Remington Model 1903A4 Sniper Rifle.

APPENDIX I

PRODUCTION OF THE

RIFLE, U. S. CALIBER .30

M1903 and M1903-A3

at the

Ilion, N. Y. Works of the
Remington Arms Company, Inc.

This document contains information
affecting the national defense of the
United States within the meaning of the
Espionage Act, 50 U.S.C., 31 and 32. Its
transmission or the revelation of its
contents in any manner to an unauthorized
person is prohibited by law.

Prepared by:

Public Relations Division
Remington Arms Company, Inc.
Bridgeport, Connecticut

May 9, 1945

[Photographs and Report courtesy of Remington Arms Company
and Roy Marcot.]

Model 1903 Springfield Rifle and Its Variations

This report is a summary of activities in connection with the manufacture by the Remington Arms Company, Inc., of the U. S. Rifle, Caliber .30, M1903, during World War II.

Additional information and copies of all letters, memos, documents, etc. referred to herein are contained in the Military Files of the Remington Arms Company at Bridgeport, Connecticut.

Model 1903 Springfield Rifle and Its Variations

FOREWORD

For many years the Ilion, N.Y. plant of the Remington Arms Company has been engaged in the manufacture of sporting firearms; largely shotguns and caliber 22 rifles. Peacetime capacity for center fire rifles of larger caliber was approximately 80 per day. Only 60 employees were engaged in the manufacture of center fire rifles in 1939.

Remington Arms manufactured rifles for the Allies during the early years of World War I and for the U. S. Government after this nation declared war in 1917. The model manufactured for the U. S. at that time was a modified Enfield rifle, chambered to accommodate the caliber 30 Springfield cartridge.

Following the sudden and unexpected events in the European War during the spring and summer of 1940, the British Government was urgently in need of large quantities of military rifles. As a result of numerous conferences in Washington to determine the fastest means of producing these rifles and supplying them to the British, a decision was reached that quickest results could be obtained by shipping standby equipment in storage at Rock Island Arsenal to the Remington Arms Company plant at Ilion, N. Y.

Equipment was moved to Ilion immediately after the lease was signed and manufacturing operations started within six weeks. Despite the many difficulties arising because of technical and manufacturing problems, the first completed rifles were ready for Ordnance acceptance within six months.....just half the time that had been anticipated.

Model 1903 Springfield Rifle and Its Variations

Mass production on the Springfield rifle had never before been attempted. Drawings, specifications and other manufacturing data had not been kept up to date and the equipment itself was In need of rehabilitation and modernization. However, so critical was the British demand for rifles that immediate production was necessary. Time could not be spared for pilot production, experimental runs or for an engineering layout of the entire rifle in advance of initial productive operations.

Schedules were first set at 1,000 rifles per day -- then doubled to 2,000 -- then tripled to 3,000 per day. To attain such an objective, a program calling for redesign of the rifle and modernization of the manufacturing process was necessary. This formidable undertaking was superimposed on the company's already difficult production program.

The entire program at Ilion presented the problem of producing, within the shortest possible time, a maximum number of rifles suitable for combat use. The first of these was produced in six months and from then on, until Ordnance discontinued rifle manufacture in February, 1944, over a million Springfields had been presented and accepted.

Model 1903 Springfield Rifle and Its Variations

Negotiations with British

The Remington Arms Company was first contacted on the subject of manufacturing rifles for the Allies in World War II when W. E. Leigh, Purchasing Agent for Munitions, British Purchasing Commission, sent a letter to E. E. Handy, Vice President, on August 15, 1940, asking if Remington would manufacture military rifles for the British. The letter advised that 400,000 rifles would be needed as quickly as possible with deliveries at 40,000 per month. The letter states, "We would prefer the British pattern of 303 caliber but would consider an American pattern of 30 caliber." Remington immediately notified the Ordnance Department of this request from the British.

It developed shortly thereafter that negotiations were under way between the British and the U. S. Government to authorize the use of Springfield rifle equipment in storage at Rock Island Arsenal in the production of firearms required by His Majesty's government.

Toward the middle of November, Mr. Leigh accepted an estimate for moving machinery and tools to Ilion and directed that a Letter of Intent be drawn providing for full preparation costs and initial raw material expenditures. It was agreed tentatively that Remington would manufacture Springfield rifles under a cost-plus—fixed-fee contract at a fee of $5.00 per rifle.

British Contract

The British contract was formally initiated with a Letter of Intent dated December 12, 1940, providing for the manufacture of 500,000 Springfield rifles with options for an additional 500,000. As previously agreed, Remington was to

443

receive a fixed fee of $5.00 per rifle. Although there was some delay in negotiating a lease for Rock Island equipment, the British Purchasing Commission requested that work proceed immediately since no difficulty in reaching an ultimate agreement on the lease was anticipated.

The British agreed to advance $4,000,000, of which $3,347,000 was for leasing the Rock Island equipment, rehabilitation of Ilion equipment, enlargement of the plant and training of personnel; $235,000 for the purchase of raw materials and $400,000 for the purchase of bayonets, scabbards and other accessories.

A supplement to the Letter of Intent was issued on April 16, 1941, providing $800,000 for two months production, during which time a formal definitive agreement was to be reached. Such a contract was signed on June 30, 1941, and covered the production of 500,000 rifles at an estimated cost of $50 each.

Lease on Equipment

The U. S. Government was withholding execution of the lease on the Rock Island equipment because of plans to consolidate aid to Great Britain. Remington was advised of this fact on January 10, 1941, when Mr. Leigh told W. R. Scott that there was a possibility of some of the British contracts being taken over by the U. S. Government. There soon followed a meeting between representatives of Ordnance, Great Britain and Remington at which the possibility of the United States taking over British commitments at Ilion was discussed.

On March 4, 1941, Robert B. Patterson, Under Secretary of War, advised C. K. Davis, President and General Manager of the Remington Arms Company, that the use of the Rock Island machinery is "in

Model 1903 Springfield Rifle and Its Variations

the interest of the United States," and that Remington should consider his letter approval and authority to employ the equipment for the British work. On that date the lease assigning the equipment to Remington was signed by Mr. Patterson.

Type of Rifle Decided
During the negotiations with the British, they expressed a strong preference for the Lee—Enfield rifle. Remington insisted that the type of rifle must be acceptable to the U. S. Ordnance Department, which indicated that the use of the Rock Island equipment was authorized for the manufacture of Springfield rifles only. Even after machinery was moved to Ilion, discussion with the British regarding the type of rifle continued. Finally, on April 7th, General C. T. Harris advised D. F. Carpenter that the British proposal to produce rifles of the Lee-Enfield design could not be accomplished without altering the Rock Island lease and further that any such change was undesirable to the Ordnance Department.

Start of U. S. Contract
Following the passage of the Lend—Lease Act (March 11, 1941), which made it practical for the United States to take over rifle procurement for the British, this possibility was increasingly discussed; and in July Remington was advised of a desire on the part of the U. S. Ordnance Department to place requisitions for Springfield rifles. On August 21st, Wing Commander A. J. Richardson, in a letter to G. O. Clifford, definitely stated that it was likely the Ordnance Department would take over the British contract. Meanwhile manufacturing operations were under way at Ilion, the plant keeping in close touch with Ordnance officials.

Model 1903 Springfield Rifle and Its Variations

Remington received letter contract DA—W—740—ORD—36, dated September 17, 1941, for 134,000 Springfield rifles at an estimated cost of $54.15 each, on which Remington's fee was $3.00 per rifle. The contract also called for 1,340 sets of spare parts at $570 per set, with a fee of $35 per set, and 1,340 sets of accessories at $950 per set with a fee of $50 per set.

Daily capacity was to be built up to 1,000 rifles, with initial deliveries on or before November 15, 1941, and completion of the full quantity ordered by July 15, 1942. The U. S. contract superseded the British contract, which was formally cancelled on December 16th by a letter from H. D. Hancock, British Purchasing Commission to E. E. Handy. On March 10, 1942, a formal U. S. contract was approved in the form of a supplement (No. 3) to the original letter contract. The formal contract called for 508,000 Springfield rifles to be produced on a cost—plus—fixed—fee basis.

Following the execution of the U. S. contract, various change orders and supplements were negotiated, revising the quantities and schedules. In March, 1942, scheduled daily production was ordered increased from 1,000 to 2,000, and in May, 1942, a change order was received authorizing an increase in plant capacity to make possible the manufacture of 3,000 rifles per day.

Partially as a result of efforts to meet this increased schedule by reducing the machine tools and floor space required per rifle, and, incidentally, to reduce cost and raw steel requirements, Remington undertook the redesigning of the Springfield rifle. A discussion of the simplification program is included in Section IV of this report.

On September 17, 1942, Remington officials

Model 1903 Springfield Rifle and Its Variations

met with Ordnance Department representatives at Rochester and discussed the financial aspects of the rifle contract. Among other things covered at this meeting was the possibility of a reduction in Remington's fees on rifles, sets of parts and sets of accessories.

This discussion was formalized in contract supplement #36 dated November 3, 1943, which reduced Remington's fee to $2.25 per rifle and $20 on each set of spare parts. The number of pieces in a set of accessories was changed with the result that the cost per set dropped from $950 to $121. Remington's fee became $4.00 per set.

Fixed Price Negotiations

The rifle contract entered a new phase of negotiations when, on January 5, 1943, Mr. Littleton, Rochester Ordnance District, called J. S. Hoffman and W. B. DeReimer on the telephone and suggested that the contract be converted from a cost-plus fixed—fee to a fixed price basis.

Because of the complications involved in making such a change....complications resulting from such factors as the transfer of the contract from the British the U. S. Government, lease of Rock Island equipment, acquisition of Government facilities and a provision for plant rehabilitation upon conclusion of the contract....several months of negotiations followed. In October, 1943, Remington executed contract supplement #35, which established a fixed price for rifles, spare parts and accessories retroactive to the first delivery under the contract.

These negotiations were voided when Col. Duffy advised W.U. Reisinger by telephone that the Comptroller General had refused to approve Government execution of supplement #35. The contract was continued on a cost-plus-fixed-fee basis.

Model 1903 Springfield Rifle and Its Variations

Termination of Rifle Manufacture

On May 20, 1943, Brig. Gen. James Kirk advised D. F. Carpenter that in his opinion the further manufacture of the Springfield rifle was uncertain. Five days later Gen. Kirk advised Mr. Carpenter that the Ilion schedule would be reduced from 90,000 per month to 75,000.

On August 6, 1943, Major Neilson advised D. F. Carpenter that the Springfield Armory had been manufacturing rifle spare parts but that production on the Garand rifle was so urgent that Remington might be called upon to manufacture spare parts for the Springfield in order to release facilities at the Armory for work on the Garand.

On September 15, 1943, Remington received a list of the spare parts which we were requested to produce. Total discontinuance of the manufacture of Springfield rifles was discussed at a meeting in Gen. Kirk's office on November 8th, at which time Remington was requested to prepare a plan for the reduction and/or complete discontinuance of Springfield rifle manufacture. Soon after that, formal steps were taken to reduce the schedule as follows:

           November - 58,500
           December - 50,000
           January - 40,000

On December 7, 1943, Remington accepted change order #39 permitting the manufacture of a maximum of 176,774 rifles after November 1. All production was to cease as of February 29, 1944.

Since that time the Ilion plant of the Remington Arms Company has manufactured spare parts and done repair work on Springfield rifles in addition to manufacturing guns and rifles of the company's design for various Government agencies.

Model 1903 Springfield Rifle and Its Variations

PROBLEMS OF PRODUCTION

In early discussions with Ordnance and other officials, 30 months was estimated as the time required to get into production if new equipment was procured. Remington agreed to produce rifles in 12 months if standby U.S. Government equipment, then in storage at Rock Island Arsenal, was moved to Ilion and full advantage taken of the company's experience and judgment in arms manufacture. Actually, the first rifles were produced six month after operations started.

The record was as follows:

March 4, 1941	- Equipment lease signed.
April 18, 1941	- 43 carloads of equipment had been moved from Rock Island to Ilion and first operations started.
October 25, 1941	_ First rifles passed Remington inspection and ready for Ordnance inspection.

Drawings and Specifications

Remington had been advised that a complete process record on the Springfield rifle was available. It was believed, however, that the dimensions and tolerances on the component drawings were not accurate since process changes had been

Model 1903 Springfield Rifle and Its Variations

made without bringing the drawings up to date. We were advised that the gages probably represented more accurately the dimensions of the component parts although not stamped with the correct dimensions and there was no information available to determine if the gages were correct. In the event that there had been any warping or deterioration of the gages it would thus be difficult to determine practical working dimensions. It also developed that no final revisions in drawings or specifications were contemplated by the Springfield Armory until test performances had conclusively proven the advisability of proposed changes.

Because of the manufacturing difficulties thus presented, the following was incorporated in the British contract:

"It is pertinent to point out, however, that the proposed manufacture of the rifles and rifle components by the Remington Arms Company represents the first time that such articles have been produced by a commercial rifle plant. It is apparent, therefore, that certain changes in tools, jigs, dies, gage limits and fixtures may be necessary to produce a weapon with the desired interchangeability of parts .... It is recognized that variances therefrom (the specifications) are unavoidable..."

Thus it was understood that the product to be produced by Remington would probably not be strictly in accordance with the U. S. specifications. Following the passage of the Lend-Lease Act, the U. S. Government took over the British contract, and, although U. S. specifications were made a part of this contract, the same manufacturing difficulties prevailed.

Model 1903 Springfield Rifle and Its Variations

Engineering surveys had indicated, however, that rifles assembled from components manufactured from this equipment would function satisfactorily and would meet combat requirements. Subsequent experience proved this conclusion to be correct. Although there were many manufacturing problems, the company has no record that any of its rifles proved to be unsafe in the field.

Production Changes

The contract with the U. S. Government called for daily production of 1,000 rifles. The first rifles had passed the Remington final inspection in October, 1941, but Ordnance inspection for acceptance was not made until the week ending January 3, 1942, when 10,440 rifles had passed the Remington final inspection and 3,706 of these had been accepted by Ordnance.

On March 12, 1942, Remington was directed to increase rifle production from 1,000 to 2,000 per day, and on urgent Ordnance Department insistence, surveys were made to ascertain maximum productive capacity. It was indicated that a daily production rate of 3,000 was desired.

As production increased, previous manufacturing problems were thereby intensified, and it became evident that major changes in design and equipment would be necessary in order to achieve the desired production level. We faced the alternative of procuring some 1,300 additional machine tools and enlarging plant facilities to accommodate them; or of redesigning the rifle so as to eliminate some parts and simplify the manufacture of others to make possible their procurement through sub-contracting. Since the necessary additional facilities could not be obtained at that time, Remington accepted contract

451

Model 1903 Springfield Rifle and Its Variations

supplement No. 5, dated June 4, 1942, which ordered technical studies to simplify the design and manufacture of the Springfield rifle. (See Section IV). Meanwhile, on condition that a redesigned rifle would be approved for manufacturing, a change order was accepted during the end of May authorizing an increase in plant capacity to permit the manufacture of 3,000 per day, and on July 20th, a Letter Purchase Order for 720,000 additional rifles was executed, bringing the total number of rifles ordered to 1,328,000.

During the time the development and design of the simplified rifle was under way rifle manufacture continued in accordance with the then applicable drawings and specifications.

Production for the year 1942 was completed almost exactly on schedule. A total of 338,672 rifles had been accepted as against a schedule of 347,000.

In the Spring of 1943, when the initial urgency for rifles had passed, it was suggested to General Kirk that production be curtailed to make possible process improvements, which would subsequently insure a product even more closely approaching the limits set in the specifications. General Kirk approved such action and thus monthly production dropped for the next few months,

In order to attain the proposed production rate of 3,000 rifles per day, it was necessary to employ a large number of additional employees. Inasmuch as the urgency of rifle production had passed, and the manpower and housing shortage at Ilion presented serious problems, it appeared to us that a somewhat lower rate of production might lead to less disruption in the locality. This was brought to the attention of Ordnance officials, with the advice that Remington would pursue

whatever course Ordnance approved. Shortly
thereafter General Kirk advised D. F. Carpenter
that the schedule was being reduced.

In September of that year total
discontinuance of the manufacture of Springfield
rifles was discussed, and on December 7, 1943,
Remington accepted Change Order #39 calling for
discontinuance of production as of February 29,
1944.

Model 1903 Springfield Rifle and Its Variations

SPECIAL DIFFICULTIES AND/OR CONTRIBUTIONS TO THE PROGRAM

In late 1940 and early 1941 Hitler's armies had overwhelmed the channel ports and there was desperate need for rifles to arm the British Home Guard, according to Sir Walter Layton. At that dramatic moment Remington was asked to produce rifles in the shortest possible time.

We accepted this urgent assignment and within 34 months had moved equipment from Rock Island to Ilion, recruited and trained personnel, procured necessary materials and produced over one million rifles.

This entire program was a formidable manufacturing and technical undertaking in which it was necessary to overcome many obstacles. In general, all of these could be attributed to the following:

1. Discrepancies and inadequacies of drawings, specifications and other technical data.

2. Equipment and tool difficulties that would naturally occur in a program involving the use of over 1,000 machines which had stood idle for 20 years, and the procurement of thousands of tools and gages.

3. The problem of recruiting and training an organization of approximately 7,500 employees, many of whom had no previous industrial experience of any kind.

4. The satisfactory coordination of a complex procurement-manufacturing program at a time when constantly greater and still greater efforts were required to produce rifles under abnormal conditions.

Model 1903 Springfield Rifle and Its Variations

It was found, for example, that hundreds of drawing changes were necessary, great numbers of gages had to be obtained at a time when facilities were already overtaxed, and perhaps most important that none of the refinements in manufacturing processes developed since the last war had been adapted to manufacture of the Springfield rifle.

To overcome some of these difficulties and to make possible maximum production with the facilities available, Remington agreed to undertake' studies toward redesign of the rifle and simplification of its manufacture. This program was authorized by contract supplement No. 5, dated June 4, 1942.

This assignment called for the redesign of the 1903 Springfield rifle to meet the following requirements:

1. Reduce the number of component parts (the 1903 rifle had 91 parts).
2. Eliminate forging operations wherever possible (29 of the components of the 1903 rifle required forging).
3. Reduce machining operations (virtually all the parts of the 1903 rifle required machining).
4. Design parts in such a manner that the manufacture of a large number of such parts could be subcontracted to other companies.
5. The changeover from the manufacture of the old to the new design rifles should result in a minimum disruption to current production.
6. To the maximum possible extent the new component parts should be so designed that they could be used as repair parts for either the new or the old rifle.
7. The new design should result in a rifle which would meet the severe performance

requirements of the Army.
8.   The entire design, engineering, plant conversion, tooling, and procurement program should be completed in the shortest possible time.

The above assignment was completed satisfactorily and met virtually all of the foregoing requirements. In August, 1942, the U. S. Rifle, caliber 30, Model 1903-A3 was approved by the Ordnance Department. The modified rifle was mentioned by Major General T. J. Hayes, Assistant Chief of Ordnance and Chief of Industrial Service, as one of the most outstanding improvements in the design of ordnance material by an industrial company. It was also cited by Lieut. General W. S. Knudsen as an outstanding example of American industrial achievement in the war effort.

More specifically, of the 91 components of the Model 1903 rifle, 12 were completely eliminated, 23 parts previously requiring forging were redesigned to be stamped and formed, and only 24 remained unchanged. Approximately 1,300 machine tools which would otherwise have been required were released for other war needs; more than six pounds of steel were saved in the manufacture of each rifle, and a saving of 50 per cent in direct labor was effected. Thus, It was possible to subcontract many additional parts which were formerly machined at Ilion, because outside facilities were available to do the stamping and forming of the redesigned parts. It became possible for the Company to undertake manufacturing schedules up to 3,000 rifles per day within the Ilion Works.

The success of this entire program can be attributed to experience, mutual confidence, under-standing, and stability of judgment and purpose on the part of both Remington and Ordnance personnel.

Model 1903 Springfield Rifle and Its Variations

IMPORTANT EVENTS

Aug. 15, 1940 - British Purchasing Commission asks if Remington will manufacture 400,000 military rifles.

Oct. 23, 1940 - Sir Walter Layton emphasizes the urgent need for rifles; estimates that five million will be required at the earliest possible date.

Nov.9-18, 1940 - Negotiations completed authorizing the use of Rock Island equipment. Tentatively agreed that Remington would produce under a cost-plus-fixed-fee contract at fee .of $5 per rifle.

Dec. 12, 1940 - Letter of Intent from British providing for the manufacture of 500,000 Springfield rifles.

March 4, 1941 - Robt. B. Patterson, Under-secretary of War, signed lease assigning Rock Island equipment to Remington.

March. 11,1941 - Lend-Lease Act passed.

April 18, 1941 - First manufacturing operations on Springfield rifles.

Sept. 17, 1941 - Remington received Letter Contract DA-W-740-ORD-36 for 134,000 Springfield rifles on a cost-plus-fixed-fee basis at a fee of $3 per rifle.

Oct. 25, 1941 - First rifles passed Remington final inspection.

Dec. 10, 1941 - First rifle presented to Lieut. Col. R. L. Bowlin.

Dec. 16, 1941 - British contract formally cancelled.

March 10, 1942 - Contract supplement No. 3 executed calling for 508,000 Springfield rifles.

June 4, 1942 - Contract supplement No. 5,

Model 1903 Springfield Rifle and Its Variations

ordering technical studies to simplify
the design and manufacture of the
Springfield rifle.

July 20, 1942 - Remington received Letter
Purchase Order for 720,000 additional
rifles.

August, 1942 - Redesigned rifle (Model 1903-
A3) approved by Ordnance.

Jan. 5, 1943 - Remington first contacted
regarding conversion from cost-plus-
fixed-fee to a fixed price basis.

May 25, 1943 - Remington advised of monthly
schedule reduction from 90,000 to 75,000
rifles.

October, 1943 - Remington executed contract
supplement No. 35 establishing fixed
prices retroactive to first delivery
under contract. (Above negotiation was
not consummated because of Comptroller
General's refusal to approve government
execution of supplement No. 35).

Nov. 3, 1943 - Remington's fee reduced from $3
to $2.25 per rifle.

Nov. 8, 1943 - Discontinuance of rifle
manufacture discussed with Ordnance
officials.

Dec. 7, 1943 - Remington accepted change order
No. 39 calling for the cessation of
production on February 29, 1944.

Total number of Remington-manufactured rifles came
to 1,084,079.

Model 1903 Springfield Rifle and Its Variations

About the Author

Joe Poyer is the author of more than 400 magazine articles on firearms, the modern military, military history and personal security. He has written and published twelve novels with worldwide sales exceeding five million copies and authored or coauthored nine nonfiction books on the modern military.

He is the editorial director and publisher of North Cape Publications®, Inc., which publishes the "For Collectors Only®" and "Shooter's and Collector's Guide" series of books for firearms collectors and shooters. In these series, he has written or coauthored: *The .45-70 Springfield*; *U.S. Winchester Trench and Riot Guns, and Other U.S. Combat Shotguns*; *The M1 Garand, 1936 to 1957*; *The SKS Carbine*; *The M14-Type Rifle*; *The SAFN-49 Battle Rifle*; *The Swedish Mauser Rifles*; *The M16/AR15 Rifle*; *The Model 1903 Springfield Rifle and Its Variations*; *The American Krag Rifle and Carbine*; and *Swiss Magazine Loading Rifles, 1869 to 1958*.

Mr. Poyer has served as editor of the following magazines: *Safe & Secure Living*; *International Military Review*, *International Naval Review* and as field editor for *International Combat Arms*. He is currently at work on a new book in the "For Collectors Only" series, *The U.S. Government .45 ACP Pistol*.

Mr. Poyer was the on-camera Military Affairs Analyst and Reporter for a major television station in Los Angeles, California. He also imported the very fine L1A1A inch pattern FAL rifles from Australia in the late 1980s.

About the Editor

Ed Furler, Jr., has been a collector of U.S. military firearms for nearly four decades. A former technical writer and editor for the oil industry, he is also an author in his own right, having written a number of magazine articles on firearms for the *Remington Society of America Journal*, *Gun Journal* and other magazines. Ed is also an expert on the Bell P-39, P-400 and P-63 series of aircraft. He has written a number of magazine articles on the Airacobra and its variations for *Air Classics* and other magazines. He also contributed to the book, *Cobra!: The Bell Aircraft Corporation 1934-1946* by Birch Matthews. He and his son restore old military vehicles as a hobby. Ed is a Life member of the National Rifle Association and lives in the Houston area.

Model 1903 Springfield Rifle and Its Variations

Books from
North Cape Publications®, Inc.

The books in the "For Collectors Only" and "A Shooter's and Collector's Guide" series are designed to provide the firearms collector with an accurate record of the markings, dimensions and finish found on an original firearm as it was shipped from the factory. As changes to any and all parts are listed by serial number range, the collector can quickly assess not only whether or not the overall firearm is correct as issued, but whether or not each and every part is original for the period of the particular firearm's production. "For Collectors Only" and "A Shooter's and Collector's Guide" books make each collector and shooter an "expert."

For Collectors Only® Series

Swiss Magazine Loading Rifles, 1869 to 1958, by Joe Poyer, ($19.95). The Swiss were the first to adopt a repeating rifle as general issue to all troops in 1869. The rifle was the Vetterli, a clever blend of Swiss and American engineering. In 1889, the Swiss adopted a small-bore rifle with a straight pull bolt and a box magazine, the Schmidt-Rubin, that somewhat resembled that developed around the same time for the British Lee-Enfield rifles. The design was so successful, that with relatively minor changes and upgrades, it remained in service until 1958 when it was replaced by a semiautomatic rifle. As with all the books in the "For Collectors Only" series, there is a complete part-by-part description for both the Vetterli and Schmidt-Rubin rifles in all their variations by serial number range, plus a history of their development and use, their cleaning, maintenance and how to shoot them safely and accurately.

The American Krag Rifle and Carbine, by Joe Poyer, edited by Craig Riesch ($19.95). A new look on a part-by-part basis at the first magazine repeating service arm adopted for general service in American military history. It was the arm first adopted for smokeless powder and it required new manufacturing techniques and processes to be developed for its production at Springfield Armory. The Krag was an outstanding weapon that helped define the course of American arms development over the next fifty years. In this new text, the Krag is redefined in terms of its development. Old shibboleths, mischaracterizations and misinterpretations are laid to rest and a true picture

Model 1903 Springfield Rifle and Its Variations

of this amazingly collectible rifle and carbine emerges. The author has also devised a monthly serial number chart from production, quarterly and annual reports from Springfield Armory and the Chief of Ordnance to the Secretary of War.

The Model 1903 Springfield Rifle and Its Variations (2nd edition, revised and expanded), by Joe Poyer ($22.95). Includes every model of the Model 1903 from the ramrod bayonet to the Model 1903A4 Sniper rifle. Every part description includes changes by serial number range, markings and finish. Every model is described and identified. Abundant color and black-and-white photos and line drawings of parts to show details precisely. 444 pages.

The .45-70 Springfield, by Joe Poyer and Craig Riesch ($16.95) covers the entire range of .45-caliber "trapdoor" Springfield arms, the gun that really won the West. "Virtually a mini-encyclopedia . . . this reference piece is a must," Phil Spangenberger, *Guns & Ammo*.

U.S. Winchester Trench and Riot Guns and Other U.S. Combat Shotguns (2nd edition, revised), by Joe Poyer ($16.95). Describes the elusive and little-known "Trench Shotgun" and all other combat shotguns used by U.S. military forces. "U.S. military Models 97 and 12 Trench and Riot Guns, their parts, markings [and] dimensions [are examined] in great detail . . . a basic source of information for collectors," C.R. Suydam, *Gun Report*.

The U.S. M1 Carbine: Wartime Production, by Craig Riesch ($16.95) describes the four models of M1 Carbines from all ten manufacturers. Complete with codes for every part by serial number range. "The format makes it extremely easy to use. The book is a handy reference for beginning or experienced collectors," Bruce Canfield, Author of *M1 Garand and M1 Carbine*.

The M1 Garand, 1936 to 1957, by Joe Poyer and Craig Riesch ($19.95). "The book covers such important identification factors as manufacturer's markings, proof marks, final acceptance cartouches stampings, heat treatment lot numbers . . . there are detailed breakdowns of . . . every part . . . in minute detail. This 216 page . . . volume is easy to read and full of identification tables, parts diagrams and other crucial graphics that aid in determining the originality of your M1 and/or its component parts," Phil Spangenberger, *Guns & Ammo*.

Model 1903 Springfield Rifle and Its Variations

Winchester Lever Action Repeating Firearms, by Arthur Pirkle
    Volume 1, The Models of 1866, 1873 & 1876 ($19.95)
    Volume 2, The Models of 1886 and 1892 ($19.95)
    Volume 3, The Models of 1894 and 1895 ($19.95)
These famous lever action repeaters are completely analyzed part-by-part by serial number range in this first new book on these fine weapons in twenty years. ". . . book is truly for the serious collector . . . Mr. Pirkle's scholarship is excellent and his presentation of the information . . . is to be commended," H.G.H., *Man at Arms.*

The SKS Carbine (3rd revised and expanded edition), by Steve Kehaya and Joe Poyer ($16.95). *The SKS Carbine* "is profusely illustrated, articulately researched and covers all aspects of its development as well as . . . other combat guns used by the USSR and other Communist bloc nations. Each component . . . from stock to bayonet lug, or lack thereof, is covered along with maintenance procedures . . . because of Kehaya's and Poyer's book, I have become the leading expert in West Texas on [the SKS]," Glen Voorhees, Jr., *Gun Week.*

British Enfield Rifles, by Charles R. Stratton
    Volume 1, SMLE (No. 1) Mk I and Mk III ($16.95)
"Stratton . . . does an admirable job of . . . making sense of . . . a seemingly hopeless array of marks and models and markings and apparently endless varieties of configurations and conversions . . . this is a book that any collector of SMLE rifles will want," Alan Petrillo, *The Enfield Collector's Digest.*
    Volume 2, The Lee-Enfield No. 4 and No. 5 Rifles ($16.95)
In Volume 2, "Skip" Stratton provides a concise but extremely thorough analysis of the famed British World War II rifle, the No. 4 Enfield, and the No. 5 Rifle, better known as the "Jungle Carbine." It's all here, markings, codes, parts, manufacturers and history of development and use.
    Volume 4, The Pattern 1914 and U.S. Model 1917 Rifles ($16.95)
In Volume 4, the author describes the events that led to the development of the British Pattern 1914 Enfield and its twin, the U.S Model 1917 Enfield rifle. The M1917 was produced in and used on the Western front in far greater numbers than was the M1903 Springfield. Skip Stratton provides not only the usual part-by-part analysis of both rifles to show how the M1917 evolved from the Pattern 1914, but provides a cross-check of which parts are interchangeable. Included are the sniper and Pedersen Device variants.

Model 1903 Springfield Rifle and Its Variations

The Mosin-Nagant Rifle (3rd revised and expanded edition), by Terence W. Lapin ($19.95). For some reason, in the more than 100 years that the Mosin-Nagant rifle has been in service around the world, not a single book has been written in English about this fine rifle. Now, just as interest in the Mosin-Nagant is exploding, Terence W. Lapin has written a comprehensive volume that covers all aspects and models from the Imperial Russian rifles to the Finnish, American, Polish, Chinese, Romanian and North Korean variations. His book has set a standard that future authors will find very difficult to best. Included are part-by-part descriptions of all makers, Russian, Chinese, American, Polish, Romanian, etc. Also includes all variants such as carbines and sniper rifles from all countries.

The Swedish Mauser Rifles, by Steve Kehaya and Joe Poyer ($19.95). The Swedish Mauser rifle is perhaps the finest of all military rifles manufactured in the late 19th and early 20th centuries. A complete history of the development and use of the Swedish Mauser rifles is provided as well as a part-by-part description of each component. All 24 models are described and a complete description of the sniper rifles and their telescopic sights is included. All markings, codes, regimental and other military markings are charted and explained. A thorough and concise explanation of the Swedish Mauser rifle, both civilian and military.

A Shooter's and Collector's Guide Series

The M16/AR15 Rifle (2nd edition, revised and expanded), by Joe Poyer ($19.95). The M16 has been in service longer than any other rifle in the history of the United States military. Its civilian counterpart, the AR15, has recently replaced the M14 as the national match service rifle. This 140-page, profusely illustrated, large-format book examines the development, history and current and future use of the M16/AR15. It describes in detail all civilian AR15 rifles from more than a dozen different manufacturers and takes the reader step-by-step through the process of accurizing the AR15 into an extremely accurate target rifle. Ammunition, both military and civilian, is discussed and detailed assembly/disassembly and troubleshooting instructions are included.

The M14-Type Rifle (2nd edition), by Joe Poyer ($14.95). A study of the U.S. Army's last and short-lived .30-caliber battle rifle which became a

Model 1903 Springfield Rifle and Its Variations

popular military sniper and civilian high-power match rifle. A detailed look at the National Match M14 rifle, the M21 sniper rifle and the currently available civilian semiautomatic match rifles, receivers, parts and accessories, including the Chinese M14s. A guide to custom-building a service-type rifle or a match-grade, precision rifle. Includes a list of manufacturers and parts suppliers, plus the BATFE regulations that allow a shooter to build a legal look-alike M14-type rifle.

The SAFN-49 Battle Rifle: A Shooter's and Collector's Guide, by Joe Poyer ($14.95). The SAFN-49, the predecessor of the Free World's battle rifle, the FAL, has long been neglected by arms historians and writers, but not by collectors. Developed in the 1930s at the same time as the M1 Garand and the SVT38/40, the SAFN-49 did not reach production, because of the Nazi invasion of Belgium, until after World War II. This study of the SAFN-49 provides a part-by-part examination of the four calibers in which the rifle was made. Also, has a thorough discussion of the SAFN-49 Sniper Rifle and its telescopic sights, plus maintenance, assembly/disassembly, accurizing, restoration and shooting. A new exploded view and section view are included. The rifle's development and military use are also explained in detail.

Collector's Guide to Military Uniforms

The "Collector's Guide to Military Uniforms" endeavors to do for the military uniform collector what the "For Collectors Only" series does for the firearms collector. Books in this series are carefully researched using original sources; they are heavily illustrated with line drawings and photographs, both period and contemporary, to provide a clear picture of development and use. Where uniforms and accouterments have been reproduced, comparisons between original and reproduction pieces are included so that the collector and historian can differentiate the two.

Campaign Clothing: Field Uniforms of the Indian War Army
      Volume 1, 1866 to 1871 ($12.95)
      Volume 2, 1872 to 1886 ($14.95)
Lee A. Rutledge has produced a unique perspective on the uniforms of the Army of the United States during the late Indian War period following the

Model 1903 Springfield Rifle and Its Variations

Civil War. He discusses what the soldier really wore when on campaign. No white hats and yellow bandanas here.

A Guide Book to U.S. Army Dress Helmets, 1872-1904, by Mark Kasal and Don Moore ($16.95).
From 1872 to 1904, the men and officers of the U.S. Army wore a fancy, plumed or spiked helmet on all dress occasions. As ubiquitous as they were in the late 19th century, they are extremely scarce today. Kasal and Moore have written a step-by-step, part-by-part analysis of both the Models 1872 and 1881 dress helmets and their history and use. Profusely illustrated with black-and-white and color photographs of actual helmets.

All of the above books can be obtained directly from **North Cape Publications®, Inc., P.O. Box 1027, Tustin, CA 92781** or by calling **Toll Free 1-800 745-9714**. Orders only to the toll-free number, please. For information, call 714 832-3621. Orders may also be placed by FAX (714 832-5302) or via e-mail to ncape@ix.netcom.com. CA residents add 7.75% sales tax. Postage is currently $3.95 for 1-2 books, $5.50 for 3-4 books, $7.95 for 5-8 books. Call, fax or e-mail for UPS and Federal Express rates, for postage on quantities of 9 or more books, and for foreign postage rates.

Also, visit our Internet Website at **http://www.northcapepubs.com.** Our complete, up-to-date book list can always be found there. Also check out our linked Online Magazine for the latest in firearms-related, magazine-quality articles and excerpts from our books.

Model 1903 Springfield Rifle and Its Variations

NOTES